"We have always understood architecture to be an intellectual construction. Which means that it is a set of ideas and concepts that are organized into ordering systems and that design is the discovery of those systems."

"There are sources that have nothing to do with architecture, they aren't history, they aren't really theory but they are sources that move us: dance, theater, nature come back into our work in direct ways."

INTERNAL
DEVELOPING INFORMED ARCHITECTURAL LANGUAGES

"As an architect you shouldn't be arrogant. You should understand that fact."

"The meaning of every project involves building up complexity, and complexity is all about gathering and organizing information."

"Architecture, of all professions, is value laden."

"An architect should create buildings that are didactic, that explain themselves, that explain the role of order in providing intellectual and psychological comfort."

"Operating in a free fashion would indicate that there is no moral modernist project. You would be free to do whatever you want. That could not be further from the truth."

"I think authenticity comes from the ability for one not to accept it as a rule, but to invent it in a personal way and define it in a manner that makes it belong to the architect."

INTERNAL
DEVELOPING INFORMED ARCHITECTURAL LANGUAGES

Tom Diehl

APPLIED RESEARCH +DESIGN PUBLISHING

APPLIED
RESEARCH
+DESIGN
PUBLISHING

Published by Applied Research and Design Publishing, an imprint of ORO Editions
Gordon Goff: Publisher

www.appliedresearchanddesign.com
info@appliedresearchanddesign.com

Author: Tom Diehl
Editors: Jake Anderson
Book Design: Eric Dowding
Project Manager: Jake Anderson

10 9 8 7 6 5 4 3 2 1 First Edition

ISBN: 978-1-951541-25-5

Color Separations and Printing: ORO Group Ltd.
Printed in China.

AR+D Publishing makes a continuous effort to minimize the overall carbon footprint of its publications. As part of this goal, AR+D, in association with Global ReLeaf, arranges to plant trees to replace those used in the manufacturing of the paper produced for its books. Global ReLeaf is an international campaign run by American Forests, one of the world's oldest nonprofit conservation organizations. Global ReLeaf is American Forests' education and action program that helps individuals, organizations, agencies, and corporations improve the local and global environment by planting and caring for trees.

Table of Contents

Acknowledgments

This effort was impacted by many events, some fortunate - some unfortunate, with each occurrences extending the timeframe for completion well beyond that which was initially envisioned. As the intent of the book is to be relevant beyond a specific set of contemporary issues the interruptions, at least at the beginning, were not perceived as setbacks but rather detours to be accommodated. With the passage of time I became concerned whether the architects would remain available to re-engage and complete the remaining work years after the initial interviews.

As they did, I owe them a great amount of gratitude as this project was only one of many typically occurring within the hectic pace that defines their professional and academic activities. With a similar debt I would also like to thank all of those at each office with whom I interacted and developed electronic friendships. An intent remaining unfulfilled was to include the names of those who participated in the design of the buildings that are the focus of the interviews. I would like to thank you for your participation in the design and follow through responsibilities as I know that the buildings attained more meaningful outcomes because of your involvement.

At the beginning and at the end of this project there was support from both the University of Houston and the Gerald D. Hines College of Architecture and Design. Funding from the University of Houston Small Grants Program provided initial support enabling on-site visits to the buildings and, of course, the ability to meet and interview the architects. After the interviews were completed, the lengthy phase required to transcribe them was shortened and made less arduous through the assistance of Laura Logan and Anita Parker. It remains greatly appreciated. Peter Gail Borden provided valuable insight regarding publication avenues and Catherine Essinger offered many timely pieces of information relating to obtaining source material. At the end of the effort, Dean Patricia Oliver provided support to help meet the goal of finalizing the book. For that I am truly grateful.

Perspectives on design are not formed from singular vantage points. They evolve and mature though the insights belonging to numerous individuals. I am grateful that many of the thoughts underlying this effort were informed by multiple and often unscripted conversations with my fellow faculty. While too numerous to list, many whom I have had long-term associations and benefited from immeasurably, both as a student and colleague, include Robert Griffin, Duke Fleshman, Kevin Story and Sharon Chapman.

Bruce Webb provided valuable commentary on several thematic aspects of the book and Melinda VanPaasschen and Jake Anderson upgraded the abundant oversights in the text, aiding in providing more cogent communication.

After the interviews, the refining of ad hoc communication into written prose, and the gathering of drawings and images, the "thingness" of a book has to be addressed. In that domain I owe an immeasurable debt of appreciation to Eric Dowding. Without his professional insight, refined graphic sensibility and ability to critique with humor, the completion of this book would remain enmeshed as an additional unfortunate event – my immense gratitude to your assistance.

And lastly, and certainly not least, is my love and appreciation for my wife Jackie. This could not have been completed without the release time you provided me to retreat to the "mole hole" for so many hours. That support and continued belief in the eventual outcome of this book was very important to its final realization. ■

Introduction

The range of architectural design directions in existence today owes it diversity partly to a heritage unknowingly ushered in at the very beginning of the modern movement. New design processes and directions replaced more normative ones demonstrated through written treatises, pattern books, and historically accepted design procedures that provided guidelines for earlier design outcomes. These guidelines were replaced with varied explorations that might be described as explorations into new methods of construction and individual searches for architectural expressions of an anticipated new norm. The resultant diversity was surreptitiously embedded into the modern design ethos as architects explored solutions for an expanding array of program types and architectural directions representing new modern realities and perspectives.

Reasons for the modern critique of earlier approaches to the design of buildings are well known. The application of various historically informed styles to the façades of buildings had run its course, not only as an indicator of an aesthetic anachronism but also in relation to emerging architectural programs such as factories and airports. The impact of World War I with its devastating commentary on preceding political realities and the technological advancements revealed by it added to the sense that there was a need for new directions. New materials and manufacturing processes entered the marketplace impacting the design and detailing of buildings themselves. With those advances, architects were given new options and greater flexibility to work with an expanded material pallet and methods of construction.

While many contributed to this revolution, Frank Lloyd Wright, Le Corbusier, and Mies van der Rohe emerged as the dominant flag bearers of new formal, spatial, and aesthetic replacements for the symmetrical and classically inspired predecessors. With the passing of these early leaders in the 1950s and 1960s, it was not long before the question of "what's next" arose. Charles Jencks, in *Modern Movements in Architecture* published in 1973, provided response to the question. In it, he included a taxonomy indicating the roots of various directions in contemporary design.[1] Interestingly enough, his amorphous and organic chart expressing these directions and their permutations suggested that they were by no means a finite collection. The suggestion for succeeding practitioners was that a new frontier for individual explorations was opening up. His taxonomy and its underlying logic not only suggested the paths forward were wide open but in some ways encouraged as a vehicle for distinguishing oneself from other more standardized approaches to design.

However, even with his contemporary perspective, Jencks himself could not avoid the historically inspired belief for a coalescing of some sort that would tidy up this tendency toward diversity and

This raised the potential of "meaningfulness" in the newly developing architectural languages.

Essentially Jencks was arguing that all buildings possessed (or could possess) both syntactic and semantic qualities.

define new design directions. In particular, ones that were, or might be, culturally knowable and accessible were promoted. *The Language of Post-Modern Architecture* was, for its time, one of the more influential books discussing the break-up of the hegemony of early modernist approaches. Jencks attempted to identify a few architectural languages that could be created and would reflect "semiotic groups."[2] For Jencks, these groups represented anchors inculcated with the cultural infrastructure and knowledge enabling architects to design buildings conveying meaning in a similar manner to which the classical orders conveyed earlier cultural links or references. His intent was to provide a design process allowing the resultant languages the ability to communicate meaning by incorporating design intentions and resultant languages into a building with the assurance that those intentions would be perceivable and validated by the users. This was part of the transition to modern architectural languages, and to the desire to remain relevant in a "classical" way.[3]

This raised the potential of "meaningfulness" in the newly developing architectural languages. In an era not completely removed from "form follows function," questions arose as to what exactly is an architectural language and how is one created? Jencks attempted to answer the question in his second book. In "Part Two" of *The Language of Post-Modern Architecture*, entitled *Modes of Architectural Communication*, he identified metaphor, words, syntax and semantics as vehicles useful for the creation of architectural languages. However, outcomes suggested through the incorporation of these terms into a design process remain problematic in directing the creation of such languages as they are often perceived as creating superficial results or do not appear to remain meaningful over time.[4]

Even the projects identified by Jencks do not represent complete conceptualizations of the elements and assemblies that define a building's design. Utzon's Sidney Opera House is an example. While the metaphorical terminology used to define the shells of the Opera House—orange segments, wings of birds (by Utzon), shells, sails, flower petals—may indicate an appropriateness or provide a sense of association in a way that contextualizes the shells, one can see the metaphoric "process" breaking down when aesthetic questions surrounding the building's base are discussed, or not.[5] The lack of an additional set of visual references. explaining the intentions these elements of the building's design were to symbolize and suggest a disconnect between conceptual aims and design development in the form of a metaphorical follow through. Instead, the building's base has a vague bunker or office building expression failing to illicit similar poetic references or experiential effects. There is no language relationship or intended metaphor in the form of plinth, island, or outcropping to create a more conceptual and formal relationship to the surrounding water below or "shells" above. This is

Sydney Opera House
Jorn Utzon, *1957-74*

Charles Jencks
Diagram from Modern Movements in Architecture

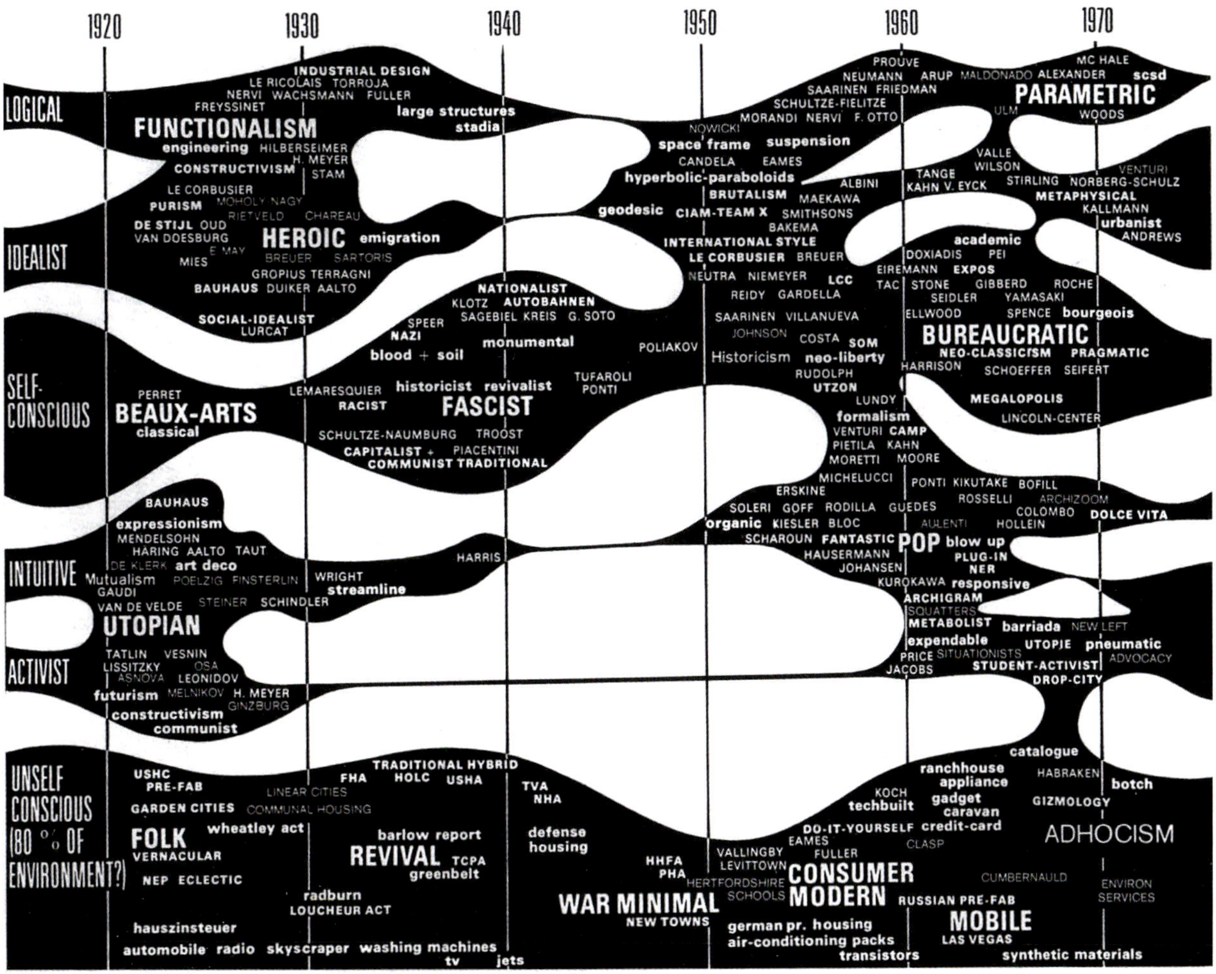

Developing a specific strategy toward language development is not Alexander's goal.

Yael Reisner, expands on the "troubled relationship" modern architects have with concepts and themes underlying the idea or definition of beauty.

not to suggest that there is no room for design outcomes whose interpretations suggest an enrichment deriving from metaphorical associations, but rather the need for a process or strategy that links the potential for multiple and beneficial readings into a whole, even if the whole is defined, usefully, as one made up of many narratives.

Jencks's use of the grammatical terms syntax and semantics brings us closer to a viable direction for a legitimate and inclusive procedure for guiding a design process. While in this application they are probably no more successful than his other modes of architectural communication suggested via metaphor and words, they have value in that they represent operations relating to a methodology for generating an architectural language. The terms provide the potential for a decision-making armature and the issues they allude to have the possibility of becoming normative attributes of a design process. With their inclusion in a design process the designed outcome possesses the possibility of a more comprehensive resolution than ones obtained from earlier epitaphs such as "breaking the box," "form follows function," and "less is more."

Essentially, Jencks was arguing that all buildings possessed, or could possess, both syntactic and semantic qualities. Through these terms he implied that on one hand it would be possible to design, from a syntactic standpoint, a structure (not to be confused with structural) or an "order" defining an architectural character with the potential to become one of the significant attributes of the building. In so doing it could endow the building with greater depth, relevance, or meaning, in particular when integrated with a semantic field. For Jencks it appears that a syntactic language could not exist on its own. On its own it would more likely become a "private" language. For him this problem was best exemplified in the early work of Michael Graves and Peter Eisenman.[6]

Developing the semantic character of a building and linking it with a syntactic order allowed it to be "coded" and rooted to an appropriateness of a particular "semiotic group."[7] The potential problem underlying this approach is that the architect is left trying to design for a specific group versus developing overall qualities or orderliness representing shared experiences in the building he or she is designing. Jencks identified this issue in references to outcomes that became too insular, possibly esoteric to the average user.[8]

It might be said that he is partially right and partially wrong. Buildings can and should integrate themselves to and participate in the culture of which they are a part. In that regard they do represent "codes" and give semantic readings. Yet the "semiotic groups" to which they were to correspond never really existed in the way Jencks probably hoped. Even at the time of the writing *The Language of Post-Modern Architecture* the (Western) world was too much of a diverse global village to think in terms of tailoring a design to a given "semiotic" group or even a set of groups.

In this regard his statement explaining how the classical orders expressed governmental presence and civic-ness, yet were interpreted differently over time, becomes the undoing of his advocating for an anchored or universal semantic role in architecture.[9] When advocating that the different meanings ascribed to the details distinguishing each classical column type are not really standards but represent simply three different versions of one type allowing for different interpretations, Jencks is essentially arguing for constantly changing semantic representation. Not only will these different interpretations occur, they will, and do, change over time. In this regard semantics is placed in an environment assuming architectural relativity.

As a basis for defining meaning in buildings Jencks loads the semantic approach with the same burden described above in the use of metaphors. Furthermore, for architects increasingly engaged in world-wide practices it would not be possible for them to understand the "visual codes" of different cultures and locals. Glen Murcutt states this well when he refers to his preference to practice only within the Australian context stating, "I

Nakagin Capsule Building
Kisho Kurokawa, *1972*

have no interest in practicing in different parts of the world, I have enough responsibility in learning and absorbing the cultural mores of my own country."[10]

Buildings have too great a need for their own design continuity and cohesiveness to be saddled with semiotic codings attempting to make them understandable, via a metaphor, or multiple metaphors, to specific user groups. Jencks's own reference to the Nakagin Capsule Building in Tokyo, designed by Kisho Kurokawa, bears this out. Whereas for Jencks it appeared as if the apartment units represented "stacked washing machines," for Kurokawa they were metaphorical references to small concrete birdhouses located in trees in Japan. In this interpretation the birdhouses are for itinerant Japanese businessmen.

Also in the 1970s, the question of what's next, was addressed from a different perspective by the architect and theoretician Christopher Alexander. In his book *A Pattern Language* he supplied a "language" consisting of pattern-types addressing a range of significant design considerations. The 253 pattern-types identified in the book range from the very large, such as Pattern 2 *The Distribution of Towns*, to the very small, *Half-Inch Trim* discussed in Pattern 240. *A Pattern Language* places the creation of form, space and place in a more systematic context with languages viewed as entities entitled patterns.[11] As Alexander states, "A pattern language has the structure of a network. ...we always use it as a sequence...since the language is in truth a network, there is no one sequence which perfectly captures it."[12] The procedure, used to provide a desired outcome, is a process of selection and integration where various combinations of the 253 listed patterns can be selected and combined to resolve the design needs of a particular project, ranging from the design of a town, a house, or a child's cave. Alexander's selection process is framed by general guidelines based upon functional associations of relevant normative pattern-types responding to emotional, behavioral, or performance needs, yet they do not provide in-depth assistance relating to insights required for the creation of visually cohering architectural languages.

Developing a specific strategy toward language development is not Alexander's goal. As stated, the sequence of patterns is "the base map from which you can make a language for your own project."[13] However, outcomes are more of a collection of patterns, not necessarily a language that is, if a language is defined visually by specific rules and strategies, aimed at generating visual coherence and understandability. An example of this is documented through his description regarding the design of a porch.[14] In the example Alexander provides ten patterns, which are used as guidelines directing the design process, yet the outcome of the resultant porch remains uncertain. Based upon Pattern 161, Sunny Place the desired porch location should face south, yet in his example this south-facing orientation impinges on Pattern 120 Paths and Goals. To accommodate the requirements of Paths and Goals a corner of the porch addition is removed. While preserving an established walking path remains a noble outcome, the resultant "language" comprising the visual outcome of the porch may be less satisfying.

Similarly, toward the end of the discussion of Pattern 159 Light on Two Sides of Every Room, the statement "Don't let this pattern make your plans too wild – otherwise you will destroy the simplicity of *Positive Outdoor Space*," Pattern 106 suggests a positive approach to a legitimate design concern.[15] However, guidelines geared toward solving potential aesthetic questions associated with the floor plans becoming "too wild" are not offered. This lack of specificity could leave many designers with a certain angst relating to the organizational strategy required to provide a configuration defining a positive outdoor space while also providing light on two sides of every room.

Alexander is more interested in the character of environmental situations and their combination. Sequencing the patterns becomes the vehicle used to define a valuable and normative outcome. However, the aesthetic outcome, versus the environmental one, is achieved through the use of established visual continuities he refers to as the timeless way,which tend to rely on language norms established through various traditional and historical styles.[16]

At this juncture the difference between Alexander's use of the term language and a "modern" interpretation must be made. It may be arguable that the topics covered in Alexander's book relate to principles governing the use of foundational rules establishing basic design principles versus describing the process for creating aesthetic coherence in modern architectural languages. As stated in the opening of this introduction, the range of design directions existent today, often with underlying interest in inventiveness or transformation, do not singularly relate to the use of timeless entities. That could constitute only one of many language options.

Today, we can see a permutation of this issue. In an interestingly titled book *Architecture and Beauty* the author Yael Reisner expands on the "troubled relationship" modern architects have with concepts and themes underlying the idea or definition of beauty. In interviews with numerous architects (or more precisely leading edge architects) and their respective opinions on the subject of beauty, Reisner suggests that any form of communal appreciation for particular aesthetic qualities buildings may possess, or aspire to, is not definable other than in fairly subjective terms.[17]

Reisner's observation regarding the troubled relationship architects have with beauty highlights the modern status of aesthetic relativism and the resultant diversity of design approaches. However, Jenck's, in identifying a design process employing the use of syntax and semantics in the creation, understanding and enjoyment of architectural languages, suggests languages do have underlying value in relation to developing outcomes with a broader reach. Buildings do require organizational attributes to give conceptual and language coherence and they do represent qualities and values, whether of an owner, company, institution, or culture. Through those qualities the potential for greater meaning and relevance increases. While not objecting to the possibility of referencing specific user groups (Re: the interview with John Patkau on Strawberry Vale Elementary School) the task of the architect is to ensure that he or she has developed design strategies providing relevance, meaningfulness, and visual cohesiveness within a broader understanding of an architectural language, even if the language is to be confrontational or challenges established norms. These qualities most often derive from internal language-based continuities and strategies. This is in contrast to, but not an avoidance of, being overly dependent on external considerations, emanating from significant design drivers such as the site and program, as those considerations contain a reduced ability to affect purely visual architectural interests.

Promoting the value of understanding and developing internal architectural language-based qualities at various stages of the design process is the thesis of this book. Related to that thesis is developing a clear understanding of the value of organizational and representational design considerations as unique yet interrelated language-based domains. Incorporating those domains and understanding the value their integration provides in fulfilling broader and often more abstract design interests architects bring to the design of a building is essential. The goal is to provide a useful and understandable path defining a design process that is more inclusive. This added inclusiveness offers the potential for greater depth of development and clarity on behalf of the designer and understandability on the part of the user, including a more encompassing and viable set of sensory experiences, ones that speak to us in a manner we not only understand but also feel.

Methodology and strategies

The shortcoming of Jencks's *The Language of Post-Modern Architecture* and, similarly Reisner's *Architecture and Beauty* is not in the value of the issues raised and discussed, rather it is in the lack of providing design strategies that support the development of language-based design processes and their outcomes in the form of realized buildings. As architects become more informed with knowable strategies underlying

Promoting the value of understanding and developing internal architectural language-based qualities at various stages of the design process is the thesis of this book.

representational and organizational tools at his or her disposal, the potential for richer design outcomes increases. A design process communicating more than subjective or lightly researched interpretations of culture, context, or metaphor is replaced by one that is comfortable with the communication and experiential potential embedded in the outcome of developed architectural languages.

The difference between a metaphor attempting to signify something that is not present, often becoming a caricature providing gestural imagery, versus a strategy whereby representational considerations are identified and embedded into the design process is significant. A representational strategy working inside the purview of architecture, versus relying on abstract references to conditions not fundamentally a part of architectural essences or priorities, has the potential to develop qualities resonating in both rational/intellectual and experiential/emotional realms. Through their rigorous employment and resultant depth in both substance and spirit, representational strategies touch both our emotional and intellectual chords.

Yet, as a strategy, understanding that all of architecture represents something (even such qualities as "cheap materials = low budget" or "garish colors = buy here/don't linger") is not fully distinct from the trap of a metaphorical approach to design. This raises the other relationship to Jencks's terminology—the use of syntax. Developing cohesive and meaningful architectural language-based concepts that operate in the representational domain requires that they be paired with concepts operating in an organizational domain to realize their expressive potential.

Herein lies the difference between searching for syntactical rules and *organizational strategies*. There is need for a process that is strategic in the use of organizational concepts versus a playful bending of rules in the form of a personal heuristic search. Jencks correctly believed the syntactic and the sematic had to be understood as a paired relationship. Yet in a manner similar to the differences between a metaphorical symbol and a representational strategy described above, the problem with his emphasis on these words as part of a linguistic addition to architectural communication was that he did not develop a methodology for allowing the various rules and codes to be integrated into a design process by "all" architects. Instead they remained just words and represent a bending of rules with the designed outcomes remaining unknown to the "readers" of architecture.

Therefore, my emphasis on *strategy* as it relates to the development of a design process integrating an enhanced understanding of the methods needed to define meaningful architectural languages. The first step in developing a viable strategy requires the understanding of the existence and *integrative* nature

The integration of organizational strategies with representational concepts and qualities is fundamental for their understanding and enhancement.

of these two primary conceptual domains—organizational and representational. A common language-based mistake is to conceptualize in one of these domains yet to under-conceptualize in the other.

An example will clarify this symbiotic relationship, but initially a bit more "practical" definition of each domain is needed. After studying the *external* factors represented by the program and site, architects usually establish a more purely architectural interest to help coalesce these forces as they do not in and of themselves typically present a common denominator generating the aesthetic qualities of the design. These interests often, but not always, fall into a conceptual domain more representational in nature and are expressed in linguistic terminology such as "The space is to appear as a "forest of lines," or the building is emblematic of the "diversity" of the corporation, etc.

However, the identification of the *organizational concepts* of the "forest" or the "diversity" of the company is not always understood in the manner in which these qualities and intentions support the expression of representational interests. The understanding and use of organizational strategies in the development of representational interests allows them to be more developed and integrated than a simple metaphor. How are the lines of the forest organized, does it have "clearings" and then denser areas? Similarly is the essence of the diversity of the company expressed organizationally in a highly organized framework or more as a random dispersal of elements comprising the building or space? The integration of organizational strategies with representational concepts and qualities is fundamental for their comprehension and enhancement. Identifying and understanding which of the two conceptual domains one is working in and the necessity for them to support and cross-reference each other is paramount for a successful conceptual strategy to be employed. This methodological aspect is what Jencks's and Reisner's efforts do not document.

The need to understand the necessity to identify and conceptualize different organizational approaches as they relate to the support of representational qualities is absolute as the representational/organizational duality is necessary for the identification of particular "*language sets*" as most buildings are composed of multiple ones. A simple example is in the two different, yet distinctly related, language sets often designed into a building—one representing the elements defining the public spaces and programmatic components and another representing an equivalent language defining private areas (similarly the service/served duality could also work). To allow a building to communicate both a deeper more knowable essence and, similarly, possess a richer experiential pallet, the employment of numerous language sets is often required and they typically have, to a greater or lesser degree, differing organizational strategies.

The need to understand that there are representational and organizational domains to be identified and incorporated—consciously—into the design process is paramount.

This is not to imply organizational conceptualization only at the level of a floor plan but rather the need to include similar organizational strategies at various points in the design process, including the material jointing or detailing level. A straightforward example can be seen in the difference of a plan organization of programmatic spaces and components that could be described as "gridded" in one schematic approach or "offset" in another. Similarly, the development of the language continuity of the building will be enhanced if similar organizational strategies are employed, or for differing conceptual intentions counterpointed, throughout the entirety of the design process. This would then include the use of similar types of organizational strategies in the section, elevation, material jointing, etc. In this example the goal, whether the detailing and jointing strategy echoes or counterpoints the plan organizational strategy, is not of significance. The significance lies in the fact that the intentions are strategic, versus a default compositional approach, in their use of organizational and representational design intentions.

The issue is not for the creation of "private" languages or languages for "semiotic groups" but rather for something as simple and useful as order, cohesiveness, and coherence, and the resultant pleasure that can derive from understanding and appreciating the underlying intentions that create those qualities. Even if the intention explores a new role for "chance" as suggested by Thom Mayne in his discussion of the Caltrans District 7 building, the need to understand that there are representational and organizational domains to be identified and incorporated—consciously—into the design process is paramount. Identifying and clarifying that process is the intent of this book. The goal is to provide a design strategy that will not inhibit the diversity that is modern architecture but will provide a framework for more meaningful and inspirational design outcomes, both conceptually and experientially. ◘

Notes

1. Charles Jencks, *Modern Movements in Architecture*, 1977, Rizzoli.
2. Jencks, p.55
3. Nikolaus Pevsner, *An Outline of European Architecture*, 1960, Penguin Books, p.661-700. Various directions and tenants unfolding in contemporary design are identified with a summary observation…the exclusion of the intellect impoverishes architecture and design…architecture can rarely afford to be silly; it is as a rule too permanent and too big merely to amuse…buildings must be acceptable in all moods, that means, must have a certain seriousness. Seriousness does not exclude a challenge to reason, but it must be a serious challenge (p.700).
4. Jencks, p.73. In the segment entitled "Semantics," Jencks refers more than once to the slipperiness and relativeness of such applications, in particular when the role is reduced to metaphor as any associated meaning is modified through changes in the culture.
5. Jencks, p.43. Or not, is the primary point. Jencks does not continue the discussion of metaphor to involve the base from which the shells perch but he does address many variations as to what the metaphorical meaning might represent. Whatever associative value may arise from a metaphor based upon stylistic aspects, if those associations are only attached to certain attributes of a building a further lessening of any meaningful associative connection(s) is diminished.
7. ibid., p.63.
8. ibid., p.63-70, include a description of the 3 versions of houses and then on p.70: "it takes years, perhaps a generation, to master"
9. ibid., p.77.
10. Glen Murcutt, lecture at the Museum of Fine Arts, Houston, Texas, 1980.
11. Christopher Alexander, *A Pattern Language*, 1977, Oxford University Press, p.x.
12. ibid., p.xviii.
13. ibid., p.xix.
14. ibid., p.xxxvi.
15. ibid., p.750.
16. ibid., p.ix.
17. Yael Reisner, *Architecture and Beauty*, 2010, John Wiley & Sons Ltd., p.13 .
18. Yael Reisner, *Architecture and Beauty*, 2010, John Wiley & Sons Ltd., p.12 .

Internal Versus External:
Strategies for informing the design process

In a world where even the most speculative and exploratory approaches to design appear possible, both in the studio and the profession, the design of buildings of cultural significance requires intentions grounded in organizational and representational strategies that prioritize "internal," language-based attributes of design. It is important to know and understand the role of decisions governed by internal language-based intentions and their relation to "external" aspects of design such as those impacted by the site, program, and other performance-related design issues. These areas, while vital, do not always incorporate visual language-based intentions that assist in maturing the design process. By including strategies for further conceptual development, more fully resolved design outcomes are created, merging additional conceptual depth and overall development with those affected by external design considerations.

It can be argued that the missing constituent in many design processes is a methodology that establishes precise positions and rules of operation. This is of particular importance in relation to the creation of architectural languages. Design intentions influenced by external issues do not carry the singularity of language authority as compared to those grounded in purely internal architectural issues. Intentions conceived in relation to these internal language-based concerns add validity and relevance to the creation of comprehensible and accessible architectural languages. Identifying the framework within which these intentions operate is the focus of this book. The goal is to illustrate strategies that add clarity and depth to the design process, informing and refining approaches supporting the development of more coherent architectural form, space, and experiential qualities.

Recent Historical Context

The word "order" does not have the gravitas it once possessed. In the recent past when one spoke of an architectural order it was not just describing the mechanical guidelines organizing columns, windows, and other components, but an underlying essence, spirit, or understandability. Issues of design intentionality were guided and informed by an underlying assumption that good design incorporated strategies that had an intended outcome that "made sense" even if the logic was aimed at transforming established conventions.

Initial challenges to established languages of modern architecture began through revisiting the direction of contemporary design following the deaths of Frank Lloyd Wright, Mies van der Rohe, and Le Corbusier and continued with a figural death suggested in two books published in 1966, *Complexity and*

Contradiction in Architecture by Robert Venturi and *The Architecture of the City* by Aldo Rossi. Strategies forwarding or revising varying directions in architecture ensued. An expanded theoretical discourse directing architectural design became the focus of a broader discussion and was manifest in two primary spheres of influence.

Theoretical debate was disseminated in journals such as *Oppositions*, which sought to provide a forum for new directions in architectural thinking. Much of the debate within the practice of architecture focused on two divergent viewpoints. Those favoring an advanced modern architectural language became known as the "Whites" and were often associated with a book published in 1972, *The New York Five*. This book featured the work of Peter Eisenman, Michael Graves, Charles Gwathmey, John Hedjuk, and Richard Meier. The projects and tenets of the Whites were critiqued by another group of architects who aligned their thinking with principles outlined in Venturi's and Rossi's books and became known as the "Grays." These architects, Robert A. M. Stern, Jaquelin Robertson, Charles Moore, Romaldo Giurgola, and Alan Greenburg wrote an article published in the *Architectural Forum* entitled *Five on Five*. Their position suggested the modernism of the Whites was less concerned with foundational design issues such as appropriate responses to the users program, site orientation, and similar more pragmatic design influences. While numerous critiques involved performance-related issues, the larger critique by the Grays focused on the formal languages of the Whites and many other accepted directions of modern architecture. For the Grays a more accessible and comprehensible architectural language was desired.

These two views frame the paradox then underlying the diversity of modern architectural directions and the languages created to define them. One viewpoint suggested a desire for greater accessibility and increased understanding of modern architecture's relevance and appropriateness to contemporary society. This approach envisioned that multiple continuities, traditions, and viewpoints be understood and maintained enabling a shared, relevant, and comprehensible language to come forward. The other viewpoint offered a desire for languages of greater transformative potential, equating architecture to a constantly evolving modern world. This position suggested architectural intentions grounded on a more innovative spirit of invention.

Unless an unanticipated event or force creates a shared design ethos, strategies for the design of buildings will remain diverse. Significance will be given to design approaches that incorporate a more expansive design process, that includes considerations lying beyond functional and pro-forma aesthetic responses. Understanding the role design intentions play as agents for the creation of unified and

It is the prioritizing and integration of language-based intentions with decisions required for the external-based aspects of design that provide the linkages and continuities necessary for creating informed architectural languages.

The concept of coherence in and of itself may be debated as design interests may rely on positions that question its conventional definition.

coherent architectural languages and the strategies required for their expression is essential. It is the prioritizing and integration of language-based intentions with decisions required for the external-based aspects of design that provide the linkages and continuities necessary for creating informed architectural languages, ones possessing enhanced experiential and problem-solving potential.

Internal Versus External

Spatial, formal, material, and phenomenological qualities deriving from design intentions and strategies that organize them yet express transcendent or "poetic" design themes all relate to what can be described as internal issues. These qualities require the development of a language to provide an overriding priority governing the external factors influencing the design of a building. External factors, such as site conditions affecting the building's placement, sustainable attributes, the plan and sectional distribution of program components, do not typically possess all-inclusive language properties with a visual common denominator necessary to bind together the entirety of the aesthetic related decision-making process. Incorporating these externalities so that they do not become a set of independent unrelated form-giving attributes requires the use of clear, language-based intentions. Language-based intentions integrate these external factors to the "larger" purely architectural concerns of the design process and prioritize aesthetic concerns over the specific and local concerns to which the externalities typically relate. External functional and performance-related ideas must be vetted through intentions that control architectural themes if coherence is to emerge. The authority of the language has to be understood and maintained from initial investigations and diagrams to the design of final detail considerations.

The concept of coherence in and of itself may be debated as design interests may rely on positions that question its conventional definition. Today, a variety of organizational types exploring diverse arrangements of elements and spaces less directly ordered are frequently employed. Examples from the work of OMA, UNStudio, or Coop Himmelb(l)au may ultimately be understood as practices defining this field. Yet these strategies do promote various intentions and ultimately a desire or belief that the design intentions can be comprehended and convey logic. This returns the discussion to the development of design strategies and the rationality underlying them.

The intentions of the heroic modernists, conceived to usher in new and transformative approaches to architectural design, nonetheless maintained a rational underpinning in relationship to the search for a "truth" underlying their viewpoints. These transformations were expressed not through new understandings of the program or relationships to the site, but through the creation of new architectural languages. The transforming visions expressed in structures such as the Robie House, Villa Savoy, and the Barcelona Pavilion established relationships between intentions and language, providing clues to new directions in architecture. While these structures did not avoid issues relating to site and program, ideas driven by those criteria were not seen as critical to the success of their transformative goals. The goals were expressed within the very nature of the architectural dialectic, with operative strategies incorporated into the creation and refining of internal language-based themes. These themes fall into two domains: one is an organizational realm, the other representational.

Organizational

While the Robie House, Villa Savoy, and the Barcelona Pavilion use established "determinate" modern architectural organizational strategies such as axial, linear, nuclear, and field forms of organization for the arrangement of space and form, today, these organizational types are joined by additional "indeterminate" ones such as splaying, wrapping, warping, and perforating. The common aspect of these approaches is that all require an understanding of the unifying strategies that give coherence to the decision making process, even if the intention is to create a more dynamic, possibly even anti-cohering effect. For successful design outcomes, clear organizational strategies have to be understood and integrated to provide well-defined expressions of the dominant architectural language and the more localized language subsets. This does not relate only to how organizational themes can impact the arrangement and definition of components constituting the plan, as is often the case, but also how the same strategies influence section, elevation, and material jointing conceptualizations.

Representational

As with the early buildings of modern architecture, design efforts can start with, or be underpinned by, a global design interest that is often representational in nature. The use of this term is not to be confused with metaphorical associations, but rather with the development of a design decision-making process. Examples expressing how representational interests can change the outcome of design are seen in three successive projects by Morphosis and are identified in shifts that take place between the design of the Crawford Residence, continue through the design of Diamond Ranch High School, and are "finalized" in the school for Cooper Union. The changes are identified, in part, through a re-prioritizing of strategies relating to the use of "standard" ordering systems to ones less conventionally organized. However, these changes in direction have less to do with differing interests in organizational approaches. Their progression is more directly related to a growing interest, on the part of Thom Mayne, in themes exploring qualities that represent more indeterminate variables, ones exploring the more mysterious side of experience.

The plan of the Crawford Residence, while not based upon a grid, exhibits an interest in modern architectural organizational principles of bays, rhythms, regulating lines, lines of extension, etc. Moving away from those interests to ones exploring a topographic representation, Diamond Ranch High School presents a less regulated plan and section given that representational interests derive from a reinterpretation and re-creation of the surrounding topography and the larger global interests of Thom Mayne mentioned earlier. However, in comparing the indeterminacy of Diamond Ranch to the organizational tools employed in the Crawford Residence designed seven years earlier, one can see a number of established regulating systems remain, suggesting a middle ground in relation to the organizational strategies employed. Different and diverse organizational systems, multiple repeated modules, lines of extension, and other ordering conventions clearly demark and link, through a system of clear formal and spatial relationships, the definition of precise architectural zones where specific language-based tools are used to identify one "topographic" zone as distinct yet related to another.

In the facility for Cooper Union, themes more overtly arising from interests originating in the realms of chance and indeterminacy impact the design of the primary interior public spaces and façades. Conscious strategies are employed creating formal and spatial conditions promoting an intended effect of imbalance, an overall disquiet-ness, and conditions where intrigue is created through the utilization of non-straightforward configurations of space, form, and structure. Previous organizational rules such as regulating lines, bays and repetitions are replaced by ones relating twisting and curving lines, angled and curvilinear elements, and other architectural components within a strategy allowing multiple indeterminate representational relationships and orientations. While many programmatic components such as classrooms and administrative areas are located using straightforward organizational methods, design strategies utilized to arrange public space, circulation routes, and exterior façades define a representational outcome quite distinct from those employed in the Crawford Residence.

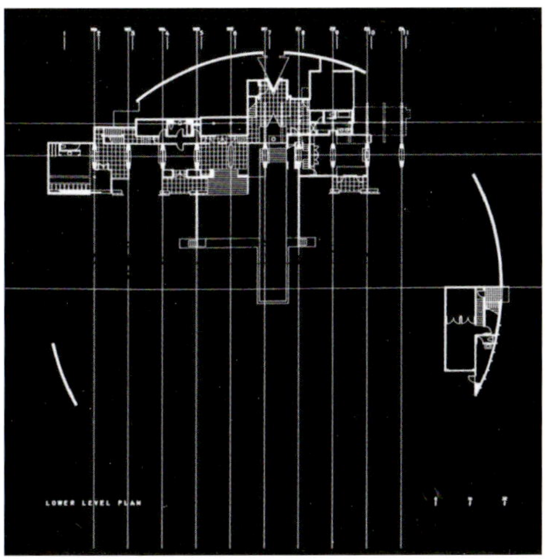

Crawford Residence plan.

Crawford Residence interior.

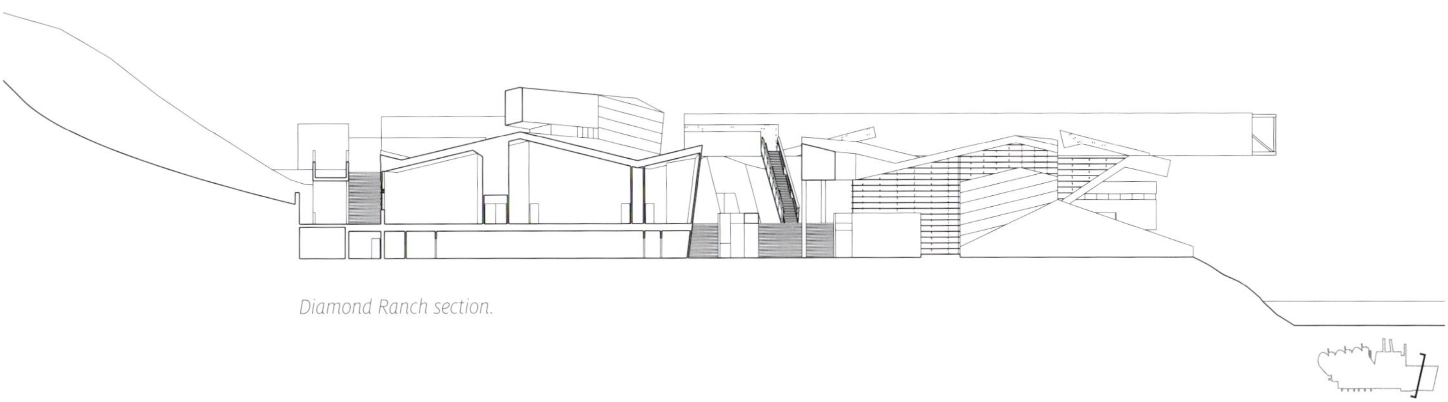

Diamond Ranch section.

Internal language-based strategies are necessary for the project's full conceptual development.

Process

Through research, investigation, or input from other members of a design team, the designer becomes aware of significant site issues as well as programmatic and code-based criteria impacting the direction of the project. This information, often lying in a different realm than considerations affecting the formation of an architectural language, plays a significant role in the project's development. However, what has been referred to as internal language-based strategies are necessary for the project's full conceptual development. It is the employment of these intentions and strategies, which transcend the required external design criteria, that mature the design effort through added conceptual depth, embedding the project with the potential to create an enriched and coherent language.

At a point early in the design process, it is necessary that the designer become acutely aware that ultimately every decision must be understood in its relationship to language-based concepts. Understanding the domain in which one is working, either organizational or representational, is significant as that understanding assists in targeting precise conceptual utilization. In familiarizing him or herself with the existence of these domains, the designer is able to utilize concepts appropriate to each and ensure that all intentions have been understood in, and vetted by, each domain. Typically, an over-reliance on one domain produces design shortfalls.

Approaches that excessively utilize organizational processes frequently have clearly organized plans and numerous architectural elements expressing strong ordering qualities, yet do not exhibit similar interest in developing a narrative for the representational nature of design. Concepts corresponding to the representational nature of a building, even if the concept is reasonably general in nature such as one promoting orderly appearances of a geometric or technological expression, are left unattended. The spaces and architectural components defining the building are typically under-conceptualized in section and elevation, often becoming generic responses created by vertical extrusions of the architectural elements developed to functionally organize the floor plan.

Conversely, processes that over emphasize representational themes do not often develop the rigor necessary to create a design that resonates on a level other than superficial metaphorical imagery. Representational concerns are not understood as having organizational biases or requirements and subsequently appear unresolved in relation to a fully informed design. The outcome of this lack of a developed organizational rigor supporting representational interests is expressed in a "thinness" defined by conceptual interests less concerned with outcomes enriched through the use of multiple organizing

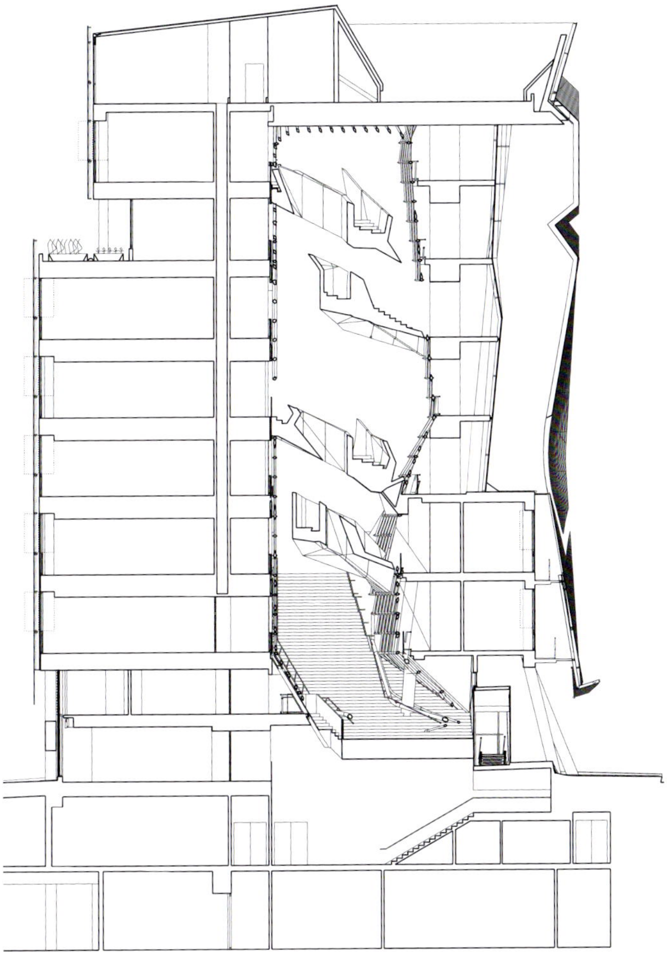

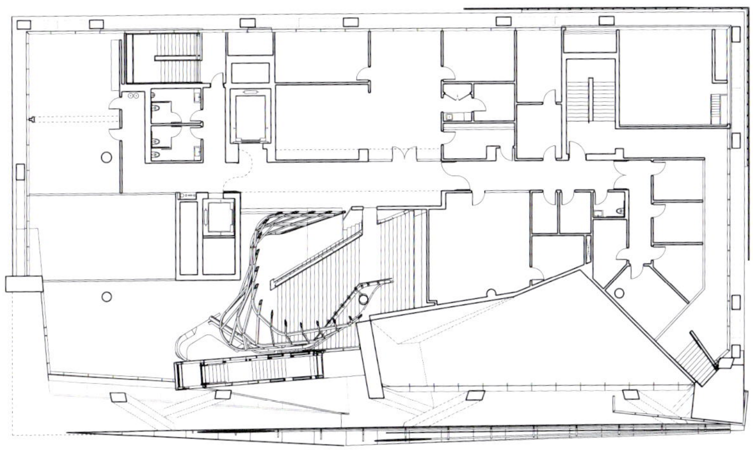

The 41 Cooper Square plan, section, elevation detail.

strategies. The use of multiple ordering systems is often replicated in the design development phase where issues such as material proportions and jointing, expressed architectural assemblies and conceptual positions established earlier in the design process are revisited and incorporated into subsequent design decisions.

Consequently, it can be anticipated that both organizational and representational conceptual fields are required for the development of a mature project. Intentions that incorporate both domains ensure that the project is not under-conceptualized. The under-utilization of language-based intentions define outcomes common to many buildings in that the external based influences derive from information that is both practical and defensible, while language-based intentions often originate from broader, more abstract positions. However, as has been stated, the external influences do not possess information having the authority of language because they are primarily *external* to purely language-based concepts. For language-based intentions to mature, architects must understand and employ a design process precisely and consciously, with a clear use of intentions emanating from both domains. Without incorporating both, one domain will be utilized as a conceptual armature without utilizing and integrating the conceptual enrichment the other provides.

Synopsis

The position language-based intentions play in the development and diversification of design narratives has been expanding from the initial heroic period of modern architecture. This tendency is documented in the diagram created by Charles Jencks incorporated in the introduction to this book. It is anticipated this phenomenon will continue as modern architecture, intertwined with the continued ascendency of democratic forms of expression and the growth of individualism in societies, will continually shape design narratives and conceptually influence architects seeking to define or re-define them. The impact of these forces, and the issues underlying them, will remain the primary stimulant for continued diversification of design directions.

The range of information impacting the design of buildings deriving from the external influences of site, program, and other performance-related aspects will remain fairly consistent. The ability of external-based information to create wholeness in relation to the larger narrative of the design, while not irrelevant, will remain secondary. Expanded design narratives will primarily be created and defined through the understanding and development of language-based intentions. It is this expanded narrative, derived from the use of language-based intentions incorporating both organizational and representation strategies, that will inform a methodology necessary to instill an experiential moving spirit into buildings.

Precedents

Given the diversity of design directions it is improper to suggest that one domain should carry greater value than another. The precedents included in this chapter present a range of diverse architectural intentions expressed through multiple architectural languages. They are included to provide a preview into the use of intentionality woven into themes discussed in the interviews conducted with the eight architects. It is to be expected that some language-based concepts originate more consciously in one domain over the other. While a more complete explanation of the integration of various intentions into the design process is addressed in the subsequent interview chapters, a brief synopsis of their use provides an initial exploration into the value of language-based design intentions underlying this effort.

The four projects selected incorporate both representational and organizational intentions into their design. There is a temptation to suggest that the Rachofsky House/Gallery and the Nasher Sculpture Center exhibit stronger use of organizational strategies and Diamond Ranch High School and BMW Central place greater emphasis on the representational aspects of their design intentions. This is not necessarily true, but the assessment does raise a relevant point. Both the Rachofsky House/Gallery and the Nasher Sculpture Center do, in their representational modes, accept a role of conferring and uplifting common values that have resided in much of architecture, past and present. The architecture of Diamond Ranch High School and BMW Central explores the potential of design intentions to challenge expectations or transform them. The importance of this aspect is that buildings will always have a semantic component, whether expressing interests of the day, timeless principles, realities driven by client values, or the banal revealed through under-informed design processes.

In each project description the representational intentions are discussed first, followed by an outline of the organizational concepts and strategies. A hallmark of these projects is that often a certain blurring occurs regarding which domain the various design intentions and attributes most clearly belong. One is sometimes forced to inquire which domain is more useful or more important to the experiential quality of the building. The blurring is valuable; it is an indicator of a mature use of strategies emanating from each domain.

Rachofsky House/Gallery

The representational aspects of much of Richard Meier's work derive from global themes adapted from the early work of Le Corbusier and are couched in general statements such as "Openness and clarity are qualities that represent American architecture at it's best,"[1] and "one must be concerned with constructing a physical fabric that is equally durable, rational and architecturally vibrant."[2] While these statements and the adopted Corbusian language represent positions that are very broad, they do set themes establishing representational attributes. These attributes qualify—whether through the re-establishment of the analytical origins underpinning Le Corbusier's early work or through themes implied in the use of words like "clarity" and "rational"—the use of white, spatial types promoting transparent linkages, precision in relation to regulation and construction, and other highly ordered aspects of Meier's work. A desire for "an emphasis on the character of the whole"[3] acknowledges representational aspirations marking an architecture defined by an expression of knowable relationships and intangible essences.

These themes extend into the organizational realm as the "knowable" and are defined through a rigorous employment of regulating systems establishing a common framework for making a unified set of decisions. These decisions, in turn, exhibit a coherent strategy for integrating architectural space and form. Spatial qualities are defined through multiple components bound together through intricate regulating systems made understandable through analysis of the ordering systems used to relate the diverse components and, more importantly, made visible as one moves through and experiences the integrated and open spatial quality of the building. A quality of wholeness is achieved by employing clear organizational strategies promoting spatial and formal alignments and multiple underlying ordering systems. Structural and modular repetitions, alignments extending, and relating one space to another and the continual reference back to a system where the relationship of one component to another can always be identified provide organizing frameworks on which elements are placed upon, aligned with, and extended from. Looser, more offset spatial qualities are allowed, yet remain integrated and true to a system regulating points, lines, planes, and masses through very clear and identifiable ordering systems.

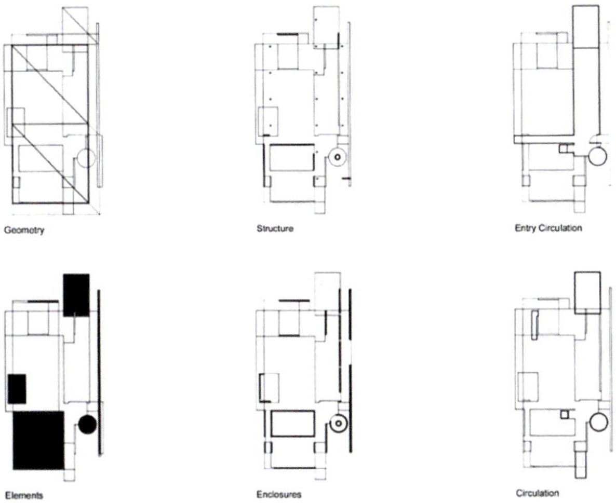

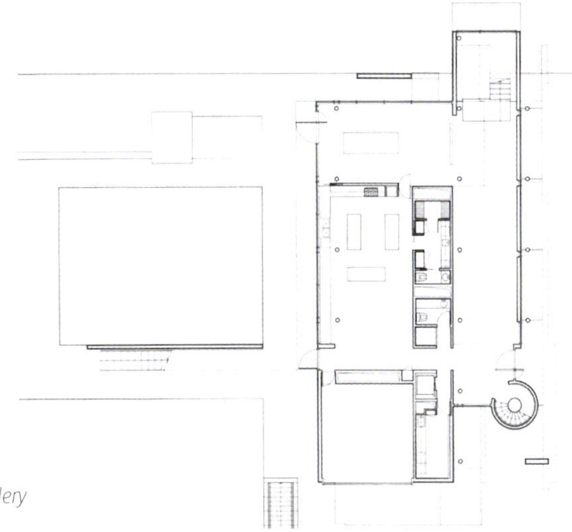

Rachofsky House/Gallery diagrams, plan.

Diamond Ranch

Diamond Ranch High School marks a transition point in the evolution of Thom Mayne and Morphosis' focus on representational aspects expressed in their architecture. In Diamond Ranch, formal and spatial coherence remains a focus, but one that is redefined to accommodate evolving global interests. Intentions representing a modification in the understanding and use of different representational aspects informing the design process begin to direct the decision making process. Thom Mayne states: "I've been interested in the space between chance and intention. I am fascinated with that as a part of life. I probably put a preference on chance."[4] While the representational outcomes suggested by Diamond Ranch differ from the Crawford Residence, understanding the need for cohering strategies remains. "Without intentions creating a guiding framework through which all decisions must pass would be like a minister directing a ballet; you probably can't do it. It is the same in design; it is the constant rebuilding or reuse of the initial intentions."[5]

In Diamond Ranch, these intentions are twofold. The reinterpretation of topography and the growing interest in relationships more casually ordered define primary interests. The transition to a different representational position necessitated the creation of different organizational strategies for the building's spaces and forms.

> The whole project becomes a resolution of two systems; the organizational strategy of the program and the conceptual land strategy. We intentionally shifted them in order to make evident the tension that exists between the operation of the school and the fabricated landscape. Everything in this project has to do with resolving this opposition. While the forms take on a certain sculptural quality as a result of these operations, they really have nothing to do with sculpture. The process is absolutely rigorous and rule driven.[6]

In the plans the organizational rules are evident, but different, as splays, rotated orthogonal systems, repetitions of ovoid shapes, and linear components all correspond to define new organizational strategies. In section and elevation similar manifestations occur as splays, rotations, diagonal sloping roof planes, and similarly organized material claddings express comparable qualities, assisting in the creation of an architectural topography.

Diamond Ranch plan, elevation, exterior.

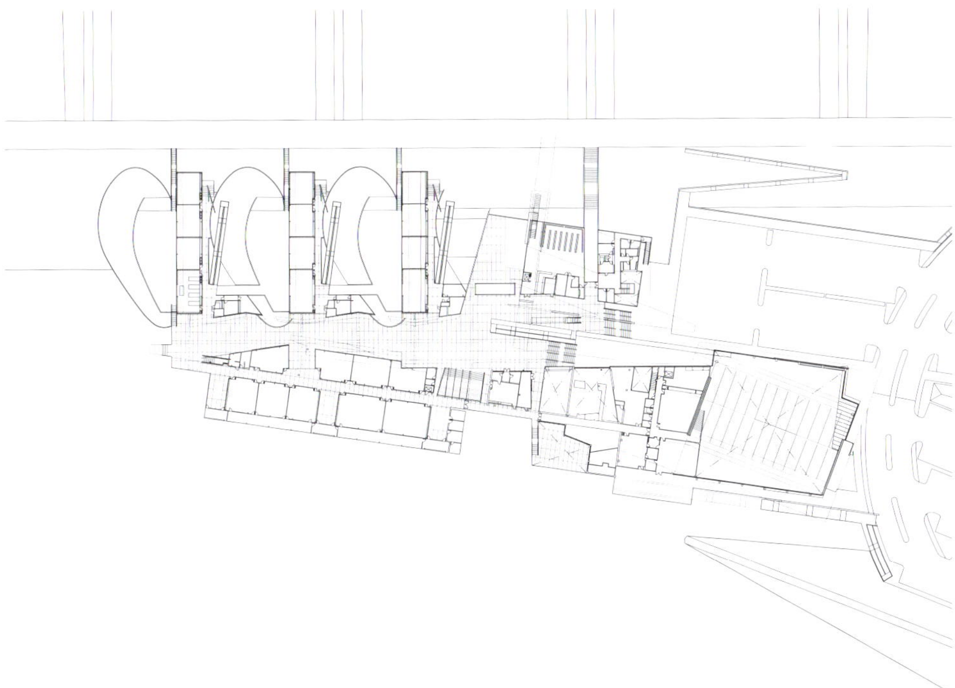

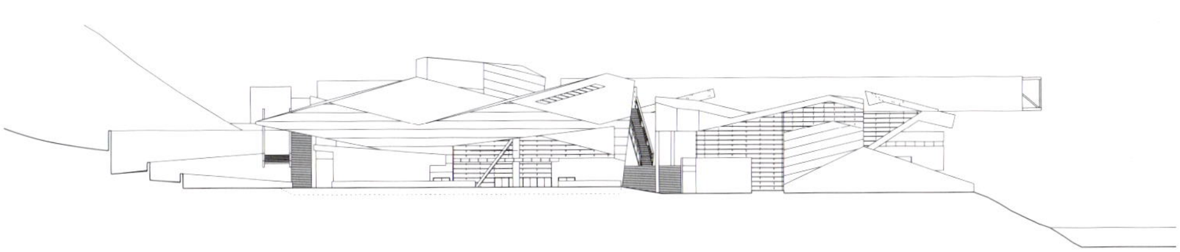

BMW Central

An "infill" building on a site measuring 295' x 950' and surrounded on three sides by existing manufacturing facilities, the BMW Central building acts as the nerve center for the entire factory complex. Movement defines the essential attribute of activities ongoing in the building, whether of product, automobiles, or people. Zaha Hadid Architects envisioned a complex linearity deriving from automobile production lines. "This project is about making space through lines. In each case, the space derives from a linear process, an exploration into the way a system of two-dimensional lines can devise a three-dimensional space."[7] Maximizing continuities was also a key spatial characteristic for the design. "In terms of my own work, I would say that after twenty years, an interest in fragmentation gave way to an obsession with fluidity."[8] The representational quality of the spaces was seen as "articulated complexity."

> In the building, we attempt to deploy architectural language and formal discipline to organize a series of connections and to orient various flows...The architecture is characterized by key decisions made early in the project: We employed only homogeneous, continuous materials such as concrete and welded steel: we strove to eliminate as many columns as possible; and we minimized the number of corners.[9]

The "obsession with fluidity" and linearity becomes an organizational strategy in which parallel bands of weaving forms, spaces, and materials impact decisions ranging from the configuration of the arrival sequence, layout of the parking lot, organization of the systems or ceiling/lighting systems. Fluidity and linearity are organized as a series of "cascades" impacting and shaping the load-bearing concrete walls, removing a structural reading from them. In addition, the organizing attribute of cascading sets of multiple floor levels provides an articulation strategy for the stairs connecting them.

Other than at the entry, the exterior elevations do not maintain the continuities of the linear flows defining the decision making process for the interior. Many of the elevations do not fulfill representational intentions focusing on an obsession with fluidity. Punched orthogonal windows and doors stand out as distractions in contrast to the seamless integration of surfaces, lighting, HVAC ductwork, sprinkler systems and other components configured by rules that employ corresponding organizing approaches defined by linearity. Cascading is replaced by pinching and abrupt terminations as exterior cladding systems intersect in decidedly non fluid methods of organizations.

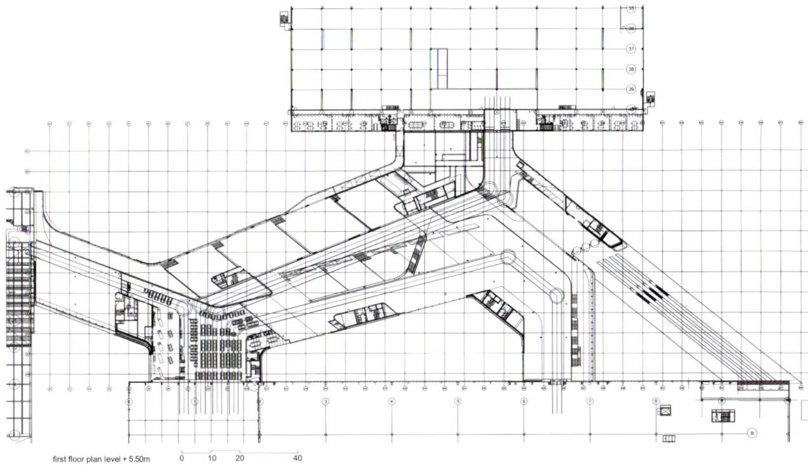

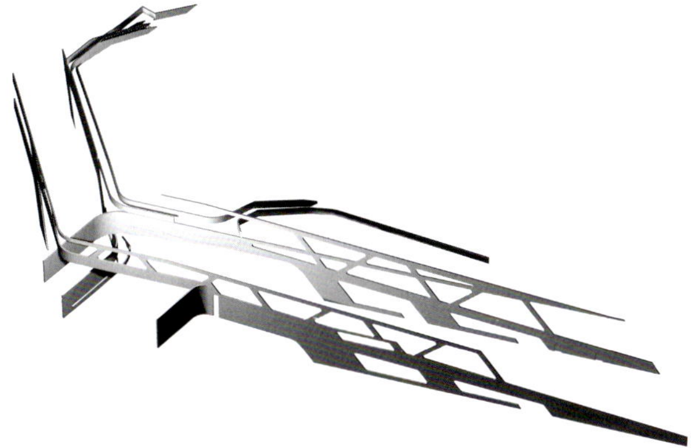

BMW Central plan, structural surface diagram, entry, interior lobby.

Nasher Sculpture Center

Landscape, or more precisely, garden-space, archeology, weight, lightness, transparency, and quietness all become representational attributes of the Nasher Sculpture Center.[10] Designed to accommodate an extensive sculpture collection and not compete with it on a site dominated by large-scale buildings and freeway infrastructure, Renzo Piano Building Workshop chose to create a building that was both archeological and technological in its creation and definition of space. Stone clad walls 2 feet wide by 144 feet long and spaced 34 feet apart mark the building and the site with a timeless presence, in turn complemented by a glazed roof presented as a thin rendition of technology articulately detailed to admit only northern light. The attributes of archeology are further reinforced through the concealment of "external" realities. Gutters and downspouts are located within the walls, which, in turn are given further solidarity through the precise mitering of the corners, achieving a look of solid stone blocks.

Representational themes are united with organizational strategies by incorporating the use of neutral ordering systems. To promote the idea of transparency the linear stone walls are organized in a repetitive array of parallel planes perpendicular to glass façades at both the front and rear of the building, extending a transparency from the front entry well into the exterior sculpture garden to the rear of the building. The regular bays and singular height of the walls, in addition to the conscious repetition of different modules, whether the stone blocks, closely spaced curved roof beams, or delicately repeating light-screening panels on the roof, all support a quietness created by the utilization of simple and clear systems of order.

Modularity, linearity, and lines of extension are also used as site organizing strategies. A tight tree module for planting perimeter trees along the sides of the site, along with segmented linear perimeter walls, provide privacy and definition to the exterior sculpture space. Trees planted at the front of the building align with the stone walls, extending the spatial quality of the exterior sculpture garden at the rear of the building, to its entry façade. An additional allée of trees in the sculpture garden aligns with the stone walls, defining the interior entry space, extending it into the sculpture court, and maintaining similar organizing rules. ◘

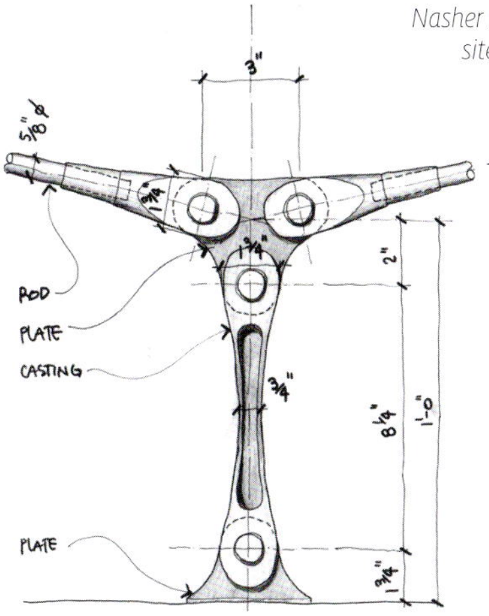

Nasher Sculpture Center site plan, assembly sketch, interior.

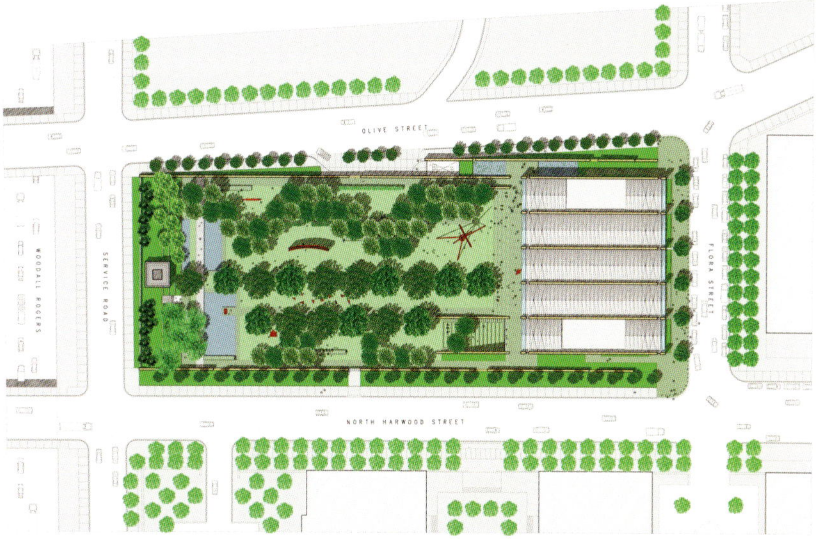

Notes

1. Richard Meier, *Introduction to the Atlas of American Architecture*, 2009, http: www.richardmeier.com
2. Richard Meier, *Richard Meier Architect 3* (Rizzoli International Publications Inc., 1999), Acknowledgments.
3. Ibid.
4. Thom Mayne, Interview with author, July 2009.
5. Ibid.
6. Jeffrey Kipnis and Todd Gannon, eds. *Source Books in Architecture 1*, Morphosis Diamond Ranch High School (Montecelli Press, 2001), 25.
7. Todd Gannon, ed., *Source Books in Architecture 7*, Zaha Hadid BMW Central Building (Princeton Architectural Press, New York, 2006), 14.
8. Ibid, 17.
9. Ibid, 19.
10. Renzo Piano, *Renzo Piano Building Workshop, Complete Workshop Volume 5* (Phaidon Press Ltd., London, New York, 2008), 152.

How to use this book

The aspect of this book that may be the most distinctive follows from a decision to "control" conversations and connect them to the use of design intentions and strategies that are the basis of this effort. The primary vehicle for establishing a framework for the interviews was the utilization of a common set of questions. As outlined in this chapter and given evidence in the subsequent interviews, the questions were asked of each architect. Given the need to allow for a spontaneity and fluidity in an interview format it is to be admitted that every question was not asked in each interview. On the other hand in some discussions the topic underlying a given question appears more than once. Yet with these interview-based realities acknowledged it can be stated that the themes underlying the larger substance of the questions are addressed in responses that are both clear and necessarily abstract, and sometimes compelling even if not always speaking to the specifics of a given question.

To further inform the reader, various methods can be employed to absorb the thoughts expressed in the individual interviews. Armed with an overall perspective concerning the thesis of the book presented in the introduction and chapters preceding the interviews, it is preferred they be read in a sequence desired by the reader. However, options exist allowing for a reading of the interviews "simultaneously" by focusing on responses to individual questions. To enable that option, questions discussed with each architect and numerically identified in this chapter are located in a linear band at the beginning of each interview. To locate the questions in the respective interviews the corresponding number(s) representing the questions asked are located in the lower left corner of each two page spread and then precede the paragraph in which the question is located.

The intent of the simultaneous reading option is to allow the reader to go back and forth from question to question and uncover the commonality or range of positions discussed in response to each topic. This method of reading the book permits a more singular focus on a specific topic. The book then becomes more of a workbook, allowing one to develop his or her position through direct research of the beliefs and positions of others.

A final note on the use of the pull out quotes and captions. Quotes delineating larger themes are lifted from the text body to capture notable comments expressed by each architect during the interview. While not project specific, these comments typically underlie beliefs that form core values and remain foundational to ideas and concepts underlying multiple design decisions. These quotes are framed with two dotted parallel lines. In a similar but more visually oriented manifestation, captions adjoining the photographs of the completed projects are also extracted from the interviews. With these captions the intent is to link ideas expressed in realized outcomes with statements that delineate design concepts and intentions. ◘

Interview Methodolgy

The thesis underlying this book is unique in two aspects, both derived from a common issue. That issue is the belief that there exists certain design related procedures which, when followed, can provide consistent and elevated design outcomes. One side of this is embedded in the title of the book itself, that "internal" language-based concepts, and the strategies required for their implementation, advance aesthetic, and experiential qualities and aid in establishing organizational "rules" that assist in forming an underlying quality of coherence. Within that requirement is the need to identify and establish the use of organizational and representational conceptual domains if one is to fully integrate a comprehensive architectural language-based design process.

The second aspect constitutes the content of this chapter. The intent is to expand upon the issues described above by utilizing an interview methodology that magnifies the organizational and representational domains identified as necessary components of a design process, ones integral to providing enhanced design outcomes. Given the diversity underlying contemporary architectural practices and a similar extensive array of discussions regarding the role design intentions play in the design of a building, it is of value to provide a framework to these types of discussions, a framework that allows for more directed responses and useful takeaways by a reader. The goal is to prevent an outcome where broad generalities and anecdotal side stories regarding a design "process" replace a more thorough discussion of topics important to an elevated outcome of a building's design.

To avoid that occurance, an interview framework defined by the use of consistent questions is useful to avoid outcomes that arise when discussions of design intent are limited to sweeping statements or tend toward topics of interest to individual architects. Questions providing a common framework for the evaluation of specific topics related to the use of design intentions addressing questions relevant to the design of all buildings is of value and also allows for a "shared" dialogue to evolve. Employing a standard set of questions in the interview format provides for a cross referencing of underlying design strategies employed by the architects interviewed and their application in the projects which are the focus of the discussion. This is amplified by forming questions directed to the use and creation of architectural languages, ones that incorporate organizational and representational strategies underlying their development.

The opposite is often evident in lectures and many written formats where design intentions are presented via verbal or visual gestures. Often general in nature, these statements provide little development in relation to the more difficult aspect of explaining how a given design intention is used or amplified throughout the design process. This lack of follow-through development contributes to an incompleteness regarding design related dicussions that, while intriguing as starting points, often remain under-conceptualized as end products.

The architects and the projects selected for the interviews have overcome these limitations. While diverse in scale and direction, they maintain a thorough development of the architectural languages utilized in the formation of their designs. The intent of this effort is to follow this, allowing an understanding of these investigations as they relate to the deeper use of design intentions. The diversity of the projects allows for that understanding to evolve through using the common and shared question format.

Furthermore, this effort is actually more of a "workbook" than a book one simply reads and absorbs. While the second option is certainly available, more insight to the various design processes employed will be gained if one works back and forth from project to project, standard question to standard question, and text to drawings and photographs in a manner allowing for a clearer understanding of the organizational and representational strategies utilized in the development of various design intentions and languages. It is also important to see it as a workbook in that analyzing multiple projects is essential to developing a greater understanding of the issues addressed by the questions and the varied responses the architects offer.

It can be argued that compressing the focus of the book to the investigation of language-based representational and organizational domains is reductive. There is room for that critique in relation to the relevance of performance and other design related considerations as a building's final design outcome is dependent upon the integration of these factors. However, if these external considerations become drivers at the expense of the internal language-based attributes, the process begins to degrade as it is then not anchored or envisioned in relation to the considerations ultimately needed to give depth and coherence to the work.

An underlying attribute of the questions accepts that all themes underlying design intentions can derive only from considerations of the site, the program, or the parti (parti in this context suggesting architectural interests, conceptual interests, client values, etc.). From an internal standpoint, these questions probe the language creating attributes of the design process. An additional goal is to explore various strategies utilized for the creation of diverse yet integrated language sets. Buildings typically require the use of multiple language sets in their final designed resolution. Diverse organizational and representational strategies have to be utilized if language-based drivers are going to enhance the overall design quality in relation to meaningful experiential outcomes.

The questions below represent those asked of the architects interviewed for this book. In the transcribed interviews not all questions may appear. To support and honor the fluidity of the conversation, some aspects of a question located further in the format may have been previously addressed at an earlier point in the interview. To avoid redundancy in relation to a topic previously addressed a question may have been eliminated. Similarly, interview topic-specific follow-up questions are often employed to expand on points raised in the response to the initial formatted question.

Preliminary Questions

1| What value, potential, or use do you see in order?

Historically the concept of order has been related to an "idea of beauty," a definition that is more difficult to determine or agree upon in contemporary architectural practice. However, ordering principles continue to be employed in the design and refinement of noteworthy buildings. They are used as design development tools in the creation of unified languages and/or secondary language sets.

This question, as a starting point, may or may not directly relate to the discipline of architecture. As such, non-architecturally specific positions may ultimately be incorporated into initial design conceptual considerations. As an example, these positions could be represented in declarations from numerous "de-constructivist" architects who have explained their design strategies as being based upon opinions that our lives are not lived out with everyday certainty or regularity, thus their architecture reflects those considerations.

This question is used at the beginning of the interview process to allow the architect to define initial parameters or interests as they relate to principles affecting the use of "cohering strategies" in their design process.

2| How do concepts of order manifest themselves in your design thinking or process? What does order mean to you architecturally?

Having discussed broad outlines or definitions of order, the initial question is followed with a more specific query exploring the relationship of order to architecture. The intent of the question is to probe the architect's perceived value of order as it relates to the use of architectural ordering systems specifically. Similarly, does the integration and manifestation of ordering systems, in whatever architectural application, occur as a tool early in the design process or as an evolving strategy, one that develops as the understanding of the design is clarified over the duration of the design process.

3| How do you employ formal/spatial ordering systems?
The discussion regarding order delves into specific strategies that, while not necessarily project specific, may underpin early design considerations as one searches for responses to issues raised by the site or program. Information provided by those considerations become "influencers" suggesting organizational ideas or design intentions that provide architectural and spatial direction.

4| Do design interests, specifically ones extending beyond those concerned with facilitating the distribution of the program and fitting the building to the site, originate within the discipline of architecture or from sources lying outside of it?
Design interests, and their domain of origin, are strong determinants affecting the aesthetic direction of a project. The intent of the question is to probe underlying interests, relating their proximity to the development of standard architectural considerations such as structure, space, materials, etc. This is in contrast to broader themes that may or may not derive from these considerations. Examples of broader design interests could include considerations establishing the structure as a place of "refuge," an exploration of "indeterminacy" suggesting interests referencing more philosophical considerations lying outside the more normative design considerations identified above. These wider design considerations have animated the architectural production of numerous contemporary projects whose architects have achieved international recognition.

5| How do these interests impact your thinking in relation to the methods employed to architecturally organize and/or represent your intentions?
Depending upon a design interest and its relationship to formal preferences, considerations of this type will have a significant impact on the design's outcome. If an architect has a strong preference for developing and refining a "normative" approach, such as the use of a geometric form of organization or a tectonic expression, that preference will direct design outcomes toward aresults creating an identifiable architectural expression lying within the norms established by organizational or language-based "rules" underpinning geometric organizational strategies or techtonic representations. Siting and program distribution concerns will not become the only design drivers. Other approaches, more philosophically oriented, can direct the design in a manner intended to create experiences envisioned to provide a project with a qualities referencing themes beyond established norms referenced above.

The transformative work of Frank Lloyd Wright, Mies Van der Rohe, and Le Corbusier can be evaluated in relation to their intention to establish transformative positions in relation to history, technology, and materiality. These visions were not singularly grounded in functional or performance-related explanations. More often they represented, or were interpreted as, visions made manifest through organizational and representational themes identified through language-based intentions exploring formal, spatial, and material considerations.

Global Design Strategy Questions

6| What are your initial concerns when you begin design work on a project?

This fairly standard question has an underlying intent seeking to determine design interests or priorities. Flushing out a client's wants and needs as well as gaining insight from varying site characteristics are appropriate considerations at the beginning of the design process. However, for many architects design interests may define avenues used to convey interests or experiential qualities that fall outside those defined by responses to the site or program.

7| When you started the design of ...., were there global, architecturally transcendent, themes you were investigating at the beginning of the design process? If so, could you elaborate?

Essentially following up on the underlying intent of the previous inquiry regarding design interests, architectural or otherwise, this question seeks to probe further into that area but now specifically relating those interests or considerations to the project to be discussed in the interview.

8| What other conceptual criteria (organizational, representational, or performance) did you employ to anchor the initial intentions?

Ultimately, all design processes exploring higher design aspirations must address and incorporate an organizational strategy as an intent versus a simple functional or performance-defined arrangement of space or material. Similarly, projects of this type typically envision numerous design aspects permitting characteristics that represent more than a collection of individual ideas solving individual problems.

Therefore, both organizational and representational strategies are employed conceptually as these are areas available for additional conceptual definition. This is in contrast to creating a design that is singularly defined by programmatic and site based considerations. In that regard this question is included to allow the architects to expand on their design interests.

9| What organizational or representational intentions arising from an analysis of the site and program were employed to organize and ultimately express your conceptual interests?
Organizational and representational strategies can be responses to the site and program. The question preceding this one was probing the use of "internal" interests of a more purely architectural nature that might impact or direct the creation of an architectural language. As that is not necessarily a priority early in the design process, this question seeks to focus on the conceptual interests that are "external" to language-based considerations and often derive from considerations such as client values, functional relationships regarding the layout of the programmed spaces, influences derived from the site, etc.

General Design Strategy Questions

10| How do you add additional depth to your initial (global) intentions?
Projects containing greater design development and maturity conceptualize a greater number of areas or components than those that are less developed. This question seeks to discover those conceptual interests and discuss how they have been employed to develop the design and to identify the specific areas of interest to which the individual architects are drawn.

11| Did you "name" or prioritize elements or programmatic areas to differentiate or give hierarchy to larger global intentions?
Many architects will give a building, programmatic zone, component assembly, or detail a "name." This name is often utilized to identify specific design characteristics, representational authority, specific organizational strategy, or a language set intended to present a special identity to that area or component of the building. The question further explores the use of design interests and intentions as they relate to specific strategies employed in areas that have an identifiable or distinct design attribute beyond those defining initial design interests.

12| As the design developed, did you use the different attributes of the organizational and representational conceptual fields to mature or cross-reference each other?
Organizational and representational conceptual considerations represent an interwoven matrix of a building's design and should not remain as seperate domains utilizing self-contained independent strategies. Further in the design process, as each of the domain's characteristics are more fully understood,

certain cross-referencing often occurs. A general example is when an organizational type or strategy is identified and reinforces or amplifies representational design interests unique to that component or area (language set). This allows the representational interests to be identified or self-expressive as per the preferences and intentions of the architect.

13| Regarding ideas that are more representational in nature, how do you explore the organizational potential of these ideas? Did you envision the manner in which the .... building was organized as representational in nature?

Building on the previous question and the use of organizational strategies to further identify and enrich representational interests, this question further explores the linkage of organizational strategies to representational interests. Themes that are representational, not metaphorical, such as "I want the private areas of the building to be 'passive' and the public areas to be 'active' often require different organizational strategies supporting design interests intended to create passive and active languages, and therefore, experiential outcomes. This may be expressed in plan and section organizational characteristics of the building or the manner in which details (concealed fasteners vs. exposed fasteners) or material-jointing (gridded vs. offset patterns of organization) considerations may be employed.

To amplify and more fully discuss themes of the preceding question, this follow-up seeks to uncover organizational methods employed at various scales that provide the broader representational themes with more detailed definition. This is specifically asked in relation to organizational strategies used to enrich the representational intent.

14| Did you see the organizational framework employed in the .... building needing additional architectural expression because as an organizational or ordering system that aspect of the design was "under conceptualized"? Conversely, was its essence envisioned as a significant aspect of what the building was to represent?

Some architects prioritize the value of clear organizational strategies or expressions. Representational outcomes such as the general "orderly-ness" of a particular organizational strategy are understood as embedded in the buildings essence and understood in the eyes and mind of the observer. Under this viewpoint the question seeks to explore whether the architect is seeing the concept of organization as defining or becoming a representational aspect of the building's design in its expression of clarity and coherence.

The question also explores the relevance of organizational strategies in that for other architects organizational aspects are simply givens, such as a 25-foot by 35-foot structural bay and the grid that derives from it. This example represents an aspect of a building's organization that may be under utilized or under conceptualized from a theoretical standpoint.

15| As the design progressed how did you link ephemeral, poetic intentions of your design to the pragmatic, functional performance concerns?
Technically a broader topic that could be understood as a global design interest on the part of an architect, this question was placed later in the interview to allow poetic considerations underlying a project to be explained in relation to the building's refinement in a more developed or architecturally understood part of the design process where functional aspects of design have been resolved, more or less, and considerations that are more purely architectural are coming to the fore.

Specific Design Strategy Questions

16| Was the expressive, representational, nature of materials, or how you deployed them, important in the design of ....? When did the notion of (or diminishing of) material intentionality become important in the project?
For some architects the notion of materiality and its relationship to the building is at the heart of the design from its inception, whether as part of a basic ethos on the part of the architect or as a response to the characteristics of the site or culture of the area. For others, the character of the materiality comprising the project developed as multiple characteristics of the design evolve and is further revealed in the material qualities of the building.

For noteworthy buildings, materiality is not just cladding but is at the heart of its character. This character is often expressed in a singular representational aspect defined by the material itself, such in the use of concrete. However, the manner in which materials are jointed or proportioned often contains an organizational and representational subtext.

17| How did you conceptualize the organization, assembly, or composition of the joint between materials in the .... building and relate it to earlier intentions?
In the design of many buildings organizational interests concerning the proportion and scale of a given component or material, and, therefore, the pattern created via the joints separating them, are

often dictated and installed via the specifications of the manufactured product. This often leads to an under-conceptualized aspect of many design decisions regarding a building's exterior and interior surfaces in relation to the organization of its material components. In other buildings, the size of a component or the organizational strategy underlying its arrangement expresses significant conceptualization. The question seeks to understand not only the architect's interest in conceptual strategies underpinning the use and conceptualization of materials and their joinery, but also how these aspects relate to earlier design interests and intentions.

18| What was your thinking regarding the expression of building systems or the diminishing of their epressions in the building? What organizational or representational strategies were contemplated in your decision to express the systems?

The degree to which structural, mechanical, building envelope (e.g., rain-screens,) and other system-type components and assemblies are expressed can become a significant attribute of a building's design, with both representational and organizational value. The degree to which these system-type expressions may be incorporated is often determined early in the schematic design phase but their detail and refinement generally occur later in the design process when greater conceptual clarity regarding intentions is more fully realized. When expressed, the representational attributes of the system-types are directly related to the manner in which organizational strategies are used to enhance the meaningfulness of their expression.

19| In refining the design did you select programmatic areas or architectural elements to privilege? If so, how were the conceptual positions expansions on, or counterpoints to, earlier design intentions?

Standard language-based expressions include dualities such as public/private and servant/served expressions of differing programmatic components in the design. The question seeks to uncover how similar but more specific design interests are served through identifying certain unique aspects of the building's program, giving them additional conceptual "privilege." An example of such an interest would be to allow the library in a law school to spatially "float" or be clad in a more exotic material in order to distinguish its importance within the larger confines of the school itself. ◘

Question Indexes

By Architect *(Question•Page)*

By Question *(Page)*

Interviews

MacKay-Lyons Sweetapple Architects Ltd.

Brian MacKay-Lyons

Hill House

Representing a project revealing a "less is more" attitude towards design, the Hill House was constructed in 2003 on a drumlin facing the Atlantic Ocean on the east coast of Nova Scotia, Canada. A wood framed residence clad in wooden shingles, the 2000-square-foot structure is comprised of a main residential structure and a guest-house, both forming and embracing a central courtyard. Allowing vernacular building traditions to overlap and influence modern language-based preferences for more dynamic forms of organization, the design of the Hill House engages multiple intentions incorporating both abstract and very real understandings of living.

The Hill House addresses cultural and physical landscapes, cultural in the form of recognizing regional climate-based building customs and physical in relation to the manner in which the Hill House integrates to the landscape. Both landscapes are intended to facilitate human needs honoring existential feelings towards prospect and refuge, evidenced in the manner in which the house captures and frames distant views while also promoting intimacy and protection through the use of multiple spatial typologies. Spaces, ranging from courtyards, covered exterior gathering areas and intimate interiors provide multiple opportunities for anchoring and exploring, attaching and detaching – essentially allowing the possibility to ground oneself to essential human desires and link to the land, sky, water, materiality and order.

1| 4| 5| 7| 8| 9| 12| 15| 10| 18| 19|

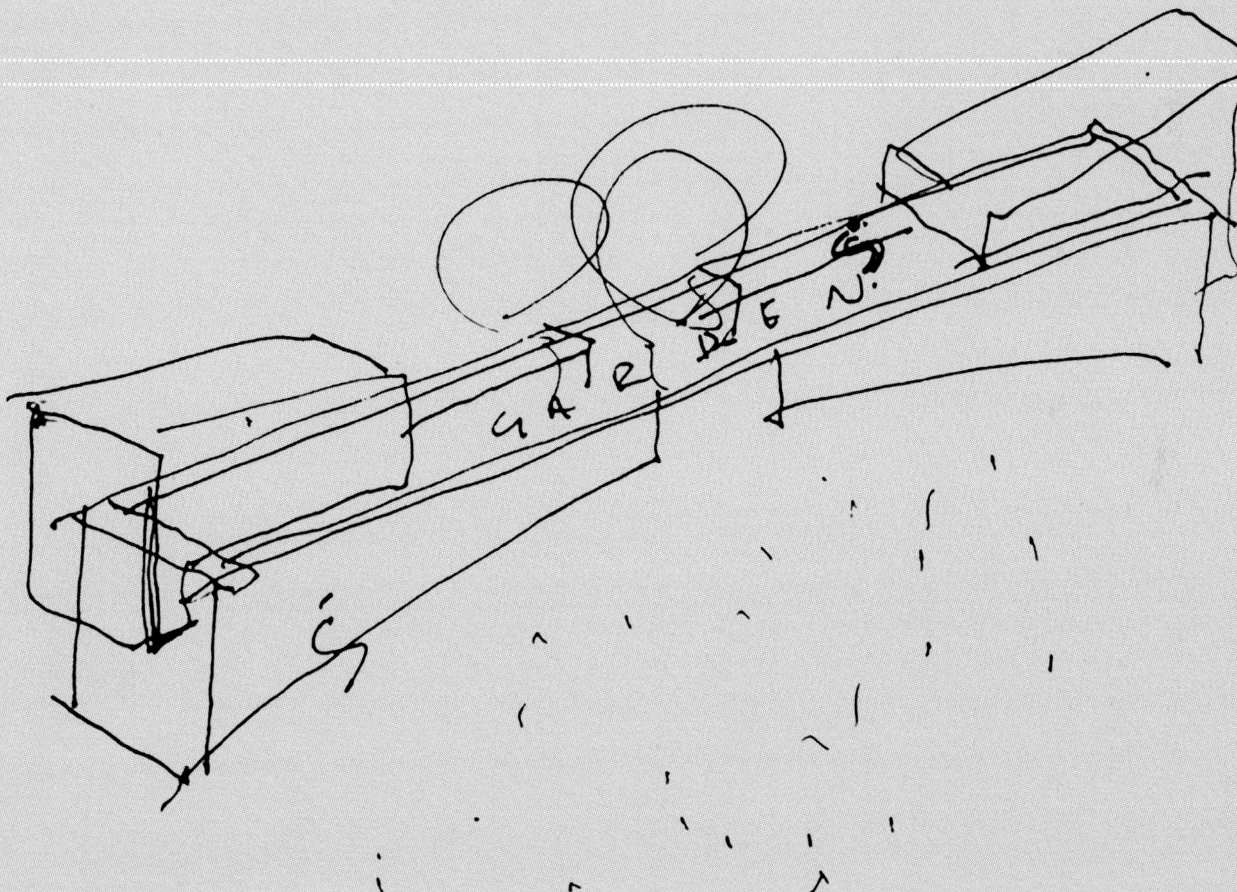
GARDENS

What architects need to do is bring order to a design outcome. In essence creating order facilitates the role of the architect as teacher. An architect should create buildings that are didactic, that explain themselves, that explain the role of order in providing intellectual and psychological comfort.

So a good parti drawing is something you keep remaking through the process. You don't just do it at the beginning.

If there is a problem with an elevation, with a section, or with a detail, I'll say, "OK show me the plan," because the diagnosis of that will be evident in plan. The right way around the problem will be found in the plan. The plan really is the generator.

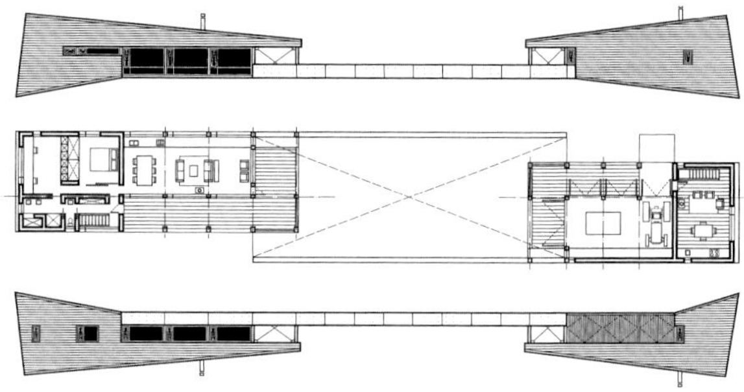

1| Tom Diehl: What value, potential, or use do you see in order?

Brian MacKay-Lyons: Today in architectural education, in architectural discourse, the word order is not used very much. There seems to be a greater interest in surface than there is in deep structure in architecture. I think of deep structure as being interesting stuff in architecture, in the Jungian sense, in the archetypes and Chomsky. He talked about deep structure. During the relativistic days we are in right now it seems fashionable to say that chaos is not order. I think that is such a facile argument that you don't design chaos, that it happens automatically, with a lot of complexity. What architects need to do is bring order to a design outcome, which brings comfort to people. There is a kind of legible or even invisible order to things that allows us to make sense of the world. In essence, creating order facilitates the role of the architect as teacher. An architect should create buildings that are didactic, that explain themselves, that explain the role of order in providing intellectual and psychological comfort.

A form of grounding then.

Yes. I'm a drummer, so I think a lot in terms of the rhythm section, in terms of structure. For me, the parti, which is another word you don't hear much about these days, is very, very important because it is the minimum amount of marks on a piece of paper that tell you the most about the order of things. The Hill House has a very clear parti: the drawing you keep remaking as you work to try to get closer and closer and closer, with fewer and fewer marks, to the essence of things. It's like in a haiku poem—how few syllables can you actually make a poem from? And that is not some kind of hollow exercise; it has to contain a tremendous amount of complexity for the whole project to succeed. The idea that that's a reductive way of working is really a kind of silliness about words, as if simplicity and complexity were opposites. Architecture, luckily, is not a verbal discourse. That's a frailty of the language to say that complexity and simplicity are opposites. A good parti is the simplest thing that contains the most content.

Frank Lloyd Wright said an architect is the master of the plan. Again, that's very unfashionable to say, but the abstraction of a plan, a diagram, or a section diagram, allows the imagination to continue to work. The image is a short circuit. Giancarlo De Carlo said to me one time, "Brian, once one is given an image you never take it back." So if you want to take your clients on an intellectual journey together, where they leave their biases and tastes at the front door, you take them along via the abstraction. A lot of architects will tell you that clients don't understand abstraction. But I find quite the opposite. The human mind has great pattern recognition skills. And that's a way to get clients to trust you and let you take them some place new. The image gets in the way of that.

The image may contrast the essence. As you're trying to understand the essence of the project, is the intent to create an abstract architectural order allowing for a coherence to emerge among the "parts."

Venturi talked about the idea of symmetry, by which he meant the commensurability of the parts. So a good parti drawing is something you keep remaking through the process; you don't just do it at the beginning. It should be able to embrace content at the level of landscape and environment at a large scale and hold subsequent refining issues together at the smaller scale. It should represent big ideas, and it should represent its own completion.

Some of this might be a function of a practice such as yours where one knows future issues that are anticipated in the initial parti. You have that ability to read into the future what a parti might represent. For someone starting out as a designer can you reel back in time to comment on what you remember of an initial parti from a project years ago and how you moved from abstraction to "reality"?

How does one generate other layers of meaning? Frank Lloyd Wright said, "If all the great buildings were burned, they would rebuild themselves on their foundations." When I am working on a project with someone in the office, if there is a problem with an elevation, with a section, or with a detail, I'll say, "OK show me the plan," because the diagnosis of that will be evident in plan. The right way around the problem will be found in the plan. The plan really is the generator.

So the plan becomes, as the design has matured from a sketch to a plan, the point of reference for sectional or elevation implications. Many have a sense that elevations have some additional conceptual requirements. Students and many designers often have a basic understanding of the building's siting or its plan, yet when they get to elevations they struggle.

Mies Van Der Rohe said elevations were the hardest. And I think that's right. I think in terms of my own development as an architect, the ability to develop an elevation, a façade, was the aspect of the design that took the longest to learn. When I try to teach my students to think in elevation, I refer to the elevation as a piece of skin on top of a section. Unless you draw the section, which has the structure in it, and the framing of the building, you can't really make the elevation. In order to make an elevation you need a plan and a section underneath it. The plan is the program, meaning that it has to percolate

The grammar, the pin-wheeling relationships in the elevations, happen in the sections, they happen in the plan, and they happen in the site plan when we make courtyards.

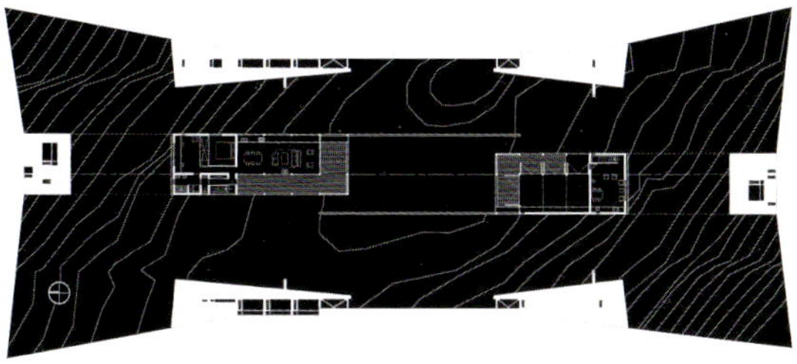

through the elevation. And the section is the structure that has to percolate through the elevation. I tell students, and people in the office, a productive person draws what they know first. It's like when you are taking an exam. You want to answer the questions you know the answers to right off the bat. I find that when you do that, when you put into the elevation the information from the plan and the section that you need, in that onion skin kind of way, there's very little else to do. You've gone a long ways toward having a façade without doing anything.

Yet at this point, the rubber hits the road, and it's very, very difficult to really do it. I think the reason it takes so long to create elevations is that there has to be a language, and it takes a lifetime to develop one, a kind of best practices way of composing things. For example, I've developed a very consistent grammar for integrating fenestration. The grammar, the pin-wheeling relationships in the elevations, happens in the sections. They happen in the plan, and they happen in the site plan when we make courtyards. Essentially, there is only one idea represented as pin-wheeling. Even if I am putting a house and a barn together to form a courtyard, the relationship between two windows on a façade, or organizing two buildings in a site plan, it is really the same grammatical approach. The grammar comes from years of practice, and it comes in our work; well, it comes from two places. The grammar, that pin-wheeling grammar, comes from looking at vernacular buildings emanating from this building tradition and understanding how a pinwheel evolves when a lower door and an upper window share a jack stud. It also comes from looking at Russian Supremacist paintings and modern art. I've found a place in my own mind where modern art and vernacular building traditions overlap, and that overlap has become the grammar of making elevations.

Of course, that's a modernist idea, the idea of a non-static kinetic composition where an elevation, a plan or section has movement, implies movement, and is dynamic. It's not symmetrical, not static.

So when you look at the architecture of Palladio and others, you see static neo-classical approaches which were also associated with class and wealth. When you look at a fish shack, and you see a door with a window along side, you are looking at folk architecture, indigenous, local, poor people stuff. The pioneers of modernism said we need a new idiom because class associations tainted the neo-classical idiom. So, if you're a modernist, and you're a democrat, you are looking for a source for order that comes from the poor.

I believe that, as a North American democrat, all culture derives from the poor. We know that jazz comes from the blues, and the blues come from Black sharecroppers in the Mississippi Delta. We know this. We know that frogs' legs in Paris come from starvation. All the great symphonies...we know that Tchaikovsky's symphonies come from Russian folk dances. We know when we lose track of the grass-roots origins, culture gets soft. So, I am very committed to that democratic idea that you look to the grass roots for culture.

Your argument then is that many modern directions are derivative of previous actions emanating from the poor; they are from a more culturally based understanding.

Picasso and the African mask, Henry Moore and African sculpture, Eric Clapton, what did he do? He studied Robert Johnson. This is extreme worldview stuff, but when I make an elevation, I avoid the Palladian symmetry because of those principles.

Because it is more democratic?

Because it's more dynamic. Earlier, you asked if there is a master plan informing the design of my residential property here in Nova Scotia. There is a grammar. And the grammar is always incomplete because of this dynamic element, this pin-wheeling element. It's like walking. Laurie Anderson said walking is a combination of falling and stopping yourself from falling. If you set up this kind of dynamic composition, it's always easy to make the next step. Yes, there is a kind of inductive master plan.

And your argument would be that it is more accessible from a meaning standpoint?

It is less rigid. You know, if a client says, "I need a window over my kitchen sink." You could say the grammar we have for organizing elevations is happily complex and rich enough to accept that. I was on the site of the Hill House one day, and I said to the client, "You need a window right here over the sink because of the view across the beach." And he said, "We can't do that." I said "Why not?" And he said, "Well, it will ruin the elevation," but we were able to show him how it would integrate with our grammar, our language.

In effect that would go back to the use of the parti; it is still going to exert an influence.

The parti tells you where the major openings go. For instance, the plan parti tells you where the solids and voids are. When we make an envelope in a building, I rather think of it as an envelope because I think of the wall and the roof as one surface, as one continuous surface. When we make holes in buildings, we do the principle holes first. You go from the general to the specific. I know this is south, and I know there is a great view, so I'd like a big hole here. The parti tells you where the big holes are going to go. What they don't tell you is

So, I am very committed to that democratic idea that you look to the grass roots for culture.

This is extreme worldview stuff, but when I make an elevation, I avoid the Palladian symmetry because of those principles.

I think architects, especially serious ones, ironically just enjoy making order.

But as you are developing as a student, or as an architect, your facility should not ever be ahead of your intellectual questioning.

Architecture is not a side component of some other discipline. Architecture is architecture. And if you want to prepare yourself for interdisciplinary work, then you should be a good architect first and foremost, ...the basis for a meaningful interdisciplinary exchange is to be a specialist.

where the salt and pepper are going to go. In our work when we make elevations, there are always the principle openings and the secondary openings. The secondary openings are very flexible as long as they obey the grammatical rules. One of those is white space. For instance, I will not easily distribute windows over a surface unless I absolutely make it a cheese grater. It is a very particular intention to do that. Otherwise, we make sure we have what painters call white space, or negative space. If I do put windows in a wall, I'll cluster them and leave large parts of the envelope blank.

So that you can honor or privilege that initial relationship set up in the parti? Then the secondary windows become, if not the salt and pepper, they become the furniture.

That's it. It goes back to the plan, the parti. I am an easy guy to talk to about your thesis because the order for me, as a musician, as somebody who thinks in terms of the rhythm section and structure, ordering ideas are second nature, and I love it. Now, we can have conversations about these things in terms of right and wrong or good and evil, or we can have conversations about these things in terms of just the delight of working, making things.

I think architects, especially serious ones, ironically just enjoy making order. Now some make order in a stillborn way; they are just not good architects. You have to have a sense of humor to go with order.

The serious architect has a desire to communicate meaning through their use of intentionality, versus the architect who might be ordering in a facile manner because he or she knows some rules of operation yet there is no attachment to a larger meaningfulness or anchoring.

It's a classic issue of facility. It's dangerous to get experienced. Because when you get experienced, you get facile. I remember in a conversation with Juhani Pallasmaa, I was saying that I think facility is the enemy of rigor. We all know the student who can do the beautiful watercolor, do the beautiful perspective drawings right off the bat, and it comes very easily to them. There is no struggle. That work is ultimately not satisfying.

You need some facility; you have to have some talent. But as you are developing as a student, or as an architect, your facility should not ever be ahead of your intellectual questioning. It's like being a better salesman than a designer. We all know the student who gets up in the three-piece suit and presents his or her thesis. What they are saying is basically "I'm going to be a good salesman first and a good architect second."

I think it's the same thing as about craft. Craft is highly overrated. I think, like Glen Murcutt, craft is given by your culture. He says 80% of his buildings are designed by his culture, and he does the semi-tailoring where he crafts the last 20%. I think craft has become fetishized in architecture; that's another thing I am really against. I don't think when you are designing you should be better at polishing than you are at conceptualizing.

That's an interesting point. Does the well-crafted model, or the drawing with beautiful line work, or coloration seduce us into believing there is more content in the project than really exists?

It is seductive. Craft has its value. Craft has meaning and value. There's no question to that, and you need it. However, what you shouldn't do is get so tricky with craft that it can somehow replace a larger meaning. So structure first, craft second.

Structure in this case is more than structural; it is structure with multiple meanings. You are arguing for your definition of deep structure, correct?

Yes, spatial structure first, structure in the landscape, structure in the sticks, posts and beams, the bones, the rhythms, and the compositional structure of two-dimensional composition or the skin. It is all structure.

4| But it is structure that is tied to an order that's tied to a meaning that is tied to a culture. Someone else might tie it to something else. I would like to follow that with a question regarding your comment about Russian Supremacists and Mondrian exerting an influence on your conceptual thinking. Do design interests such as these, those extending beyond one's concern with facilitating the distribution of the program or fitting the building to the site, originate within the discipline of architecture of from sources lying outside of it? I am interested in fleshing this out.

That relates to another issue that is disturbing to me, the word interdisciplinary. It's usually code for not being good at anything. The discipline of architecture is an integrative discipline. I tell my students, "If you are going to be an architect, you have to be comfortable being the dumb one in every conversation." The building inspector knows more about code. The carpenter knows more about a piece of wood. The banker knows more about financing. The planner knows more about planning. You will always be the dumb one. But we are integrative. We are the art director in the film. We are the conductor in the orchestra, and you have to know a little bit about a lot of things. Now, I believe very much in disciplines. There are disciplines, and there aren't many of them—you know mathematics is a discipline, and architecture is the supreme form-giving discipline.

In our work, when we make elevations, there are always the principle openings and the secondary openings. The secondary openings are very flexible as long as they obey the grammatical rules. One of those is white space.

There are only three languages. We have a visual language, a numerical language, and a written language. Architects seem to be the best at the visual, formal, spatial language. I think architecture is not a side component of some other discipline. Architecture is architecture. And if you want to prepare yourself for interdisciplinary work, then you should be a good architect first and foremost, which is a mistake a lot of people make.

We have students who say, "I want to be like an artist." So I say the best way to collaborate with an artist is to be an architect. When I sit with Richard Serra at his dining-room table, and we sketch together, he is absolutely not interested in my understanding of fine art. He is sitting with me because he knows that I know something about buildings and being an architect. So, the basis for a meaningful interdisciplinary exchange is to be a specialist.

To where you can dialectically raise the bar and have a conversation adding additional input, meaning, or content to the conversation?

It wouldn't help that conversation if I said I also paint on Saturday afternoons. Who cares about that?

But you obviously have an interest in form, we all do…

But architecture is the medium for that. It's through the discipline in all of the senses of the word. You know, practice takes practice; you've got to stick to your knitting. That allows you, ironically, to be open to find a way to channel your interests in so many other things. Rather than being a pure spectator at an art gallery, you can mine fine art for things you can actually use in architecture. So there's a kind of pragmatic "How can this be a part of what I do?" It's through your own discipline that you can engage other ones, whether you engage Mondrian or Russian Supremacists.

Right. When you are looking at a painting or a sculpture or an automobile, whatever it might be, you are looking at it within the framework of your own thinking. You might ask, "What were the design principles, or what were the themes underlying that work of art or that taillight detail, and how do they add value or legitimacy to my own investigation?"

You can look at or listen to the choreography of a jazz concert, of the music's structure, the structure of the performance, and you can process that through an abstract relationship to your discipline, a sequence of spaces or the way that the music was choreographed.

So your argument would be…

You have to have a discipline, you've got to have a home page, and you've got to have a toolbox. Ideas used by students often reference everything but architecture. I had some students this semester who said, "Well, you know I am interested in sustainability." I said, "OK, that's fantastic. Learn to be an architect. If you want anybody to hire you develop a toolbox of architectural skills, you will then be hired because you are a good architect. If you're interested in sustainability, and you are not prepared with proper architectural skills, you will drive a taxi. You won't be able to do anything for the planet except recycle your garbage. However, if you obtain proper architectural skills, you can practice the principles of sustainability. People will pay you to do it, and you can change the world. So be a good architect." Now some of those students end up leaving school because they don't like the sound of that. The others are all over it and…

That further legitimizes your comments.
I believe in the discipline, but it's just a toolbox.

Many architects do make references to conditions beyond architecture. I am interested in ferreting out positions that explore fundamental issues in architecture through statements such as, "Yes, those themes and ideas are important, and I do use them, but I don't use them as if they are creating an initial spark brought in from outside the discipline of architecture."
I don't read Derrida, because I believe Derrida thinks that architecture is a subset of literature. Architecture is not a subset of anything. Architecture is architecture. If you think you can get up every day and not open your toolbox, you are not going to be an architect. One of the biggest tools in that toolbox is what I call structure.

But again, you go back to structure having multiple meanings.
So back to order... That's our job.

At a basic level all architects do is organize parts.
Poetically. You organize them in a sublime way and people will have deep emotional and spiritual relation to them, which is important. It's not order in the Nazi sense of order for its own sake. It's order to clarify and enrich human experience.

5| So how do these interests impact your thinking in relation to methods employed architecturally to organize and represent your intentions? We have just discussed the possibility that there are interests that come from outside the discipline of architecture.
Ecology, geology, climate. When I am talking about the Hill House, I am talking about the Ice Age and what it did to the landscape, and I find that very, very interesting. I'm just happy I've got a discipline, called architecture, which provides a vehicle allowing me to explore and expand on these interests.

You don't find it interesting just because it is a personal fascination to you; you find it interesting because it allows you to further anchor the house or to further...
Exactly. We need authentic sources of content to make something meaningful. We're practitioners of pragmatics. We will take it where we find it. If we can find it by digging down 200 feet to the Ice Age, then that's where you get it. And I don't think there's anything doctrinaire about it. I think it's totally pragmatic. Charles Moore said to me one time, "There are two kinds of history courses. The ones taught by historians, and the ones taught by architects.

That idea of setting up an order, it is about an order that you can feel and enjoy, to feel secure in and feel good as a human being

We need authentic sources of content to make something meaningful, we're practitioners of pragmatics.

When I am talking about the Hill House, I am talking about the Ice Age and what it did to the landscape, and I find that very, very interesting. I'm just happy I've got a discipline called architecture which provides a vehicle allowing me to explore and expand on these interests.

The detail is not a detail, it is thematic.

practitioners, and they're just different." Architects mine history, and they do great damage to it, but they use it, so it's a pragmatic thing. You have a reason to learn. The need to make a building gives you a reason to be curious. It gives you a purpose and curiosity. You need something.

Curiosity in the form of design interests and intentions, whether underlying global concepts or detailed issues, informs the process.

Yet that statement about the global or the detail is a kind of a non-issue anyway. In literature they have that term "metonym" where the leaf can be the tree, when someone is talking about the leaf, they are really talking about the tree. So, if I'm thinking about how to make a windowsill, in a thin-skinned façade, I'm thinking about that as a representation of climate which washes over the building. The detail is not a detail; it is thematic. When I make windows; without trim, I am making the peasant window, I am making a democratic argument about society and about keeping the rain out. Keeping the rain out is not just about performance. It is being didactic or representational about your understanding of climate, of culture. The detail and the concept are the same thing. It's a social idea, an environmental idea. There's an economic or democratic idea. There are so many layers, and that is fine. It's not just a window sill. It is not just to keep the rain out. But if you remove the issue of keeping the rain out from the discussion, you have disembodied it.

So each decision is grounded on the technical side and the poetic or representational side.

Windows are not lipstick on the elevation. They are not graphics. You can't take the technical dimension out of making an elevation.

Many elevations are loaded with lipstick, and it is not just a technical problem. Elevations often don't have design continuity because people do try to represent something beyond basic spatial and formal acknowledgments of public space versus private space or themes beyond configurations documenting a response to the site.

A couple of generations ago we were closer to making things. When we constructed elements at a Ghost Project, we made our own things. I can tell you many participants didn't know what a window was, what a window box is, casings, aprons, stools and things. They had no idea what the language was even about. And that did not just derive from the weather related considerations. It also considered aesthetics.

It is also about the process of putting a window in a wall, the idea of a window box as something you make as a

I would say for me there are always two landscapes: the cultural one and the natural one. If you are an architect, and you are interested in making things, you are interested in culture. The Hill House is about these landscapes.

The concept is the archetypal idea, which represents a natural idea and a cultural idea at the same time.

fabricated unit that you put in a wall in a certain way from the outside. So you put the casings on before you put the box in the wall. That is a process learned by making stuff. The reason you see so many lipstick elevations in architecture school today, or in practice, is that there's a greater distance between making and designing than there used to be. It's like our grandparents knew where their food came from. They were smarter about that because they knew where it came from. Now we have no idea where it comes from. So a window is something you buy as opposed to seeing how it is made. When the technical aspect disappears, things become graphic.

And it is because of that incomplete understanding of how buildings are put together that architects have to fully comprehend that buildings are a kit of parts, both figuratively, in terms of the conceptual, and literally in terms of the assembly process?

In the big corporate offices today the people who wear the Gucci clothes are on one floor and the people who are so called technicians are on another floor. They don't talk, and they don't get along. People like Daniel Libeskind will design a building and have no idea how it actually stands up and just assumes that the structural engineer will put the bones in the chicken. If you work in a small scale, like we do, you are closer to how things are made and that gives you an understanding of this relationship between technology and aesthetics.

7| We will now return to global design interests specific to the Hill House. When you started the design of the Hill House, were there global, architecturally transcendent themes you were investigating?

Well, that project really started with the landscape. I would say for me there are always two landscapes: the cultural one and the natural one. Now it is not very fashionable to talk about the cultural one because there is nature envy these days, and aspects of green washing are the current fashion. Man is evil; man has screwed up the planet. Mother nature is perfect. Giancarlo De Carlo was showing these pictures of Umbria to me, and he said, "I bet you think this is nature." It was beautiful, bucolic, verdant landscape. He said, "There is nothing natural about this. This land has been cultivated for 5,000 years by humans. In Italy, nature is something you eat."

In Nova Scotia what we are seeing here is also not natural. The forests that were here when Champlain arrived are gone. This crap that has grown up here in the fields is weeds. It is not nature. There is nothing wonderful about a white spruce tree that is programmed to die in 50 years. There is nothing particularly beautiful or aboriginal about that. If you are an architect, and you are interested in making things, you are interested in culture. We are in the culture business. And I think it is very damaging to our toolbox if we talk about "Mother Nature" all the time as if cultural things are somehow less important. We are in the culture business. We should just acknowledge that and get on with it.

The ruins outside the window where we are sitting are 500-year-old ruins. When they built that house they thought they were building something permanent. Nature makes a fool of all of us. The human ethos to build is a powerful and satisfying thing.

The Hill House is about these landscapes. The natural landscape that has driven it, as we discussed, is the Ice Age, when the glaciers came, and they scraped all the soil off down to the shale. When they retreated and the ice melted, the dirt that had been plowed out from the Canadian shale melted out in long piles, long northwest lozenge-shaped piles on the axis of the retreating glaciers. And it produced a wonderful landscape like the finger-lakes in upstate New York. So you get islands out of that, you get cliffs eroding and making beautiful beaches, and you get farms on hilltops. It's a beautiful thing.

From that natural process, which is really the day before yesterday time-wise, comes agricultural pattern. So the whole genesis of the architecture in the region where the Hill House is located derives from building on top of the drumlins and creating courtyards. There's an acknowledgment of a front and a back in the landscape and a desire to be in a microclimate by creating wind-protected, sun-capturing places between buildings. This house absolutely does that. It is a pin-wheeling plan just like the farmsteads. You can say it's really local because it's like every farm on a drumlin in Lunenberg County, and you can say it's absolutely not local. It's like a Neolithic, fortified farm in Scotland. There are two narratives about these things: there's the super local story and the super not local story. The concept is the archetypal idea which represents a natural idea, and a cultural idea at the same time. When you climb the hill, you realize there is this great prospect realized in the form of an expansive view. Now there is another problem. There are accelerated wind speeds and a need for refuge. Glen Murcutt is very clear on this dualism, prospect and refuge. So when we designed the Hill House, we did what every farmer does in Lunenburg County. We went on top of the drumlin and said, "Shit, it's windy up here. We need a courtyard." So you make a courtyard. Now you've satisfied the prospect and refuge desires. In the Hill House, the spatial strategy indicated in the parti drawing shows both aspects. On one hand, you have the courtyard making for a place of refuge on the hilltop. On the other, given the views, you honor the making of prospect. It is helpful to set views across the courtyard. So, to look

So, to look outward, ironically you look inward, which helps in satisfying that need for anchoring.

outward, ironically you look inward, which helps in satisfying that need for anchoring.

The other primary issue in the project, which is very deep structure, is that the drumlin is on a northwest axis and the house is on a north/south axis, because it is parallel to all the pre-existing stone walls and hedgerows and other cultural markers. It is saying the building gets its orientation and form placement according to cultural rules. It gets tweaked, and its elevations are informed, principally, by natural rules.

In this case natural rules are...
The sun is the biggest one.

And in terms of a pre-existing fabric, what are you also alluding to at this point?
All of our projects have an implied diagonal to them because there is always this tension between the cultural patterns and the natural patterns. The reason the parti implies an open diagonal through the site is that the ridge of the drumlin, the cow path, is the lazy person's way of walking along the long axis of the drumlin and not taking on the slope.

So the project is fitted to a cultural tradition of walking along the ridge of the drumlin. It is anchored to the top, but it facilitates the path.
The most important line in that drawing is the line that is not there, which is the diagonal of the path that cows would take walking the ridgeline. Nature and culture are deeply embedded in the parti drawing.

8| Following on that, what additional organizational or conceptual criteria did you employ to anchor the initial intentions? In what you have been describing, you have been talking about order as the house is fitted to the site in terms of the sun, of the geographic lay of the land, of humans accessing the land and how those aspects were grounding attributes. If we look at this same parti drawing, there are additional conceptual criteria employed to anchor these intentions. There is a very clear duality between two pin-wheeling anchoring planes represented through the garden walls. You have talked about this in terms of how it is organized on the site, and obviously that's given the project a specific footprint. However, there are additional issues. When we look at the parti drawing, there is a suggestion of other "pure" architectural intentions.
Yes, one I am very, very interested in is this minimalist ethic, not style, but doing more with less. For a long time I have been interested in this issue of borrowed space that the Japanese are fond of. So, the space between two structures, if it is conceived as the project, is free architecture. It doesn't cost anything. The idea that you can make a modest project into a monumental project by embracing exterior space is really interesting to me, because it is making something with almost nothing.

In the Hill House the courtyard space is expressed as part of the parti.
Yes, someone asked me after a lecture in San Francisco, "What would you like to be doing in ten years that you are not doing now?" And I said, "I would like to make buildings that are more silent but say more. Talk less. Say more." That interests me a lot. That idea of setting up an order, an order that you can feel and enjoy, to feel secure in and feel good as a human being, that you created from almost nothing. That is really wonderful. In every field we have this concept called elegance. Vitruvius talked about "claritas," clarity. If you are a scientist, like my wife, you know elegance is represented in extracting the most significant findings from the fewest number of subjects. Elegant design of an experiment...when Teller wrote the formula for the hydrogen bomb, it is not that anybody could not envision the formula, it was that he could do it in about a hundredth the amount of chalkboard space than the other scientists of his time. It's not that they didn't know about the hydrogen bomb. They just couldn't express it as simply. In every field there's this idea of elegance.

Elegance, in a way, is a global strategy. Should that be a starting point?
Well it's a sustainable strategy, to use a word that's over worked. To me, that idea of economy of means is how I would define minimalism in our work. I talked about it in social terms as lack of pretension, plainness, but it is also appropriate in terms of the use of resources. My background is in urban design, so I think that if you make a good town square, the buildings on the town square can be simpler. If nature is wonderful, and you can harness nature in architecture, then the job of the architect is simpler. You do something really simple. You don't have to shout it, because you are borrowing the power of nature. So the idea of less, of less is more, is very valid.

Describe the pinwheel organizational strategy. The parts comprising the project are linked by clear, regulating lines, and yet they are flipping, shifting.
In the diagram there's a red line in the plan. That's the centerline. The main house is on one side, and the barn, or guesthouse is on the other. The "interior" spaces of the two buildings completely bypass one another. Remembering the themes of prospect and refuge, the thing is to look out to the landscape by looking in to the courtyard. In order to make that work you're going to have to sidestep a little. You are looking past the other

That idea of economy of means is how I would define minimalism in our work.

I would like to make buildings that are more silent but say more. Talk less. Say more.

So the idea of less, of less is more, is very valid.

building. So they look inward to one another, but they also look past one another.

There is also, in the parti drawing, a series of references to a structural module. There is a kind of secondary order within the structural rhythms. One is at 12' and another is at 10'.
It is major, minor symmetry. It is to express or represent priority. The house is more important. Its structural rhythm is larger. It has more glass, a higher level of finish.

The residential component has a larger structural module. It has more glass. It has a higher level of finish, and volumetrically it is larger. Is it then fair to say that you wanted, on one hand, to maintain the continuity of the two by using a simple structural pattern or rhythm, yet on the other hand to gain hierarchy. You adjusted the scale?
That's right. Being averse to symmetry as a good modernist would.

9| There's a subtlety there that I find intriguing in terms of how one takes a more minimal palate and then adds additional meaning to it. Beyond the architecturally transcendent issues we have discussed, what organizational or representational intentions, arising from the analysis of the site and program were employed to express additional conceptual interests? You have used the terms the "stretched skin" or "shrink-wrap." Also, we have discussed the structural grid as an additional organizational strategy that is not about the diagonal line.
It is important to talk about the arms of the courtyard. What you are seeing when you are looking at the black line in the parti drawing is the foundation. You are looking at what is in the ground. It holds the building down in the wind. You experience that by arriving at the front door, which is the red dot in the drawing, an access point to the house. That is your introduction to the regulating line that wraps around the foundation, goes along the kitchen counter, and extends out as the wood bench and the concrete wall embracing the courtyard. The most expensive aspect of this house is where that system of concrete meets the system of wood because of the extreme wind loads on top of this drumlin. So the anchoring and the setting of the heights of the place where the wood frame takes off is where the rubber hits the road. Now, having said that, which is a kind of layer cake story, the plan story is, where the "wall" is, the windows are smaller. Where the wall isn't, the windows go right to the floor. So in the main house the windows go right to the floor and give priority to the western view across Hirtle's Beach and toward the village, which is the best view, the big view. The guesthouse gets the view of the beach to the southeast and the cove, which is very intimate, and links the whole house to the water's edge. Remember, you want to do two things. You want to stand on top of the hill, and you want to put your feet in the water. The "stand on top of the hill" experience is from the main house looking west, where the foundation and the concrete wall isn't expressed so the glass can come to the floor. And the intimate view, where you put your feet in the water, is from the other one. So the parti tells you where those principle floor to ceiling openings can be. The elevations are given by the plan or by the macro-environmental read of many miles. This view is all the way down the coast for another 200 miles. So when I am looking out this way, I am aware that we are really referencing a 200-mile-long coastline.

Now, the building is kind of hunkered down in response to the wind which is why it has the low profile. It is also to express this idea of refuge which is reinforced through the battered outer walls.

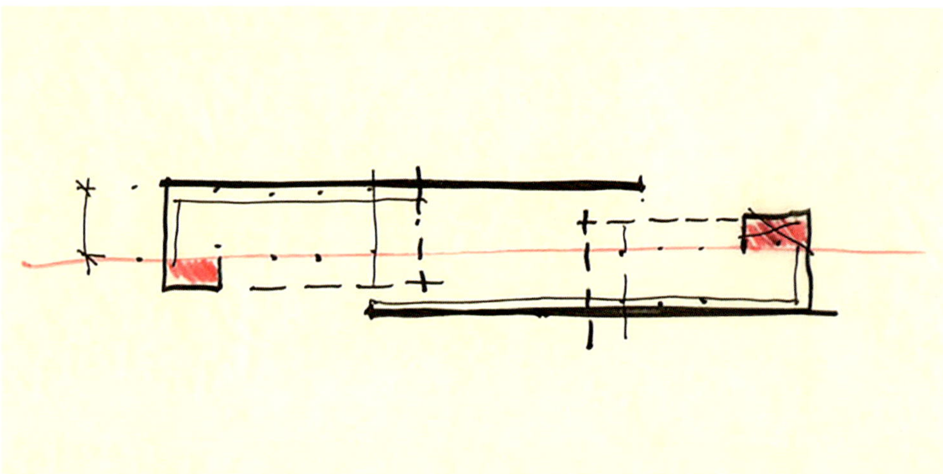

So they look inward to one another, but they also look past one another.

It is major, minor symmetry. It is to express or represent priority. The house is more important. Its structural rhythm is larger. It has more glass, a higher level of finish.

Similarly I know that the soil on this hilltop comes from somewhere in northern Canada. It gives me a lot of satisfaction knowing those things. And in a building like this, the principle objective of the building is to be a didactic instrument, a landscape-viewing instrument. The building is not a thing, but an enabler of landscape understanding. So the thing-ness of the building, or all of our buildings, is really almost irrelevant. Yet it has to look like something. So I decided to make it look like a rock outcrop in silhouette on the hilltop.

Let's take that thing-ness, that image as a rock outcropping, relating to what you were referencing, and compare it to the notion of the materiality of the building and what it represents.

The cladding is four layers of eastern white cedar shingles, 4" exposed to the weather with woven corners, which is a 500-year-old tradition. So it's like feathers on a duck. It is all about keeping the water out and being responsive to the labile, changeable climate. The wintertime temperatures hover around freezing, above freezing in the day, below freezing in the night. So you get this freeze/thaw, wet/dry cycle and the building materials are tortured by the weather. We have the highest weathering rate in North America. Not because it is cold, but because it is not very cold. The shingles, the local shingles, are perfect because they are like feathers on a duck. They are always in motion, expanding and contracting. And that's a great material response. The reason there are no overhangs is, again, a connection between the Spartan aesthetic of the vernacular and the minimal aesthetic of modernism connected to the climate.

There is a good overlap there. In this particular costal climate, if you put eaves on buildings, the building will leak. If you cut them off, it won't. If you have overhangs, you get ice dams on the eaves because the snow melts off the roof over the living areas and doesn't melt off the eaves. Because of this very, very particular climate, if you want it to leak, you build eaves because there will be ice dams. That's great for modern architects because you can do this very austere stuff.

What that allows is the building form to read as an articulation of the line of the hilltop, almost like a rock outcropping. When the sun is behind the building, in the morning you just see the profile. When the sun is shining from the west, it becomes very evident that it is a building. It either disappears into the landscape or becomes very prominent. Now, the building is kind of hunkered down in response to the wind which is why it has the low profile. It is also to express this idea of refuge which is reinforced through the battered outer walls.

That is an interesting comment, as refuge is now part of the language of the building itself, representing the concept of refuge, as well as a literal place of refuge defined by the courtyard between the two buildings.

It is kind of like a protective gesture given that the building is more or less solid on the narrow ends and then opens into the courtyard in that protective manner, reinforcing the refuge quality of the courtyard. Having set up this language of the very mute, trim-less shingle building I am very, very interested in the material irony of mass because of the detailing, and because of the way the shingles are scribed to the ground. As the base line of the building is scribed right down to the earth, to the top of the hill, and the roof has no eaves or overhangs, this ironic massiveness is expressed. The thinnest tissue-paper thin type of construction, in some light, looks like it is made of stone. So is it tissue-paper, or is it stone? I love that irony. That is taking advantage of a local building tradition and combining it with modern architectural ideas to create something particular to a place...something that you can only do here.

The thing that I try to do, because of the site reading, is to create this very attenuated, very fragile courtyard orientation. That is counterpointed with this very, very massive external rump of the building. By making the big incisions, seen as voids, extensions of the courtyard, and small incisions containing windows I am playing with that line of separation. How much can you take away from a mass and not completely destroy its essence, its role? Where is that line?

In your lecture in Houston you made a statement, "When I start a project, I determine whether it is monolithic or elemental."

This building is absolutely monolithic.

So, is there a point when you wonder if the project has veered away from that monolithic quality?

Yes, there is a fork in the road design-wise, where you can choose to go down either fork. What I have learned over the years is that monolithic is cheap and elemental is expensive. Elemental usually isn't affordable given the kind of clients we have. We don't have the rich clients of the Hamptons. Our buildings are extremely cheap.

The other thing is our climate. I'd describe the climate as being very demanding, and it favors the monolithic. Additionally the society that I operate in it has a kind of irreverence for authority that is kind of Celtic. You know, "F... you." So, the idea that the buildings are mute and monolithic fits very well. There are a lot of reasons for going monolithic—cost, climate, and culture.

So this house, placed in the cultural and natural landscapes you have referenced, contains a monolithic

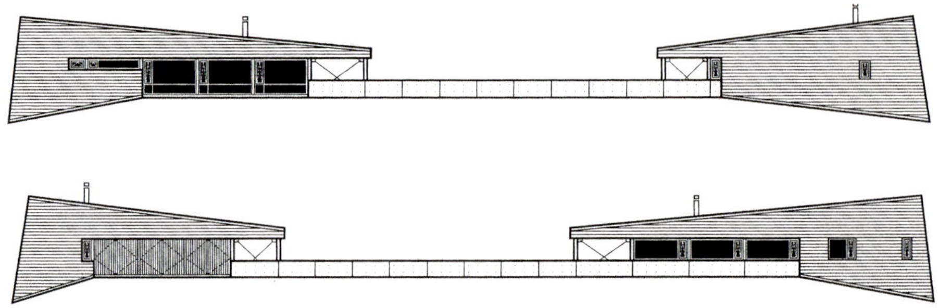

The main regulating line in these elevations is the seven-foot height above the floor line that is consciously low so as to frame the landscape more powerfully.

I am very, very interested in the material irony of mass because of the detailing, and because of the way the shingles are scribed to the ground.

It is really an understanding of the lightness of this type of construction and the groundlessness of it that allows me to undercut the structures with big sheets of glass right where you expect it to be solid.

architectural language reflective of those conditions. Yet it is not entirely monolithic. There are the dynamic modernist interests you have also mentioned. I would like to return to pin-wheeling as an organizational concept as it can relate to design development issues. I see it in the long horizontal openings, in the details...

The two structures comprising the house are the big dipper and the little dipper. The pin-wheeling comes from two sources–one is modern art, painting in particular. I have been drawn to De Stijl and Russian Suprematism paintings with their modern kinetic compositional language. And from a construction standpoint the pin-wheeling comes from looking at fish shacks and barns and seeing that a window above and a window below share a common jack stud, and they flip or pinwheel around it. Those are structural and regulating lines assisting in organizational themes.

Vertical regulating lines?

And horizontal lines. The main regulating line in these elevations is the seven-foot height above the floor line that is consciously low so as to frame the landscape more powerfully, to enlarge it by taking the sky out.

Or it can be seen as compressive, a cropping, where the building crops the photograph of the sky. Instead of thinking about building from the ground up I like to think from the roof down.

Specific to this house, or in general?

In general, but this house is a good example. I would say our buildings aren't built on the ground. They are hung from clotheslines. There is always a datum line in our projects which is an abstraction; it is a baseline that is some distance above the ground.

12| You are referring to a datum line. In this example we are talking about a line in the elevation, the seven-foot line. There is also a datum line in plan, the red line. There's a series of datum lines that is used. As the design developed, did the use of these organizational concepts also migrate or cross-reference into representational themes?

The datum line in the elevation is the top of the windows, and the windows are seven feet, which is actually closer to the eye level than normal, and as I mentioned, the sense of the ocean is enhanced because most of the view is without sky, and the line is absolutely horizontal, aligning with the horizon line of the ocean in contrast to the undulation of the topography. We work with the idea of the two datum lines created using the horizontal line of the ocean and the seven-foot line, the clothes line, from which the building appears to be hung.

You become aware of the topography representing a contrasting condition flanked by the datum lines as they provide a context from which it is viewed.

Whether as datum lines, pin-wheel organization, an incision, or a clothesline these all represent additional organizing strategies that integrate with your monolithic cultural landscape representational interests.

Well, they are organizational absolutes yet the interest in hanging buildings from the air as opposed to building them on the ground is also cultural because this is a ship building culture. Wooden buildings have always been conceived in a manner similar to boats, built by boat builders and moved around a lot. There are buildings in the village that used to be out on an island. They move them in on the ice or they float them on rafts. Buildings are moved all the time as wooden structures are easily moved. That barn we just built last week was brought from over 200 miles away. Buildings are moved. Consider the idea of buildings without foundations, buildings on stilts. If you look in the fishing villages, you see buildings on stilts, on thin little chicken legs. It is really an understanding of the lightness of this type of construction and the groundlessness of it that allows me to undercut the structures with big sheets of glass right where you expect it to be solid.

What I am hearing is that on one hand there is a monolithic quality, yet there is also an understanding that the buildings are lightly assembled and that can be represented.

There are ethereal qualities and lightweight qualities. How you expres that is to take the knees out from under it. To show it, or to be not afraid to do so because you understand the material culture in which you are operating. The compositional device allowing me to contrast the roof with the curvature of the hill by taking away the mass, in part, at the ground is natural if you grow up in a ship building culture. Buildings float, they float on an absolute horizontal line, and it's called the ocean horizon, and the seven-foot line is echoing that horizon which is the world's best level.

Recapping some of your intentions—there are the monolithic conditions at the ends of the house which are counterpointed by the lifted and eroding framework at the courtyard, which allows for views and simultaneously creates a place of refuge. Then there is the construction-related aspect providing a reading of the structural grid, rhythms, which are wrapped with a monolithic yet "thin" skin. The battered angles of the walls provide an additional psychological foundation while visually anchoring the house to the ground

I am more interested in the "platonics" of the universal: the sun is the sun, the wind is the wind, and they are universal. ...These become a way of informing your architecture by taking notice of issues relating us to the cosmos. It is important to get one out of one's own little idiosyncrasies, and realize you are insignificant.

The work that we do is extremely local in its materials and its understanding of climate or even social mores. But that has to be in equal measure with the platonic and archetypal, what I call universal things.

You must consider the global stuff, yet I think the way to arrive at general principles for any field is through intensive study of the particular. You can get to the global from the local. ...I believe in internationalism as a modern architect, yet I think being regional or local promotes specificity.

with the roof being a geometric compliment to those battered angles.
Or comparable to that. The building bows low at the courtyard so that it doesn't block the sun. That's the low end. It makes a kind of bowtie on top of the hill. That's a formalism. Why make it 85 degrees if you can make it 90 degrees? There is a side of me that is a classicist at heart. The idea of pure form hiding here is very important.

That refers to the idea of geometry possessing latent meanings that are still available for clarifying purposes—i.e., why a square is seen as having a more profound or platonic quality.
If you look at the structures from their narrow end, they look like tilted cubes in the landscape, borrowing from fine art, like a Donald Judd work. Ironically, I find the word regionalism to be a trap. I don't like being pegged as a regionalist. I am more interested in the "platonics" of the universal: the sun is the sun, the wind is the wind, and they are universal. When you move from place to place ,you have a different relationship with the sun and the wind. If you're on top of a mountain in Utah, there is a problem in the high desert with solar gain, and the building needs a ball cap, a way of protecting itself from the sun. In a place like Nova Scotia or Scandinavia you want to capture the sun and block the wind. The sun and the wind are universal, but they play out differently in different climates. We need to make the most of those conditions and respond intelligently to the elements depending on where we are located. That is the universal; the cosmos is in there. The beavers cut trees down on a certain moon because they understand how not to have wood that rots. So to the cosmos you can add the moon, the sun, and the wind. These become a way of informing your architecture by taking notice of issues relating us to the cosmos. It is important to get out of one's own little idiosyncrasies and realize you are insignificant.

In that regard you are saying your work with various design intentions represents an involvement in a discourse on modern thinking.
Yes, and architectural history and cross-cultural premises. The work that we do is extremely local in its materials and its understanding of climate or even social mores. But that has to be in equal measure with the platonic and archetypal, what I call universal things. When you talk about the 90-degree corner or the cube in the landscape, and you see it in a light that allows you to not know whether it is wood or stone, or concrete or steel, then it touches Richard Serra, it touches Donald Judd, it touches Japanese castles with their battered walls. It is very important to me to connect with the archetypal, because I think in those terms, like the courtyard on the hilltop. I remember staying in a farm on the west coast of Ireland. It was a courtyard farm on a hilltop. It is archetypal. You can find one in Italy. The fact that there is this universal context is also a kind of modernist idea referencing the global village. We are all really first cousins. Humanity is one thing.

So it would be fair to say that for you, maybe all of us, there are certain existential connections that we are ultimately able to participate in, and that we share common goals and hopes.
Absolutely. You must consider the global stuff, yet I think the way to arrive at general principles for any field is through intensive study of the particular. You can get to the global from the local. Monet painted water lilies in his backyard, but it wasn't all about his backyard, and Andrew Wyeth, when he was asked why he painted the same hill in Pennsylvania over and over in his Snow Flurries series, said, "Because I wanted it to be all the hills and yet a very definite hill." To me it is a frailty of language to say there are regionalists and internationalists. I believe in internationalism as a modern architect, yet I think being regional or local promotes specificity. What comes with that is what we call sustainability, understanding the principles the farmers knew. I just hate that word. Sustainability is just common sense, good design. The local is your friend; the global is your friend.

15| You want to be regional in a sort of international way.
Yes, I've been called the North American Glen Murcutt, which is a great compliment. It represents somebody whose practice is emblematic of a way to choose a model that is appropriate to a given locale. That is what I'm trying to do, but in a completely different climate, including the cultural climate.

As the design progressed how did you link the more poetic interests with the pragmatic, functional, or performance oriented concerns?
There is a book, *Precedents in Architecture*, and in the 4th edition it has diagrams of the Hill House on the cover. In the forward to the book the authors use the project as a proof that the poetic and the structural are linked opposites. He describes our parti drawings for the project as extremely structurally clear as partis, while he describes me as the poet of place. So this idea of poetry of place is not inconsistent with the universal archetypal timeless "structure" ideas. You can be extremely rational and extremely poetic at the same time.

Does that relate to simplicity or minimalism as approaches having poetic underpinnings?
There are different words you can use for the deep content of things. Archetypal is one I use a lot, timeless is another.

So this idea of poetry of place is not inconsistent with the universal archetypal timeless "structure" ideas. You can be extremely rational and extremely poetic at the same time.

I am trying to get at the archetypal. ...To make that explicit you have to get rid of everything else so, therefore, minimalism.

In the kitchen the counter participates with and expresses the embracing courtyard wall, providing architectural continuity tying interior and exterior spaces together .

Meaning that there are some embedded qualities or certain understandings that the building represents or carries over time?

It relates to minimalism. To convey universal or timeless principles that Emanuel Kant described in his aesthetic writings as the sublime, you have to diligently pursue that path because you will never get there. You have to take away almost everything else to lay bare the universal principles that provide deep emotional meaning. Similarly, Jung talked about this in his work on archetypes, his archetypal experiences representing universals like the cave or the womb. I am trying to get at the sublime. I am trying to get at the archetypal in a Jungian way. To make that explicit you have to get rid of everything else so, therefore, minimalism.

Does that not relate to the materiality and detailing of the Hill House? As the shingles are scribed to the ground to promote an idea of anchoring or corners are detailed without trim boards to create a representation of an outcropping or a more monolithic element?

The geomorphology of Nova Scotia was formed by drumlins deposited by glaciers retreating from thousands of miles away. They carried granite boulders that were rounded through the tumbling caused by the movement of the glaciers. That geomorphology goes back to the Ice Age, yet it connects with a more recent material culture of shipbuilding. In the mid 19th-century half of the ships built in the world were built in Nova Scotia, so you have a biased material culture toward wood and away from masonry. Masonry was only used in the ballast of the ships. The Hill house is, in effect, a wood drumlin.

From a construction standpoint the granite boulders were round and hard to make into square stones and there were few masons; therefore, it was difficult to make a stone box, so they didn't. They did not want to use masonry to build a house a story up from the ground, so they minimized the masonry and brought the wood down to the ground. The geomorphology produces difficult stones to work with and the material culture, with its bias toward carpentry, means that when you build a building you minimize the amount of stone and maximize the amount of wood. Instead of bringing the stone up, you bring the wood down to the grass. That's the story of the material culture of Nova Scotia, and it is clearly expressed in the Hill House. The carpenters win. They take their craft all the way to the ground and minimize the use of masonry. The result is you make a building expressing an ironic massiveness. I've always played on this, as when you take the climate of Nova Scotia into consideration it favors taut skin envelopes, so you have no overhangs. You have the sort of solid looking forms because they're not attenuated to an elemental language. They're monolithic. As I said, there's this ironic monumentality in making a monolithic form that is scribed to the ground and appears absolutely massive yet you could put your foot through it. The Hill House is made out of light timber frame. So the irony arises when you make something tissue paper thin, which I believe is something I invented, in the sense that you ever invent anything, yet it all comes from primary sources, in this case the vernacular, yet the corner detail makes a difference. If you were to hit a woven shingle corner with four and a half layers that are alternating, you've got a corner you can drive a truck into. There's no way the weather is going to penetrate the envelope, and a monolithic essence is achieved. If you were to add a corner board, you take away the massive monolithic expression.

Therefore, to achieve the monumentality you detail the woven corner, and you achieve the sense that it's carved out of one material. There remains a structural quality but with a thin skin. Ideally, if I had a steeper roof, it would have been clad in shingles also. The Hill House is a good example of mirroring a material culture expression in a language that has evolved. The house is an important point on the line and evolution of this theory.

I think there are two temperaments in the arts, maybe everything. There is this attachment to being novel all the time, which I feel is futile. Then there's the temperament toward working out ideas over a lifetime.

The Hill House is part of a series of projects building on the conditions of material culture and artistic expression. I think there's energy in contradiction. In the Hill House it is the contradiction in the massiveness expressed through the minimalism of a house with no eaves, woven corners, and a building of essentially one material. That provides energy to the work.

10| In the Hill House, and possibly more specifically to its interior at this point, how do you add additional depth to your initial global intentions?

In the minimalist game you're trying to make details less expressive, to disappear. Sometimes when you let them appear, then they become significant, more representational. In the house there is an exposed truss. It follows the pinwheel ordering strategy. The seven-foot height demarks a line represented with solid or glass wall below and openness above with the truss defining an area of transparency. The wood at the ceiling reads through, permitting an openness at the ceiling so the volume doesn't get truncated. There was a need to do something, so it takes a form. The form becomes an image. The image is not important to me but given that you need one, it has to look nice and is a byproduct of the overall intentions.

In the kitchen the counter participates with and expresses the embracing courtyard wall, providing architectural continuity tying interior and exterior spaces together. The workbench in the barn engages with that same relationship so there is an expression of order or connection in the detailing. The concrete wall is extended by the counter, and the trivet is the functional part of the counter, so we do the big thing cheap, and the small thing expensive. The small thing is a 13'-6" long trivet of soapstone where the washing and the cooking occurs. We treated it not as inlay, but as a second floating plane.

So the solidity of the concrete is reading through at an appropriate location.
There is concrete in some places, a counter in some places, a trivet in some places and a workbench in the garage, yet they all define a layer from which the windows spring. We are relentless about these sub-ordering partis.

It represents a second horizontal datum that might not be everywhere, but it is the height of the concrete "foundation," the top of the anchoring wall that the thin, yet solid, wood box sits upon and becomes an additional sectional organizing strategy as one moves vertically. There is not only the seven-foot datum representing a universal ordering system, but there is also this second datum line relating a number of elements.
They're kind of everywhere. Other than that there are not a whole lot in this house. There's the library ladder, and there are the sliding doors to the bedroom that are hanging from the seven-foot datum line. If I could make it all go away, I would. That's the difference between us and just about everybody else. Ultimately, success for me would be to have lots of meaning and almost nothing to look at.

I will use that to return to the gutter and downspout for a moment. My interest in that is how you captured the water in a manner that makes it disappear.
Around here we call that a Yankee gutter, and it's a recessed gutter. I would never do it in our climate over an interior space. I would only do it over an outside space because it fails. We hide the gutter and take the water underground.

Similarly, the downspout is treated in a very pure manner, a circle. A lot of downspouts are circular, but this onc was treated as a very singular expression. It disappears...
It's pure, just a pure thing. The same can be said of the cross bracing. The cross bracing resists wind loads as this is the location where the wind will try to lift the roof off the house. There are two squares of threaded rod and turnbuckle cross bracing at the courtyard walls under the roofs. In light timber frame construction dealing with the vertical forces of gravity is easy. Dealing with the lateral forces created by the wind is hard.

They are similar to two small aedicule on the corners of the porches, and they pinwheel with each another in plan. They are integrated and become embellishments of the parti, forming a kind of space, a cube actually. It's kind of a privileged place in the scheme because of the visual effect of the structural expression. Dealing with the wind is visually foregrounded and should be expressed as it is a functional expression of the environmental conditions created by extreme winds.

Ultimate success for me would be to have lots of meaning and almost nothing to look at.

I take a lot of pleasure in finding relationships to the history of architecture, to the history of place, to the work of other people who I admire.

However, the monumental presence in this house is the view to the landscape not a view toward the fireplace.

18| In the Hill House it's fairly obvious that the systems are not a significant visual architectural component. However, in this house the fireplace can be considered part of a heating system. How was the fireplace considered conceptually? Is its freestanding look a part of the culture, or was its selection or location in the house grounded on other architectural considerations other than providing an appropriate heat source?
It is a piece of garnish, a freestanding woodstove, which is a more efficient heat source than a fireplace located in a wall. In this case it was something preferred by the clients as they loved this particular manufacturer, and they assumed we would install a wood stove instead of a fireplace. Had a standard fireplace been part of the program, I probably would have integrated the fireplace into the concrete wall. However, the monumental presence in this house is the view to the landscape not a view toward the fireplace.

19| In refining the design did you select a specific programmatic area or architectural elements to privilege, to give added architectural intent or meaning?
Well, as mentioned, in the Hill House the privilege is the view as a prospect and anchoring as refuge. It goes back to the drumlin and houses from Neolithic hill farms in Scotland and Ireland. You go there for security, as in some sense it is like a fortified farm, and you also go there for prospect, to see who's coming, and to see out. Prospect is being on the hill to have the big view and when on top of the hill the view becomes 360 degrees. The view is so powerful you don't want or need anything else so the essence of this project is not the building. It is the experience of the landscape and the procession of getting up there. The place is about landscape, climate, and geo-culture. We kept coming back to those three qualities in this house. If you tap into them deeply enough, in effect you almost don't need to privilege anything in relation to building. The building can just be pedestrian, banal...

Yes, the privileging then becomes place, view, and anchoring. It is refuge, all of those existential experiences and deeper meanings tied to the poetic domain.
Exactly, and poetry, or the word poetic can stand for the timeless, sublime, things we do not always think of as poetry or poetic. For example, when people say our work is highly crafted, I almost laugh, as it is not. If there is sophistication in the craft, it is because of the culture it inherits. The material culture is smart and individuals are dumb in comparison. By that I mean the craft intelligence in our work is not created through us; it is created by the culture, and I am open to that. I have the good sense to listen, and I'm not imagining we invented anything. This idea of craft in architectural discourse these days usually means to fetishize craft using elaborate words that have no real intrinsic meaning. I am not really interested in that as a topic as a craft culture comes out of a sense of the place and one's understanding of it. Actually, you do not have to do much. It is in the air you're breathing. Malcom Quantrell wrote a book about our architecture with the title *Plain Modern*, and he made a really good point in that book. He noted that when you come out of an intact material culture, you don't need an à priory theory to begin building. The theory is in the air. It is all around. You just have to have the eyes to see it. That is why I don't take any pleasure in novelty or similar trends that move through architecture. I take a lot of pleasure in finding relationships to the history of architecture, to the history of place, to the work of other people whom I admire. ◘

Olson Kundig Architects

Tom Kundig

Chicken Point Cabin

At times architecture responds to needs beyond the physical and structural necessities required to enclose space and the functional necessity to solve programmatic needs. For Vitruvius that responsibility was defined as "delight". Chicken Point Cabin considers the issue in responding to a simple client request: "Make the house as open to the water as possible". The 2,000-square-foot residence, constructed in 2,000 organizes itself around a central space in the form of a "C", utilizing "solid" components of the program including the kitchen, storage, bedrooms, etc. These solids frame open programmatic spaces containing living, dining and food preparation activities that occur throughout the day. The organizational strategy also allows the house to function as a foil to noise and activity occurring occasionally on a street located adjacent to the back of the property.

While in the Chicken Point Cabin siting and views are fundamental to providing delight, more tactile experiences of a similar nature also occur in language-based attributes of the design. Honoring the industrial heritage of the logging industry prevalent in the northwest region of the United States, Chicken Point Cabin provides connections via the use of concrete block and steel. Steel elements designed as industrial furniture and components capture the built fabric of the region and accommodate life experiences by transforming them into "gizmos". These gizmos stimulate the imagination and provide tactile links–and delight–to material representations that recognize genuineness as a form of emotional and intellectual connection.

There is nothing we do that doesn't have some implication of order to it. ...Disorder often has something to do with muddy thinking or unclear thinking. It's more about our understanding of that.

Let's be clear about that. In most architecture we commit to you can argue that there is an underlying order.

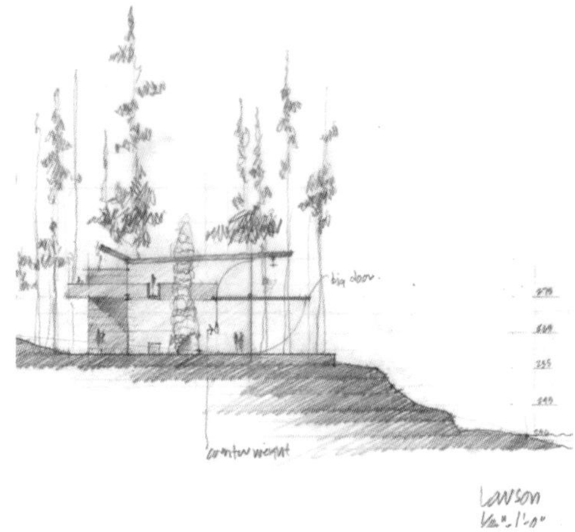

1| Tom Diehl: What value, potential, or use do you see in order? I want a point of reference. I am not trying to have you define architectural order.

Tom Kundig: If you talk about order in anything, nature is order. Chaos has order. That's what people with a more scientific background suggest. Science is nothing more than trying to understand the manner in which things work. It isn't actually the way things work; it's trying to understand how things work. Anything we do as human beings, conceptually or physically, whether it's a built structure or an organizational proposal, is all about order at some level. There is nothing we do that doesn't have some implication of order to it. If you talk about the value of order, well, it's fundamental. At an atomic level it's all about order, and at the cosmic level it's all about order. To say that we do things with disorder is not true. We can do things that don't have as elegant a resolution of order, an understanding of order, or there may be an unclear resolution of order but there will be some expression or need for an order. Disorder often has something to do with muddy thinking or unclear thinking. It's more about our understanding of that. I suppose at some point you could take it to the next level and argue philosophically that disorder actually is order because, in fact, the disorder is based on some sort of underlying rule-making that may be beyond us to articulate.

So how do concepts of order manifest themselves in your design thinking?

You hope that architecture is resolved at the level that it works both functionally and aesthetically. Let's be clear about that. In most architecture we commit to you can argue that there is an underlying order. You can also argue that better architecture has a greater sense of order at either a cosmic level or philosophical level. Who knows what that is. When I start a design, I don't think I'm necessarily pulling out those subjects, whether atomic, cosmic, metaphysical or spiritual. I don't think I personally have compartmentalized those subjects and check off a list as in "That was it. That was it. That was it," but I do think the older I get the more I understand what we are culturally, what we are physically, maybe even spiritually. There's a rational intuition or intuitive rationalism or whatever you want to call it in my approach to architecture. Some academics might argue that that isn't articulated clearly enough to decipher. Frankly, that is unimportant to me and does not represent an issue I think I need to figure out. It's great for somebody else to decipher or understand. In fact, I can sit back and say, "That's terrific," but, what I'm trying to do is get in touch with those things that we as human beings are always trying to do, and I'm convinced that we are always trying to look for an order, whether we can articulate it or not. So if I'm committing architecture, I'm looking at a situation, I'm looking at a conceptual landscape, I'm looking at a cultural landscape, I'm looking at a physical landscape, client landscape, technical landscape. I'm looking at all of these things in sort of a stew-like way, or in a miasma sort of way, and I'm trying to figure out what is the elegant solution for this particular situation.

So would it be fair to say that while there is no checklist in the development of your process, you are sensing how these variables, by that I mean the client, interpreting the program, the site, material use, etc., are cohering?

Exactly, I always say that architecture is the resolution of conspiring vectors. You've heard Glen Murcutt describe architecture as the intersection of the poetic and the rational, so there is this rational basis and then there's this other poetic part. It's hard to articulate that. The rational actually is a relatively easy one to articulate: You are given a set of parameters or orders and if you're a modernist architect, you are looking for efficient, elegant, rational, "form follows function" type of values. It's not about stylistic beauty, whatever that is, and it's dangerous to define what beauty and design represent, yet I think beauty is the nature of things coming together beautifully!

Often I will describe to students that one typically has to have at least two points to support each decision. One should be supporting functional and performance criteria and the other should support aesthetic concerns. In your sense of a rational and intuitive/poetic combination, would you say that there is a greater use of one or the other in the beginning of your design process?

That's actually a really good question because there is, for me, a defined beginning point. A greater percentage of my intentions at the beginning of the design process are trying to rationally figure out the nuts and bolts of the situation. How does this set of circumstances that I've been given by the client, the site or whatever, how does it work on a quantitative basis? As you begin to understand the quantities of what you're dealing with, the physics of it, the hard science of it, from that understanding you begin exploring the ideas of invention, and maybe delight. So you're trying to reinvent this in a way that addresses the human condition. You are saying, "No, we're humans, we have this need, sense, whatever you want to call it, to make something that makes us smile, makes us thoughtful." It's that next level that changes us from mere atoms circling a proton to humans.

We need to activate that spirit.

Understand and activate that spirit. Ultimately, you can melt us down into our component parts of water,

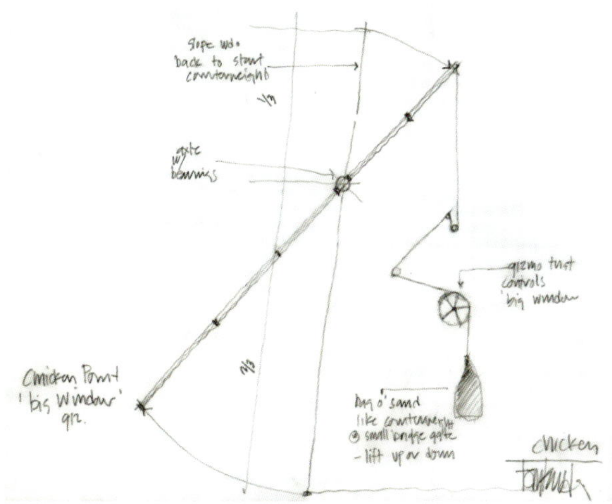

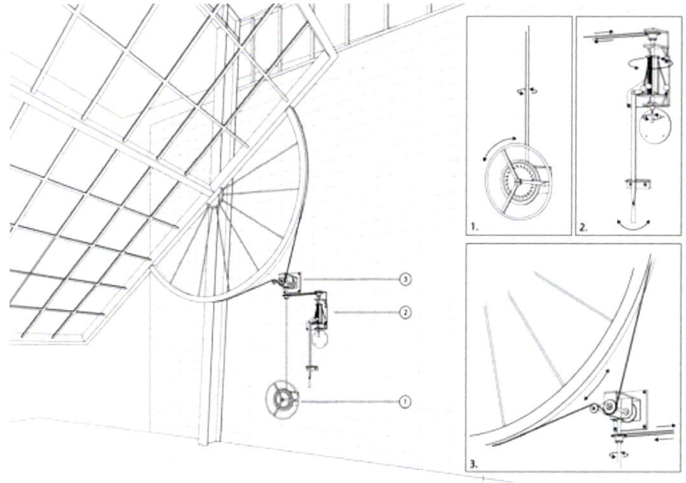

I first try to understand what are the underlying physical vectors I'm dealing with, the art of the science, and then from that I try to find the poetry.

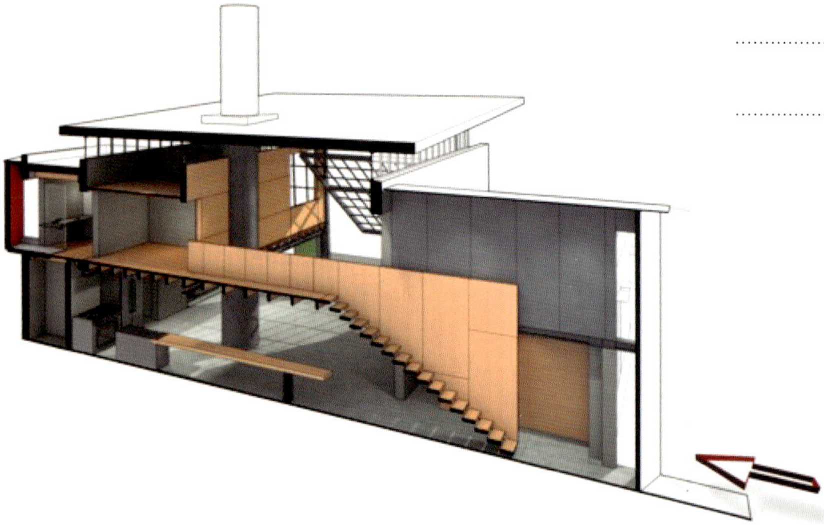

You are trying to understand how to make a relatively complex pile of conflicting issues comprehensible.

So if I'm committing architecture, I'm looking at a situation, I'm looking at a conceptual landscape, I'm looking at a cultural landscape, I'm looking at a physical landscape, client landscape, technical landscape.

2| 3|

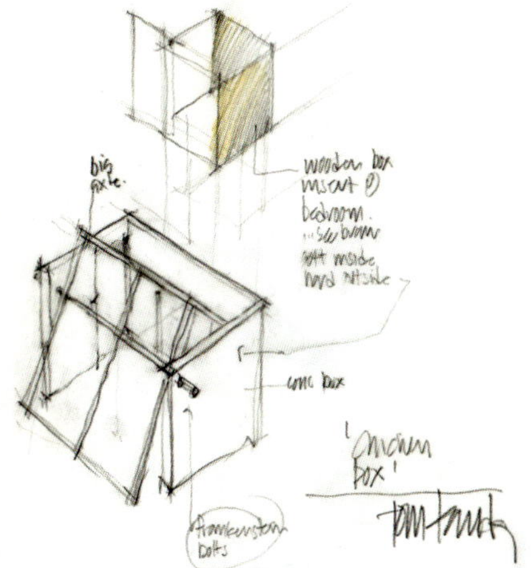

I try to be more optimistic about the architecture I'm doing in that it can open to the landscape, it can be a box of wonders in a way that engages you into the wonder of light, space, and the cosmos.

atoms, and minerals, and there's not much that distinguishes us, but when we're finished, there is a spirit in us. You can take all these perfect percentages that make us up, and yet there is the mystery of life, the mystery of doing architecture, the mystery of doing art, mystery of writing a sentence that you may not be able to. You know there are so many ways of writing a sentence that it could go from a statement of facts with no particular underlying order to being so poetic that you almost don't have to read the sentence. And everything we do is like that. If you're skiing, if you're a downhill racer, there are places where you know the rational underpinnings of everything you're doing, all the physics, the environment you are in, your physical form, but there is a point where, as a true pro in downhill skiing, you take that stuff to the next level, the poetic level, which is harder to define. We've all done it in physical activity. We've all done it in musical activity. We've all done it in artistic activity. It's a rare moment, but when it happens, it's pretty special. All of a sudden it's the musician that knows the mechanics, but then discovers the soul. But what is the soul?

So at the beginning of your design process, as you mentioned, you are concerned about the nuts and bolts of the site, program, client interests, etc. Initial investigations also include a tendency toward searching for themes that are going to allow you to bring a spirit to the place in a way that one can sense an underlying essence of what I will call the poetic of coherence. Is that a fair assessment of the early phases of your design process?

Yes, yet I think that might be different with certain architects. Some architects try to understand the spiritual nature of the thing, and then they make order out of that. Not me. I'm more the opposite. I first try to understand what are the underlying physical vectors I'm dealing with, the art of the science, and then from that I try to find the poetry. Steven Holl, for example, is good at starting with the poetry. He'll do his experiential watercolors, and then architecture out of that. It's terrific that he can do that, but it's baffling to me to try to start that way.

2| That's interesting, as this effort is not about attempting to codify a process where it is suggested one concern has to precede another. What does order mean to you architecturally?

I think you *sense* order, regardless if somebody is starting a design process like Steven Holl, or starting it like a rationalist. I think you just understand it. I don't care if you walk into Holl's St. Ignatius Chapel or a Glenn Murcutt house, those are two different approaches to a resolution of a poetic space and they're both beautiful. Tell me Ronchamp wouldn't move anybody. Well, I wouldn't necessarily be able to get to create a Ronchamp as a designer, but Corbu did. If one walks into a Glenn Murcutt or a Peter Zumthor building, it's still a poetic building. It's still got order. They both have a strong sense of order because of the way they're assembled. But they come from different worlds, different perspectives.

3| How do you employ formal ordering systems? At this point we are not exploring their use, I'm really trying to understand the strategies employed. What thoughts can you offer in terms of how you employ formal ordering systems?

I think one is always trying to use formal ordering systems. It's not completely different from solving a storage problem or a physics problem. You are trying to understand how to make a relatively complex pile of conflicting issues comprehensible. It's like writing a paper. You write down all these great ideas and then you try and find a thread. I can use the example of skiing trees because I grew up skiing in the mountains. You have all these trees in front of you and basically what you are doing is, you're trying to find order through those trees or you're going to hit one. That's what I'm always trying to do. You can look at order as the relationship between public and private space, material hierarchy, etc. There are lots of ways to describe how to make order out of a relatively complex set of issues but that may come from my rationalist background. Obviously, Chicken Point Cabin and another project of mine, Studio House, are classic courtyard schemes. They both happen to be closed in this case. There is a semi-transparent glazed space where the public comes together. There is no sort of metaphysical jumping-off point, but there is a desire to make order out of somebody wanting a bunch of classrooms, or somebody wanting a big gathering space. Then, like with the musician finding the soul of the music, the parti, that overlying idea begins to assemble the elements. Then you take it to the next level. How do you articulate that idea in the use of materials, structurally, and environmentally? Then you respond to the next layer, the tectonic level, the landscape level. How do you protect those interiors that have large areas of glazing? So the overhangs, the eyebrows, the wrap of the rooms around the big glass space all have multiple interwoven reasons for being.

There are five reasons for the central skylight at our offices in Pioneer Square, Seattle. It's day lighting, it's our ventilation system, and it's our art piece as the sun goes through the sky. Right now the sun is on the west but it does this big sort of graphic as you walk in. It's

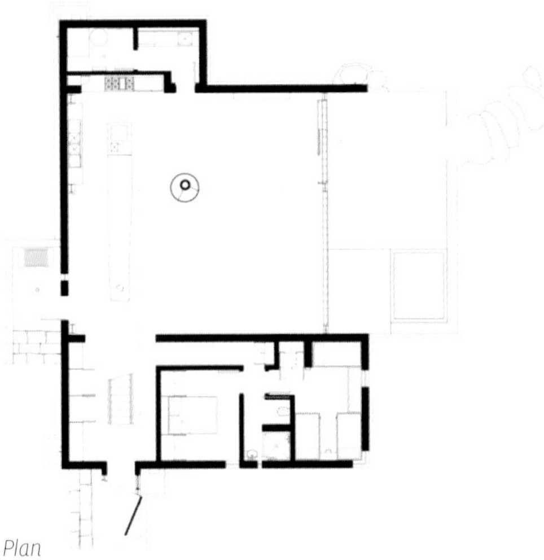

Plan

Whether it's working in a construction site, and you begin to understand the heaviness, the gooshy-ness, and the complexities of mud and concrete or whether you're helping Harold Balazs build a sculpture and you're grinding miles of welds, those are all outside of what one might say is a definition of architecture yet they have a significant relationship to architecture.

also research and development, it's a science piece because it can't be over 3 ½ tons of glass and steel and it's also our irrigation system. That's the kind of overlay that you're always trying to build. I think that's the main thing in that one is always building that idea of clarity, which is order, and authenticity, which is another order. Materials are materials. They have characteristics. They are not to be used in a manner for which they are not intended. Engineering in a modern sense is often exposed as in that's just the way it works. It is the guts as one sees in a body, the ribs, the shoulders. You can see how things work, the body works. It's a modern aesthetic, and it's a value system.

When you said "building that idea of clarity," in this day and time we see designs as having very complicated versions of order, or more specifically I could say non-orthogonal attempts at organizing.

It's Frank Gehry. It's Deconstructivism. There is the reconfiguring of the box.

So how do you respond to those kind of organizational strategies? I'm diverting off the word clarity by not linking it exclusively to the more common use of the orthogonal. Do a greater use of orthogonal relationships suggest to you a stronger sense of clarity?

I think it's a relevant question as I ask myself similar ones. Obviously Chicken Point has a curve on the window and occasionally I'll do a curve, but it is always based on an idea connected to the conceptual function of the space. The curved roof on Studio House was to bounce light back into the photography space. There's also a financial aspect, and there's a constructability aspect that comes into a lot of these projects. I have financial and constructability constraints as many of my projects are built in a remote space or place. I'm a practitioner in today's time and place. In 50 years if CNC machinery becomes available on site, and one can manufacture components in different ways, even if they are a complex shape, they will still have to, for me, be underpinned by a rational reason. Whether it's shaped by the wind, shaped by the sun, or shaped by something happening internally, culturally, for me there has to be a reason. It's like why a flower blooms the way it does, but for me the orthogonal is constructability. It is tectonic assembly. It is the nature of many materials, and there are financial underpinning reasons that benefit from the logic of orthogonal-based construction.

So that relates back to the larger process, larger intentions, i.e., establishing a method by which one can successfully make space, organize components, unite diverse materials, etc., in the making of a cohering strategy from the initial global vision down to the details you've incorporated in the Chicken Point Cabin.

That's exactly right. When I'm put in a situation of making an arbitrary shape—what I would consider an arbitrary shape—I'm almost always disturbed by that as I don't have a rational basis for making the decision, and therefore I'm not sure. I don't know how to answer the question, and I could jam myself up trying to make a decision. But if all of a sudden I discover a shape formed by acoustic criteria, or whatever the criteria, providing better performance qualities well, that's the shape.

Prior to a process where we ground decisions on a rational basis we feel like we're just composing or manipulating form.

Yes, yet again, composing might create a sense of order and a perfectly reasonable one. When you go to St. Ignatius, you see the various shapes of those rooms. At the time St. Ignatius was designed, I was in Steven Holl's office helping him put the building together, not developing concepts for the project. It was interesting to see how he shapes a room—it's stunning, it's beautiful. I'm not always sure how I would control a design process such as his, but clearly that's an ordered space for them.

4| This revisits ideas concerning order that are not easy to define, but you know it when you experience it. It links to the next question. Do design interests, specifically those extending beyond ones concerned with facilitating the distribution of the program and fitting the building to the site, originate within the discipline of architecture or from sources lying outside of it? We haven't really talked about that.

What do you mean?

For example, the whole deconstructive phenomenon could be argued as a critique on culture, i.e., culture doesn't make sense like it used to so why should architecture be bound by "old rules"? The direction many of the deconstructivist projects followed was established by interests well outside the bounds of classic modern rules of order.

You are asking, "Does architecture ask the same questions as art"?

Yes, in a way.

Does architecture challenge us, or should it intentionally challenge us to larger, global, cultural issues? Frankly, my opinion of architects as artists is a little worrisome. I think architecture is not art. I actually think architecture is more of an applied art, and in that it could be an art. I don't think, as maybe what Steven

Naming comes out in the proces. It is part of a strategy or a follow-through on an earlier intention. ...it evolves from a set of linked decisions that share in the making of a common identity, a name

Holl does, that architecture is more of an art form. Maybe what Coop Himmelblau explores is more of an art piece because there is more of a conceit, saying this is our commentary on where culture is today. Maybe in some ways anything we do is a reference to where we are and our place in time. In post modernism and deconstructivism there is the potential for a cynical side and a type of social commentary. With my work I try—and people may argue that it doesn't look optimistic—to be more optimistic about the architecture I'm doing in that it can open to the landscape. It can be a box of wonders in a way that engages you into the wonder of light, space, and the cosmos. It is actually an optimistic architecture.

So would it be fair to follow that up by saying your references are more focused on the discipline of architecture, yet they are attempting to aspire to connections that might be a bit transcendent?

Exactly, and I think that the Chapel of St. Ignatius is like that. I think it is very optimistic. I think Frank Gehry's Experience Music Project is very optimistic. There is an exuberance there. It's about the positive nature of what is occurring here in Seattle. Rem Koolhaus would probably disagree, but I think in some ways the Seattle Public Library is optimistic.

In a sense, it returns us to a word used earlier, authenticity. Many say there is an accurateness to Koolhaus's critique. The same could be said of Venturi's questioning the direction of modern architecture as realized in so much of post World War II production.

Absolutely, he was asking *totally* fair questions about modernism. If he was poking fun at conventions, or maybe it was irony, he was pursuing it thoroughly, and he rooted it in a very clear understanding of what modernism had become. It's like the early modernists who were actually better architects than later ones, or we are, because they were taught using Beaux Arts rules. They knew Beaux Arts rules, and they knew order. It may have been a supplied order, in other words they had established organizing rules, established proportions, but they understood the value of that. It is like musicians that understand music before they become jazz musicians. A true jazz musician understands the tradition of music that predates jazz.

Students get a book on my work, and they say, "Oh, I think that's cool. I am going to do one of those." And that's exactly what it's not about. In fact, my emphasis on pursuing rational underpinnings is based, in part, on how performance criteria has everything to do with my personal upbringing. The landscape where I grew up in northern Idaho, with it's extraction industry, impacted my root being, not theirs. If I do something that feels authentic, it is in part because I know it origins. It's not based on seeing or being influenced by somebody doing something that was a riff on that. As a kid, I grew up seeing Jean Tinguely's artwork and sculpture and I loved it. As a kid, that had some sort of resonance whatever it was. Can one argue that I invented some new direction or did this come out of nowhere? Absolutely not. It's coming from all sorts of references, Scarpa details, Scarpa walls, big mining buildings, and logging buildings with these huge crazy things that move.

Let's take that back to the question of the use of sources lying outside the singular domain of architecture.

Absolutely, they there are. I did not want to be an architect when I was a child yet many things I experienced

5|

I try to keep things simple enough, straight enough, clear enough so that when the poetry can be conceptualized, it happens very beautifully. It comes out of the process.

as a young adult had an architectural influence. I was climbing mountains from about 15 years old to probably 27 years old. Clearly, climbing mountains is not about architecture per se, but it *is* about how you engineer a poetic experience, how you use hardware, your body, how the gear is as an extension of your arms and hands. How do you prepare for what we call elegant light climbing, alpine style climbing? It all has reference to what I'm doing now.

So whether it's Tinguely, whether it's climbing mountains...

Whether it's working in a construction site where you begin to understand the heaviness, the gooshy-ness and the complexities of mud and concrete, or whether you're helping Harold Balazs build a sculpture and you're grinding miles of welds, those are all outside of what one might say is a definition of architecture yet they have a significant relationship to architecture whatever that it is, good or bad. What I try to make clear to students is that they shouldn't let the professor tell them what to think, yet they should listen to him or her and try to understand what is being implied in broader terms. What is often being explained is their perspective, their experiences and that may be really important. But ultimately, make up your own mind when it is an appropriate time. That may take a long time. In other words, it's like Japanese watercolors: To learn ink penmanship you have to draw something like 2,000 bamboo shoots in one stroke. All you're doing is making one stroke, yet understanding how to make a bamboo shoot through drawings requires practice, practice practice. It's about understanding the fundamentals of something. Picasso, I think, did a painting, something simple on a canvas and then it was sold for hundreds of thousands of dollars, and somebody said to somebody

I understand how issues of construction impact design, and I understand the necessity for conceptual underpinnings.

I'm trying to figure out if I'm beginning to understand the problem in a larger way, how do I order, how do I organize this problem. Additionally what is the underlying reason that expresses or organizes the issue?

else, "He just did that in three minutes!" and the person next to him said, "No, he did that in 30 years." Similarly, while we are obviously not practicing architecture as children or internalizing those experiences, they can ultimately affect our architectural development if we understand them correctly. It becomes really important. Everything matters. All of a sudden you're looking at something, and it makes you smile. "OK, I get it. I understand. It touches me."

5| Can you describe how these interests impact your thinking in relation to the methods employed to architecturally organize and/or represent your intentions? Would it be fair to say that the methods employed, more often than not, are attempting to create an initial simple construct for the carry-through of more developed relationships? In other words, you haven't had the temptation to make something more complex in initial diagrams. Is that right?

That's correct. I'll describe to students sometimes that I don't necessarily have large budgets, and I cannot allow myself a continuous string of indulgences. A lot of these projects don't have that many opportunities, but they may have an indulgence.

An example in the Chicken Point Cabin being the gear mechanism and the tilted window wall.

Yes. Six and one half tons of glass and steel, well, that's an indulgence, but the building is simple enough that I can evaluate the indulgences with an understanding toward the overall. Something at the detail level becomes a larger detail that becomes a crescendo. It's important. It comes from the idea of the building, seems appropriate, seems authentic to the place, culture, and to what is happening inside the building. It's like, the skylight here in the office. It's clearly an indulgence for us. That may be a round-about way to answer the question, but I try to keep things simple enough, straight enough, clear enough so that when the poetry can be conceptualized, it happens very beautifully. It comes out of the process.

So in your sense of methods employed to organize and represent design intentions, you know that the poetry will come because you have a preference for a clear starting point, usually understood, at least architecturally, via simple orthogonal relationships. That organizational simplicity tends to set the foundation for a more developed, usually tectonic, poetry.

Exactly right, the poetry will come out of the process. It may be frustrating, and you may not understand it at first, but if you keep trying to understand the problem or the issue, all of a sudden it's like the names of these parts and pieces of the building coalesce. Why is it called Chicken Point? Why is it called the Brain? People always ask me that. Why is it called Delta Shelter? I didn't start those projects calling them the Brain or Chicken Point. It comes out of what is appropriate. I'm just finishing a project called Shadowboxx. For the longest time it was called the Bumble Bee Hut because the lane in front was Bumble Bee, and we just called it the Hut. Shadowboxx is a reference to an important book for both the owner and me. I introduced her to it. It's the old classic *In Praise of Shadows* by Tanizaki. There are implications in that little book that are explored, in a way, in the design of the building. There are intentions that reference the book.

Naming can have value as it puts boundaries, usually language-based, on decisions that are appropriate. One can name or identify something as a tectonic assembly and make a series of consistent decisions that may add a level of clarity, or it can be named Shadowboxx suggesting any number of added architectural intentions not governed by the site or program, yet the implications are often helpful to the design process.

Absolutely, you can name rooms, name details, something comes out of it, puts a hook into that thing and clarifies it. I don't start with a name, I don't say "Ok, this is going to be Meadow House or this is going to be Shadowboxx."

That's where naming can suggest something superficial or metaphorical. One of the architects interviewed was concerned with my use of the term representational. He felt it meant exactly what you're just describing, as if representational implied a stylistic or metaphysical starting point.

Naming comes out in the process. It is part of a strategy or a follow-through on an earlier intention. The gizmo thing is an example. I do have clients where these start to happen. I don't think they're particularly new, the gizmos. They've been around, but it comes up. The Chicken Point gizmo was purely a response to something that came from the owner. They just wanted the building to open up to the landscape. With my background working for Harold Balazs or as a kid working at a sawmill and seeing big things being moved with tools aided by human power, it was not difficult to imagine a large movable window as at Chicken Point Cabin. That's just the creative spark when someone suggests something, and you have this legacy with certain perspectives, and you know it's possible. You don't know how you are going to do it. You just know it's possible, and you work with someone on the engineering side, and it comes out of the process. I didn't start out thinking

that I was going to put in an operable window that a six-year-old could open. That's not the way it works. So now when people come, and they do, they sometimes will say, "Well, I'm hoping we have a gizmo." It becomes gimmick-like, and you don't want to start that way. You might feel more comfortable doing that kind of stuff based on history, as with a style, but that's not the way a "name" appears. It is from the process. It evolves from a set of linked decisions that share in the making of a common identity, a name.

7| Now we will shift to initial design considerations of Chicken Point Cabin. When you started the design, were there global, architecturally transcendent, themes you were investigating? This is a carryover from some of the previous discussion as I'm trying to establish, in the beginning of the design process, what type of issues anchored your initial design intentions? Were you more concerned about a site-based concern such as getting the cabin oriented correctly, or was it closer to a broader, more personal interest such as "I have this itch about technology that will be explored in this project"?

You don't come to a project with a clean slate. I know this landscape like the back of my hand. It is a very familiar place to me, but the owner came from Michigan. The owners had their own desires and wants. They came to me because they had seen Studio House, and there was, from their perspective, a sympathy with that project. Yet, I have reference points. I do like the idea of architecture being morph-able or movable. That has always been something I'm interested in. I'm not an architect that wants everything to be in its place. I like it when owners can move things and how weathering changes things. It's just my DNA. So certainly before Chicken Point I would imagine how a house could be changed or how can a building morph. I remember thinking, "Isn't that great that they can take a garage door in a saw mill and have it open up using an incredible cantilever to let this big front loader out." Why did they do it "that" way versus using hydraulics and electronics?

That's in part what I'm trying to document, that architects obviously work with themes established within the discipline of architecture but there are other sources lying outside that discipline that are sources of creativity.

That's exactly right. You build up your references. You build up your experiences. Rick Joy and I talk about how it's OK, probably better, that one often develops better

Then you turn that corner and all those vertical proportions immediately go to the horizontal. The window, the view, the lake, the mountains, the sky, all are horizontal. And that's all intentional.

Yes, simplicity, clarity, employing the yin and yang of something that's very soft with something that's very hard, transparent with opaque, and so on.

architecture when older because you have more, I call them tools, in the tool belt. You just develop more strategies for solving a problem. At this point in my life, at 54 years old, somebody comes to me with something they want, and I've got a number of tools I did not mentally possess earlier in my life. Even with my great experiences as a kid, they weren't necessarily completely developed. It took me time to build up an encyclopedia of references. I think you should have at least a 10-year apprenticeship in an office just learning the issues that a practicing architect must deal with before you can really be skilled in this profession. The kind of architect I try to be is the soup to nuts kind. I understand how issues of construction impact design, and I understand the necessity for conceptual underpinnings. It took me 10 years or more. I had to do the boring stuff. I had to draw the bamboo shoots 2,000 times. I had to figure out how to

But if you have an authenticity with the way a material works, an authenticity with the way it looks, that governs the way it should be assembled.

work with clients. It's a great profession, but it's a very difficult profession to understand.

So, regarding the design process, for those who are thinking and thoughtful and want to develop a project from soup to nuts, there are these larger global strategies or interests that may suggest a specific or unique solution. They may range from how I can marry mechanical and human power to open a large transparent wall or contemplate a cultural reference, such as, "I am going to address the building's role as a social condenser in this project." It then becomes about what specific organizational strategies are employed, and what I am trying to represent.

But then how you run those is the magic of the individual. In fact, when clients comment on how much I am involved in the project, I say I have to be intimately involved in the project. My and other architects' role is critical to the project as we are the ones trying to make architecture out of our client's interests. It's like going to an attorney. You are giving the input, but you're not constructing the case. The client for Chicken Point, Jeff Larson, was interviewed for a *New York Times* article by Pilar Viladas, and she says of course he has a lot of influence on the project, yet he goes on to say, "I'm a neurosurgeon. I hope you hire me to be a neurosurgeon, but you're not going to tell me how to do my neurosurgery. I did the same with Tom. I hired an architect, and I expect him to do the architecture of the building and yes, Amy and I made our comments, but we're not telling him how to do his architecture, just like I don't want anyone telling me how to do my neurosurgery." Obviously, we should respect a client's values and their input, but it's important that architects, including myself, sometimes forget that we're actually pretty well trained. At a certain point in our lives we become pretty damn good at being architects. I don't know when that happens. Some individuals feel confident at an earlier age. I started to feel I was a pretty good architect between 37 and 40. It took me a while.

Sometimes you feel like you can control the conceptual side of the design process but have no clue about how to put a building together.

After you do the working drawings, and you explain your intentions to the contractor and the sub-contractor, you know that he knows a whole lot more about the specific trade he is involved in than you do, but you have to explain the architectural side of your intentions.

Yes. As Brian McKay-Lyons said, "You can feel like the dumbest one in the room." You are feeling a little humble at that point.

Yes, and you should. As an architect you shouldn't be arrogant. You should understand that fact. A friend of mine once said that an electrical sub-contractor got real uppity with him on a situation, and my friend finally had to say, "Wait a minute. I understand you know a lot more on this issue than I. You're an expert in that. But I know a lot more about what you do than what you know about what I do. I need you to follow what I am trying to do." I think that's true. I think architects shortchange themselves. How many times have you heard, "I'm shocked at what he or she knows about issues relating to architecture." It's rare. A lot of times you will talk to somebody in another profession and they will quickly prove they don't know anything about architecture; they don't know what they don't know. We know a lot about a lot. We deal with all these vectors, all the parts underlying a design, all the conceptual

That's where the richness comes in, because a successful decision or design is one that addresses two or three questions; functional, technical, and poetic. Sometimes the answer isn't always obvious.

issues, and then its construction. We are like conductors. We don't know how to play the oboe or maybe the viola or the piano, but we're conducting this pack of experts into a larger whole. Football–same thing. Maybe the coach is the client, but we are the quarterbacks. We're not necessarily running the patterns, but we're trying to make sense out of this larger, complex, unfolding situation.

8| So let's take that conducting role into Chicken Point Cabin. Beyond any larger global conditions you were interested in, what organizational or representational intentions arising from an analysis of the site and program were employed to organize and ultimately express your conceptual interests?

Well, ok. It's almost back to an earlier answer where I really do try to look at the site and plan and, again, there are these conspiring vectors that I look at rationally. What are the issues and design opportunities? Certainly landscape, it's a certain place in time and space, and there is certain criteria from the clients. At this point I am collecting data so the employment of the intentions is more rational, and I am trying to understand and activate the larger underlying issues. It's as if a human body were simply chemicals that had to be put together and all you have in the beginning is this big pile of chemical goo. Once you understand the strategies for organizing that goo to make a human body, then how do you make it wonderful? How do you glean additional intentions from that pile of goo and take the next step, the step into an architectural realm?

In that regard if we go back to where you referenced service and served organizational conceptual strategies, or public and private understandings of organizing the program, are you saying that in the design of Chicken Point Cabin there were larger searches into various organizational strategies?

Yes, but initially you are trying to understand the underlying idiosyncratic situation to then begin organizing. Is it an onion-skin layered type of organization? Is it actually layers that transition to a core? What is the appropriate reaction for the site? Places like Chicken Point and Studio House have a very clear residential ordering principle. You can order just about any house that way, whether a dumbbell scheme, a "U" scheme, maybe an "H" scheme. There are public spaces, there are semi-public spaces, and there are private spaces. There are diagrams, 3 or 4 or 5 organizational diagrams that you can use to organize just about any house. And they are completely appropriate.

If everything works well, you can begin to unlock the mystery between those yin and yang variables, I always say you're looking for the yin and yang in every situation. You don't see black until you see white or you don't see white until you see black. You don't feel cold until you feel heat. You don't feel heat until you feel cold. You don't have prospect until you have refuge. Yet, you don't start out thinking, "Well, I'm looking for the extremes." I don't start out like that. I'm trying to figure out if I'm beginning to understand the problem in a larger way, how do I order, how do I organize this problem, what is the underlying reason that expresses or organizes the issue?

So at Chicken Point Cabin there was a desire based upon the site's magnificence for the capturing the view. Were there other factors or design interests influencing the project's organization?

Privacy was an issue, privacy from the neighbors on the flanks and the privacy from the back of the site because there are neighbors right behind them. Yet one is holding on to the most important component of the site, the transparent view to the lake. You arrive through a mixed stand of trees. You come to the front door, which is intentionally tall so you have this vertical relationship. You enter, you turn the corner, and the horizon goes big with the characteristics of the site, the lake, the mountains, the landscape. In other words, your perception, your experience, as you enter the front door is vertical. It's a big, tall door, and the spaces between the trees outside that door are vertical. You are confronted by the stair, which is also this big element with vertical proportions. Everything is about this big vertical proportion and vertical circulation because of the stair. Then you turn that corner and all those vertical proportions immediately go to the horizontal. The window, the view, the lake, the mountains, the sky, all are horizontal. And that's all intentional. Its understanding the context issues of the property—the site character, the trees, the landscape, the sun, the southern orientation as organizational drivers. It is all of that yet it was primarily based upon the function of privacy because you want privacy in the cabin.

So the house becomes a portal at one end with a spectacular view and simultaneously a frame not only creating the portal but also protecting the flanks by not permitting unwanted views into the cabin. From those criteria let's return to your statement regarding the diagram. Those conditions could be met with a "C" or with a "V" as well as a "U" or an "H," yet everything is orthogonal. Would that be because of other criteria or interests mentioned earlier?

Yes, simplicity, clarity, employing the yin and yang of something that's very soft with something that's very hard, transparent with opaque, and so on. Actually an

It's a spiraling process; you're going somewhere. You are always re-editing and re-thinking and changing.

An old architect once said this to me..."You're not really an architect until every line you draw, you understand what that line means, not only to the plan you're working on, but you understand it in section, you understand it technically, and you understand it in elevation."

earlier scheme was an "H" because the backside was actually glass at one point with an inner garden at the back. The garden would be enclosed at its back and visually would flow through the interior space out to the lake. That scheme was not selected for budget reasons and for their sense of place

So, did Chicken Point Cabin become orthogonal because of cost considerations or other interests? Delta Shelter, Rolling Huts, most of your projects have a dominant orthogonal structure. I would like to expand on that. Would you say, "Yes, it is orthogonal, because that is a cheaper way to build," or "No, there is something more meaningful in the orthogonal." Are you initially setting up your projects orthogonally because there is a clarity there that you appreciate, that goes beyond...

Seeing it?

That's what I'm wondering.

That's true, but it's also the nature of materials. Metal can obviously be bent into a shape, but it typically comes in orthogonal profiles or rectangular sheets. That's the way you get it. It is a whole lot easier to work with the given. Maybe some would say there is a mundaneness to that, but if you have an authenticity with the way a material works, an authenticity with the way it looks, that governs the way it should be assembled. You know, it is a working shape, not one shaped for aesthetic purposes. It is more poetic and less arbitrary than if I made a big circle or some other shape just for visual purposes.

It's fair to say that your statement ties back to themes of authenticity. There is an argument, under a global position or interest, which returns to this matter of authenticity that can be found in the orthogonal as a part of the logic of construction, found in letting materials be what they want to be.

Exactly, there is a rationality, a reasonableness in those aspects. It's not indulgent for indulgence sake. An indulgence can come at the appropriate time, after I have understood the nature of the problem.

Is there a different kind of authenticity? Earlier you were comparing Steven Holl's design process and yours. Referencing St. Ignatius you said, "I'm not sure how I would control the design process," referring to how he starts with watercolor sketches. It sounds like, in your description, he is exploring or searching for what he wants a building to represent. He's less concerned about the plan's organizational attributes at the beginning.

It is more of a phenomenological reference, more about experiencing this building and the authenticity of what you feel, how your perceptions change when you move through a building. It may not be fair to say that about his process, but that is definitely how he thinks about places.

10| Moving further into the design process when you are located in what I will call the architectural domain—whether that is exploring the quality of light, materiality, or a subset of a larger interest, etc.—how did you add additional depth to initial thoughts in the design of Chicken Point Cabin?

For me, the design process is where the richness develops as you spend more time with the client, spend more time with all the converging factors, the compromises, the opportunities, all these things. You are bringing together issues that are seemingly in conflict, or maybe in concert with each other, yet you are trying to assemble an idea out of the situation. The more you explore and edit that situation...it's almost like answers are there, but you have to remove the weeds and chaff to find the kernel. That's where the richness comes in because a successful decision or design is one that addresses two or three questions: functional, technical, and poetic. Sometimes the answer isn't always obvious. You've worked the problem, you've edited it, and you've asked if it is making sense. It's not a linear process. That's why design takes time. You push forward all your ideas and then begin to edit down to the essential one. The poetry then comes out of that process.

Sometimes when these issues are not supportive, they throw you off balance and make you think about another approach. Sometimes it blows you away because suddenly you find another pathway to resolve the issue. Yet it's not like you've forgotten the DNA

that allowed you to get to that point, but it readjusts it. Sometimes it's helpful and sometimes it's not.

Later in the design process when one typically has confidence in the design approach, and details are being refined, how do you utilize your design intentions? Do you find a way to trace design development ideas back to earlier concepts? In your houses there appears to be an interest in thickness complimenting thinness. I can say that is an interest you might start from or go back to. Are those legitimate topics in your mind?
One learns how to use one's tools. Sometimes they are proportional tools, and sometimes they are technical tools. The tools are almost like the rules of the road. Are they the Fibonacci series or the Golden Section? I'm not exactly sure it would be a mathematical analysis, yet if there were an actual mathematical analysis, they would follow exactly that kind of study. I think there is an intuitive nature about how to make decisions based on your own personality, your own situation and your background. Those, naturally, are going to influence the decisions, and I do think they are intuitive. There is so much about what we do that is an intuitive leap. Academicians would argue that is cheating, that it is not really trying, but I disagree. I think to be in touch with those perspectives is something that only comes with years and years of practice, with tools that you develop naturally. You talk to downhill skiers—they are going 70-plus miles an hour. They are not really thinking about what's happening with their legs, but they are definitely in tune with everything that's going on. It's like the inner game of skiing, of tennis.

In my own design process I used to feel this element had to be one inch or one foot. Now I look at the design, or the component, or the wall, and say it has to be "this" long, what feels right in relation to the context or intention.
You're right. An old architect once said this to me..."You're not really an architect until every line you draw, you understand what that line means, not only to the plan you're working on, but you understand it in section, you understand it technically, and you understand it in elevation." Of course, I thought it was BS, but he was right. I've been designing for so many years now that I can actually lay down lines and often there is this wild thing that happens where clear relationships appear that validate an intention almost magically.

11| When that clarity occurs, whether through a rational process, intuition, or "intuitive rationalism," do you find yourself naming or prioritizing elements

Sometimes when there are these little details or these little moments, if they really are authentic they come out of the process or the evolution of the idea.

The idea of materiality informs the plan, informs the poetry, informs the function, informs the tectonics.

Material is a reference to the cultural context and the landscape context. Northern Idaho is big rustic machinery for old mines and the logging saw mills. Its CMU which is for these tough industrial buildings that are made out of a material that comes naturally from the surrounding area. I always associate certain materials with certain places and certain landscapes.

I've always been attracted to anything that has a beauty based on function. I have a hard time imagining what beauty based on just beauty really is.

or programmatic areas to differentiate, give hierarchy to, or establish a relationship to larger global intentions? Earlier we discussed the Studio House, the Brain, the Delta Shelter...there is a certain naming aspect that you use.

I call them handles—naming represents short cuts or shorthand for different assemblies or areas within a design. For me they have a reference or meaning beyond the name in order to provide direction. A similar non-architectural example is a hot rod term, which is "French" headlights or taillights. If you know the term, then you know exactly what to do.

In that regard, in a more architectural context, naming might reference an assembly or detailing process intended to create a specific visual outcome, yet naming can allow a connection linking the design to another intention having nothing to do with earlier, more primary ones, such as organizing the project to capture the view of the lake or allowing that view to be enhanced by incorporating the operating window wall. Yet naming continues to be a standard or regular part of your methodology.

That is correct, yet sometimes people will ask me, "What are you going to call that?" That is not the way it works. It is not image based; it's part of the design process.

12| Are there situations in the design process where you might be thinking, "Since the building is sited properly and functionally the layout works, I need to think about this project in terms of what I'm trying to represent."? As the design developed, did you use the different attributes of the organizational and representational domains to mature or cross-reference each other? As an example, I was reviewing the exploded axonometric drawing of Chicken Point Cabin that documents the surrounding CMU wall. Then above that is the assembly highlighting the window wall system, the transom wall system, and the floating roof. Conceptually it seems you are exploring issues such as having a solid stereotomic container, that contains components which have additional functional and organizational roles, but are envisioned as having distinct tectonic expressions.

Yes, that is accurate, yet it is almost a seamless moment. I wouldn't be able to define when one realm blends into another. In fact, it might even be better to imagine the process as being a spiral process where I am thinking about what an appropriate material might be, even conceptually, because I am trying to consider all these

convergences relating to the issues you're describing and bringing them all together. It's not a linear process. I don't even know if there is an appropriate line in the sand where I say, "Ok, I've established this. Now, I'm going into phase two, three, four, five, or whatever." That's not the way I work. In fact, I'd have to say that is probably the reason that I sometimes enjoy smaller scale work. It allows you to imagine its totality. It's almost like industrial design. You can imagine it in a morphing, completed form, but you are juggling all the pieces at the same time. I think in large buildings, it is difficult to juggle all the pieces at the same time. That is why there are so few large buildings that really work effectively as architecture. They may work great from a scenographic standpoint. An exception might be Peter Zumthor's Spa at Vals, which is genius and is a pretty large building. He was able to keep that clear in his head.

So you are saying your design process is almost a continuous cross-referencing or spiraling between multiple issues yet quality projects will have organizational conditions, a "structure" will be used to provide a kind of glue, an ordering system. Maybe at a point in the design process you realize you have been thinking about a project primarily from an organizational perspective, but in the spiral reference you gave, it suggests your design intentions are continually questioning or evolving. Organizational concepts can represent more that just ordering systems and conversely ideas that are more representational in nature typically need organizational strategies.

It's not a circular process; it's a spiraling process. You're going somewhere. You are always re-editing and re-thinking and changing. You sort of sense it. I'm not sure that I would be able to describe it exactly, but, back to the music analogy. I know when it feels right, when it feels connected to the equation, and when the equation is edited, elegant, efficient, and poetic. How do I define it? I don't know how to put it into words.

So you would say, the "U" organization was related more directly to site considerations and the notion that there is a stereotomic container enclosing a series of tectonic assemblies or components may have spiraled from that condition. Did you see that organization having representational considerations or did it evolve strictly as part of organizational responsibilities derived from the site or client programmatic considerations?

Primarily the "U," or "C" derived from the organizational requirements as dictated by the site, the material realities of the situation, plus the budget, yet it is a

I do know that the "C" was, in plan, clear about the idea of providing prospect opportunities and a place of refuge, and that is more than an organizational intention.

relevant question. I do know that the "C" was, in plan, clear about the idea of providing prospect opportunities and a place of refuge, and that is more than an organizational intention. You have the refuge aspect created by the wrapping quality of the "C" where inside the "C" you are comfortable. You are cozy. Then you have prospect revealed via the window looking out to the horizon, the mountains. and the water. That was intentional, whether the U shape, the C shape, an open box, etc. This house has a road behind it. That's partly the reason for the refuge part, to remove you from the realities implied by the road. A lot of similar houses I have designed open to the forest in back and to the horizon in front. I will use the forest itself as a refuge. In those houses it is not a C building plan; it is a C landscape plan with the forest providing the wrap of refuge.

14| I can see that. In part you are saying the organizational quality does have some representational or meaningful qualities attached to it. You are organizing the existential qualities of prospect and refuge. It is very clear in that regard as it is configured in a way to represent or create a place of refuge. Did you see that organizational framework needing additional architectural expression because the U form of organization was too under-conceptualized or was its organizational essence envisioned as the significant aspect of what the building was to represent? I realize from what you just said that these things are working simultaneously, but what I'm trying to explore is the fact that house was organized as a U, and it was oriented toward the lake view, but those issues do not speak to your design interests concerning materiality, or technological expression, or construction-based aesthetics. Why is Chicken Point Cabin CMU. Why isn't it clad in wood siding?

That is a completely fair question. You could have made it in wood, and shingles, basically the back of the box. That would have been a perfectly fair response and appropriate. There are other converging factors, one of which was that it is a major fire area, another one being the client wanted absolutely no maintenance, and there was a tight budget. So, all of a sudden there was a series of corresponding bricks. You're bringing all these issues together, and you're trying to figure out which brick fits here, which brick fits there. So, the idea could certainly have been expressed in a number of materials. These particular materials were chosen based on a number of existing factors, primarily site and landscape factors.

I would not deny any of that. That's valid. But did you have an architectural interest in wanting this powerful, so stout, or confident container signifying refuge such that it couldn't be wood, because wood isn't visually "stout" enough and therefore the need for CMU or concrete? I'm wondering about the number of issues or intentions that affected how you came to this decision. Was there some kind of added representational quality that the organization didn't cover?

This may not be emphatic or clear enough for you, but I could easily see the box clad in wood given other circumstances, or rammed earth, but maybe not brick. There are ways that I would make decisions, and they tend to be function based, and to some extent the sense of the materiality is important, obviously. I could see Chicken Point in board formed concrete.

Architecture is not a diagram. Architecture is something you leave out in a natural landscape. It is in a climate and has forces working on it. ...It's not an abstract white box set in the landscape. It is actually a functioning working object, and as it grows older it gets better.

But I can envision where you might have said, regarding brick, that, no, it couldn't be brick, because even though it might have solved all the criteria of maintenance, fire safety, etc., it's just not right. Brick has other qualities attached to it symbolically.

That's exactly right. I could see it as a steel box, like Delta Shelter or something like that.

So is a reason you are saying that maybe Chicken Point cabin could not be clad in brick is because brick has too many associations with other stylistic representations in architecture whereas, steel and concrete and CMU and wood boxes have associations with more singular authenticity?

I always associate certain materials with certain places and certain landscapes. In that particular landscape, brick just doesn't exist out there because of the nature of the material that is locally available. If Chicken Point Cabin were located in Virginia, or where there is more of a brick sub-culture, it probably would make sense. Material is a reference to the cultural context and the landscape context. Northern Idaho is big rustic machinery for old mines and the logging sawmills. It's CMU, which is for these tough industrial buildings that are made out of a material that comes naturally from the surrounding area. The aggregate is there; even the Portland cement is there and the sand is certainly there. It is a material that is ubiquitous in all the inexpensive buildings. The steel is certainly there, in the sad yet evocative rusted structures. So, there's a larger material context that makes sense to me and is appropriate for this rural area.

15| As the design progresses, how do you link ephemeral, or poetic intentions of your design to the pragmatic functional performance concerns? I am calling some of these aspects poetic because they have obviously been thought about and designed, whether as a proportional issue, a material issue, etc. Do they refer to preferences that suggest intentions or meanings you have developed over time, or would it be that these poetic inspirations arise through certain project specific aspects?

That's a good question. Regarding the gizmos, the fear I've always had, and in some cases, it has become true, is that these devices become kind of a fetish or a kind of gimmick. And, all of the ideas, including the Chicken Point Cabin idea, didn't come because I'd always dreamt of doing this big window wall that could be cranked with a counter-weight and some gears and levers. It came about because I had some experience with certain machinery in my youth, and the client made a statement, and with my physics background I said, "Oh, well a person can do this." That's really bottom line important to me. I do have clients that want to hire me because they want a gizmo. I tell them that's not the way it works. The way it works is, you don't want to do a gizmo, but if there is a need for a gizmo because there's something wonderful and poetic about something you experience, heck yeah, that's why you might hire me. That doesn't mean you get a gizmo. Sometimes when there are these little details or these little moments, if they really are authentic they come out of the process or the evolution of the idea. Maybe it's not obvious, but that reality should be part of the fun of putting a building together.

Maybe I can follow up. In the sense of poetic intentions there is an aspect suggesting that whether poetry comes through authenticity via an exposed steel angle used as a connector for bolting the wood joists to a steel beam, or whether in designing the handle for the front door, would you say that the idea of poetry, and I'm hesitating to define it as such, is something related to authenticity?

Yes, but it is like the reason you and your son like to work on his 1972 Challenger. For whatever reason there's a poetry to it, but there is also an authentic poetry to it. Obviously it is a gilded lily in some ways, but there's an exuberant authenticity to it, and that's why you are attracted to certain experiences or things, whatever that thing is. I've always been attracted to anything that has a beauty based on function. I have a hard time imagining what beauty based on just beauty really is. I'm not exactly sure how to define that, because obviously I, and most of us, have a sense of beauty based on nature. Well, nature is basically a function; it is a function driven thing. It has to be to survive. It has physics involved. It has forces involved. Survival involved.

If the beauty is through function, I'll return to the door handle, and argue that there is more to its design than just function. So from where do you think that is derived?

I agree. If you look at a Shaker chair, why does a Shaker chair function so beautifully as opposed to a folding chair. There may be numerous explanations, but I do know that one quality is that it is created with care, created under the umbrella of function, but under that umbrella with poetry. The Japanese architects, Japanese equipment, and Japanese tools are just stunningly beautiful. There is something—it's an intuition—but you know it when you see it, and it feels right. When you are designing something, you actually do know when that moment happens, and there are certainly a lot of moments when you know it doesn't happen, maybe when it's only halfway there.

16| To carry the material issue through, was the expressive nature of materials or how you deployed them important in the design of the cabin? We

know the answer is yes, but when did the notion of the play of material intentions become important in the project?

Almost from the beginning, and that goes back to my earlier answer that all of this stuff is just a swirling spiral where the material informs the plan, informs the idea, informs the poetry, informs the function, informs the tectonics and you are slowly circling the wagons. You are slowly figuring it out, like jazz, you are slowly figuring out the conversation as you proceed.

So would you say, because of the expressive nature of materials, you would never be able to do an all white house, or a house of a more or less singular material.

Exactly, because that's a diagram to me, and architecture is not a diagram. Architecture is something you leave out in a natural landscape. It is in a climate, it has multiple constraints affecting it. There is a functionality. there are forces it is dealing with, forces that affect the structure, gravity forces, forces like wind, earthquakes, climate forces like hot, cold, windy, rainy, snowy. It's not this abstract white box that is set in the landscape. It is actually a functioning working object, and as it grows older, it gets better.

How do you conceptualize the organization or composition of joints between individual pieces of materials? As an example I will return to the design of the front door. There is the Mondrian form of organization arranging the panels that spin off of the peephole. While I can assume that the peephole is there for the typical need to view through a solid object, the organization of the panels could have been accomplished in a number of ways. The jointing strategy then becomes of note as an idea.

It was an idea of reinvention. Sometimes I will use the location of a peephole to accommodate family members of different heights, for a small kid I'll have it low, for an older kid I'll have it a little higher. I think that is important. It's like hot-rodding a car. You take a commodity idea and make it your own. You imagine a particular function, something you need, and then you re-imagine it. The skin on the front door...clearly, the door is larger than any single panel you can buy, so how do you take these two specific conditions and make a larger whole that re-thinks both the skin of the door and the location of the peephole? The rectangular peephole becomes both an organizer of the metal panels and part of the manufactured essence of the door. It becomes integrated into the field of spot welds, and becomes a part of the jointing system rather than just a hole. You make it your own.

In that regard this isn't only about a joint or a peephole. I could expand the issue of the meaningfulness of a joint into the conceptual interest in letting the door rust. Is your interest in those qualities largely because they provide added character marking the passage of time? What values do you see expressed in those kind of intentions?

Well, the value of these issues, and they are important, is because that is something that I do not have control over. I think in a manner a little bit like listening to jazz. There are conversations occurring between the musicians, and those conversations sometimes rely on the nuances of surprises, the nuances of risk, of letting something happen without having ultimate control. Because ultimately we don't have control over our lives; we don't have control over anything. And it's insincere and almost narcissistic to imagine that we have control over everything around us. These issues represent a wink and a nod saying, " I don't own this house, and I don't own this weather or the situation here." And actually, to embrace those parts of life is what makes it all interesting.

And it makes it a better house.

For me, yes. When you ski the trees, you don't know your route through the trees. If you assume you knew your route, you're going to hit a tree. What you're doing is taking your skills, wit, talent, and speed and making minute and large decisions very quickly as you're going through the forest. It is one of the most thrilling experiences, because you are going like a kayaker in rapids. You are experiencing the nature of this place. You have some control over it, but you don't have ultimate control over it.

That touches on the part of design dualities that bring added meaning to why we love something, or why we appreciate it. We appreciate the understandability of the aspects we are familiar with, yet we are also drawn to the mystery embedded in the other "aspects."

Someone just recently asked me what was one of the most important books I read as a kid. This is almost embarrassing to say, but it did have some importance to me. It was an Alan Watts book called *The Wisdom of Insecurity*. I was about 16 years old. It is a short book. In it he says you can't do anything about the past, you can't predict the future, but you can experience a given situation right now, and it is often a very insecure situation, but the best part about that is that it *is* insecure. ■

The rectangular peephole becomes both an organizer of the metal panels and part of the manufactured essence of the door. It becomes integrated into the field of spot welds, and becomes a part of the jointing system rather than just a hole. You make it your own.

Patkau Architects

John Patkau

Strawberry Vale Elementary School

Strawberry Vale Elementary School, completed in 1995, is located in Victoria, British Columbia, Canada and includes programmatic elements standard to a typical elementary school. The school encloses 35,446-square-feet which include 16 classrooms, a gymnasium and library, plus administrative and support components. In addition, Patkau Architects "invented" additional program in the creation of "learning support pods" and devoted extensive effort to integrating the building into multiple site and environmental considerations.

The school's form gives expression to these factors in addition to incorporating architectural responses to the local culture and its diversity. These deliberations, in addition to the normative nature of the program, informed the design outcome of the building, suggesting the building's design would encompass both standard criteria and unique tenets. Additional architectural themes developed the organization of the circulation, the expressive nature of the mechanical system and the conceptual integration of materials. These investigations, in both their conceptual and constructed expressions, are documented in stereotomic and tectonic understandings, material texture, scale, jointing, and assembly manifestations, all contributing to the realization and expression of multiple design intentions.

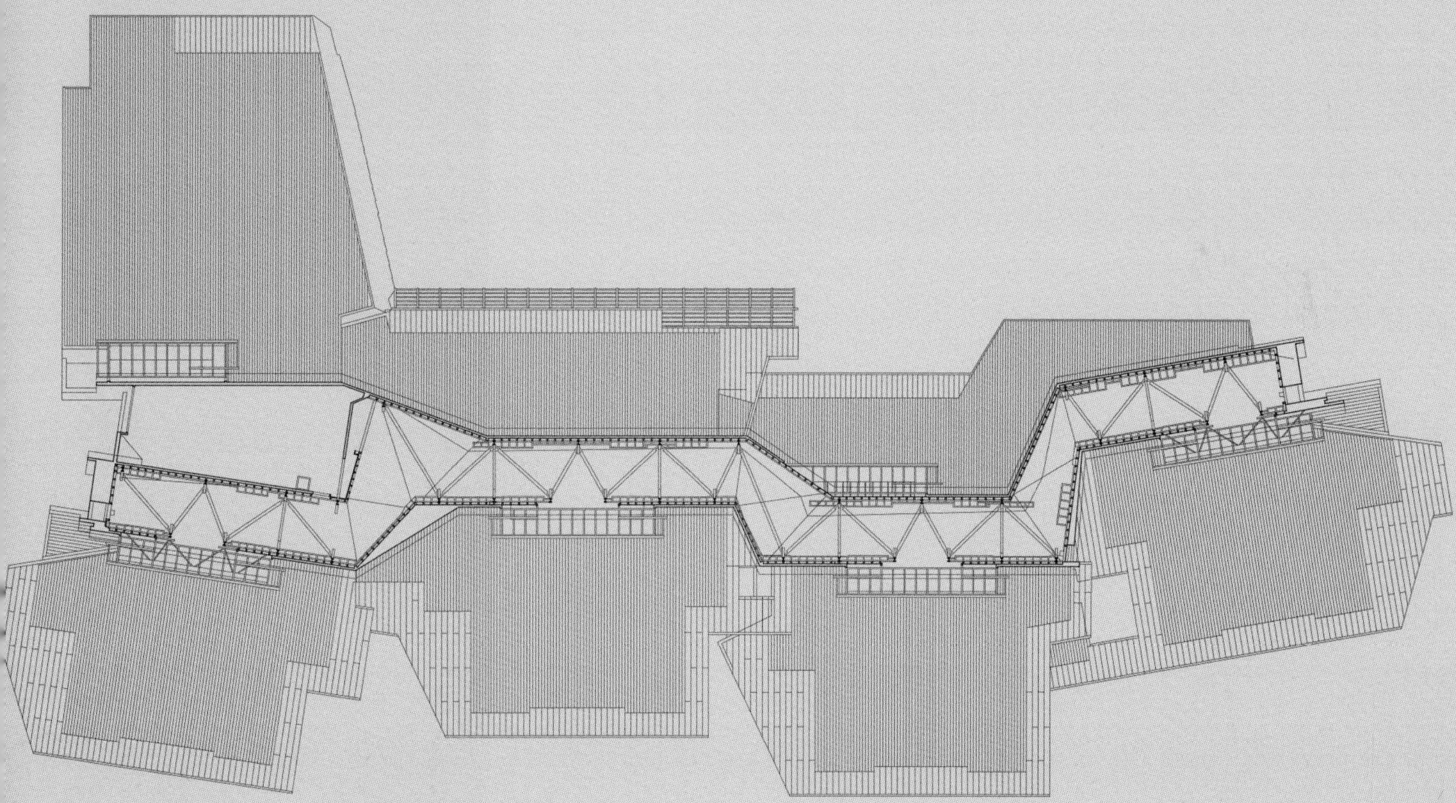

I would say that Patricia and I have always understood architecture to be an intellectual construction which means that it is a set of ideas and concepts that are organized into an ordering system and that the design process is the discovery of that ordering system.

At the same time there are a variety of investigations that are beyond the specifics of a given project that have to do with our own interests in how we develop our design language.

There's the language of splays, and then there are the extensions or offsets of lines through some of the walls.

1| Tom Diehl: What value, potential, or use do you see in order?

John Patkau: I would say that Patricia and I have always understood architecture to be an intellectual construction which means that it is a set of ideas and concepts that are organized into an ordering system and that the design process is the discovery of that ordering system. Through that I mean that it is not that you begin with the ordering system; you end with the ordering system. You discover the ordering system in designing the building. Until the ordering system is complete and cohesive and in a sense resolved, locked together, as in the jam jar kind of thing when, if you roll it down a hill no piece would fall off, until you've achieved that, the design is not complete.

Nothing can be added or taken away.

Exactly. So the notion is that you begin with certain principles which are relevant to the project, and you build from those. One starting point may be the program, the site, the environment, construction techniques, etc. But what you're really trying to do is to assemble an intellectual ordering system, make it coherent, complete and adequate to describe the project, but not more than it requires. You don't want superfluous components in that ordering system. Simpler projects would have a simpler ordering system. Potentially simpler in what terms, I don't know. So the idea of order is definitely a precedent to all of us, that without order you can't act.

So it is, for you, a kind of a frame, one to promote coherence, whether it comes from the program, whether it comes from the site, whether it comes possibly from an external issue.

Absolutely. It could be an external condition; it could be a desire to represent an idea. Which could absolutely produce an ordering system. For us, when there is a part of a design that doesn't appear to be resolved, which does not reflect the idea, to us that condition suggests that the ordering system is not adequate, that we need to enlarge its capacity to solve problems. That means inventing additional components to allow you to solve or resolve the entire project. You keep inventing additional components until you're able to resolve the project entirely.

So the concept of an ordering system as a singular issue is not a singular belief structure so to speak. It might be more accurate to refer to the use of ordering systems.

The design process requires multiple systems, and they could have many different dimensions. They could be material, geometric, etc.

2| How do concepts of order manifest themselves in your design thinking or process, i.e., what does order mean to you architecturally?

Our buildings are dissimilar to each other in many ways based on their circumstances. You might look at the interiors of Strawberry Vale and say that there's a Deconstructive aspect to them. That was not what they were about. They were about something else having to do with an attitude about being a rural building versus being an urban building, where the geometries were the geometries of nature, the irregular geometries of nature. If we were doing a project that was in a urban context, it might have a very different ordering system reflecting the nature of its situation. Somebody whose position was underpinned by a Deconstructivist point of view would have a similar geometry or architectural language regardless of the context.

For your projects, do site specificity and the client's program become initial drivers for the organizational and representational qualities of the building?

Yes, those issues are secondary for some architects because for them there's this larger issue, a larger cultural issue that is expressed in the character of the formal or material quality within the building.

4| I'm trying make the distinction between those kinds of starting points. I'm not arguing for one over the other. Some architects use broader, more global intentions and some don't. So then, for Patkau Architects, do design interests, specifically those extending beyond ones concerned with facilitating the distribution of the program and fitting the building to the site, originate within the discipline of architecture or from sources lying outside of it? Is it not fair to say that Patkau Architects tends to start within traditional architectural points of departure?

I would say that's true. For example, it's not suggesting that architecture is autonomous; some people have suggested that architecture is an autonomous discipline which owes nothing to anything outside of itself. Certainly we believe that architecture is part of a larger cultural and physical environment and needs to be aware of those things and respond to those things. At the same time there is a variety of investigations that are beyond the specifics of a given project, that have to do with our own interests in how we develop our design language. For example, it would be very unlikely that we would develop interiors of a character similar to Strawberry Vale today for a variety of reasons. Strawberry Vale represents an interest we were focused on in 1996 when we designed the building, but we've moved to a different place. Today, those interiors would be very different. Even though they are founded on principles, they are founded on ideas

They were about something else having to do with an attitude about being a rural building versus being an urban building, where the geometries were the geometries of nature, the irregular geometries of nature.

It's very easy to discuss Strawberry Vale as a response to specific site or programmatic circumstances. But that's not the complete explanation.

about appropriateness, and there are reasons why they look the way they do. Those reasons aren't as compelling to us today, and other ones are. We've changed.

What I'm hearing is that while there are foundations of architectural principle that you are drawn to, you are not linking your process to a singular approach. There are broader concerns you find yourselves being drawn toward.

It's very easy to discuss Strawberry Vale as a response to specific site or programmatic circumstances. And we will do that. But that's not the complete explanation. There are other factors that are less conscious, perhaps certainly having to do with personal sensibilities and the interests that arise from them. In our practice Patricia and I are often at odds regarding many issues including what represents an appropriate sensibility for the project. There is a push and pull in the development of all our projects. We think it is for the better as nothing goes untested because there's always a challenging point of view. Hopefully the value of the ultimate solution has been tested against alternate proposals, whereas if I were practicing on my own, there would probably not be as rigorous a process because there are many questions I wouldn't ask as I can only bring my own perspective. So even that comes into it: the fact that there are those fundamentally different and personal ways of seeing the world that are unique to each individual and are different.

That's interesting as it makes the work more modern regarding the essence of a building. The process does not start with a fixed idea but with a dialectical process or a multiplicity of viewpoints intending to be more inclusive.

In fact, as a conscious intention we have always wanted to expand the issues we deal with in our projects. We've attempted to take on more and more issues. As an example, issues of sustainability are important issues that we wholeheartedly endorse, and we've incorporated them into a range of other issues. They are not the most important. They are not the least important, just one of many as is local culture, etc, etc. It goes on and on, and whenever we become aware of another way of thinking about architecture in another dimension, we try and bring that into the discussion as well.

Which confirms your earlier statement that you see architecture as an intellectual pursuit. Would you say that the reason for an intellectual pursuit is not for itself? But rather it is part of human nature that we can aspire, through design, to provide more feedback, to provide more quality moments?

Beyond the obvious practical requirements of society, I think the primary reason that we design buildings is for the intellectual gratification of constructing a complex ordering system and resolving it. That's our motivation and hopefully the result of that is a building that offers great value and use to its community, but that's not our only motivation. Our primary motivation is that desire to engage in an activity, refine that activity, and gain satisfaction from that resolution.

4.1| How do the more purely architectural interests, those derived beyond considerations related to the program and site, impact your thinking in relation to methods employed to represent your design intentions? I'm trying to find out what has the most relevance as a starting point.

It certainly is all of the above. Our projects are intentionally very expressive of context, and context can be

I think the primary reason that we design buildings is for the intellectual gratification of constructing a complex ordering system and resolving it.

Our projects are intentionally very expressive of context, and context can be the site, it can be the culture of the client, and these can be instructional. Context can be environmental. Our projects have attempted to be expressive of all of those things. ...attempted to try and understand, is an architecture appropriate to the heterogeneous North American culture.

In projects of the vintage of Strawberry Vale, we were very interested in expressing the way buildings are constructed, making the construction of the building legible, and making that an important part of the experience and richness of the building.

the site, it can be the culture of the client, and these can be instructional. Context can be environmental. Our projects have attempted to be expressive of all of those things. At the same time there are definitely important larger concerns. For example, one of the things we have always, yet not always, attempted to try and understand is an architecture appropriate to the heterogeneous North American culture. We are not a European culture. For example, the postmodern use of European buildings as icons is culturally inappropriate for a large segment of our population because they are not Europeans. They are Native Americans. They are Asians. They are Africans. They come from everywhere. And so we have intentionally thought about that issue and tried to understand what an architectural order could be that would be inclusive of those different cultures. When we discuss Strawberry Vale, I'd like to refer to that again, because finding something that has an expressiveness of humanity interests us, as that is what comprises our society. There are people here from everywhere, and so we need to find an architecture that is capable of being a good fit for all of those people. This is interesting because the whole issue of globalization and local culture is a very challenging one and because there is such a diverse cultural history in North America. Our local culture is not based upon a singular culture as much as site and climate

6| We'll shift to your global design strategies. What are your initial concerns when you begin design work on a project?

I think initial concerns exist on many levels. There is obviously the base research that every architect does about the site, the orientation, the program, the budget, and appropriate construction technologies. We do all of that in the

In a heterogeneous culture, creating an architectural language that was in itself heterogeneous might be an appropriate expression.

beginning. We also try and bring in larger questions about sustainability, about appropriateness, about local culture, all of those things. We also bring to projects an interest, which evolves and changes from project to project, about certain ways of organizing architecture which lie beyond the project. For example, in projects of the vintage of Strawberry Vale, we were very interested in expressing the way buildings are constructed, making the construction of the building legible and making that an important part of the experience and richness of the building. We currently are more interested in making sure that spatial qualities are clear. Strawberry Vale School has very powerful spaces in it, but in some ways the spaces are in competition with the expression of construction. We are currently interested in suppressing the construction language in the interest of making more legible spaces. Although different, both past and current interests can be seen as beyond the requirements of the site or program.

Because we are very self-critical, and we look at our previous work and try and understand ways in which we might understand it being unsuccessful, we can respond to our projects and are driven to move away from what we've just done by virtue of that self-critical process. Every project is put under harsh criticism and is viewed as having a variety of unsuccessful components that we try to avoid in the future.

In that context your initial concerns in a new project are often a critique of previous concerns.

We look at what we've done, and we say, "Well, that wasn't as successful as it might have been, or as appropriate as it might have been, or that's no longer as interesting an intellectual endeavour." So our initial concerns are constantly changing.

There is obviously the base research that every architect does about the site, the orientation, the program, the budget, and appropriate construction technologies. We do all of that in the beginning. We also try and bring in larger questions about sustainability, about appropriateness, about local culture, all of those things. We also bring to projects an interest, which evolves and changes from project to project, about certain ways of organizing architecture, which lie beyond the project.

That was an intention brought into the project because of a prior concern with the issue of finding an architectural language appropriate to this fused culture arising from so many different places. That interest was larger than the project itself.

There's a very strong discipline in the building, regarding the use of materials...

The enhanced environmental concerns and the cultural one relating to heterogeneity are represented through a multivalent project.

The desire to move, or move forward, is very much embedded in our culture and that comes into the criticism...

Yes, and so what I suggest is that the architectural language is necessarily changing from project to project. When you look at architects whose career is basically located within a single formal language, and I'm sure you can make an argument that those languages are rich, that they can support an evolving sensibility and a maturing sensibility, but I find it odd when a building that was designed at age 30 and a building that was designed at age 70 are so similar.

7| When you started the design of Strawberry Vale School were there global, architecturally transcendent themes you were investigating at the beginning of the design process? As you have referenced themes of this type, could you speak to the specificity of their use in Strawberry Vale School?

In the case of Strawberry Vale, there were a variety of them. One of them was the idea that in a heterogeneous culture, creating an architectural language that was in itself heterogeneous might be an appropriate expression. When you observe the building with this intention in mind, you see a variety of building materials in a variety of roles. There is a variety of forms and materials making up the building. That was an intention brought into the project because of a prior concern with the issue of finding an architectural language appropriate to this fused culture arising from so many different places. That interest was larger than the project itself.

So the character of the school, signified by it's relationship to the site and by the diverse cultures represented through the student body, created an architectural interest that grew into a design intention aimed at allowing those using the building to interact with it on multiple levels?

Yes, all of those things. We thought that would be a better fit than a singular identity. This project was also very important in that it was a milestone project in our own development of an attitude toward nature. Up to this point, we had primarily viewed nature aesthetically from an environmental and experiential point of view. This site was semi-rural at the time. We were on the edge of a nature preserve. Because of that there was a very conscious attempt to bring nature in as an aesthetic appreciation, which is characteristic of many of our earlier projects, but there was for the first time a very serious attempt to understand nature as a system. So this project deals with a lot of sustainability questions in terms of its relationship to its natural context, how water moves through the project, the materials from which the building is constructed, etc. All of those things were viewed not exclusively as aesthetic questions but as systematic questions, an environmental system. So that was larger than the specific project. This was our first serious attempt to architecturally deal with environmental sustainability and express it architecturally as opposed to simply deal with all the mechanisms.

There was a very conscious attempt to find the right thing. For example, we were very careful to use only second-growth lumber and build as much as we could out of lumber because that's the local building material, and to avoid using large members that are typically first-growth lumber, which is rare. Similarly, in lieu of those large wood members, we used steel, which could be recycled. There were a variety of intentions throughout the project, which talk about that and make it architectural. There's a very strong discipline in the building, regarding the use of materials, which is founded on environmental principles. This was dealt with rigorously, architecturally, even to the point where, for example, the roof construction is differentiated between the insulated portions of the roof and the un-insulated portions of the roof. The language of the roof changes. The idea was that all of these environmental relationships would be manifest in a coherent architectural way that would be thorough-going through the entire project, and readable.

So, the enhanced environmental concerns and the cultural one relating to heterogeneity are represented through a multivalent project. Those are dominant themes transcending interests that are purely architectural.

8| Given these transcendent themes are broader by nature and not always purely architectural concerns, what additional conceptual criteria did you employ to anchor your initial intentions?

Let's discuss the plan. To begin with we looked at a variety of organizations including multilevel organizations and ultimately came to the conclusion that a single level was best not only because it was an elementary school, but because that would allow all students to have equal access to the surrounding site, nature, playfields, and things like that. I'll tell you a little bit about the development of the site plan, but in relationship to that, the school basically fills the available site. We came to the conclusion that, for a couple of reasons, we wanted all the classrooms to be oriented toward the adjacent park. That meant that they would be south facing to facilitate this connection as well as day lighting strategies within the classrooms. So the 16 classrooms that make up the school, if we made them in a straight line, would have been longer than the site. What we decided to do was to put them into clusters of four where we nested

We adjusted the location of these secondary spaces to respond to the rock outcropping so the orthogonal geometry begins to become irregular.

The principle circulation spine was defined by the adjustments of the classroom pods to the topography. That's where the larger scale irregular geometry comes into play.

some classrooms behind other classrooms but they all connected to the exterior. So what that allowed was, by moving one cluster slightly behind another we were able to shorten the length of the school while maintaining the constant relationship of all classrooms to the south and to the park. That generated the idea of the cluster of four classrooms from which we then generated secondary non-programmatic components located in the shared spaces adjacent to the classroom clusters.

9| It appears to be an organizational concern based upon site considerations so let me fold in this question. As this was not a direct language-based consideration at this point in the design process what organizational intentions arising from an analysis of the site and program were employed to organize and ultimately express your conceptual interests?

Well, let me go back to the secondary components for a moment. They are actually spaces that were intended to have a variety of support components. We proposed a series of movable carts that would support different functions. There would be a cooking cart, an art cart, etc., that could be moved into those spaces. We adjusted the location of these secondary spaces to respond to the rock outcropping so the orthogonal geometry begins to become irregular. We could have organized the four pods into a regular manner but they were organized in an irregular manner to accommodate rock outcroppings, which one senses in the site. Also, each pod was put at a different elevation to minimize excavation. They move up and down in section following the changes in topography that create some very interesting spaces with strong sectional characteristics. Those were the organizing issues from where it all began. We then took the other components of the program supporting the classrooms, i.e., the administration, the libraries, a little computer room, the

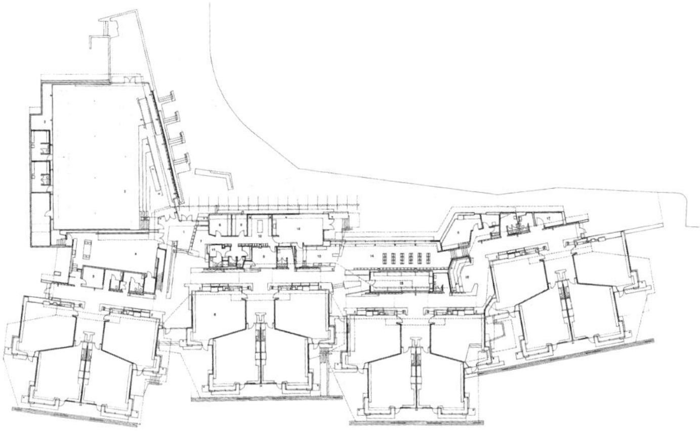

Plan, offset organization of classroom pods.
Linear bars organizing diverse program components.

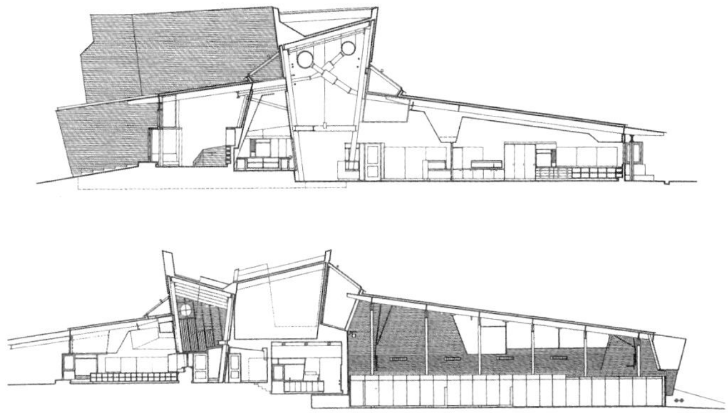

Building sections

gymnasium, the multi-purpose room, and put them on the north side opposite the principle circulation spine. The principle circulation spine was defined by the adjustments of the classroom pods to the topography. That's where the larger scale irregular geometry comes into play.

You use the word "nesting" to describe the relationship of the offset pods. Do you use words as signifiers to give a clearer picture of what you are trying to establish with your concepts? As one looks at the plan, it is easy to identify what you are describing in relation to the nesting of the four classrooms. When I look to the service pieces or the support pieces I see a strategy of linear bars or masses layered together. Is that another type of nesting or did you see it as a different area which required a different organizational strategy?
It has a different organizational strategy because it's made up of a variety of program components which are dissimilar, whereas the classrooms are repetitive elements. There is a very different program type on the north side of the building as opposed to the south side.

Pushing that a little further, the program components on the north side have been organized with an identifiable linearity, whether the linearity of the variety of program spaces you've just referred to or the linearity of the support components located on the north end of each classroom. There appears to be an organizational strategy employed to relate the dissimilar components. There is a defined organization, in the form of the repeated pods used for the classrooms, and another linear-based organizational strategy for the associated support components. Is it more accurate to say one is service and one is served?
At this point the section really comes into the discussion as well as the plan because we developed a service spine located above the circulation spine. The height of that portion of the building did a number of things for us. It facilitated our mechanical servicing but also our environmental systems. That was part of a natural ventilation strategy where air is drawn in from the classrooms and from the spaces at grade level on the north side into the corridor. It rises as it warms to the high point of the spine and then is drawn off. The section, the generic section, has two low sides upon either side of a central spine and the construction of that spine was made into four components, one associated with each of the four clusters of classrooms with an irregular connection between them. The linearity you see is partly a function of the generic character. If you were to isolate one of the segments, and if it weren't for the fact that we have jogged them back and forth to respond to the site, they would have been on a flat site and would have been one straight line; the direct linear geometry would have been there. It's actually simply a function of a straightforward, logical way to construct and organize that segment of the plan.

I'm sensing three prime organizational strategies employed. There are the offset nested clusters of classrooms, then there is the circulation based spine segment that aligns with and follows from each of the offset cluster components, and then that spine segment begins to generate an organizational follow through into the linearity of the support components on the north side of the building. So while there are three distinct organizational components, they are all an outflow from the strategy employed to organize the classroom clusters.
Agreed.

We were discussing how additional conceptual criteria were employed to anchor the initial intentions. Discuss that same question as is relates to the section as, when I look at the cross section, there is a dominance about the spine. It is certainly privileged as you were describing in relation to circulation, expression of building systems, and for use in sustainable-based strategies, yet I am also seeing architectural language issues. One, the angling out or splaying of the upper walls creates a clear orthogonal relationship with the sloped roofs over the side support areas. The other sectional aspect is the orthogonal base composed of the windows and their rectangular geometry in a somewhat open or irregular composition. In section that tendency adjusts as you move vertically. There are no orthogonal lines of any sort when you move higher in section. What is of interest to me is the conceptualization of the section in terms of the architectural languages employed. There is the orthogonal simplicity of the base that becomes less regular as the building rises in section. I see a certain continuity of an organizational strategy, even though adjusted. I'm trying to explore that issue in section.
What is happening there is that the lower levels of the building are orthogonal, although not in the overall, but in the local areas. This is the simple response to the fact those geometries are easiest to use, and the upper levels are shaped by larger environmental forces, by the need for water to flow off the roof, etc. What happens is the zone for people is driven by the needs they have. As this is a publicly funded school, very efficient and useful systems of construction are required, ones that do not waste space and can be subjected to all the net to gross considerations and accounting procedures necessary to justify a public expenditure. Above that, though, the forces are different. People don't inhabit those upper reaches directly, but other forces are obviously impacting the building. The rain falls on the roof and needs to be

People don't inhabit those upper reaches directly, but other forces are obviously impacting the building. The rain falls on the roof and needs to be moved away. The language of the building takes on the language of environmental response.

One idea that we had is that the interior of the school, because it's conceived to be in a semi-rural community, has a natural character. ...but it's almost forest-like in its quality. The notion is that there is a topography.

What is happening there is that the lower levels of the building are orthogonal, although not in the overall, but in the local areas. This is the simple response to the fact those geometries are easiest to use, and the upper levels are shaped by larger environmental forces...

moved away. The language of the building takes on the language of environmental response.

Accommodating users, construction realities, and responding to environmental concerns. I like that in the way they respond to the pragmatic necessities of building. You gave me very authentic, useful, and practical answers. Now I'm going to inquire about the architectural side. We can ask the question in terms of why you maintained a 90-degree relationship in section between the slope of the roofs at the spine and those over the secondary areas. Explain the architectural interest in that.

Actually, one idea that we had, this is an idea less compelling to Patricia than to me, is that the interior of the school, because it's conceived to be in a semi-rural community, has a natural character. Whether or not that's an appropriate consideration is another matter, but it's almost forest-like in its quality. The notion is that there is a topography. The ground plane of the school is like a topography of rock outcroppings, and the upper volumes equate to trees with branches and masses and their irregularity. There is an intention to create a sense of naturalness. There is sort of a self-conscious naturalism about the interior that fully orthogonal geometry doesn't support.

Nature doesn't plant trees in grids.

Exactly, and the trees don't necessarily always grow straight out. And so the intention is that walking through this space is like walking through a forest.

That thought derives from defining the circulation spine's character by expressing a more "natural reading" of it's experiential qualities. It's not orthogonal. In section the building honors or privileges the spine architecturally in terms of this representational concern. From a performance viewpoint the building responds architecturally to environmental and architectural concerns.

I wouldn't completely agree with that because I think that the fact that it has height and a more dynamic character doesn't necessarily assign privilege to it. I would suggest that what we've attempted to do is to find the appropriate form for each of the components of the project and that the nature of this space, which is a circulation space, a mechanical servicing space, and a collector for natural ventilation strategies, means it's a tall space. The fact that it's a dynamic space, where people are not sitting, thinking, and working but actually just walking through, is in harmony with that more dynamic expression. I don't think that that privileges the space because the classroom has been very carefully considered to create characteristics that are appropriate to it. In fact, I can see an opposite argument being made which is that the classrooms and their clusters of pods, and the way they are organized, is the driver of the plan. Everything else is simply responding to that. And so I understand, but I don't accept the fact that that signifies "I'm privileged."

We are now moving into design development strategies. You've spoken to the nature of the site as an organizational concern and the organization of the south side of the building is derived, in part, from the rocks of the site. The north side has a different organizational approach. Were there other organizational attributes that we should discuss?

Well, yes. The north side is the entry side, the more public side, where cars arrive and the building is actually more closed on that side, whereas it's open to the park on the south. All of the support functions became a buffer between the public activity at the front of the building and the classrooms at the back. So there was

There's a two-fold objective of appropriate material characteristics for use, but also a desire to minimize material use. If we didn't need the element, we eliminated it.

On the south the roofs are all sheltering and open, whereas on the north there are more massive, sculpted kinds of forms having a significantly different character.

a very careful understanding of the very different characteristics on the north side, which is the public side, with cars, parents dropping children off, buses, all that sort of stuff, and the natural quiet side on the south. The program is organized in response to that and the building forms change as a result. On the south the roofs are all sheltering and open whereas on the north there are more massive, sculpted kinds of forms having a significantly different character.

10| It gives a more civic presence to the school. So by this point in the design process you have situated the building on the site, the layout of the program has been approved by the client, and a number of architectural issues, both personal and professional have been addressed. How did you add additional depth to your initial design intentions?
The surfaces of the building were rigorously developed in response to our fundamental objectives. In the interior we minimized finishes, because we wanted to reduce the number of materials and the impact of that material use.

When you say minimize finishes...
Eliminate elements of the project where they could be eliminated. There would be no ceiling in the spine because we didn't require a ceiling in the spine. There would be no cladding of the structure on the upper regions of the building, but there would be cladding or millwork components in the lower regions for a couple of reasons. One is because kids are circulating at this level and they might bump this elemental framing and it can be kind of tough on kids, so we introduced appropriate surface components.

The majority of the surfaces in the kids' zone are refined smooth surfaces that are kid friendly whereas when we rise above the kid zone, we simply strip those things off because we don't need them any longer. We let what was required to build the building be there. There's a two-fold objective of appropriate material characteristics for use, but also a desire to minimize material use. If we didn't need the element, we eliminated it.

Then there is the companion issue of your architectural interests of letting the building be expressive of its constructive nature.
Yes. So there was the thought, whether realized or not, that this would be instructive to the students, that by allowing them to see how the building was constructed, they might begin to understand something about construction and architecture that they wouldn't otherwise have been able to perceive. There was that desire.

I would add the word authenticity. It was more important to sense the school in terms of how buildings are built, i.e., this is the authentic expression of the constructive nature of the building versus a conceptual concern regarding unmasking. You stripped away for different reasons.
It was about that, too, sure. We were concerned that the building would have material presence and be a convincing artifact, yet authenticity is a word that can have some issues associated with it so I'm reluctant to use the word authenticity.

State your concerns.
The concerns are, and this is outside the discussion of this project, but what is authentic to you is different than what is authentic to me. I remember there was an advertisement for a product and the slogan was "more authentic than real," which is a real head twister. So what is authenticity? At the time of Strawberry Vale we certainly wanted the kind of material credibility, detail, richness, and a textural presence that you get when you allow the building's construction to be manifest. Certainly in a project like a public school, which typically has a very limited budget, one is trying to get richness any way possible because you can't afford expensive materials.

So additional depth, whether it's a material issue, a constructive issue, a programmatic issue, etc. Are there specific issues you find your office continuously mining?
Well, at the time of Strawberry Vale there definitely was the idea of a constructional language which transitions from the mass, sort of rock-like base, to the more fragmented components of the upper reaches of the building. There is that transition from the stereotomic to the tectonic. There is the metaphor of a forest that is there as well. There is the functional consideration for the material character that is appropriate for kids, and there is also the desire to have an interior of multiple materials

Well, at the time of Strawberry Vale there definitely was the idea of a constructional language which transitions from the mass, sort of rock-like base, to the more fragmented components of the upper reaches of the building. There is that transition from the stereotomic to the tectonic. There is the metaphor of a forest that is there as well.

One of the things we were exploring with the idea of heterogeneity was to develop a variety of interior characteristics that would be appropriate to the activities going on there.

expressing a multivalent character that is heterogeneous and creates an architectural language that might speak to the diversity of the building's occupants.

11 Did you "name" or prioritize elements or programmatic areas to differentiate, or give hierarchy to, the larger global intentions?

The spine was called the spine, and that has significance because it is the backbone of the project. The classrooms were called clusters, but they could equally have been called pods as they had an identity as an element. In that sense, the naming demonstrated that they were, in a sense, given priority over the other components. All the other components are local. It's the spine and the cluster of classrooms that are unique to the project, and so they were given names.

Local in this case meaning they were kind of secondary.

There was one gym, and it was in one location. But there were four clusters of four classrooms, and there was a continuous spine that tied them all together. So components or assemblies that had a stronger architectural role tended to acquire a name.

"To give them an identity"...In your strategizing, in the naming of assemblies, did you begin to see certain architectural attributes that...

Yes. One of the things we were exploring with the idea of heterogeneity was to develop a variety of interior characteristics that would be appropriate to the activities going on there. So the spine, which is an active space, physically active on the part of the user, is visually active. We wanted to quiet down the classrooms because they were where the work of the school occurred. We looked for something that had a more serene character and would also be a better backdrop to all the students' activities. They didn't want the visual activity of the other parts of the building; they wanted a much quieter kind of visual activity. In addition to that, we wanted interiors that would be very good in terms of natural light. The white layer we added in the classrooms doesn't exist in the spine or the other big spaces. It was added to the classrooms as part of a day-lighting strategy. We wanted a more luminescent interior with a higher quality, yet a kind of light that was more even and less dramatic. Where we had an over abundance of light at these glazed reading nooks, we exposed the structure of the building because having this over abundance of light, we didn't need the quiet surfaces.

How did you establish where that distinction occurs? Is it an architectural "rule" or did it equate to, "This

just feels right proportionately."? Is it fair to say there is an interest in creating multiple elements by detaching or separating various components? Is that a fair corollary in that there are times when one uses a certain theme because you know how it works and we understand its potential?

I think there is a language, a formal language, which is an evolving language, which often runs from project, to project, to project which is where these forms come from.

So one may say there is a history of "detaching."

It is all part of the "elemental-ization" of all these components, of breaking the building down into its component parts.

12| As the design developed, did you use different attributes within the organizational and representational conceptual fields to mature or cross-reference each other?

Definitely. I think that, as we noted when we were at the school, starting with large scale plan and sectional characteristics of the building and adjusting them to the topography through an offsetting technique, both horizontally and vertically, an organizational strategy becomes embedded in these offsets. When you move to the level of detail at a variety of scales, the offset reappears frequently in the project. It is really about creating an animated line, about creating movement in a fluid, rather than static kind of order.

The offsetting derives it's origin from the site, both in plan and section, creating a kind of an animated line or space. Would offsetting as an organizational or even representational strategy include an extension to the outside where some walls extend beyond the building envelope and reveal themselves as planes? I realize that "extension" is different than "offset" but under what you just said, under a larger interest in a non-static organizational pallet, were extensions and splays seen as subsets of offsetting, or seen as related non-static ordering strategies?

Offsetting is one device; splaying is another. You're quite right. The walls are splayed in section by tipping outward various secondary masses, and some are tipped inward. There are the diagonal beams that cross the sort of meandering circulation spine. Then there are minor splays in various components of the building including large splayed plan forms. There's the language of splays, and then there are the extensions or offsets of lines through some of the walls. They all extend beyond the building. In all cases those are

It is really about creating an animated line, about creating movement in a fluid, rather than static kind of order.

In all cases those are different strategies to achieve that kind of animated character, that dynamic character. Everything seems to be setting things in movement.

We intended light as if it were really like the sun shining through a small clearing in the forest—otherwise one just has skylights.

different strategies to achieve that kind of animated character, that dynamic character. Even the plan form is sort of like movement in that you can imagine the way the shape of a snake is similar as it moves across the ground. It's a wiggling quality. Well, the plan form has that wiggling quality too. Everything seems to be setting things in movement.

That's interesting. I'm going to rewind a bit. Earlier you were talking about how the pods were offset because of the boulders and siting conditions. Now there's a kind of global conception in relation to offsetting. It sounds like one can argue that there is an architectural intent paralleling the siting considerations relating to an organizing strategy corresponding to an interest in dynamic vs. static orders. Would it be fair to say that as a global architectural intent there is an interest in a spatial configuration or a spatial creation that suggests an interest in exploring offsets or extensions, etc., over fixed or aligned connections?

I would say that certainly more of myself than Patricia. I have a fundamental preference for these more dynamic forms and more animated forms rather than static forms. It's not to say that we don't have projects where we explore the static quality such as the church that we were talking about earlier or even the art gallery that we did in Ontario. Those projects have that kind of static quality, and we certainly don't believe that one is better than the other. It's really a question of appropriateness, but there is, certainly in my own case, an innate preference to move to that kind of language more readily. It doesn't take much to get me going that way.

One other aspect, certainly in North America, is that there are lots of non-urban architectural opportunities. We've done a lot of work in those fundamentally natural

We've done a lot of work in those fundamentally natural conditions. ...we have responded to that wildness by being freer, more animated, more dynamic.

Concrete in this project is treated as a massive monolithic component, which are big, bold blocks. The steel and the aluminium are typically perceived to be thin. The aluminium mullion is the chubbiest piece of metal on the job. What we really want to do is heighten the character of materials by pushing them to their extremes.

conditions. In those circumstances I definitely favor a more animated, more lyrical kind of expression as a global approach to those kinds of contexts, and they're clearly not necessary. You can build a Palladian Villa in a rural context, but we have responded to that wildness by being freer, more animated, more dynamic.

Then concluding these issues, at one level you have an organizational strategy. You are saying, "I have offsets, I employ splaying and extensions, and they're all there." Those are the organizational strategies, yet they are, as you said, representational in that they derive from the natural, non-urban site context you have been describing.

At the same time we've done similar modeling work connected to other projects, but they are independent studies that are really just exercises, formal exercises ,and they tend to have that quality. There is often a formal preference for a specific character that is an overriding preference.

In the end there's a hesitancy to discuss the forms one is drawn to.

Similarly, there is the work of other architects I'm attracted to, and other architects who are equally accomplished whose work I'm less attracted to. It's simply because the work of one strikes a resonance with me. It's not to say it's better; it just resonates with me.

13| Do you believe that the school was more representational or organizational in its aspirations?

I would say that it was...balance is the wrong word, but I think it was intended to address both of those issues, very much so. Certainly there is a very clear programmatic organization, which organizes the classrooms relative to the other components of the building program in a very clear way. There's a very strong organization of the components within the program to each other and to the site. Then there are all of the site responses that are very organizational in character.

At the same time we were really interested, as I mentioned earlier, in expressing issues of heterogeneity and the diverse culture in the region through establishing a language that employed a diversity of architectural components. So we have sheets of galvanized metal for the roof, we have boards, we have columns of steel, we have concrete masses, and we have primary and secondary structural members that are different materials. We have materials for different kinds of finishes, and they've all been very carefully organized to work together in diversity. That's part of the larger idea of expressing a diverse culture that we talked about earlier. There was also the desire to talk about the place of the building in nature, and the strategy of reimagining a forest with the building as being a natural phenomenon which is an expressive thing. I think that it attempts equally to address both of those issues, as well it should. Projects don't always do that.

15| That's true. Many architects, it appears, often focus on organizational strategies leaving the representational qualities under-conceptualized or establishing default expressions in relation to materiality, construction representation, jointing concepts, etc. I would argue, to your credit, yours is a much more balanced approach. Returning to the questions, "How did you link ephemeral, poetic intentions of your design to the pragmatic, functional performance concerns as the design progressed?"

Well, that's a good question. We were very conscious of trying to create a poetic expression. That's part of where the representation of nature comes in and the idea of this lyrical, linear dynamic quality.

That's the path and the forest in some ways?

Very much so. There was a very conscious attempt to create poetic expression and an aspirational, inspirational environment—something that would move people: such as the way light comes in to the interior volumes. We intended light as if it were really like the sun shining through a small clearing in the forest—otherwise one just has skylights. That was very high on our list of important things to accomplish. I would say that it is more successful with the smaller projects, and I think the Strawberry Vale School is the largest project where I would say we've been successful at accomplishing that. When we've moved to larger projects, they, I think, do not have the same successful poetic quality. They tend to be more diagrammatic or more

We conceived the building in its materiality; we did not conceive the building and apply materials later.

We exercised as much control over these systems as we could in order to have them support the overall aesthetic of the building.

conceptual and less poetic. And my ambition is to do a larger building that has that kind of accomplishment. One of the things that we're constantly striving for is to design a large building to the same level...I don't really feel that the larger projects we've done have accomplished that. We've done two large libraries both of which have some very strong dimensions but I wouldn't say they're poetic. And the other university buildings that we've done similarly have good qualities but I would not call them poetic.

16| At this point, relatively far in the design process, we know the building quite well. Design decisions may now revolve around material nuances, smooth versus textured, exposed versus concealed fasteners, etc. It is at that point in the design process where these questions originate. Was the expressive (representational) nature of materials or how you deployed them, important in the design of Strawberry Vale School? When did design intentions in relation to material expression occur?

The answer is that it was a very preliminary thought. That issue is something that's thought about right up front. The forms of the building are derived in part from the character of materials. Obviously the mass is easy to accomplish in concrete and the light stuff up top is easier to accomplish in wood. We know those materials, and it's not that we created those spaces and forms, and then we found the appropriate materials. We conceived the building in its materiality; we did not conceive the building and apply materials later. A minimalist language can also be equally material driven. It's just a different side of the same coin. You can heighten the perception of materials through reduction rather than, in our case, through elaboration. Our material pallet is elaborated to make materials come forward as an actor in the design, but that can be true in a minimalist language as well.

So at Strawberry Vale would it be correct to say that conceptually there was an interest in going from a continuous surface to segmented surfaces or disconnected surfaces? Or would it be more correct in that wood comes in separate pieces, concrete comes in...

I think it's probably more the latter as that is how the material comes. That cast in place concrete is typically a monolithic material, and wood, as a structural material, comes in boards, and planks, and timbers, and steel comes in I-beams, and so it's really a very direct use of those construction materials.

17| How did you conceptualize the organization or composition of the joint between materials at Strawberry Vale and relate the resultant outcome to earlier intentions?

I'm not sure about that. I would say that the joint, and there are many expressed joints at Strawberry Vale, is not elaborated. The steel tends to be set on the concrete or be cast into the concrete in a fairly conventional, fairly direct way. The wood is attached to the steel in conventional ways. The steel is connected to itself in conventional ways. I would say that in this project we did not invest in re-imaging the joint. We simply accepted conventional joints. In other projects we have invested in re-imaging the joint, but I wouldn't say that was true here.

And would that be because it's a product of limited budget, and you're trying to work with conditions as found or as existing?

I think that was a large part of it. It is in some ways a common project. It is a common building; it's not a jewel. It doesn't have the opportunities, although it's a highly elaborate and complex design, that occur at a larger scale. We had to accept many conventional conditions. Plastic laminate is not a material we choose to utilize. We have lots of plywood in terms of the millwork. I'm not a big fan of plywood. I prefer lumber, but nobody would imagine building all that millwork in lumber anymore, and the fact we were able to accomplish wood plywood lockers as opposed to pre-manufactured metal lockers,was a major breakthrough. That makes the building much more tactile and friendly than it would be if those corridors were all lined with metal lockers.

I want to go back to an issue you brought up earlier. You talked about an interest in thinness when I was looking at...

That's absolutely an expressive issue. Definitely, we wanted to establish the identity of different materials. Concrete in this project is treated as a massive monolithic component, which are big, bold blocks. The steel

To really stretch that expressive range so you're not operating only in the middle zone. That was part of our thinking regarding the visual responsibility of materials at Strawberry Vale.

and the aluminium are typically perceived to be thin. The aluminium mullion is the chubbiest piece of metal on the job. What we really want to do is heighten the character of materials by pushing them to their extremes.

By their extremes you mean their performance extremes or their compositional extremes?

Their expressive extremes. I guess you could say that making concrete extremely slender would be an expressive extreme, but what we wanted to do at Strawberry Vale was juxtapose the massive character of concrete with the slender character of steel and aluminium. The wood in turn had its own characteristics. We definitely wanted to stay out of that middle range, which tends to neutralize. We pushed the concrete to larger masses; we push the metal to slenderness.

Then there was a desire to give the material pallet its greatest potential for expression in terms of it being authentic. That's not right but to give it...

Its full expressive range. It's interesting, when I started architecture school, we went to a lake for a week at a "sketch camp." We had a drawing instructor, and we spent the week drawing, and one of the things he taught us was that, and there may be masterpieces that take exceptions to this, but he said, "To achieve a full expressive range your drawings should have areas that are black and areas that are white, and if it's all in the mid gray tones, it's going to lose its expressive potential." That actually stayed with me, and in photography you tend to want that as well. You tend to want to have areas that are extremely dark, and areas that are light. Get that expressive quality—to really stretch that expressive range so you're not operating only in the middle zone. That was part of our thinking regarding the visual responsibility of materials at Strawberry Vale.

It was our intention that the constructed nature of the building be legible. ...We really did intend that the building be available as a lesson in construction.

That contrast is part of the spatial structure of the building. One understands places of movement as opposed to places of repose. Therefore, the spatial character of the building changes in response to the programmatic use of the space.

Sometimes when there are these little details or these little moments, if they really are authentic they come out of the process or the evolution of the idea.

18| What was your thinking regarding the expression or lack of systems in the building? What organizational or representational strategies were contemplated in your decision to express the systems?

Well, there were actually several reasons for expressing the systems. One of the reasons was the desire to eliminate materials. If we didn't need it, we wouldn't use it. So a ceiling would obscure the view of the ducts and pipes in the upper reaches of the spine. It was not required. It was simply a use of materials that we could avoid, and with the intention of minimizing material use in the project we end up, by default, expressing the systems. At the same time it was our intention that the constructed nature of the building be legible, so that if somebody was interested in understanding how a building works, how a building stands up, how it's enclosed, how it's environment is qualified and tempered, those things would be visible. We really did intend that the building be available as a lesson in construction.

You've referred to the expression of steel and how it becomes a part of the understanding of the building or the understanding of the components of the building. You've also mentioned how the steel constitutes an expressive nature of the spine and plays a part in defining that element. Does that description also apply to and organize the layout of the ductwork? Does the ductwork have any additional expressive attributes and intentions or is it primarily about following an efficient path in the ceiling? Was there an added architectural interest as with steel or concrete in that you wanted to splay or offset them in concert with other similarly organized parts?

We spend a lot of time designing the location and distribution of all the systems. By and large we were successful and in a couple of cases it didn't get constructed the way we wanted, but this happens. We were very careful to investigate this potential, yet obviously their role is primarily in support of their mechanical engineering role. You have to address that responsibility directly, but there are choices within that, and we exercised as much control over these systems as we could in order to have them support the overall aesthetic of the building—within the limits of what you can do.

19| In refining the design, did you select programmatic areas or architectural elements to privilege? If so, how were the privileging concepts expansions on, or counterpoints to, earlier conceptual intentions? We're now really fine-tuning the design at the end of the process.

Some detail-oriented examples of the expressive character of materials and elements are found in the painted doors and operable windows found within the glazing system. Moving components were painted a color whereas the fixed components of the exterior glazing system were left the natural color of aluminium. We wanted to reinforce and accentuate those components of the system—the parts that are more dynamic, that you actually work. There's very little color in the building but the plastic laminate in the little kitchenette or little sink areas in each classroom have color. And that color changes from classroom to classroom. As does the color of the doors and the operating windows. Those were all attempts to make the areas people inhabit the most, having the closest contact with the building, a little bit more animated, a little bit more expressive.

So those elements could be conceptualized as another layer of design intentions?

Yes, and obviously the central spine is, I wouldn't say exaggerated, but it certainly is a generous vertical space that offers a very different character than the spaces to which it provides access. That contrast is part of the spatial structure of the building. One understands places of movement as opposed to places of repose. Therefore, the spatial character of the building changes in response to the programmatic use of the space. There are a lot of devices, spatial devices: color, the character of detail, the more rugged animated quality of the spine relative to the classrooms, etc. There are many devices which are used to give that type of emphasis.

To continue that kind of differentiation, is there anything we've been discussing on the interior that is relevant to the exterior. Maybe it's more that there is the front public side, and there is the back private or park side.

It's very common in our projects to differentiate different exposures in response to context whether it be the public vs. the natural side, or the north vs. the south. We typically look for, or have looked—whether that's still true today I'm not sure, but we have typically looked for reasons to differentiate, and we've taken advantage of opportunities to differentiate.

That seems to have been a global interest up to now. Would that be to define a hierarchy such as...

I wouldn't say hierarchy as that implies that there is a hierarchy. For us it's not hierarchical. It's more about differentiation, about giving different parts of the project an appropriate identity while maintaining their place in the whole. ◘

Moving components were painted a color whereas the fixed components of the exterior glazing system were left the natural color of aluminum. We wanted to reinforce and accentuate those components of the system—the parts that are more dynamic, that you actually work.

Morphosis

Thom Mayne

Caltrans District 7 Headquarters

The headquarters building for District 7 of the California Department of Transportation Department is on the east side of downtown Los Angeles, located catty-corner to the City Hall which was completed in 1928. Encompassing 1.2-million-square-feet, the program, primarily comprised of offices for various levels of staff comprising the District 7 workforce also includes a café, a daycare center and a retail area in addition to conference, exhibition space and a parking garage below grade. However, the most architecturally significant program element, both functionally and experientially, is an exterior public plaza and amphitheater.

Caltrans District 7, completed in 2005 represents the largest building of those discussed in the interviews. It documents a more conventional building type, that of a mid-rise office building. This factor was significant in its selection. A more prosaic building type with a client limited by the expenditure of public funds, Caltrans District 7 is a building with limitations typical to many architectural commissions. However, of greater significance is the level of architectural development incorporated into its design. Caltrans District 7 explores environmental efficiency, integration to the urban fabric, and employee comfort in a building whose language alludes to freeway infrastructure and the dynamics of movement represented through automobiles traversing miles of Los Angeles freeways.

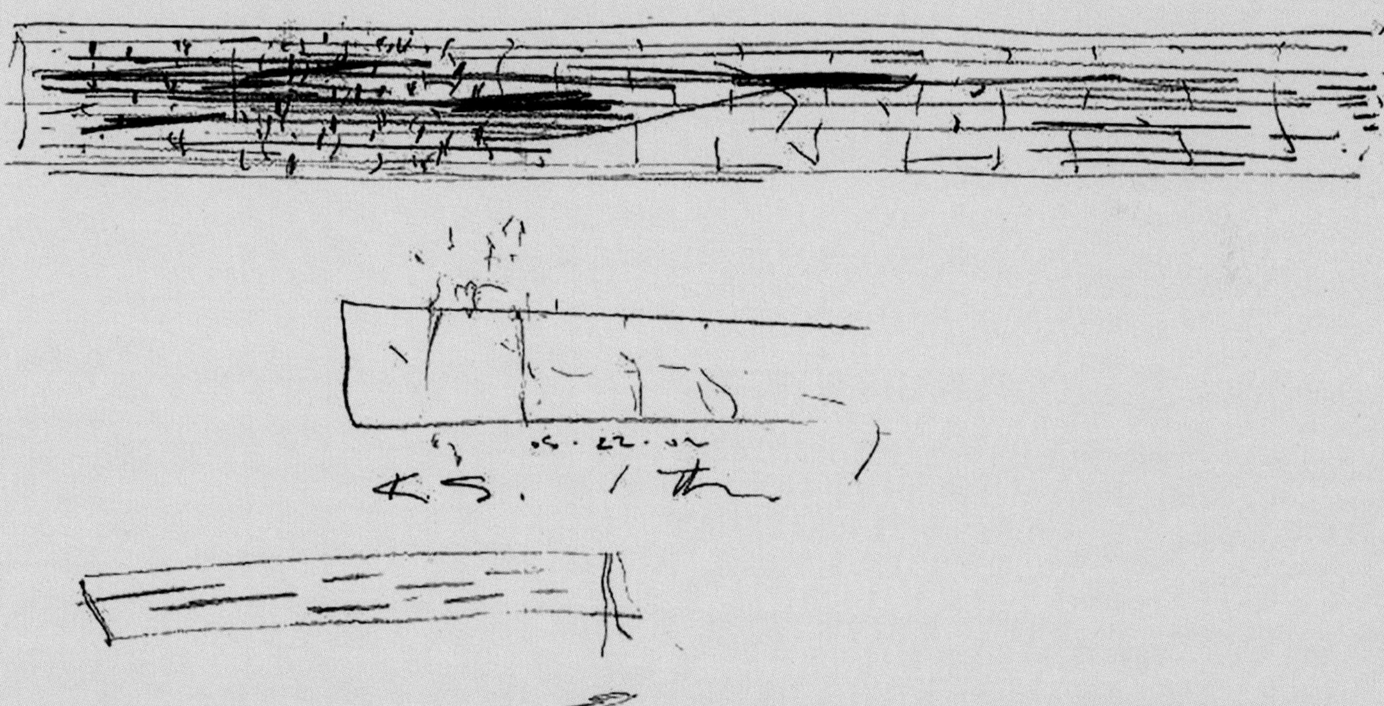
05 · 22 · 02
K.S.

If it's a serious work of architecture, it cannot be understood solely in terms of form. It operates on environmental, human and urban paradigms, and is somehow fundamental to the cultural and political dealings inherent when people function in the world.

If you look at how the world operates, it has little to do with rationality; it has to do with an incredibly complicated subconscious and how we deal in immensely irrational ways to control our world.

By the end of the 19th-century there was no longer a preference for single systems of order—there is an understanding of the need for multiple orders.

1| Tom Diehl: We're going to begin with preliminary questions that are beyond the scope of the Caltrans building but not beyond the scope of design intentions. What value, potential, or use do you see in order?
Thom Mayne: Let's start with order. Making architecture essentially orders and concretizes certain aspects of space and form in order to create coherency. The interesting part is that these ordering strategies essentially shape behavior. I'm not talking about style—architecture impacts quality of life issues, it affects the way we live, work, behave, etc., but it's the shaping of behavior that's the big issue. If it's a serious work of architecture, it cannot be understood solely in terms of form. It operates on environmental, human and urban paradigms, and is somehow fundamental to the cultural and political dealings inherent when people function in the world. So, if what we do is organize things, then the question is how we define order. Now things get stickier. Some people would say, "Well, Morphosis, do they order things?" They are looking at a certain convention of order defined by a type of regularity, an idea of repetition, a notion of the Euclidian. We can go right back through many epochs in western civilization to understand where that comes from.

So, the question of the essence of order is based upon multiple considerations. Is that how you see it?
Modern architects look at the world from the end of the 19th to the beginning of the 20th centuries and see a period of profoundly fundamental change. These were times of philosophical and theological change that reshaped how we see and think about the world. In simple terms, there was movement from static to dynamic, from fixed to open, and it was challenging very basic tenets of how we organize the world in terms of our thinking. It started from Darwin who attacked our notions

Crawford Residence: section

of who we are, where we evolved from. Then along came Freud who established an understanding of the reality of the subconscious, which had not existed before. What he really did was attack rationality. If you look at how the world operates, it has little to do with rationality; it has to do with an incredibly complicated subconscious, and how we deal in immensely irrational ways to control our world. It has direct effects on how we behave politically, economically, how our decisions affect the stock market or cause us to become involved in Iraq. No one would claim any more that these are purely rational decisions. They are highly subjective—loaded with subconscious stuff. Add to all this that Einstein was re-working our understanding of the physical world. Parallel to all this change, there was the avant-garde explosion in art, music, theater, literature, etc. You can look at Stravinsky; you can look at James Joyce. Wherever you want to go, you can see it and pair it with technological developments, such as the camera. You can look at Duchamp's "Nude Descending a Staircase" as an absolute direct reflection of reality at that time. He's clearly looking at Marey, but he's developing a new interpretive position. He's no longer painting; there's no nude. There's descension. There's the space between the legs of the moving "figure," He's interested in a completely different subject that was unheard of 50 or 100 years earlier—he's most definitely not painting the figure. Rather, he was painting conceptually and suddenly the whole world shifted from figurative to conceptual. Art exploded, the whole art scene, including architecture, which can be seen in Mies, Corbusier, etc.

Ultimately there were shifts taking place politically with the idea of social democracy. Marx and Engels rewrote the notion of industry and economic relations. The direction of the world they were anticipating was actually taking place. And out of all that began the exploration of a new sense of social and cultural order.

4| As you are elaborating a cultural context embracing change and invention, let's more closely relate that to design. Do these types of design interests relating to creating coherence, specifically ones extending beyond those concerned with facilitating the distribution of the program and relating the building to the site, originate within the discipline of architecture or from sources lying outside of it?
You must look at how these broader ideas affect notions of organization as it relates to the creation of coherence. What does coherence mean? Coherence is already an interpretation of a broader construct dealing with these various territories that I'm briefly describing. We're now looking at organizations. And what is happening? To begin with, a single strategy and a specific hierarchy as

At Caltrans, you still see multiple ordering systems. Each of the skins slips or moves past the next one.

seen in pre-20th-century architecture no longer dominates organizational intentions that were, at that time, focused on the expression of a singular idea. It was a basic Renaissance position focused on axiality, bi-axiality, symmetry, etc. But by the end of the 19th-century there was no longer a preference for single systems of order—there is an understanding of the need for multiple orders. Multiple orders align with the reality of modern programs and allow architecture to become much more complex. Renaissance orders were already breaking in the 19th century where the Beaux Arts model couldn't handle a tall building, where it was unable to deal with huge exhibition spaces, factories, etc. New strategies were needed in real and pragmatic terms to align with new problems.

What I'm interested in is that change in alignment, and I'm recognizing that this notion of a single strategy is no longer philosophically viable or pragmatically useful to solve the kinds of problems we're addressing. Of course, this reality has ramped up radically in the last 20 years, as the economic aggregate has increased and the size of the scale of the work has increased. We're now building big chunks of cities very quickly with a single architect. If people remain interested in the diversity of the city, it is clear that a single position, a single order, will not achieve that end.

5| Describe how you use multiple strategies or intentions. How do these interests impact your thinking in relation to the methods employed to architecturally organize and/or represent your intentions?
We start with the assumption that multiple strategies will be employed in a given project, and then we work to resolve how various systems are translated into the architecture and linked together to become a part of the whole. The Crawford House is probably a good example of how we think about these issues. We began by inscribing a landscape circumference defined by an incomplete wall. Layered into this defined space was a series of three different obelisks that provided lines and structures to start organizing space sequentially. At that level, we operate within conservative, almost conventional, terms. However, there were additional elements overlaid that behave differently. I've seen the rhythms of the house described in terms of syncopated jazz—which I think makes sense. The various seemingly non-sequitur moves begin to divide the site spatially down to the level of rooms. There is then a T section imposed that is a conceptual idea that also incorporates the distribution of ducts for the HVAC system. It is structure, it is duct, it is the organizational line.

In that project, we became very interested in the narrative of movement. We used pacing to establish the increment of rhythm, to define the movement of the site. Fairly early on we were challenging the notion of "house," as we began to understand the project more in terms of augmented landscape. We were scraping and forming the site to develop a new coherence to something that already had a biological, ecological organization. We were giving it an order based on a set of functions for a house, but we could easily see how to translate the concept into a school, a recreational facility, etc. Rather than working with a building on a site, we were interested in creating a much more complex interactive set of systems that work to tie building and landscape together. Architecture was becoming less about the thing and more about the relationship between things.

Have these types of organizational intentions, as concepts, moved forward into othe Caltrans building?

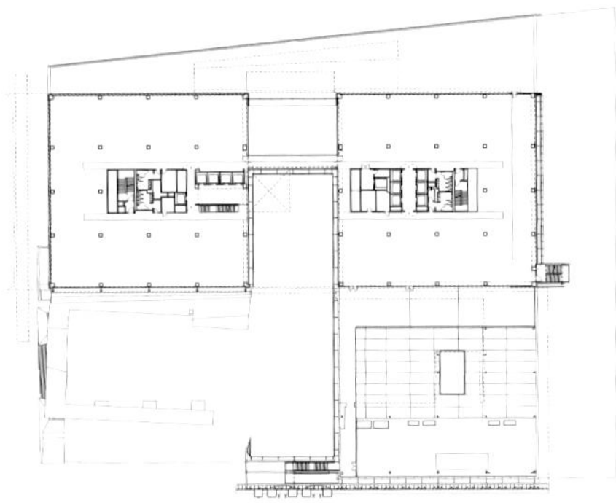

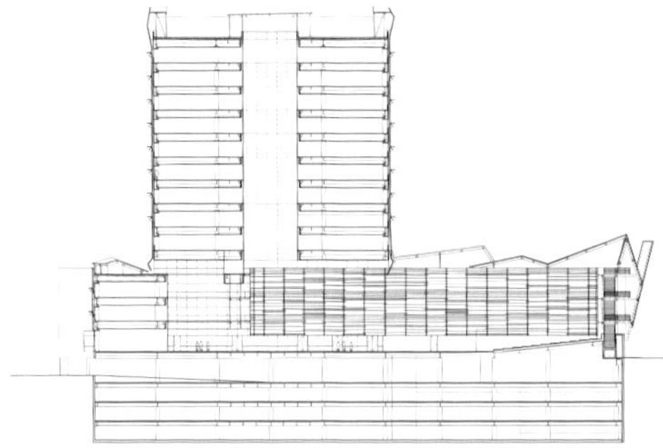

Plan, section

Caltrans is a simple generic office building...
We questioned whether in fact an office building is generic.

When you look at Caltrans, you still see multiple ordering systems. Each of the skins slips or moves past the adjacent one, therefore allowing each one its independence.

In a traditional approach in which one works with a single order, each piece has to follow, to be beholden to, that order. We are saying each of these multiple elements takes on a different role: one operates to take the sun away, one operates structurally, and one operates as the skin separating the inside from the outside. Each of them is allowed to have its own independence and express its identity because they all have a very clear relationship to an organizing structure. What I'm interested in here is the relationship between the various pieces that make up the whole. You could say it's a simple kind of model, a politically democratic or egalitarian model in which there is a group of individuals whose relationships one to another might be very nuanced or complicated. It can be a very tricky subject, dealing with the degree of independence and individuality vs. the amount of connective tissue that fosters coherence and allows for the expression of collective aspirations.

It does speak to the relationship you're talking about, that is, seeing architectural elements as a group of linked "individuals." In relation to your design process, how has this migration away from singular, or fewer, ordering systems to one with multiple integrated organizational strategies with a more open-ended approach evolved?
7| For example, when you started the design of Caltrans, were these envisioned as global, architecturally transcendent, themes you were investigating at the beginning of the design process?
Caltrans is an interesting example, and it also reflects on how we start a project. Caltrans is a simple generic office building that gave us a place to start. We questioned whether, in fact, an office building *is* generic. It's only assumed to be generic, and I thought, "Ha, that's interesting," because I've never worked in an office space. As architects we need a messier space, we need taller ceilings, and we need a shop. Design is a dirtier hands-on kind of work.

So, I began to question whether there's such a straightforward notion of a 1 to 1 relationship between architecture and function. My attitude tends to move toward the relaxed—a church can make an absolutely incredible residence, or it can be used as a restaurant. The goals of architecture today are more complicated and make that 1 to 1 relationship less relevant. Although we couldn't actually solve the office building part of the problem, we set to work on other problems that were related to these preoccupations. At Caltrans, we differentiated the workspaces and actually inverted them in many ways. For example, management is located toward the interior spaces while workers are located along the exterior, windowed wall. This project became a very different kind of pragmatic problem in which we were making assessments and asking broad questions from which we could establish architectural positions other than those of the formal. In this early phase we were asking how architecture can participate in the broader problems of urban, environmental, functional, and humanistic issues. We were looking at a broad range of problems and potentials, focusing mostly on the latter. We asked ourselves, "What are the territories that are of interest, that are compelling, and that we think will allow us to make a contribution?"

We start this kind of thinking prior to any notion of where we're going with the physicality of the building. At the early stage there is no problem-formation yet. We're absolutely black, empty, and open. This is the hard part, probably not dissimilar to an author facing a blank page and it's difficult to describe to students, other architects, even clients because the process is not happening in an analytical way, or it's happening both in an analytical way and in a synergistic way. We're consumed with the assessment of multiple things, multiple territories, and we're making inner relationships and associations of the territories we define.

For example, In the case of Caltrans, we were located next to City Hall, so early on we made an assessment that urbanistically the building would be secondary to that structure in height—it would not be a tower. We made an assessment, based on its location in the center of L.A. and given that L.A. has a dearth of public space, we would prioritize the creation of public space for the project. The client did not ask us for the space. The city could care less, so we did it as a somewhat idealistic aspiration. We knew that at some point the city would become more urbanized and would eventually have an identity less associated with the car. We're actually very conservative in that way. I don't believe in an absolute adherence to a conservative or a radical position. Sometimes we are interested in conserving and maintaining; sometimes we're interested in challenging and innovating—it would be impossible to identify us in one camp or the other. The point is to make assessments as to where you can make connection and meaning. Sometimes you need to reinforce a convention or some principle. At other times, you are challenging that or interpreting that. It could be both. In all of our projects I need issues to work with. I am not a tabula rasa person, and I think our work is much better in the city where we have stuff to work with.

It can be a very tricky subject, dealing with the degree of independence and individuality vs. the amount of connective tissue that fosters coherence and allows for the expression of collective aspirations.

We were making assessments and asking broad questions from which we could establish architectural positions other than those of the formal.

The point is to make assessments as to where you can make connection and meaning.

We are going to be really comfortable with an infrastructural language because we conceive of the totality as infrastructure, as opposed to thinking of it as a building, and that is what interested me.

Our first move was to commit to the creation of public space while our second move was to deal with the massing so that the building would be smaller, non-competitive with City Hall. The early factors that informed the design approach are three-fold. There were ordering systems that arise from programmatic intentions, those that arise from urban space intentions, and those related to social considerations. Our job was to overlay these disparate ordering systems in a way that will hold together as a whole.

So, there are global themes employed in an appropriate manner for the program you have.

I make assessments relative to the hierarchical, representational status of our institutions. This building is an administrative site for people who build and maintain our freeways. In dealing with a unique institution such as this one, we look for a direction that speaks to that uniqueness. Add to this the complexity that arises with a budget of $140 per square foot! It's ridiculous. The budget was a little bit higher than that of a parking structure, yet we were still trying to find a place for architecture. So immediately we're saying, "OK, this is going to be kind of a tough building, and we're going to be completely comfortable with that." Freeways are concrete, a little bit of steel, galvanized metal for signage, an extremely basic kind of language. We are going to be really comfortable with an infrastructural language because we conceive of the totality as infrastructure, as opposed to thinking of it as a building, and that is what interested me.

Infrastructural ideas led to that big "100" sign at the front façade. We knew that this was to be a building that would express itself in very straightforward way and that will represent the nature of the institution both literally and interpretively. At that point we had yet to start the project, but I had a conceptual understanding of where we were headed. With vague ideas of infrastructure, freeway, the intended scale of the building, its relationship with City Hall, its relationship to Main and First Streets, we were ready to start the design process.

8| So, there are strategies you know you can use, as appropriate, when dealing with representational aspects. Do these typically represent initial concerns?

We don't start from dead zero. The gestational process can be slow, but the idea is to get to a place where we can posit an idea, and loosely call it a theory. It is not really a theory in the scientific sense; we state some sort of a premise, and we have a certain set of interests, and we pursue those interests and build them into the project, and then we repeat the assessment process. We look at what we've got and decide "Now, does this operate in the way I thought it would operate, given the premises I stated?"

At this point, at the beginning of the design process, you are offering up intentions in order to anchor a theory and, simultaneously, critique their appropriateness.

Correct. Let's say a particular intention appears to be less useful and contains diminishing opportunities. That is recognized and abandoned, and we start again, looking for something with greater opportunities.

So then you're talking about the dialectics, about the intentional side of design having more to do with your philosophy, your intentions in a broader sense than the pragmatics of the site or the program.

Exactly. However, the thing that I don't think people understand is what actually happens in the practice of

The thing that I don't think people understand is what actually happens in the practice of architecture versus what happens with a theoretical set of ideas. In a practice, we are making different assessments for every project, most of them deeply rooted in the pragmatic.

I wanted it to be a dynamic element related to movement; movement would be referential to the raison-d'être of the institution.

architecture versus what happens with a theoretical set of ideas. In a practice, we are making different assessments for every project, most of them deeply rooted in the pragmatic. At Caltrans, we were working with a very tight timeframe and budget which necessitated a super-efficient structural chassis, made of a 30' x 30' grid. eighty percent of the building was thus super-efficient (read minimally expensive) which allowed us to spend time and design energy on the other 20% where we invent solutions to "opportunities" beyond program such as the light fixture cantilevered over First Street. I know that First Street, unlike Main Street, is a connective tissue and I wanted to build an element that would hang over the street to engage the public – I wanted it to be a dynamic element related to movement, movement would be referential to the *raison d'être* of the institution. We developed an enormous truss upon which the line that was referential to the stream of taillights and headlights one sees on a freeway would be displayed. The scale needed to speak to the scale of the City of Los Angeles, which is a big place. My thinking was that I've got a client, an institution that makes freeways, and this building is part of the freeway. It is not a street sign. It is a line of light and an opportunity. It's an invention.

I further wanted the building to represent dynamics. I cantilevered one frame (I couldn't get two), and I wanted it over the street, which became sadly impossible due to budgetary issues. As we look at what we are willing to lose, we get strategic. We say to ourselves, "Well, there's not only one possible move, I've got a few things I need to do here." As it is built, one enters up the stair at the forecourt, through the plaza with space for 1,000 people to gather or pass by. This is the location where the building became civic infrastructure. This is a place we can really talk about the freeway; we just built the infrastructure, the skin, and the sign.

8.1| Yet you were able to realize the "100" sign. Was that not a part of other organizational or representational concepts employed to reinforce or anchor your initial intentions? How did the addition of the "100" sign enter into your thinking as it related to these conceptual domains?

It's iconic and generic in a similar way. It was one of those opportunities where we could express additional intentions. Going back to your question on order, not only is it forming organization in a spatial sense, or language coherency in terms of the project, the sign is also one part of a singularity. In my case, I'm making a singularity out of multiple systems versus out of a single system. In

We are committed to the idea that architecture can be made out of multiple diverse parts. They don't have to align; they can have their own independence and still make sense. Not only do they make sense, but in giving them independence, something else takes place at a phenomenological level.

I am making a singularity out of multiple systems versus out of a single system. In that regard, the sign was not envisioned simply as a sign but as a component of the larger set of intentions. When it finally comes to the status of a piece of hardware, or a door or a secondary or tertiary piece such as the "100" sign, you go right back to the trail and find your way back to the idea.

that regard, the sign was not envisioned simply as a sign but as a component of the larger set of intentions.

I imagine that architecture is a lot like filmmaking. Behind every good film is a director and a team that understands a particular set of intentions. All I do is direct an office; I'm the one that steers the ship. I say, "That's an interesting idea, but that will be for some other building." It's like what you mentioned earlier. You can look at all the pieces and if you are doing your job correctly, they all make sense and cohere. When it finally comes to the status of a piece of hardware, or a door or a secondary or tertiary piece such as the "100" sign, you can go right back to the trail and find your way back to the idea. If you can't, you have to reconstruct it. That's the basic issue of architecture which has to do with creating your own system of thinking. You develop these ideas as a method for proceeding with your work, and you use organizational strategies to keep it coherent. If you get lost, it is obvious when you see the building—if you see several miss-matched themes, and you say "Ha! There's a series of intentions, or decisions, that are not fitting together." If you have multiple systems, the more diverse they are, the more they require greater conceptualization and a thorough process to glue them together so that they do not read as unrelated objects, non-sequiturs, but they have a meaningful connection that makes sense.

When you're looking at the layering at Caltrans, you're looking at the series of decisions we've made. One asks, "Is there coherency? Are there singularities of how the elements and assemblies are organized? With a series of layers of elements going one way, an object going another way, another system containing the letters, the structure, and the stair, two skins, and the light fixture, is there some commonality in their behavior? "We have to look at it and say." There's a singular thinking here, a way of putting diverse things together that makes a coherency that makes sense to us. "We are committed to the idea that architecture can be made out of multiple diverse parts. They don't have to align; they can have their own independence and still make sense. Not only do they make sense, but in giving them independence, something else takes place at a phenomenological level.

10| That relates to the potential for enriching the design process. How do you add additional depth to initial global intentions?

The stair at the front façade is an example. With the tight budget, we wanted to allow the egress stair to form part of the façade. It is part front sign, part structure, and part

I am going to move to broader issues, using generic materials and move toward organization, and organizational ideas.

stair. Conceptually, what I was fascinated with was what we could do with the skin. We had two skins. One was solid like stone with voids left in it, which we wanted to appear very crisp. Again, we are paying homage to history. The gray Swisspearl fiber cement panel siding is "stone"; very rusticated stone and super elegant. But because of how we put it together, there is no mortar at the joints. The "stones" sit next to each other with a clean connection meaning the grout-free corner is just perfect, yet it is also perceptually paper thin, very similar to Pei's East Wing at the National Gallery.

If you look at architecture, you learn some lessons. We created a solid surface another way, and all of a sudden, it's perceptually thin. I'm fascinated by this. Part of the building clearly makes reference to solidity. It is stone. And in fact, the client liked it because it was very elegant—they appreciated that we had treated the institution with respect.

They liked the solidity, or they liked the thinness?

No, thinness is not part of it. They liked the stone. It was very crisp and very buttoned down. It was gray and the color palette was like a classical building. All of a sudden it just appears; that's what I'm interested in. It transforms the reality of the material. It's thin and non-structural, and then it's not—its use becomes blurred. I'm always looking for those dualities. To me that's modern. Now I have a contemporary building, and I'm showing it for what it is. I'm going for multiple readings, trying to get as much complexity as I can out of a simple building.

Not only do design decisions have to make sense, but they have to lead to some payoffs. They have to do something. Architects can no longer think solely in terms of "design." It has to be tactical, strategic. For me, what

I'm going for multiple readings, trying to get as much complexity as I can out of a simple building.

The role of the façade was then open to interpretation. It was no longer connected to the most simple, basic pragmatic notion of "window." It completely freed us.

Our intention was to express another aspect of movement through randomizing the placement of some of the windows as a method to achieve another kind of continuity.

happened with the Diamond Ranch High School project is that it became apparent that my types of investigations, having to do with the specificity of material, the process of making, and the articulation and the relation of those things were absolutely irrelevant to the client. I realized it would be difficult to proceed on this trajectory unless I moved to singularly wealthy clients. So, when we had the opportunity to design Diamond Ranch High School, I had to relocate my vision of architecture. The timing coincided with the work we were doing at Crawford and JPGA (Japan) with regard to an augmented landscape strategy. As we moved conceptually to the broader idea of landscape, ecology, the treatment of the site, things reversed. The idea of augmented landscape became primary while the notions of detailing a "building" became secondary to that initial strategy.

Augmented landscapes, if I'm interpreting the phrase accurately, are now more of a restatement of a landscape from a material standpoint.

That's right. We were looking at different ideas required to carry larger projects. I'm an architect who is interested in materials. It will still come down to making choices, but we can't be finicky. The choices are going to have to come from a broader domain that includes the land.

If materials in earlier projects were following on the idea of "self-expression" by individual members of the society, now "society" is taking on a greater role under the theme of augmented landscape, the wholeness of society so to speak. You are moving on to broader issues.

Right. I'm going to move to broader issues, using generic materials and move more toward organization, and organizational ideas. We're going to go to a broader reformation of the idea of space, and we're going to move toward organization and spatial characteristics of architecture at the expense of materials. The materials can be generic. That strategy has stayed with us, largely due to the reality of budgetary issues. If we're given another opportunity with the same scale of work but with a larger budget, I still have this material resource to go back to as a way of conceptualizing the building. I'm totally capable of going back to the detail as being conceptualized as a part of a language instead of being simply an instrument of construction.

In that regard the southern side of the western façade has a solid plate running up the façade, and then it has perforated aluminum that slips over and goes up. It has that little slit. Similarly there are the handrails that slip on past the stairs, the light fixtures in

We will go back and forth between the readings of the building; there's no composition anymore, the outcomes and their readings derive from our intentions.

the plaza that slip or offset from one another. I am trying to bring all of the details into conceptual focus. Are those instances that you would say, "Yes, these are a part of this understanding of the building as infrastructure, the building as a kind of an individual set of elements, as individual members of society cohering?" Now we are at the level of smaller scale components reinforcing larger global intentions.

We are making clear discretionary choices of where we're going to put additional emphasis, but it won't be contradictory to what the building is about. It will build up and enrich an idea that is a sub-set of earlier, broader intentions. Holistically it will give importance to a particular place.

I've been fascinated with the idea of the auto-generative. You set out an idea that has no specific a priori solution. I go back and forth, sometimes in my hand, and sometimes it comes out of the studio, but I remain most interested in the broad idea, and I recognize there are multiple valid solutions. I like the openness of that, and I like the way it allows for the element of surprise. It's how I've always worked. It's what Morphosis is. That is why Morphosis is named Morphosis.

My design process operates on a strategy, a methodology, and not a solution. I go back and forth; the work is collective. I will outline a strategy, a direction, and the rest of the decisions are a consequence of the strategy of layering, independence, and pragmatics. We will go back and forth between the readings of the building. There's no composition anymore. The outcomes and their readings derive from our intentions.

10.1| So, an overall strategy is in place that employs layering, the independence of various elements, and pragmatic considerations. In terms of specific details that have been used in Caltrans to create secondary or tertiary organizational orders, describe some of the ideas, at a later point in the design, you were exploring.

A building façade, from the beginning of time, has been about the compositional relationship of windows and solid. Even a window wall does that. We're still looking at the scale of the mullion, and guess what? All of a sudden, it's completely rooted in functionality, light, and view. The relationship of the pragmatics to how it affects the interior, the relationship to the exterior, and its composition are duly connected.

I really became aware of it at Caltrans once we put the second skin on. It became obvious. We didn't care whether the windows were operating on an inside skin of a two-layer system or as the façade in a single layer system. There had to be a successful balance of factors like the amount of heat they take in, the view, and the quality of light. So, the windows become purely a performance issue whose job is to balance those three things. From the inside their position is derived in relation to human needs. Outside is irrelevant. I have a neutral skin that, strangely enough, reads solid. All of a sudden, it's scale-less. I got very interested in this; a hulking, brooding building that has no scale. We gave it randomness and movement so the façade became free. That was our goal. Our intention was to employ another aspect of movement through randomizing the placement of some of the windows as a method to achieve a different kind of continuity.

Let's continue that regarding secondary and tertiary organizational strategies.

What defines the façade? It's opening and closing; it's a high-performance façade. It's closer to an automobile than a building, and it opens and closes based on sun conditions. We are organizing little random pieces, philosophically on some level, but they were also representations of open shades. We left the horizontal voids, but we curved them and made them three-dimensional. This gave the façade some texture, but the texture didn't have to do with any scale. It was on its own. The role of the façade was then open to interpretation. It was no longer connected to the most simple, basic, pragmatic notion of "window." It completely freed us. All of a sudden, some of it does this, and some of it does that. Now the ground and vertical are connected. We are looking at the continuity of ground, façade, and crinkled area at the top, giving some reference to a tripartite top, shaft, and base arrangement. It still has a kind of leftover idea that the top has some meaning, or role, and it is expressed in the traditional sense. But the primary role is now performance, and the aesthetic is open to interpretation. And that was a huge shift.

Yet it is possible to say, that while your process is more open, more fluid, more random, it is still governed by a larger global ordering intention. You are saying "I don't work within a fixed single system anymore. It's not the way we are looking at the world, or the way we live our world. It is not the way society operates. The world is a more complex structure, and in that regard, randomness is one of the realities we explore." Your concerns and your decision-making process link back to that larger intention. On one hand you say you're comfortable organizing components in a more fluid manner; on the other hand you're still strategizing that that process is related to these larger representational intentions.

Since very early on, I've been interested in the space between chance and intention, fascinated with that as a

Since very early on, I've been interested in the space between chance and intention.

part of life. I probably put a preference on chance. Look, if you analyze our lived world, who we marry, when we have babies, where we end up in our life, where we travel, what we do for a living, etc., it is not a purely rational process. I'm fascinated with chance, and literally, everything you look at is going to be somehow by chance.

But you're also fascinated with the knowable.
Yes, the space between intentionality and randomness. You're going to see, of course, that I'm highly conscious. I work with intentions. I'm highly controlled. Now we're talking about chance in an entirely different way. I'm not a Robert Altman, who puts people together to see what happens. That's a little too loose for me. I'm going to put people together, but I'm going to be closer to say, Woody Allen. I'm going to give them a series of random events to see what happens, but I'm going to put some stuff in there to make sure there's some glue. I will be the guy who says "Cut" and "Let's try that again."

Let's tie it back, because we're sort of at an existential moment here. On the one hand, I have this interest in chance, and on the other hand I have this interest in telling the story, the narrative. In the end, and here is the existential question...
I'm saying our life is prioritized between attempting to control it, given this crazy world we live in, and the reality of chance behavior. That's the contemporary world. Also, I think it deals with conflict. Through it all there's an underlying idea of conflict. For me, to be a 21st-century human being, the most compelling thing that each of us has to deal with is the notion of how we understand our world, and how we deal with confrontational situations that you read about in the paper every morning. It's the feeling I have when I'm sitting at Rose Café eating an elegant breakfast reading about Mogadishu or about a thousand

The building grew out of the institution. The institution is constantly emerging. It represents a freeway with no end...So the building emerged from those conditions. Everything is moving out; everything is connected to openness, to unfinished-ness.

What I am fascinated by, which all of our work deals with, is fragments. The fragment is seen as a new totality that has its own future.

It is not complete or "finished." It's open-ended. That fascination comes directly out of influences going back to the '60s; I was looking at Archigram and all kinds of similar characters. This was my beginning point. You will see in all of our work that there will always be pieces that will be perceived as "unfinished," not unfinished as an error but as part of a transition.

It's a new notion of completion. What we're challenging is that we don't see things as static; everything we look at today is understood in broader terms.

Let's have this conversation about what finished means.

people killed in an avalanche in Peru; I could go on and on. We live in a world where we're continually confronted with the range of human behavior, chance, individuality, etc. Socially, that forces us to come to grips with these complexities in the human character and the world.

Do you think you can say you're fascinated by conflict because you live in a fairly stable society, or that you live in a society that allows you to think about this versus dealing with the outcomes of a less predictable environment?
Of course! I'm a totally privileged character. I'm privileged to even be able to philosophize, to be able to conceptualize a notion of how the world exists. But I have to say, I'm from a situation where my father left when I was eight, I came out of a very tough neighborhood, and some of it's very personal. As a young man, I lived in a tough neighborhood and had to survive, and I know the reality of that world.

I'm asking because for a student, or even another architect reading this or hearing one say, "Well, I'm very interested in conflict," I could see where that could travel in a lot of different directions that you probably wouldn't support, because now it becomes conflict as a badge or metaphor.
Let me just say the act of taking apart or deconstructing as an artistic method is completely valid, but that's not my work. I construct things, and I construct buildings in a certain way. Caltrans is absolutely clear on that point. The building grew out of the institution. The institution is constantly emerging. It represents a freeway with no end; it is a network and not a geographical thing. So, the building emerged from those conditions. Everything is moving out. Everything was connected to openness, to unfinished-ness, and the structure is expressed as if left unfinished, as a frame. You see what you really want to see, which is also the infrastructure of the freeway.

But what I am fascinated by, which all of our work deals with, is fragments. The fragment is seen as a new totality that has its own future.

Maybe we are establishing a new compositional strategy. The random pieces or details at Caltrans may be elaborating a developing modern idea. And maybe the prior one isn't quite replaced, but still we're producing something that is somehow challenging what came before. It is not quite as simple as getting rid of something because you are revealing the process of replacing it. I think the fragment, as a part of a new totality, is about that.

It's a new notion of completion. What we're challenging is that we don't see things as static; everything we look at today is understood in broader terms.

The position suggests a fallen tree has ecological and biological interactions that are just as useful to life as a living tree. Now we understand the life of a tree in its true ecological meaning vs. the image of a tree.

The perception of the fallen tree as a new understanding of what unfinished might represent has expanded the search into the potential for multiple meanings or functions.
This Pellegrino bottle is finished when I drink it and throw it away. But it's not at all finished. It gets reused or something else happens to it. If I put it in the right recycle can, it's going to end up as some other piece of glass. Now it is literally like genetic material. It has children; it's located in some other glass bottle. Depending on what happens to the green in the glass, it goes to other green glass families. It has some sort of ethnic background, green glass vs. white glass vs. yellow glass. You cannot see this as a finished thing. You can see it as part of a connected system. When you understand that there are millions of these made a week, what you're going to ask your students to study is not to design another glass bottle. It's going to take a completely different approach, and I think a lot of the things we're talking about have to do with unfinished-ness, openness, etc. They deal with broader thinking to understand the world. I'm talking about simple expressions of that. When you look at the unfinished-ness of something, that perception engenders a broader educational, philosophical, and ideological discussion. Let's have this conversation about what finished means. What I'm talking about is an emblem, a symbol of an idea. There's another level of the reality in that realm.

But that's why you can say this is not about composition, because from the Crawford House forward, or wherever you want to make the dividing point, many additional issues have been on the ascendant, rather than following more limited architectural explorations. Now it's that the meaningfulness of design intentions deriving from these larger biological, ecological, etc. interests is more relevant. Caltrans embodies multiple readings, which before the Crawford House were limited and fewer, more purely architectural issues.
But a lot of what we've been talking about has been symbolic, or representational in your terms. You could approach your personal psychology through a psychologist, and he/she is going to look at the nature of your connections to your world and see the nature of those connections and infer how they relate to specific problems or opportunities. You could deal with a psychiatrist, and you're going to be seen as a chemical entity and

I've been interested in a biological idea of order versus a traditional compositional one for some time, it comes with chaos, which is not random, but controlled random, so you look at the façade and there is a randomness to it, as I am establishing an idea of texture to the piece.

Architecture has to reach the self, what we call the soul, it's expressive, and it has to take us someplace, like all art.

this discussion will not be about behavioral issues. To the psychiatrist you are a set of chemical connections. The way you think and the way your body operates is only chemical. That's all it is.

So now we understand the various types of schizophrenia. What we thought previously was craziness is, in reality, chemical! There is chemistry operating in your brain, and it makes you behave a certain way. It has to do with depression. It has to do with all kinds of mood shifts and with the amount of energy you have. That's the discussion that's going to happen with the reality, in physical terms, of architecture. It will focus on the biological and chemical. The physical thing, that's another discussion.

Similarly, the discussion we're having is concerning the representation of the world, as we understand it. The things we're talking about with Caltrans are representational issues. If we talked about building performance in terms of LEED, that is a different discussion. Our building in San Francisco is LEED platinum. We took the air conditioning out of three quarters of the building. That we can quantify. So now we're not in the symbolic discussion; we're in the reality discussion, and we can confirm the design equates to saving a million dollars, or the power requirements for 660 homes. We can quantify the amount of heat we take into the building and quantify it's 55-feet wide. We can put natural light on both sides and significantly reduce the amount of artificial lighting required. We can actually quantify it in those terms. Now we're talking about two parallel tracks.

The reality of building biologically is quantifiable and scientific, versus the representational aspects of building, which are more subjective, more symbolic. I think a good architect deals in both on parallel paths. It is possible to build a building that symbolically talks about these performance issues but, in reality, does not significantly address them. Or you can design a building that in reality does address the issues, but has no interest in expressing them in a broader way. I think it's one of the things that's unique to architecture. Only architecture as an art form deals in these parallel worlds.

Right. You could have a scenographic BIM building created in the hands of the wrong architect where the numbers would be right, but in the end, the spirit of invention we like to see animating a building would be left aside. It would become nothing more than the standard generic building one drives by and doesn't notice. It has no life impact or considerations of that nature. Those parallel worlds do not merge. One becomes dominant and one becomes marginalized. Your interests have been such that you can see BIM not simply as a tool, but something to engage the design and meaningfulness of the decision-making process.

That's interesting, because for me, in the '60s it was very ethically acceptable to put solar panels on your roof. They were just big flat ugly things that messed up the neighborhood and produced inexpensive hot water. It was ethically and ecologically useful. For me, architecture is something much more complex, and is not just engineering. Architecture has to reach the self, what we call the soul. It's expressive, and it has to take us someplace, like all art. And so, you do this in a way that somehow affects a person. It's not the engineering or the rational part of you; it's a part of humanism that is part of our subjective world. It is an extension of how we define art. It has to somehow move us and be compelling.

What I guess is important may not always be correct, but finally it is what is essential that matters, that connects to reality. The design intention one is investigating, which is compelling and interesting, does have to behave conceptually, intellectually, and experientially in the ways your are envisioning. If one admires and explores these things and then is unable to follow through in the execution, there's a bit of a dilemma.

I'd be in a conceptual dilemma in that I am acknowledging these issues are important to me, and I've attempted to express them, but somehow they're not embedded in the reality of the building. It would be obvious there's a misalignment of intentions. It would be the same in any personal part of one's life.

I think that's where, whether the design issue is sustainability, the use of fragments, or an indeterminate form of organization, you are saying, in all those conditions they are only relevant to the extent that they ultimately cohere. Fragments can cohere if there is intentionality, or a meaningfulness of organization and representation, to where there is an expression of intentionality.

Yes, without the intentions, creating a guiding framework through which all decisions must pass it would be like a minister directing a ballet; he probably can't do it. One has to make a decision in one's life. I say this, I do that, and I don't get distracted into something else. It's as simple as that. It is the same in design; it is the constant rebuilding or reuse of the initial intentions.

12| This reuse of intentions is part of the process of adding depth to the design. Let's return more directly to Caltrans. As the design developed, did you use the different attributes of the organizational

It is the same in design; it is the constant rebuilding or reuse of the initial intentions.

One of the representational principles was dynamism ,typically expressed in a form of randomness where we used offsetting, slipping, etc.

and representational conceptual fields to mature or cross-reference each other?

In the office I have championed differentiation and the prioritizing of everything specific or idiosyncratic that can be connected to a particular project. This has been within urban terms, landscape terms, formal juxtaposition, and organization, and with other relationships—looking at how they can be integrated into the more pragmatic aspects of the work. The work has not been language based. It's been problem based. This relates to the interrogation and assessment of the problem and has to do with the types of interests or questions we are trying to address while relating to the specificity of the project. Ultimately the language comes out of that. Of course, any conceptual continuity between projects has to do with the preferences that are part of my own intuitive self. These aspects are now institutionalized at Morphosis as a result of my position as thought leader of the firm.

At Caltrans the chassis of the box was a result of an assessment of the problem having to do with time and money. An initial organizing aspect was as simple as that. I had to see how my own design interests could accommodate this reality. It was going to lead me to something a little different than previous projects. Ultimately Caltrans does have similar ideas in terms of organization and on and on. They evolved from the same broad kind of thinking, but the realities affecting the design approach at Caltrans affected the outcome in a very different way.

For example, the structural chassis is not only simpler, it is the simplest. It is a 30 x 30 grid. Done. There is nowhere to take it. It is a 100% pragmatic project, not counting the little light piece we pushed out along 1st Street. So, I am starting with the absolute simplest possible chassis in the form of an organizing grid, straightforward service core locations, MEP components all being pretty typical stuff. But now I have my architectural interests and intentions, which become the departure point for architectural investigations. When we begin to design, we consider the site, the built-in framework required including underground parking, and then this is where I step in. What can I do with these givens? I can peel a little bit away. We can carve the middle out a little and we can add a public courtyard, but we are still dealing with the "realities."

Along with the simplicity of the chassis, all the aesthetic devices take on a dual role as functional devices. So, we externalized the fire stair. We let that become part of the skin which is part of the idea of building as infrastructure. The skin is now is a performing skin; it is not just an aesthetic layer. It deals with modulating the west and east heat load. On the skin, we can go to work on the static orthogonal organization of the grid and make it a little more dynamic in the form of its organization. We allow it to peel away and fold onto, or above, the ground. To that we add a complete piece in front of the building giving it a presence with the scale of the city and the 100-address marker, which we were exploring in terms of L.A. signage and infrastructure as themes.

15| I would like to integrate those thematic issues to an additional one. How do you link ephemeral, poetic intentions of your design to the pragmatic, functional performance concepts as the design progressed?

That's the definition of an architect.

Yes, but better architects continue to employ design intentions throughout the length of the design process and conceptualize various realities down to the last detail to advance poetic or multiple design intentions.

The use of randomness is another expression of movement. You see it in the way the lights are organized in the plaza and in the large exterior light piece. There is enough repetition of the theme of randomness and how it becomes organized that you get it. It becomes a quality of the building relating to the expression of our architectural interests, not with the pragmatics, but in the iconographic representation of Caltrans.

Well, the broader, poetic, lyrical, and aesthetic considerations you deal with are literally architecture as a cultural act. It has nothing to do with function whatsoever.

Hypo Bank: Plan, Section

We were very interested in the infrastructural nature of the freeway. We became totally comfortable with concrete, with galvanized metal, with very simple materials, as they are exactly the materials from which freeways are made.

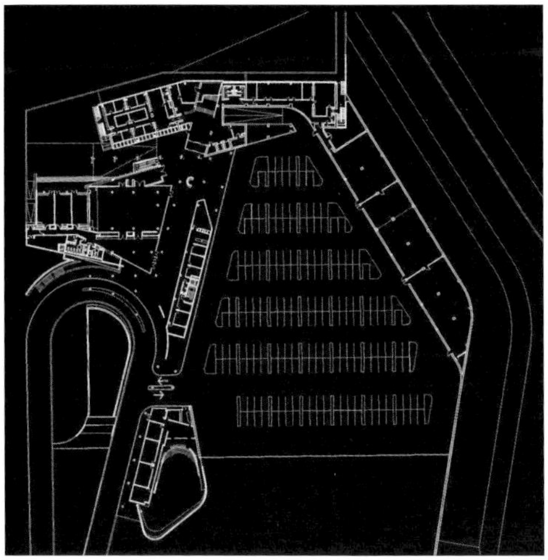

Well, the broader, poetic, lyrical, aesthetic, considerations you deal with are literally architecture as a cultural act. It has nothing to do with function whatsoever. The culture of architecture has to do with the interpretation of these things within aesthetic terms. So everywhere you look (in your photographs)...you see the skin. The skin gives a shape. Ok, we have random "eyes" in the façade...I've been interested in a biological idea of order versus a traditional compositional one for some time. It comes with chaos, which is not random, but controlled random, so you look at the façade and there is a randomness to it, as I am establishing an idea of texture to the piece. I am also allowing the eyes to look as if they are open. I am playing a game where they open and close. We wanted some of the eyes to be active, as if some are left open, the idea of movement again.

13| Somewhat of a representational theme of sorts, would that be correct? Regarding representational ideas of that nature, how do you explore the organizational potential of these ideas?

Well, one of the representational principles was dynamism typically expressed in a form of randomness where we used offsetting, slipping, etc.

Every feature of that sort is a separate system, each having its own ordering or relationship authority. If they have a genuine authority, then they will have a clear relationship with each other. They each have their own rules that are discernible—one element follows this rule, another follows that one. Everyone gets it. The use of randomness is another expression of movement. You see it in the way the lights are organized in the plaza and in the large exterior light piece. There is enough repetition of the theme of randomness and how it becomes organized that you get it. It becomes a quality of the building relating to the expression of our architectural interests, not with the pragmatics, but in the iconographic representation of Caltrans.

16| Relating to that then is the expressive nature of materials, or how you deployed them. When did the notion of material intentionality become important in the project?

We were very interested in the infrastructural nature of the freeway, in its organizational nature, and its effect on Los Angeles. We were interested in how it represents a continual evolving process, its unfinished nature, and that it is effectively always in a state of flux. From that assessment, we became totally comfortable with concrete, with galvanized metal, with very simple materials, as they are exactly the materials from which freeways are made.

We will parallel them, and that is going to have more constructional and material equality to a freeway than to a building, and we will leave it at that. Definitely the front came right out of that. We were aligning to pragmatic realism; we were aligning to representational realities that, in this case, are the symbol of the building.

4.1| On that representational issue, and your mention of being interested in a "biological" order versus an "architectural" order, it can be argued that those interests lie outside of architecture, beyond any given building you might design. In other words, would you look at a building as being a vehicle for the exploration of those issues?

Absolutely. In Caltrans those interests manifest themselves in a very different way than Hypo Bank. In Hypo Bank if we talk about an idea of nature, the building is much more didactic and literal as it grows out of the site. There's a big, low piece that grows up and out from an augmented landscape and is a large gestural statement. CalTrans operates on the chassis on a large urban site. It's a simple box that you can't get rid of. I was initially uncomfortable with the box, but I have since come to appreciate the qualities in the work that connect to the ordinary. It's essentially a straightforward building—a large number of our cities are comprised of such straightforward buildings, and that's OK.

That gets into the issue of what is anchoring design decisions, what holds them together. You were touching on that. You were saying, "Well, we are trying to bring this folded plate out. I wish I could have brought some program with it, or some public space with it." In the end you have this idea. It's part of the augmented landscape theme, or it might be part of the interest between intention and chance. In that regard, how are you using your interest in biology or augmented landscape that is more representational in nature and pairing it with an organizational system that will aid in the definition of or amplify that interest? How do you integrate the two domains?

There are going to be certain projects that are automatically more in line with our conceptual or architectural interests. Those interests, depending upon how broad they are, and how interpretive they are, are a priority. They are issues that I have ownership of and have been working on for several years. Every project could be criticized or discussed in terms of its connection to its relationship between a particular set of projects and the common or similar intentions underlying them. A very sophisticated client, which should be all clients, will automatically choose an architect whom they feel is connected to their project. That's the point. Again,

CALIFORNIA DEPARTMENT OF TRANSPORTATION
CALTRANS

We don't want to approach the building and see security symbols. We are going to reinvent and make it part of the landscape. To aid in the redefinition of security the benches are placed in a random pattern following our organizational strategies.

It is bottom-line about values. ...design is also about incorporating the client's values.

if I have a discomfort with this project, it is probably because of the sheer amount of pre-existing conditions. The site, the infrastructure, the budget, already lock me in to a certain degree. These conditions may be in conflict with aspects of my architectural interests.

If somebody really wants to understand this condition in terms of the culture of Morphosis, they should do nothing else but look at Hypo Bank. If you look at that project, you are going to find the client values and architectural interests line up. We could shape the form, or the chassis, much more in concert with our broad idea as opposed to being constrained as we were at Caltrans. The organizational or representational qualities of the chassis were in alignment with our broad intentions, and we achieved a building of programmatic differentiation, multiple systems, a formal structure's relationship to functioning spaces, and various levels of complexity that were all considered and agreed upon by the client. The offices at Hypo Bank are all different. The client liked that as it aligned with working life in a small town in Austria where some people have attic offices, some have a corner office, and they are all different.

In terms of office buildings, the US is reliant on a standardized, almost Soviet system. At CalTrans they wanted the same office, the same window, and the same ceiling heights. Those strictures came with the program, with the big box infrastructure thematic. In Hypo Bank, we were able to look at the bank's culture, and the shapes emanate from what we saw. Some people have an office with a 20-foot-high ceiling, and some have a little low piece that comes down to the height of the window. They loved that. We built the village. The enormous differentiation, strangely enough, is a good fit for the average person. One of them gets this office, one of them gets that office. Each office is different, but this one is uniquely yours. There is some sense of ownership. It's not a place where interchangeable automatons work, and that brings a sense of pride to the people who occupy the building. Given my interests in differentiation, it's no wonder that I am much more comfortable with Hypo Bank. For your reader it would become very obvious that in this case our office found a client, a use, a functionality, and performance goals all the way down the line where the client's values and our values were absolutely compatible. It is bottom-line about values. You should inform your students that design is also about incorporating the client's values.

We have a value connection based on certain notions of the human character operating within a social work environment, with transparency and on and on. I am way out of alignment with many of the basic value issues at CalTrans. So, I step back, as I am not able to engage the problem I am really interested in, which is the work force. I am dealing with secondary issues such as the building's skin and clearly with urbanism. The realized scheme was the only one that incorporated a plaza with the added human and urban dimensions.

What is intriguing to me is that you were able to expand the program on multiple scales, including the addition of the plaza. Then in the plaza if we look at the benches...

The benches are security devices, required by law. We said, "We don't want to approach the building and see security symbols." We are going to reinvent them and make it part of the landscape. Because at that point in the design process, we already had a clear notion of what the project was going to be.

The issue of security could have been solved with round bollards four feet high.

Exactly. Our job is to realign that convention so the perception does not immediately evoke thoughts about security; instead it deals with some other human factor. The benches provide seating opportunities for people while maintaining the necessary security criteria. To aid in the redefinition of security the benches are placed in a random pattern following our organizational strategies.

So, you incorporate the issue of security yet resist the use of bollards to avoid an inappropriate visual image. Similarly, they are arranged in a random fashion or are dealing with the space between chance and intentionality. Developing on or going beyond those general design themes mentioned, can you describe design intentions as they relate to the benches such as the relationship between the curved pipe and the floating concrete piece? There is an architectural idea there. What were you trying to represent?

You could also mention the use of light. A minimum light was required in the evening, and we didn't want elements in the space in the form of light poles. So, what do we use? The supports for the canopy and the entry threshold became options. We created a space that we wanted to define architecturally. We created a threshold, and then we used the lifted benches for light because we did not want to represent security, whether with bollards or conventional lighting standards. As we had already filled the space with benches and landscape elements, we didn't want lighting standards, so we took elements and made them multivalent; they do more than one thing. The structure that lifted the bench also became the lighting solution. They also provide a little bit of light on the façade, a kind of moonlight at night. Then we had the

Everything comes out of an iteration of something else.

We talk about ideas collectively, ... the larger idea is that they operate in a system that is predictable. The work is not personal or private. It is not compositional. It is three-dimensional, and it is organizational from the start. What you see as randomness are chance behaviors that come out of complexity.

big light piece defining the edges of the amphitheater. It was an assessment of the problem connecting the demands of project functionality with formal and spatial ideas, and sometimes the functions, such as security, can indicate themes that are, visually speaking, not qualities one wants to feature.

19| There appear to be other areas that are representational in nature. The north elevation is where there is an understanding of a kind of topography. With the random placement of the benches, the splaying of the elevation, and the offsetting of the lights in the plaza, there is a constant organizational strategy under the theme of movement. When you arrive at the building, those elements give the building its architectural spirit of invention. At this point in the design process were you privileging certain aspects of the design? How were these concepts expansions on earlier conceptual intentions?

To contrast the solidity of the chassis I incorporated additional intentions. With the plaza we were orienting it to the street and developing the infrastructure and landscape themes. We tried to incorporate and represent ideas of transparency into what is essentially a solid building. Everything comes out of an iteration of something else. That is where this notch came from. We notched it to give the illusion of transparency. We put this one little column behind when we pushed the glass back. We wanted the sensibility of the larger cantilevering. The stair comes out to add transparency. If you look at it, you see through it. You see you are constantly being surprised. A solid thing turns into a transparent thing. The skin becomes really film-like. You find nuances when you keep looking at something. It seems quite simple, but you keep discovering new things. It has richness, a visual complexity. It belies the simplicity of the initial brief.

That sense of wanting to continually invent or have surprises, does that emanate from your interest in chance or randomness?

It would be like asking about a particular piece of music or something. It just is. And you articulate it. The ideas then become clearer. After that it's one's personal approach to developing those basic ideas. After that I can't tell you. I will look at a line and then make another line. Why, because there might be another opportunity. The interest or investigation might be connected to the broad idea of the landscape theme, so there is a general direction I am pursuing. The broad idea is a notion of architectural landscape that emerges via research we have been working on for a while. When you get something like Hypo Bank built, and you can re-evaluate the approach because we are finding a new typology that is neither building nor landscape, I am comfortable that we are moving forward with our research. When we received the commission for Giant in Shanghai, we took the theme a step further where the whole building surface is landscaped; it is a more literal landscape. Now we have a building that is completely hybridized. Is it a landscape or is it a building? The particular gestures are very personal. They come out of a process that just happens, yet the general approach is absolutely traceable and can be evaluated in relation to precise design intentions. We can ask, "Where are we in our 15-year engagement with this particular interest? What is the next step?"

Similarly, you can look at a project underway for a competition in Milan and say, "Oh I understand." In that project one can see that while the project is bigger and more urban, the design issues explored in Caltrans are contributors to that effort. You could go to Cornell or to a café we are designing in New York, and they have nothing to do with that interest. It is a completely different project. It goes to other design interests, to other territories we are exploring.

Here is what is interesting. On one hand it is possible to say that relatively recent design interests explore themes of chance, augmented landscapes, or biological themes to give projects a wider range of conceptual territory, yet on the other hand there remains an interest in rational, definable strategies. I would like to discuss those two conceptual domains in relation to diverse architectural directions. For 10 years there has been an interest in the biological and the rational.

The biological is rational.

Yes, but it gives you the flexibility to understand non-orthogonal approaches playing off an orthogonal approach. At one level there is the use of rational, modernist architectural organizational principles. In your projects there are always regulating lines organizing diverse elements whether in plan, section or elevation. Yet, in the last ten years those lines, while having a very clear organizational strategy, are deployed differently. They are saying they don't need to be orthogonal or don't need the same level of rationality. That's what I'm interested in in terms of...

The key is the relationship to the biological world. What you are envisioning are organizational methods to produce predictable behavior. At Giant we were working on an abstract level, and what you are seeing is a different notion of organization that doesn't prioritize literal repetition and the right angle. It is working on much more complex notions of organization that are parallel to our biological world of flora and fauna. What you will see maintains our interest in coherency and structure and order because it operates in predictable behavior parallel to our biological systems. It is all based on that. I am

19|

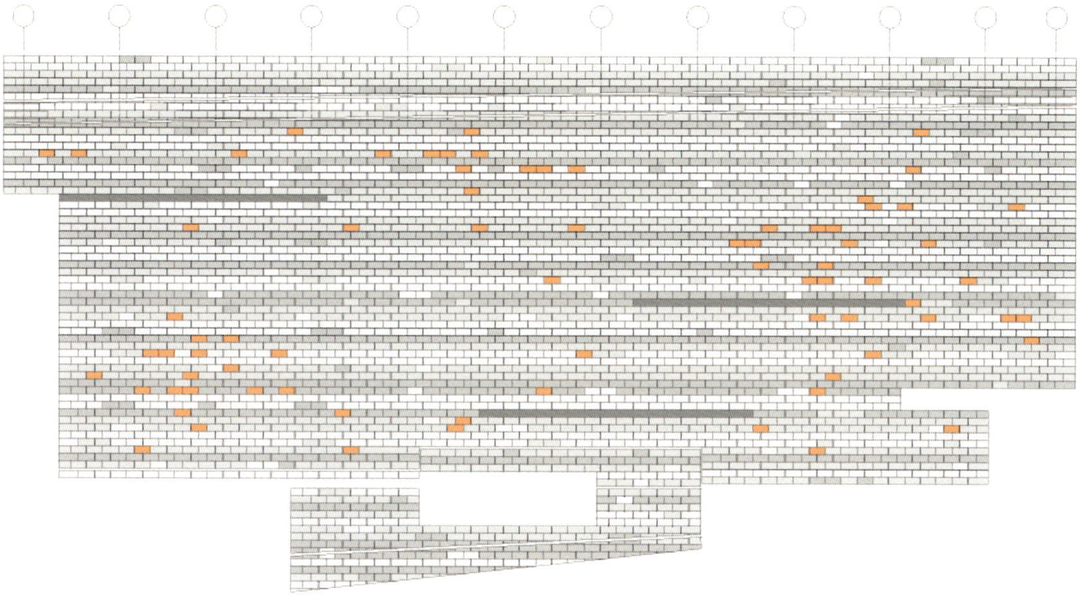

I am interested in that predictability and in producing systems which engage in different methods of creating predictability as a basis for organization.

interested in that predictability and in producing systems which engage in different methods of creating predictability, as a basis for organization.

There is a need for an aspect of predictability in the creation of systems that engage in different methods of production. This is the basis of organization. When you look at a creation, you are looking at what operates systematically, and you are understanding, even if subconsciously, what gives it coherence. It is not private, personal form-making, and it is not about a tradition of creating a private language. Our method is highly discursive—the elements of the buildings we're discussing are worked on collectively in my office.

To describe our system at the office, we talk about ideas collectively, and we can engage in them personally with discriminations such as "Oh I like this one vs. that one." But the larger idea is that they operate in a system that is predictable. I can take each different idea and give one to every person to arrive at alternative iterations. Or I could do 50 of every detail and while they would all be different, they would operate with the same premise, the same set of rules. All of the work in the last 15 years has become more disciplined in the use of that approach. The work is not personal or private. It is not compositional. It is three-dimensional, and it is organizational from the start. What you see as randomness are chance behaviors that come out of complexity.

Walking through a forest you see that one of the trees has fallen down. Of course that is chance. Is it chance that it is one tree vs. another tree? It could have been hit by lightning, a beetle could have eaten it, and it may have gotten old and fallen over. But you will find the way it fell and how it fell is decipherable based on slope, soil condition, or the event that made the tree fall. You might see that other trees have fallen, but it would still be a certain type of what one could call randomness. It is a scientific randomness, a highly organized type of randomness caused by known, understandable events.

In a similar way I am interested in the notion of trees that are not in a grid—they are denser or sparser, there is a level of fern growth, the level of rock, diverse soil conditions. There are threads that go through and each one has its own set of rules that do not operate the way the trees do or how the rock formation does. Each one has its own authority, and I am interested in the idea of looking for parallel methods of organizing architecture visually. I'm interested in bringing that forward into our architectural world.

The tools we are working with have changed. Luckily for me, we are working in a digital environment. That makes the 90-degree angle and literal repetition irrelevant. The computer does not care what the specific angle is – to the computer that is meaningless, unlike the environment in which I learned to design and draw, where the use of the T-square prioritized basic geometries.

Allowing for a type of order. Your interest in predictability and authority are really a part of saying there is still an order, a know-ability, which you are after.
Of course, yet there are differences. Look at the Emerson School. Look at the Perot Science Museum.

Does not Caltrans fall into a situation where there is a challenge attached in that there is the possibility that a building of this program type could fall into an overly "predictable" order given the constraints manifested in the program, the client and the site? Yet, you incorporated an interest in the public realm, by asking, "How can I bring a certain experiential, understandability or joy? How can I bring a predictability that comes through more complex orders?" Caltrans does not represent randomness for the sake of randomness. This randomness is to bring a spirit, or to explore a fuller understanding of what order can be or what order can represent through a series of cohering parts.
Simply put, Caltrans represents a project and program containing a lot of given material, including the frame, resulting in a kind of order that derives from the radical pragmatism of structure. And by radical pragmatism I mean at the start of the design process I already have a huge amount of order derived from multiple constraints emanating from the site, the client, and the budget. I am now bending, challenging, layering that order with another more complex order that is also multi-disciplinary. It's going to involve urbanism, surface effects, graphics, landscape, notions of movement, notions of structure, more complex ordering systems, etc. I am going to layer that or integrate it into the order I have been given. The economic realities of Caltrans predetermined a simple ordering device, which you see as a basic box. If an outcome is going to be successful, it will be due to our ability to re-write, re-imagine, or re-invent so the intentions can expand beyond the singularity of the initial simple order be that a box or whatever difficult constraint might exist in a given project. That is exactly what CalTrans is about, engagement in terms of how much can an architect transform the generic. ■

Architecture, of all professions, is value laden...

Appendix

Finally, I think architecture is a social act. The difficulties of practicing in the US, which is quite different from practicing in Europe or Asia, is that, most architects here work in the private sector. It is problematic because architecture is a public act. Young European architects are nurtured in public work, whether housing or schools. So, Europe's young architects are already nurtured in projects that would be impossible to not see as having social or political representations. In this country, most people don't even recognize architecture as a political act, which is astounding to me. Most students see it as, and I think it's extremely destructive, they see design as a formal act. I make jokes with them. I'm really rough at this level. I say, "Well, then you're like a cake decorator." Nothing against cake decorators, but I see architecture as a little beyond that. We need cake decorators, but we probably don't need them that much, or that many of them. I think architecture is a bit more complicated. In fact, more than a bit more complicated, but finally it's a social act. For an American architect, you have to reach a certain place in your life, if you ever get there, for that realization to kick in. For me it was the school.

The school would be Diamond Ranch?

Diamond Ranch. I remember Richard Weinstein went out with me when it was finished. He was the dean at UCLA at the time. He walked through, and he'd known me for a long time, and he said, "Thom, this must be really meaningful to you, because this is the first time the aesthetic act and the social act have come together." He was completely correct; it was true. For me, this was the first time a social and aesthetic act came together in a public building.

And was that because the program was a school, that you were able to bring intentionality to the site, program, and representational issues in a public building?

Absolutely! It's actually a broad program that I was able to utilize. It wasn't a café or restaurant, or a residence or a boutique. He knew that meant something to me. I was already close to 50, and that's when you're really touching architecture. Now I've got a 3,000-person school. I'm able to involve myself politically and invest myself in my country, my state, my culture, and say something, have a voice. That's all I wanted in my life—and not design wise. I wanted a voice in society, and design is a part of it. That's my language. I speak it; it's how people listen to me. That's literally the language I use. I want architecture to have a voice, to participate in shaping society, in shaping behavior. The school is the first time I could produce something that provided the opportunity to shape the world in which we live. It started with questions of what is a school? How does the school participate in education? You cannot look at the school and not scratch your head, because it has nothing to do with a conventional building, it's shape language, its organization, how it relates to the site, everything about it. The students get it.

What I think happened is they just understood it as being of the moment. And that's the beginning of architecture. You don't have to understand it. It's compelling or even startling because you don't see that many things that are of the moment, because we are often living in past moments. The point being, this is what architecture is about. That somehow, you're interacting with the world, and you have some force. Otherwise, what is the profession? The law profession, the medical profession, they have a voice, and that voice is immensely important in terms of the ultimate values that shape our world.

Architecture, of all professions, is value laden; it touches urban, it touches ecology, biology, and it touches humanistic activity. It touches all the functions we've been talking about, whether it's a hospital or a school. We are the ones that actually put a lot of this stuff together, integrate it, and concretize it. And it becomes symbolic. You can rethink what a classroom is and what a school is, and on and on. And you can reconstruct, meaning you can rethink and revalue, how we live day-to-day life. That's finally what architecture is. We all do it in different ways, whether it be Steven Holl, Eric Moss, or Frank Gehry. It doesn't matter. They're serious architects, and they understand these kinds of terms. In fact, if anything we need more of them, and more differences. Totally OK, because we know cities aren't made of similarities.

We live in an enormously pluralistic society, and that pluralism is changing really basic things at a rapid rate. If you understand the world in those terms, then you expect architecture to be equally diverse, to not have a dominant style. I want to walk down the street and see a street full of different ideas. When I hear somebody in our Caltrans building say, "It's really somber," or "It's really tough," I'm thinking, well, I can accept that. Some call it the Death Star. That's kind of cool. We have to have some brooding buildings, some tough buildings, buildings that are somewhat uncomfortable to people, and I'm okay with that. You always want to be comfortable? Is that our role? Sometimes, I want to be entertained, but other times I want to be left with something I'm going to be troubled with, like one is when one reads something challenging. You are left with a thought and it's going to work on you for a long time, and it's not comfortable. It's not what you thought it was going to be about. One is opened up to something, and his or her world is expanded, and that expansion is useful. It makes one think and reevaluate who one is: who they are as a citizen, as a father or mother, as a leader, as a man, women, etc. Architecture has to participate at that level. ◪

NMDA

Neal Denari

Alan-Voo Residence

The Alan-Voo Residence addition represents a program-type that often provides opportunities to investigate conceptual interests not always realizable in projects of a larger scale. Evolving design interests, typically representing an architect's broader theoretical positions, are often explored in residential programs with the clients providing the breadth and flexibility to allow these interests to gain conceptual traction. The realization of these interests in a "beta" format, links conceptual themes with constructed clarity, often becoming a sub-structure for further development in subsequent projects.

Located in Los Angeles and constructed in 2007, the Alan-Voo Residence is a 1,000-square-foot addition to an existing house of a similar size, representing the first of two phases, with the second phase being the reconfiguration of the existing house. The clients, engaged in film and graphic design professions, required additional space for a family of five and desired a residence more accurately representing their combined visual cultures. The addition unites those interests with architectural positions. Both the client and architect were attracted to larger thematic considerations which could be expressed and experienced architecturally. Themes lying beyond those affected by the site and the program, representing interests such as the digital versus the material, the human versus the abstract, cohesiveness, connectedness, and ubiquity, were primary factors underlying multiple design decisions.

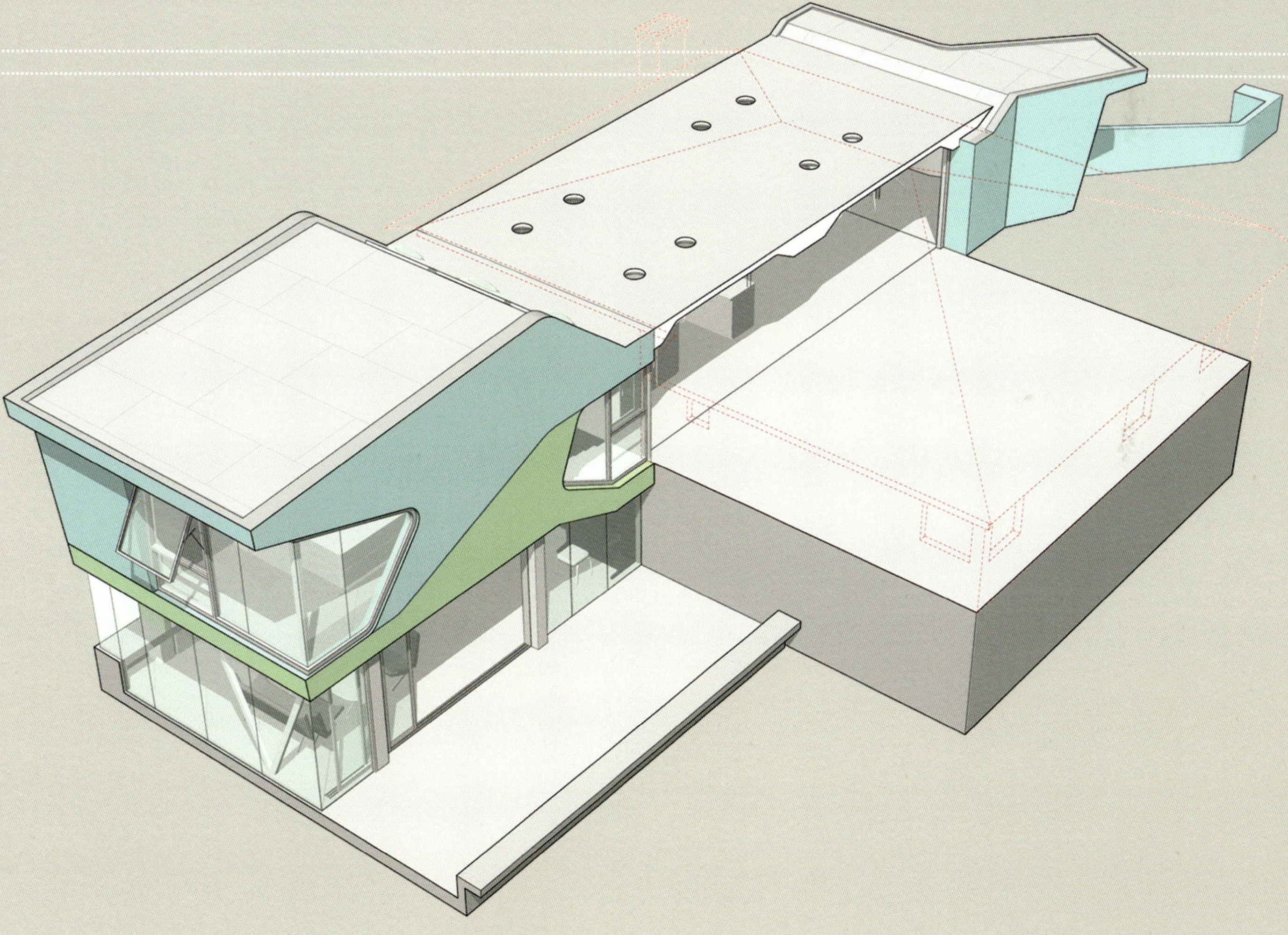

I think precision is something that becomes a kind of tangent to order in that one is searching for a particular kind of exactness, to terms, to words, to projects, so that they reach a kind of apex.

For us there is no order unhinged from the geometric and material properties.

I was still deeply interested in technology as both a transformative device and as an entitiy that was lingering out there with a set of visual references—modernism, machines.

In the Alan-Voo Residence, it is really trying to produce collaboration between the possibly open-ended and a discrete and rather defined project.

1| Tom Diehl: What value, potential, or use do you see in order?

Neal Denari: The classic idea of order is that nothing appears out of place; decisions are executed as they should be and there is logic behind order. You can't have order with randomness; you can't have order with illogic. You can't have order without the kind of smart reading of the phenomenon in front of you. That's how you're going to generate order. Of course, we know that order can come out of cultural demands and your own sense of discipline that cuts across who you are as a person but also from within the field.

For me order comes from aspects that, on the one hand, derive from the growth of a formal language we have worked on and developed over a period of time that is cogent and coherent. There are directions that wouldn't be allowed within that world, or are in the spirit of that language; there are aspects that would be displaced or are of a different agenda. On the other hand, order can come out of the logic of geometry and the logic of how it is used in relation to the architectural discourse and the cultural discourse. The architectural discourse has to do with history, pragmatics, and material logic. The cultural discourse becomes all of the issues that want to challenge axioms, truths, and so forth and can override the architectural discourse because one believes in it more than one respects a particular architectural doctrine.

In this case you are referencing a kind of cultural discourse on order. In that regard, the cultural conception of order becomes impactful at some level...

Exactly, going back to the issue of logic relative to order, we know that architecture is to be practiced with the highest regard for logic because it is a big expensive heavy discourse that's played out in a way that impacts a lot of lives, especially public architecture. If you are exploring randomness, or the chaotic, regardless of what you are trying to do as a mirror to the world, you probably want it to be incredibly precise. I think precision is something that becomes a kind of tangent to order in that one is searching for a particular kind of exactness, to terms, to words, to projects, so that they reach a kind of apex.

2| So then in relation to broad concepts of order or additional themes such as exactness, how do concepts of order manifest themselves in your design thinking or process, i.e., what does order mean to you architecturally? Would you say that there is a cultural dimension defining the way you organize or order your projects, as well as an architectural one? Can you split the two, or is discussing how you combine them a better way of getting at it?

Let me just talk about the architectural side first. Then we can talk about architectural techniques, such as grids and other devices that order projects. We know that buildings are made up of parts and pieces, even if you pour it in concrete. Structure, for me, on a tectonic level is much more instrumental than the way in which the program goes together. In the office we are always thinking and researching how grids become designed and then manifest themselves in new ways in structural systems understood as points and lines in a field. If you transition from points and lines to sheets or thin surfaces or similar conditions, those techniques then change what the ordering system would be. For us there is no order unhinged from the geometric and material properties. I'm not really interested in order as abstract systems for which we will decide after that how to approach a project. In that sense, we are very close to the material practice of architecture in the way in which it is ordered.

Would it be fair to say that order, while it is a system for clarification, is not a strict overlay? It is more...

Yes, in that sense we are less of a classic type of formalist office and more of a new school formalist office that finds limitations in the same way that orders generate limitations or decidability in a project. When we developed the continuous surface projects and they became more surface dominant rather than line or vector dominant, the whole issue of how you end things, what the limits are, how you trim and bifurcate surfaces...all of those techniques became a set of tools helping us to generate order. For instance, a number of projects in the 1990s were about banded parallel extrusions. Super dominant in one direction and absolutely reiterative, like a filmstrip, in the other direction. And I was quite happy to use heavy ordination in section and slight adjustments in plan to be able to generate a collaborative language. So, a lot of issues relative to order in a classic sense have come about because of how plan and section work in a Structuralist sense even though we are thinking about fluidity and the infinite and ideas that can't quite be tied down in terms of X, Y, and Z axes.

So where do you think that came from? And by that, I mean the sense of a migration of order from a classic modern version to an order that is, maybe cultural, maybe personal. Can you articulate that a little bit?

In the 1980s, we saw Deconstructivism happen, which was a radical rethinking of issues modernism was trying to articulate. If modernism, say represented in the De Stijl project, was about a conceptually thick center and a weak periphery, the conception of weakness

Section

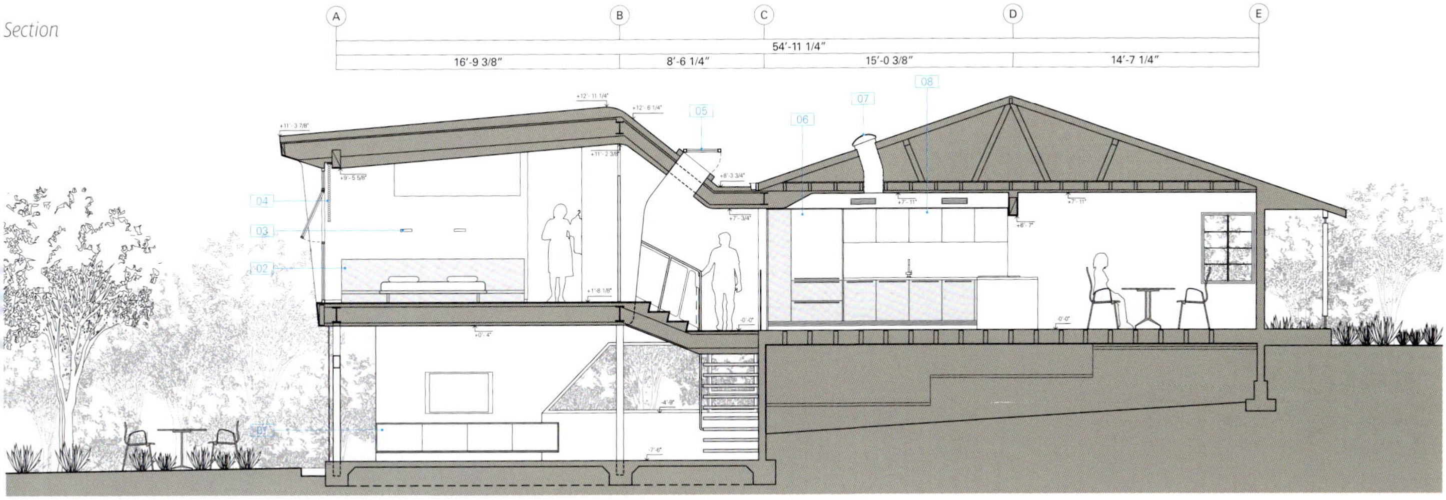

and the lack of limits became the modus operandi in Deconstructivism. Everything was a vector into an infinite space, whether it was Frank Gehry or Daniel Libeskind or others. When I was around 30, that was the contemporary landscape. It compelled one to think about one's own work. The cultural project at that time was super theoretical and super referential to Derrida and his philosophy. I was partially interested in that, but I was still deeply interested in technology as both a transformative device and as an entitiy that was lingering out there with a set of visual references—modernism, machines. By the time of the electronic paradigm, whether practiced or imagined, around 1990, it was as if there weren't any codes for new architectural languages and what the electronic paradigm would become. It is all essentially pixels and zeroes and ones and fluctuation. Now it is going to be about immaterial references, the stock market as opposed to the heavy world of institutions such as boats, airplanes, hospitals, prisons, etc. Suddenly it was how could I get my work to be more economical, more abstract, do more work and be more effective in terms of making an architecture that could refer to these new conditions.

At that time, it was how to think through and develop geometries and material conditions that could operate in that open-ended world. I was not interested in shifting the formal references from hard geometries, such as airplanes and machines, to less structured references such as clouds or the body. I am not at all interested in that. In that sense, there was a lot of continuity in the work. It is still about linearity and it is still about relatively defined conditions, but as in the Alan-Voo Residence, it is really trying to produce collaboration between the possibly open-ended and a discretely defined project. There are architects whose work is obviously more open-ended, more cellular and infinite than what ours tends toward. If you look at it, at times it appears classically composed. There is proportion going on. We are still interested in proportion. There is compression of space followed by an explosion of space and so forth.

So is it correct to say that dominant global interests were emanating from technological references while maintaining a sense of abstraction, even if articulating a different direction, with both becoming vehicles for expressing space, form, etc.?

Yes, I wanted to figure out a version of that economy but maintain a formal exploration through projects that had a certain zeitgeist quality about them. In other words, to really reflect and argue on the Venturi position that states that one can't separate out the formal aspect because in the end it doesn't matter if it's a historical project or an abstract project. It is a discourse, and it is an element in the equation that the work should support something other than proprietary interests, your fetishes, or your desires. That gets at the heart of your project. I am actually interested in encoding and decoding our work. I believe that there is a kind of semantic quality to it and you can read it. I am not trying to deliver messages that are literary or poetic.

Is it fair to say that you were sensing that the abstractness of Mies van der Rohe was a bit more transcendent than the specific references to the 20th century of Le Corbusier and this was appealing to you? Or is it more correct to say that technology was what you saw as the modus operandi to bring meaning forward or to expand upon Venturi's sense that modern architecture needed to make additional connections beyond abstractions?

The main thing that was happening at that time in relation to the expansion of the electronic world was that it became very conscious to everybody that a global society was now upon us. China in 1978 or '79 changed after Mao, but in America we didn't really know what had been going on in China for a long time, as we did not have a relationship with them. But in the 1990s, the computer became common and companies like IBM, Apple, and especially Microsoft started delivering the idea of ubiquity. Computers are the same in China as those we have here. You have the same information. Then the rise of the web created an even greater sense of the possible power of ubiquity and individualism. But if you're an architect and you're thinking, "Well I learned about place and place form relating to the local, isn't this ubiquity a problem?" Yet I've always embraced, not to a complete blind faith, that there isn't a local condition. I was really curious as to what the absolute power of homogeneity was going to do to architecture. What were the new kinds of vernaculars that were going to develop?

I would say it more openly now, building in Los Angeles or Bangkok is different. here you can build with wood and steel. In Bangkok you build in concrete. Formerly I would probably say, "What are the opportunities of those materials?" As an architect who is not stylistically diverse I had to start thinking about arguing for and defending potential signature deployment around the world where somebody could say "You are just part of a global system now, aren't you? You are just a product or brand." That's where I became really obsessed with how the business world and money became more powerful than architecture. How could we do something that would not compete but would operate as a device that could become powerful in its ability to

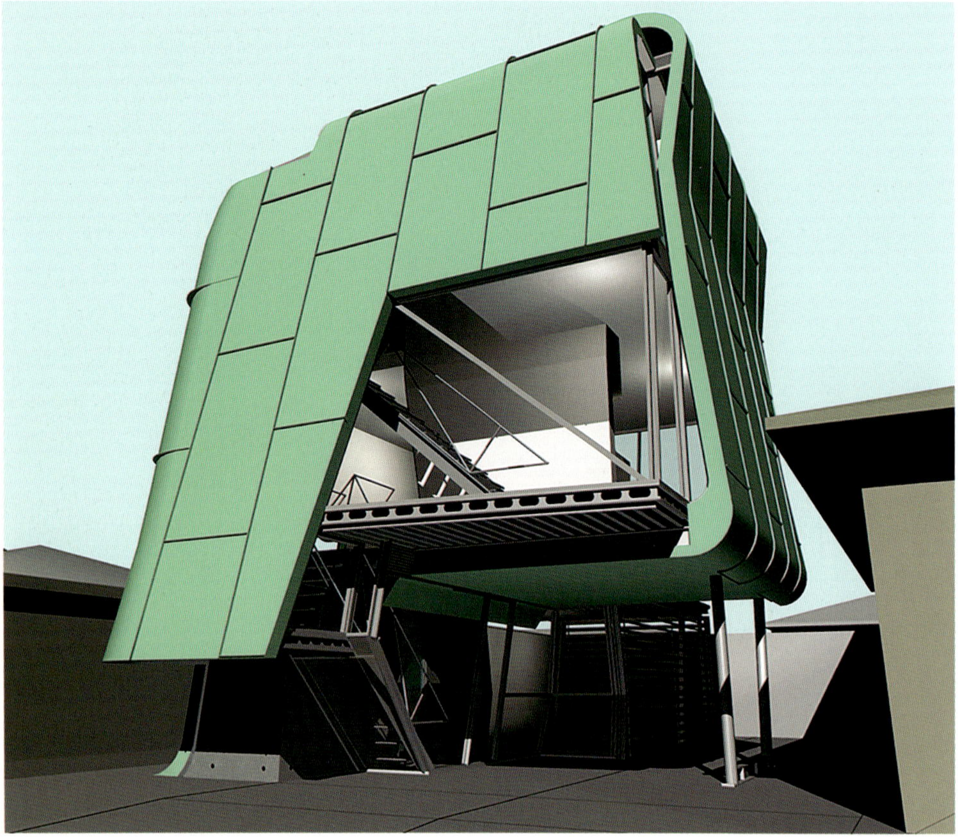

This sense of representation came partially through the idea of the generic, meaning it's just a surface—it's not decorated, it's not modeled in any way; it is two-dimensional. ...That's an important aspect. I made a conscious decision to try to maximize the optical effects of the two-dimensional curve as opposed to struggling to model and build curvature.

Top:
Vertical Smoothouse

Bottom:
Interrupted Projections

We had begun to find something that oscillates between the described and the fixed, because it was material and built and was not moving, yet optically and psychologically it just didn't feel that way.

capture life and spirit without doing it in a vernacular way? One outcome was we developed this kind of surface geometry.

So that provided a grounding in experiential qualities affecting life and spirit but with a global or more universal outreach?

I was interested in confronting the issue and had some ambivalence at the same time. For the most part, I was excited about computerization. I was curious that all of the companies were saying the same thing: "We will take you wherever you want to go. You're one click away." These corporations were trying to distinguish themselves, yet they all have the same products and the same intent. Their products and services were meant to be delivered to Africa, China, the United States—to every corner of the world. For the first time after air travel, which could get you to any point of the world, this was the next big paradigm shift, yet there was no object involved. Before, the airplane and other products of industrialization were the big references. Now, who cares about the box? There is nothing physically involved. In that sense, there isn't another device to architecturally grab onto. You have to figure it out abstractly.

So then there was a realization or understanding of a cultural milieu emanating from global ubiquity. From that, because there was a certain "nothingness" tied to the method of transmission, a relationship to abstraction was explored. Is it then correct to say that as a culturally transcendent vehicle, technology was the "abstract" strategy employed?

Yes, somewhat. Technology is a loose term. In some ways in architecture, it is a misnomer because building technology in its brutality is so much different than

the concept of the post-Newtonian world. What interested me was also written about in *Supermodernism: Architecture in the Age of Globalization* by Hans Ibelings. In it he states that one can make a glass box, make no apparent form, put in the floor plates, wire it up and get the furniture in, but you basically let people do what they do which is, in fact, humanity becoming the formal project.

This is a lot of what Ito has been about. Similarly, with Tschumi, although his is more of a project about the choreography of people. I was from the school of thought that wanted to have a project about form played out and not be abandoned in an era without a formal referent, or where a critic could say, "You shouldn't have a project about form because it's not important anymore."

Whether we use the term grounding, anchoring, or similar terms, there was a concern or an interest that formal strategies had a role to play.

Yes, very much so. At that point, intellectually you can think about what kind of project would be the most relevant to the conditions of the world. I never wanted to create a project that was holding up a mirror to the world. While there is some of that in everybody's work, I wanted to see if there was a project that could enter the conversation and become relevant. This became the continuous surface project, which we developed in the 1990s. It had a big impact in the architectural culture, and still has. It was an interesting euphoria. We felt that relative to shaping shape, in the classical sense, we could ground specific conditions, bodies in space, surfaces, and delimitations with opacity, as opposed to making the project about infinity, i.e., the Miesian project. We had begun to find something that oscillates between the described and the fixed, because it was material and built and was not moving, yet optically and psychologically it just didn't feel that way. That's what we really have been trying to achieve in the work.

It appears the concept of the continuous surface became a representational concept trying to point to a common denominator or a commonness to which people would gravitate. Was it a way of reinventing or giving architecture a new meaning in that the goal was about the relevance of architecture in this evolving world of...

We were seeing it as a way to design a new primitive, not like in the plastic art sense or in the computer sense, but in the platonic sense as a closed form. Our new primitive was essentially the surface that could go anywhere and

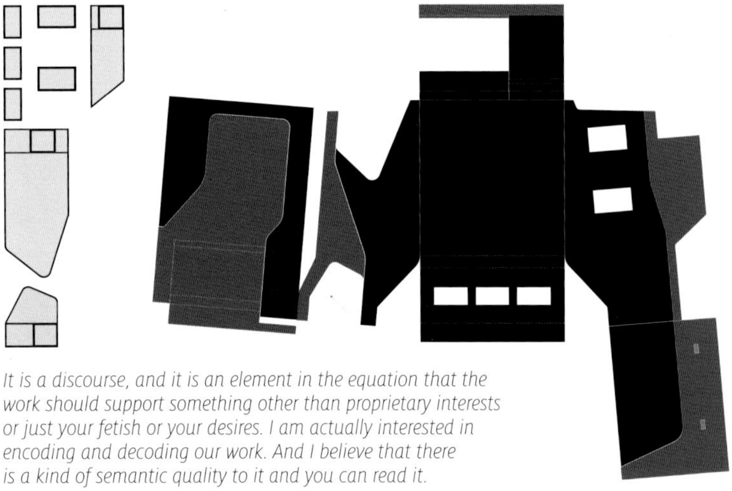

I believe very much in the optical, meaning that what you read and what you see, if it is an abstract form of the optical, you can find pleasure in it.

If modernism was about trying to open stuff laterally in terms of landscape, we wanted to do it in every dimension possible.

It is a discourse, and it is an element in the equation that the work should support something other than proprietary interests or just your fetish or your desires. I am actually interested in encoding and decoding our work. And I believe that there is a kind of semantic quality to it and you can read it.

do anything. Let's say a loop, or an unfolded Klein bottle or something similar. We wanted that to be a kernel from which everything would essentially emanate, an element that had a lot of vitality and a lot of life but wasn't closed. That was what we were searching for in this new primitive, which really became operative in that sense. When we get back to the issues of order and so forth, it has to do with the rules relative to X, Y, or Z axes and then the introduction of the diagonal, the radial, or turning corners. This goes back to formal languages. This sense of representation came partially through the idea of the generic, meaning it's just a surface—it's not decorated, it's not modelled in any way; it is two-dimensional. That's an important aspect. There really was a moment in which we asked, "In the future If we're going to build, we need to build with the same amount of money that everybody else builds, with nominally." I made a conscious decision to try to maximize the optical effects of the two-dimensional curve as opposed to struggling to model and build three-dimensional curvature.

So, was it also from the means of production or methods of fabrication that you saw as a strategy, one that not only had larger aspirations concerning ubiquity and technology but also had a constructive-ness about it.

Yes, from the very beginning. I would say that was very, very conscious. It was the coming together of my pathway as an architect. How could I make sure that the skills, the talent, and the ideas could reach a kind of commensurate level of dependability? Call it the professional aspect. Thom Mayne and Frank Gehry are kind of role models. They had to figure it out. That was a figuring out moment for me, and it was a moment where a conceptual project, a geometric project, and a project on constructability all merged.

You also mentioned being interested in the two-dimensional from a graphic standpoint. Let's discuss that further as it sounds like it represents another large issue.

In many ways, this idea of the surface came conceptually from the notion of a map or a sheet that did not have any information on it, taking out the textual and delivering the purely graphic. A similar and additionally important reference for me was the painter Robert Ryman who paints essentially white paintings. To this day, he is my favorite painter. People ask, "Why is he your favorite? There is nothing going on." My response is "It's all about the way in which white paint goes on to a surface." Getting that level of abstraction relative to a surface allowed the geometric premise to come forward and become the content.

By geometric premise, you mean the continuous surface?

Yes, the geometric premise of how many possibilities can we open up within the order and the limitations inherent in manipulating a two-dimensional curve. As I said, we weren't interested in three-dimensional curves. One could argue you couldn't build a three-dimensional curve if you weren't dealing with topological geometry, so then maybe you weren't pushing your work far enough. I agree with that to a certain extent, but two things are relevant. One, I am not an unapologetic formalist. I don't say, I just do what I do, and the only progress that matters in architecture is creating the most extreme form. However, I actually like it that people think I am that way. What that means is the work is producing an effect.

There is a meaning or connectivity that is being felt at an emotional or human level.

Exactly, but one grounded deep down in economy and constructability. The relations on a human and emotional level represent the give back from what was conceptually embedded into the work. Later the abstraction of the surface became a little more graphic because instead of one monochromatic surface we created joints in the continuous surface creating opportunities for more tones. That's really a recognition that the graphic component of the project, even the more superficial aspects of it, have become more operative and meaningful in that I can explore and understand the world and its media, including the methods of communicating in terms of people's lives. Architecture needs to do more, even if it is not telling stories or delivering content, like watching TV or reading the newspaper. We are articulating psychological differences in space. I believe very much in the optical, meaning that what you read and what you see, if it is an abstract form of the optical, you can find pleasure in it, as opposed to being baffled as to what an architect or artist is trying to say. People don't walk around my projects and say, "What are you really trying to say here?"

What you are saying is that this investigation has indicated there is a deeper, resonance, more at a gut level, but it can also be at a broader cultural level.

Also at an unspoken level. But the techniques are based in mass media. Two things we deal with quite a bit are low contrast and high contrast. Two colors like red and magenta, which vibrate, versus green and white or black and white. We are playing with those things that allow your eye to really track shapes and figures or ones that basically produce ambiguity. And they both work together in our work.

So, in this regard, the order is one of an experiential nature initially. To the extent that one can see other

... sloping surfaces between floors where we can, where we have the opportunity to explore or document volumetric excess. Getting away from the stacking, stratification, and so forth is something we have been interested in because that's a hallmark of modernism.

layers or strategies, fine. But your goal is not to create a body of work that has to be analyzed for someone to "get it." Your intent is to allow people to interact at an emotional or visual level, which functions as a grounding, and then to the extent that the work unfolds further, that's up to the observer.

One term that I've started using in the past few years to describe the work is stop action. Stop refers to the fixed, and the fixed relates to the graphic. If you look at a number of profiles spatially in the project, you can read it like a section or an elevation drawing.

That's the stop part. The action part is when you get out of the artificial mode of receiving and move into the depth of the space, which becomes time based and fluid. It is collaboration between photography and film. That is what I discovered in the development of these kinds of sheet and surface projects, which have limited yet strong profiles. I'd work on them in section quite a bit. I am really hands-on with the work. I draw and model. I am kind of a new-school version of a guy from an older generation.

3| How do you employ formal ordering systems? In some respects, this has been discussed. If one looks at photographs or walks through the house and it touches them, they think it's nice, the question then arises, "How did he get there?" I know that it is not just shaping a curve or line. In that regard, whether it is concerning the Alan-Voo Residence or a larger issue, once you have the continuous surface, there is something you are doing to organize that curve. So there is an organizational format. What "shapes" the continuous surface?

Of course the surfaces have to deal with the conventions of architecture, which are floor and wall and roof. Those

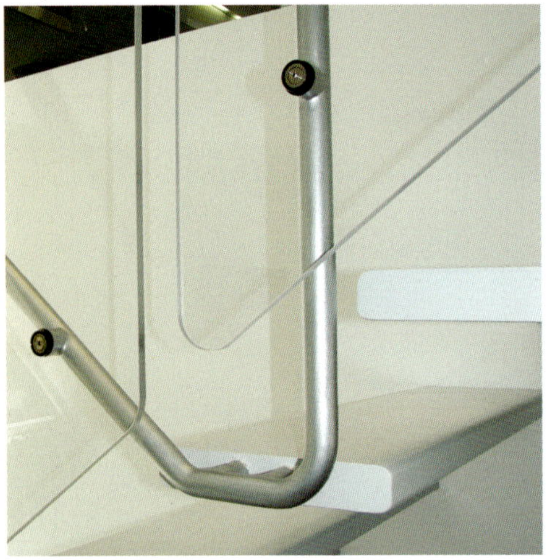

To me it is less about wanting to build something precise as it is about the constructed aspect of the work representing the way in which someone is going to perceive the project.

We were both intrigued with the relationship between a material world outlined by lived necessities, a notion that architecture is a discrete thing in a more ubiquitous world and that for the most part people's lives are lived in a world of ubiquity.

The appearance of our work is precise, one might say refined, in that regard, the role of "technology" is a bit more transcendent.

For us, allowing the surface to migrate and have different trajectories that are not required to obey discrete modernist rules of regulation is important.

are the ways in which it is typically described, whereas I use a slope or a radial condition to take a corner away. Taking the corner away is an organizational trope; it changes modernism from something about the poetry of the right angle or planar geometry. Yet there are floors and roof conditions, so to a certain extent it is not simply a softening of the orthogonal nature of modernism. At the same time, the conditions of building govern that. Not everything can be sloping and not everything can be free. Relative to the sectional profiles in two-dimensional curvature, you have to extrude those profiles, and we think of extrusion in a lot of different ways.

To give coverage, you mean.

Yes, to essentially produce depth and accommodation. So, extrusion can happen in plan along a pathway. In many of the early projects we were extruding only on straight lines, having a particular dimensional depth or width that would accommodate two structural bays or three offices or...and then we either repeated the extrusion or we would repeat and shift the extrusions so that in the direction of the extrusion you get a build up of complexity.

Are you saying that the extent of this might come from something as basic as the number of repeated offices or structural bays?

In terms of the program that's partly correct. But we are also probing, trying to do as much as we can spatially to eliminate stratification. We want to achieve a sectional blending.

Define sectional blending. Is it in terms of the curving condition?

Yes, as in sloping surfaces between floors where we can, where we have the opportunity to explore or document volumetric excess. Getting away from the stacking, stratification, and so forth is something we have been interested in because that's a hallmark of modernism. The project of the diagonal or the "in between" is essentially why the continuous surface emerged. We were trying to break down the singular relationship between X and Y, between stratification, between a singular experience...

If modernism was about trying to open stuff laterally in terms of landscape, we wanted to do it in every dimension possible, but in an economic way. You can model three-dimensional curvature all day but maybe not be able to build it. On the other hand, philosophically, three-dimensional curvature may be working too hard to try to undermine or overcome the limitations of doctrinaire modernism. I'm probably not the only one who would say that doctrinaire modernism is the launching or reference point for all the architects you are interviewing. Coop Himmelblau's work uses the five points of Le Corbusier; the same could be said about Enric Miralles, perhaps even more emphatically. The work is often cloaked in another language, but it is there.

So there is a historical connection. There is a linkage. Are there architectural preferences or architects that you would reference as having an impact on your thinking?

I would put myself in the Corbusian mold for the first part of my career. I went to Europe, lived, and studied there. I understood, literally, relative to the term order we have been discussing, the linear versus the painterly, the figural versus the abstract, and the nature of grids, the nature of assembled steel versus poured concrete. Le Corbusier is definitely the most important motivational architect. His work provides the best lessons, rather than learning them in school through a processed history. Look at both the generation above me and at my generation, people like Ito, Thom Mayne, Wolf Prix, and Zaha Hadid. See how those techniques and principles are played out in everybody's quirky, formal, and materialistic manners. Hadid's Phaneo Science Center is a Corbusian project. Ito's Mediatheque is a Corbusian Project. The columns, the floor plates, the materials are different, and they offer completely different experiences, but there are commonalities in their points of origin. I am formally within that tradition. A lot of it has to do with the ground plane and what the building is in relation to the ground plane. We know for Corbusier, it was levitating above the ground. I'm certainly not the only one who saw the possibilities in the in-between. From the mid-1950s on to the end of the 1960s Parent and Virilio's concept of the function of the oblique continued this form of exploration, which is both a landform and a discrete object where the diagonal and continuity come into play.

If I take as a general reference Le Corbusier's modernism as an influence in relation to your work, there is also the sense of technology...the sense that you don't read the surface condition in anything but through a thinness that derives from a preferential attachment to technological advances. You are not curving thick stereotomic members or planes. Technology is part of it, both in the expression of thinness and in the overall sleek metallic quality of your projects. Fit that in a bit, if that's appropriate.

There is an idea of technology that is relevant as having cultural potential, an aspect beyond the hardware. I think this is what you are getting at. A building is a relatively low-tech thing so impressions of technology

are very powerful. Richard Neutra painted wood posts silver because he wanted them to appear metallic. I'm not sure I would paint wood silver; I would just demand that it be steel and feel a little bit more comfortable. The appearance of our work is precise, one might say refined. In that regard, the role of "technology" is a bit more transcendent.

That's a better way of putting it. It is the precision and the refinement that is more important than the technology. The technology seems to be the method by which one can get there. Would it be that the intent, the narrative side, is about the value of refinement or precision?

I think it is an important point to talk about. It is a point on which Tom Mayne and I are on completely opposite sides. Everybody wants to build their work well, but the issue of its appearance, if it is too taken care of, may represent a level of fetish that can be seen as a misguided discourse, which can become too introverted, too self-referential. Beauty becomes too overwhelming in its ambition.

I've always been unapologetic about that. I want the work to represent our conceptions. I would say I'm not a classic modernist in the sense that I want everything to be the smallest, tightest, joint-free...we've been experimenting with wide joints as well as thin ones. That comes from car construction, which influences us in the definition of joints. Not everything is a 2mm joint like that built into manufacturing a car. There is extruded black EPDM and I really like that. I like it on an emotional and an aesthetic level. It comes out of how you put something together.

This connects back to the curiosity about technology. You are on the right track and I would never dissuade someone about inquiring what technology represents in our work. It is not apples to apples as if a building is as high tech as an airplane. To me it is less about wanting to build something precise as it is about the constructed aspect of the work representing the way in which someone is going to perceive the project. The lay person might notice something if it is built poorly, but when it is built well, the craftsmanship often fades into the background. I am happy about that because it means nothing is getting in the way of one's pure experience of the project. Thought of in another way, this allows for our interests in the cultural aspects of technology to come forward.

5| How do these interests impact your thinking in relation to the methods employed to architecturally

So, it is about identity, refuge, and protection. They threw out protection and refuge as representational interests but wanted identity.

We used the continuous surface conceptualization as a way to envision merging pathways, to integrate them optically on the level of the diagonal. The intent was to rethink the idea of the continuous surface not so much as a skin, but to also explore how it could impact the infrastructure, to give the effect that the horizontal and the vertical have been overcome, have been challenged.

organize and represent your intentions? On a number of your projects realized or unrealized, whether there are a series of parallel bands or there is one large continuous surface that envelopes or frames an entire structural system, there is...

One thing to reference is scalability and the potential for coherence that allows. If something is simple enough and not too idiosyncratic, then you can scale it. Not just repeat it, but you can also scale it. That gets back to modernist abstraction; a cube is a cube whether it is small or 60 meters tall. Our world of the surface and the primitive has that kind of scalability, and I think if an architect wants to have the ability to operate at a number of scales, then that's really important. For example, someone who might say, "I only work well at the scale of a house and when it gets bigger than that I don't know what to do." To me I've always said, "Airports, chairs, I can handle it," because there is a scalability of intent. I am not going to approach an airport fundamentally differently than a house. And that has to do with the repeatability of the geometry, or the ability of a surface element to repeat and produce a meta-envelope, or a series of scalable objects that produce "invelopes" as I call them, as a counter to the envelope in the sense that allows one to work in a variety of scales. In bigger projects, you should be searching for an intimacy as well. It's not just simply click "scale" and enlarge it, and you're done. Not at all. You have to explore multiple levels of scaling, as the body is still the ultimate scaling reference. In this house, we use things like a limited set of radii or angles that reciprocate about a mirror line, techniques that produce geometric coherence even while we hope for complex responses. For me, coherence is really a means to structure unpredictable experiences, as odd as that may sound.

When you are using the word primitive, is it tied to something that is effectively essential and basic and it needs to be readable in a manner that is not obtuse?

The first part is more correct. Some would say that the term primitive implies a certain reductive quality. I wouldn't say that. I would say that our new primitive is not reductive, but it is simple enough to be called primitive. Our primitive seeks to inject vitality into something beyond modernism. For us, allowing the surface to migrate and have different trajectories that are not required to obey discrete modernist rules of regulation is important.

7| When you started the design of the Alan Voo residence, were there global architecturally transcendent themes you were investigating at the beginning of the design process?

In our meetings what was interesting was that the clients essentially reiterated my interests. We were both intrigued with the relationship between a material world outlined by lived necessities, a notion that architecture is a discrete thing in a more ubiquitous world and that for the most part people's lives are lived in a world of ubiquity. We hold this belief primarily because of the new paradigm of electronic access. Twenty-five years ago, we couldn't say it the same way, but today we can. The clients represented a unique set of individuals who were trying to figure out and understand what space represented in two realms. One realm is the immaterial and the other the physical. During the 1990s when many architectural practices leveraged form-making into a stronger cultural discourse, they were attempting to expand the usefulness of design beyond just an avant-garde position. Now architecture had to be something that was not just about shock. I'm speaking for myself, but the general debate centered on how

design could become a conduit for supporting people's lives and experiences versus political positioning.

It's no longer just about the lived world of getting in the car and going to the store. It's getting online or getting connected to another part of the world. What I'm trying to confirm is did they see in your work a representation of the way they imagined the world was going to become or because it had characteristics and relationships to the world as they envisioned it?

I think they wanted to have a new paradigm for what the home is, one which did not have anything to do with home as an enclave or a vessel, or a repository for memories, which is globally what a home is usually envisioned to be. So, it is about identity, refuge and protection. They threw out protection and refuge, as representational interests but wanted identity. So this house was, as our client called it, a brand, a brand product for their family. Their brand was that they are close knit but are also digitally autonomous people. While you were taking photographs of their house one of the daughters called her mother from her bedroom and the other one texted her from her bedroom because they are shy and didn't want to come out while guests were in the house. They use technology to go through the doors as opposed to opening them. They were perfect clients.

The global perception of home and work or home and retail, these worlds are typically thought of as being single entities for primarily one purpose. They wanted the house to feel like it was always and everywhere all of those things at all times. If they are online shopping, they are shopping. If they are watching TV, yes, they are relaxing, but they may be watching a particular type of movie or event or subject that connects them to the outside world. If they are just sitting in the backyard having a drink and listening to the wind rustling through the trees, that's another type of experience. All of them had to come together in this place and in the performance characteristics of the house. That could include the glass, lightness, and blankness. These had to mix with a kind of geometric sensibility allowing them to feel as though they were not at home, not shopping, not in a museum or a cultural institution only, but in a sense at all the institutions linked together simultaneously.

8| What additional organizational, representational, or performance criteria did you employ to anchor the initial intentions?

Precision isn't the morality of the project; the key to the story is that I don't operate in a free fashion. In other words, operating in a free fashion would indicate that there is no moral modernist project. You would be free to do whatever you want. That couldn't be further from the truth. The impression that the project is vital yet liberated is what I want, but back at the office, the process is disciplined.

Every other conversation was about where the project stood in terms of the ideas—digital versus material, the human versus the abstract, cohesiveness and connectedness in a family but a family that will change and mutate in terms of its organization, ubiquity—it was all about that. Those were the themes that interested both of us and really drove the project.

Basically, we go back to the idea that modernism is about employing the Dom-Ino frame where the floor plates and the columns are seen as "structure" and the stairs are seen as "infrastructure." To develop our intentions we began to imagine how infrastructure could vertically change—to integrate with the idea of continuous surfaces. We know that ramps and stairs are what we have to use. Yet instead of expressing stairs and elevators as independent armatures, as infrastructure to the larger systems of the building, we used the continuous surface conceptualization to envision merging pathways, to integrate them optically on the level of the diagonal. The intent was to rethink the idea of the continuous surface not so much as a skin, but to also explore how it could impact the infrastructure, to give the effect that the horizontal and the vertical have been overcome, have been challenged. We play that out graphically as much as we play it out in surface geometry. For instance, the color of the exterior façade continues into the soffit and ceiling of the living room, but only partially so. It runs around the perimeter of the room then dies into the wall, creating a kind of movement to the space. However, that does not happen randomly. Because we use radial transitions between straight lines, there's hardly any curvature that's a multiple compound curve in our work. Everything is usually from radial conditions connecting to straight conditions. There is a lot of flat surface geometry in our work that I like geometrically, but it's also good for construction. The economy in the zones of curvature has to be there, and so as disciplined configurations they need to be working in repetitive numbers. Angles need to mirror and become recursive, not everything is freely configured as we don't want everything to be a haphazard kind of world. We will go back and adjust dimensions to make things work in a recursive or mirror fashion. We employ a limited number of elements in a system. I would not say that goal is similar to an industrial designer's challenge to design a lamp using the fewest number of parts. I'm not trying to get it down to zero, but I am not interested in the machine-derived idea that one line does one thing; therefore, one needs many diverse lines to design a project. Of course components must be employed again and again to be able to be logical, to be constructible.

I am sensing, from a global position, you want the notion of precision to be a part of the existential nature of the project, that it has a sort of reading of precision, not in terms of seeing a Cartesian geometry, or craft for craft's sake, but that one will perceive a sense of refinement, or mystique through a rigorous application of your ideas.

I want to throw it back out there as a kind of moral modernism, moral, in this instance, having to do with rules. Like anything, when you invoke the word moral, you think of the human condition and that its opposite is a sort of immoral project. Of course, there is no immoral project in architecture, but for some there is a "moral" project suggesting that one designs within certain parameters, and if you don't you have a problem. Precision isn't the morality of the project; the key to the story is that I don't operate in a free fashion. In other words, operating in a free fashion would indicate that there is no moral modernist project. You would be free to do whatever you want. That couldn't be further from the truth. The impression that the project is vital yet liberated is what I want, but back at the office, the process is disciplined. That's part of the heart of what your book wants to be about as you are trying to suss out the way in which a sense of order and rigorousness comes into work, one that has the ability to shuck off the limits yet be meaningful.

As modernists, we are not all marching in the same lock-step manner. One can go his or her own way, but there is a rigor and a rational process allowing the project to cohere at a level beyond simple composition.

One of the other corollaries to this is that somebody would say, "Well where is the experiment?" It's all tight. There is not a bad corner in the place. It's worked out. There is no *Red Badge of Courage* or *Scarlet Letter* anywhere, no sense of suffering. Either you couldn't work it out, or you intended some sort of icon for the experiment, to which somebody might say, "Look at that. That's going to leak." Leak means experiment. That's the issue I'm always tying to communicate, that to make a project precise doesn't mean you've given up the experiment.

I would argue that there is a sense of the aspirational nature of the human desire that we respond to. Whether through craft, which is a form of precision, or whether it's through the type of precision we were talking about, which is exuberant and something to be sought after, that, in and of itself is an experiment intended to connect to the human spirit. Those are loftier goals and in those goals there is always something we should be seeking to achieve. In that, there is experimentation.

It's really important to recognize that. It can become problematic to communicate to an audience who might define what experimentation looks like, i.e., it is more failed than successful, experimentation is not tight, it is loose, etc. It would not be experimental if I did the same thing every time. If it were crafted really well, then there would be no experiment. But "rough edges" do not automatically translate into the experimental. I am not interested in polish or slickness. I'm not interested

I'm interested in precision as an element to deliver an argument. It is a lot about how to use precision as a conduit for reading the project, to have an argument played out, which is the experiment.

The association with materials, at least in the old sense, is that they add tactility to the hand, to the touch. I really prefer visual tactility.

The two impressions of the project are important. From the interior of the parent's bedroom, i.e., the pod, with the bed dominating the space, the wood giving it weight, it was less about warmth, as it was about anchoring.

in sheen as an idea of luxury. I'm interested in precision as an element to deliver an argument. There's another story to tell.

It is the relationship of ideas from top to bottom, or maybe from the bottom to the top.
The more we build the more I think we become effective at communicating that. Nobody really reads our work as slick, polished, Foster-esque, high tech, or something like that. It is a lot about how to use precision as a conduit for reading the project, to have an argument played out, which is the experiment. Whether it is an experiment in spatial perception, which a lot of our work is, or whether there are art-practice aspects such as issues of perspective, inclusion, parallax, infinity, and subjects such as that, those are where the experiments are, and I feel if they are not crafted well, we cannot deliver the argument for the experiment.

The experiment is compromised at that point because your reading of the experiment is reduced to being distracted by other conditions that were not part of the intentions.
Anish Kapoor or James Terrell do not go out and build badly. They spend millions of dollars to build something incredibly precise.

16| We, as individuals, do want to be inspired, and we do want to sense that at our best moments we can do something special. That is where we have to be careful about craft, precision, and our choice of materials or what their effect will be over time. Was the representational nature of materials at the Alan-Voo residence important ?
Regarding materials, the fundamental aspect is that the house is built with all the standard building materials: steel, wood, stucco, drywall, and paint. It was not a project which, given where we were and what we wanted to accomplish for this family, was going to be innovative or experimental at the level of construction. We needed to execute it, and we needed to deal with the steel frame. Initially, it was a project about resolving structural issues because the bottom floor had so much glass and we really wanted to maintain that quality. Given that the clients were coming from the graphic world, we wanted to employ basic materials in a way that would give us the greatest amount of effect. We used stucco with a sand finish; you can hardly see any grain at all. From five meters away it almost looks like plastic. The grain of the terrazzo tile, the countertop, and the wood are basically micro grain levels, but they are noticeable relative to the blank abstraction of the drywall and the stucco. As a design intent we wanted those components to be expressive in relation to their being framed by the reveals, and to read the reveals. We wanted the blankness to receive the color enabling the joint between the two colors to be more pronounced, really tight and really graphic.

So the smoothness and the color contrast is a part of the "materiality," but in another sense, its purpose is to accentuate the curvilinear line.
Yes, one might say it is the lack of materiality. The association with materials, at least in the old sense, is that they add tactility to the hand, to the touch. I really prefer visual tactility.

There is no embedded meaning to the material nature of the exterior. It's more the graphic or the follow-through of what the clients are about, or about the nature of ubiquity. It's a universal palate.
I would say the only material condition that the exterior directly references is something that refers to the Neutra project in that all the steel is painted silver. Steel isn't painted white or green. As steel, we could paint it any color we wanted. But using a conventional understanding of a graphic reading of what steel is, you have to paint it silver as it is galvanized, but architecturally you don't leave steel unpainted. If you choose to do that, even more so when you paint it white, the steel components are put into a level of abstraction because they become monochrome and undifferentiated. However, in this project steel needed to be silver. I'm not sure that that's the office credo for every project, but I would not paint steel green or red, but it may be white in the future.

On one of the columns we have an anodized aluminum infill with exposed fasteners. We wanted all the assembly to look similar. Additionally the framing and the jambs for the sliding glass doors are all aluminum. They all represent a metallic world.

It represents a connective tissue to the machined, refined, techno-primitive scenario, whether it is structure or whether it's the frame at the windows allowing glass to connect to stucco.
It's definitely about hardware. Some people have given me a hard time about that. They say, "You need to get rid of that; that's your old self. That's your modernist reference self. You should be pursuing something much more singular than that." In that sense I haven't over-thought it and determined whether they are right or wrong.

9| Beyond architecturally transcendent issues what organizational or representational intentions arising from an analysis of the site and program were

employed to organize and ultimately express your conceptual interests?
In the Alan-Voo Residence we had to double the square footage of the house from 1,000 to 2,000 square feet. After analyzing that from a financial point of view, we knew that we couldn't afford to double the square footage by tearing the house down. We started with the idea of adding to the front, yet the option of building a second story on top of the existing house wasn't spatially interesting. Later it became pretty obvious we would have to put the footprint of the new addition in back of the existing house.

There is an 80-year-old coral tree from which the addition would have to be set back. That determined the footprint for how the house would be deployed on the site and set the "zoning" envelope from which we worked, from which a third was defined by the city, a third by the tree, and a third by the budget.

In all projects, you excavate where the opportunities are. You maximize those opportunities to the point where no one feels as though the building has been unduly governed in a repressive manner, such as conforming to zoning criteria. Of course, that's not strictly a trick. It is saying you can't let the building completely design itself out of constraints. They simply articulate a field. Here's my field, and now I pursue my experiment within that field. If the field is narrow or broad, that's what it is. That's standard practice.

Meanwhile while we were carrying on a strong conceptual conversation, we were having a conversation about color, atmosphere, etc., relative to what the interior environment would be and moving to the point where they would say, "We don't want any art on the walls." In the interior, they wanted a monochromatic house rather than a polychromatic house. Those considerations were running parallel as they were not present in the diagrammatic schemes.

From the beginning, they were very tuned in to the representational nature of these kinds of decisions.
Super tuned in, very articulate, really smart. They "got it" on every level.

It appears that the clients, and therefore the project was almost, from the beginning, very much about these larger representational issues, the meaningfulness of what could be. It had little to do with size and square footage and those kind of pragmatics.
That conversation was about the first two days. They trusted me to deliver the pragmatics of the project. Every other conversation was about where the project stood in terms of the ideas that you and I have already discussed—digital versus material, the human versus the abstract, cohesiveness and connectedness in a family—but a family that will change and mutate in terms of its organization. The issue of ubiquity; it was all about that. Those were the themes that interested both of us and really drove the project.

10| How did you add additional depth to your initial intentions? I would like to discuss two examples. We were talking about the reveal, the planar surface condition and layering aspects of the material conditions. Those are the kind of issues that were not conceived earlier in the design. Similarly, under how you add conceptual depth to initial design intentions, I am interested in the entry transition. When

I believe a building works the best when it conventionally works well, but in addition I am interested in the building working on all sorts of other levels. Those levels, as they pile up, that's when the building works really, really well. ...I think the representational and organizational conceptual realms are deeply intertwined and that one doesn't follow the other in some linear manner.

We wanted to deliver that level of splitting hairs between the engineered grain of counter material and the grain of the terrazzo which has references to found conditions in nature but is too uniform. It's too industrialized and that splitting the difference between the human, the natural, and the artificial reflects the whole ambition of the house.

you come into the house, you immediately enter this abstract world of whiteness and it starts immediately on with the living room floor.

After we resolved the siting strategy, and the strategy for where the volume was to be placed, the issue of the landscape as a horizontal device arose and whether it moved in underneath the addition or into the ground floor plan. That pushed the bedroom up in the air rather than into the garden. An early iteration did explore having the parent's bedroom down, which permitted access to the garden from their bedroom door with the public space lifted above it. We finally realized that inverting it was better. In that sense it is more traditional in that public space in California is typically connected to the exterior and the private space will try to capture the view.

On the ground floor, you wanted that plane to have minimal distinction between inside and outside?

Not only on a literal level, as the patio does extend out a few feet, but we were also interested in the volume of the garden vs. the ground plane. If the project was about a levitated mass, we wanted to have an opposing, yet simultaneous agenda. The first was to make the mass buoyant by pushing the supporting structure back into the volume and let the ground plane enter in. We made the volume relatively dramatic in terms of the profile so that your eye picks it up. This was not about a heavy thing over a light thing; it was simply about surface opacity over surface transparency. By the time we carved out the big window and painted the two relatively light green and blue colors, there was a sense of lifting off. Contrasting this on the inside, we wanted to balance that. That is where the idea of gravity entered in.

The two impressions of the project are important. From the interior of the parent's bedroom, the pod, with the bed dominating the space and the wood floor giving it weight, was less about warmth as it was about anchoring. We used a dark bamboo floor as a grain but mostly as a tone to work in counter-distinction to the buoyant floating and elevated aspect of the addition. Like a refrigerator there is a program on the inside and a program on the outside. In that sense while the lower volume is deeply connected to the idea of transparency, the upper bedroom volume became what they called a pod—it was insular. That's why we wanted to give it a certain weight, so it would feel anchored.

To give the pod a certain identity, were the material considerations, both in terms of adding a sense of gravity and as a counterpoint to the whiteness and abstractness of the terrazzo floor, part of using the materials conceptually versus functionally?

Yes, the theme continues when you move into the bathroom. It has a green glass tile floor. Your foot doesn't quite feel like it is hitting a surface because optically you see depth. We wanted to make the space very aquatic and different than the weight and gravity of the bedroom, a different program altogether.

You are using materials to define different experiential or representational qualities of the independent spaces. The wood floor anchors and gives gravity to the bedroom. When you move to the bathroom, a different kind of "float" or lightness is reasserted.

The materials are used in both logical and conceptual approaches. We ultimately wanted the feeling to be between the aqueous nature of the sky and water represented in their blueness and greenness. That color world becomes ambiguous—it doesn't refer to

In the 1990s when we started working with this surface idea in an attempt to innovate, we tried to forget about conventional notions of column and beam.

terra firma, it refers to the liquid and the atmospheric. Meanwhile, wood, which is terra firma, represents the gravity of the interior world.

Let's talk about the living room and the kitchen; we were referencing the texture of the terrazzo tile and that of the counter. Tell me your thoughts regarding the added conceptual depth that these material issues brought to the project.
Let's start with the terrazzo which we know from the 1940s through its use in public buildings and in more conventional structures such as drugstores. What has been the continuing interest in that material is the idea that, again, a bit like the wood you have a sense of weight and gravity. I look at it as easy to maintain, yet the surface qualities, because you can pour it, align with an injection molded technological world but connect to terra firma in the expression of the aggregate. We couldn't afford poured terrazzo floor for the living room so we found A terrazzo tile. The FLOOR is a gridded tile version of the intention to use terrazzo.

The intention was to give the material an earth bound connectivity but also of a high tech sense?
The connection between the countertop and terrazzo, as old school as terrazzo is, was more of an engineering aesthetic than say, cutting a slab of stone. The counter material is also cast, cropped, engineered, and articulated. It's like gypsum wallboard. It's a wet material that goes through an industrial process to make it a dry material system. It is the same thing with terrazzo tiles. It's a wet material that arrives to you as a dry fitted system. This generated a consistency between the two materials that we felt was more appropriate than cutting stone. We wanted to deliver that level of splitting hairs between the engineered grain of the counter

The idea of being able to display structure a bit more so that you can rename and rethink when and how you will use surface versus line is an outgrowth of our investigations.

material and the grain of the terrazzo used on the floor. That splitting the difference between the human, the natural, and the artificial reflects the whole ambition of the house.

I am going to refer this relationship back to your larger interest in ubiquity in the sense that terrazzo is a common material, and it is distributed throughout the floor as a continuous surface. As you incorporate it into the counter it maintains that spirit but with a subtle grain difference.
We didn't use the tile in the lower floor; we just used the concrete slab as it is. In some ways, including the glass tile of the bathroom floor, there are four materials, five if you include the paint on the stairs, but the whole project was intended to feel coherent in the sense of continuous surfaces while allowing for the differences we spoke about earlier.

There is a nice migration from concrete on the lowest floor, being closest to the solidity of the ground, to the similarity of the terrazzo tile at the living room floor, and then the counter, being an elevated version of that and finally the glass tiles at the bathroom floor being a further elevation and separation from the earth. There is a progression from grounded and more organic to industrialized and ethereal.
Nothing is really perverse about the use of the materials. There is not a standard underlying logic. I'm interested in those forms of convention, especially when they create transcendent effects.

11| I am going to spin your clients in on this. Did you name or prioritize elements or programmatic areas to differentiate or give hierarchy to the larger global intentions? The clients called the bedroom the "pod," and the stairwell the "sky space." As a part of your design process, do you tend to do that?
Probably not. Referring to the kitchen, we didn't name it anything. We knew that the kitchen would be a gathering space because it was literally at the intersection between the girls' rooms and the public spaces. In many ways, it probably represents the physical port where they gather and hang out as it is the in-between space. Even though they don't cook frequently, they wanted an amazing kitchen to add to the themes of the house, somewhat as an icon. It feels like the moment where design at all scales came together. It is more of a piazza than the lower space. The lower space is a destination. The kitchen is a hub but we did not name it or use the idea of a hub to direct the design.

12| As the design developed, did you use the attributes of the organizational and representational conceptual fields to mature or cross-reference each other?
I think you are talking about the relationship between a Meier example...where there is a faith between a relationship of a building grid, material modules, aligned relationships of elements, and there is a deep underlying rational logic. That rationality builds in terms of how the components work, how they respond to program and how they are going to reach an intended apex of being uniform but also allowing for a process that makes the most out of rational relationships.

We definitely don't start with a technique that will allow us to get to that type of resolution. I have the same interest, which is, I believe, a building works the best when it conventionally works well, but in addition I am interested in the building working on all sorts of other levels. Those levels, as they pile up, that's when the building works really, really well. For example, if something is thinner because the material choice allows you to take away dead weight, or you can perforate something as it adds an engineered rigor, you know there is a moment where it works. I think the representational and organizational conceptual realms are deeply intertwined and that one doesn't follow the other in some linear manner. There's definitely not a procedure for working through organizational and representational issues that we employ every time. For example, here's the site, now let's put a grid on the site just to see what we are talking about. I don't start that way.

Let's return to a conversation we had earlier when you were referencing the structure being revealed and concealed, or terms similar to that. Describe structure in the Alan-Voo Residence as representing something not part of a classic modernist approach.
I think in the 1990s when we started working with this surface idea in an attempt to innovate, we tried to forget about conventional notions of column and beam, to forget about that as a canonical device. You know, in modernism columns mark space. They mark repetitive fields; they mark the intersection between occupation and the work of structure itself. To be able to get beyond that was to forget about, to overcome, to displace, to marginalize the sensibility of how structure and space come together. We started thinking about opaque surfaces as having some fantasy of being structure and skin all at the same time. It was more about double hulled construction and monocoque construction and getting rigidity out of curvature as opposed to weakness out of curvature. That displaced the idea of an independent columnar structure in a number of projects we worked on. We would take the surface and fold it down so we could get vertical structure out of it.

In relation to the conceptual use of color we went through months discussing intentions regarding levels of artificiality, levels of reference to the printed world, the commercial world, the aquatic world, etc.

We did not change the material that we WERE using; we did not suddenly go from a plate to a vector.

That allowed the columns to go beyond a singular expression of structure. The V columns certainly are part of the design and their geometry relates to the geometry in the elevations. Would it be correct to say that in some way this returns us to a global intention concerning the ubiquity of things? Why is one to have separate intentions expressing individual ideas stating "Here's my structural grid, here's my circulation system as unique expressions." What you're implying is that all of the warp and woof or the yin and yang of things is being bound together through intentions blurring the idea that there are certain standards we are to maintain when it comes to modernism, whether it comes to structure, with materials or similar manifestations.
Absolutely, it was an idea that things weren't so discrete, the idea of the envelope, the partition, the floor plate, etc,. could all become renamed or rethought: the ramp, the stair, the envelope, the perimeter, the infrastructure. All of these things could find a different set of relationships. The critique of the modern project derived from its analogous relationship to the machine, and as a machine, one part does only one thing. In our investigations, components were rethought as gelatinous where a surface could perform as a ramp, a platform, a partition, as a roof, etc. The evolution of the work continued. This goes back to what I was saying before; we do not start with an a posteriori idea of structure. Therefore, formally, in our projects there is a deep relationship between expressed structure but not in a sense of expressionism, which might be conventional. We might have embedded structure as a part of a continuous surface. For example, in the High Line 23

project in New York City we have intumescent paint on the structure inside. It's not wrapped with any drywall. We aren't trying to mushroom it or trying to hide it—it is expressed for what it is. At the same time, there's a lot of structure that is in the perimeter walls that you never see. It's a total hybridization between deep abstraction of surfaces and seeing the structural vectors of the project.

It is interesting in that regard that the issues of hybridization and ubiquity link back to the digital transformation of so many things. Whether of images, sound, or construction there is logic implying that conventions, such as structure, can be freed from a single purpose or a single reading. Ubiquity, continuous surfaces, structure, encoded with multiple roles, etc.,—all suggest different interpretations than the ones we are familiar with in terms of traditional modernism.

Early modernism didn't allow much variety or differentiation. The idea of expressing structure a bit more so that you can rename and rethink when and how you will use surface versus line is an outgrowth of our investigations. In modernism, the points are all structural devices and the lines are all free. Those were the tenets. Now, we will just as soon have a load-bearing wall as we would have a point-loaded structure, because I don't adhere to the tenets of that early modernism. I am not alone in that.

The evolution of the design tenets defined in the early Renaissance to their overcoming in the Baroque occurred in the span of hundreds of years. If early modernism equates to the Renaissance we are now in a baroque phase. The rules set up in the Renaissance took 300 years of adjusting to allow Borromini to curve the stone with little regard for structural considerations. In some ways, we are dealing with similar conditions in our rethinking of modernism.

I agree. I look at contemporary architecture as a compression of history. Through the 1990s when computerization started influencing design directions, and in 2000 with the commissions for the Seattle Public Library, the Bird Nest in Beijing, and other mega projects, it was a bit like, "Let's see what can we do now." I make the argument that from the late '90s up until the crash in 2008 it was a "just do it" time period. In other words, let's build these buildings because we have new tools, robots, digital fabrication, and so forth. Let's just consider various approaches, build them, and let the dust settle. Then we can analyze what we approaches measure up. I called that the Nike Period.

I always wanted, as they did, to have conversations that were probing through cultural history and references, rather than simple taste or instance. Nothing is ever relegated to simple taste in the project. We vetted it on a cultural level.

The interesting thing is that in the wake of the economic crisis the work is seen as, "Well that was a giant experiment in excess, and we will will not see that again because we have sobered up." For me this more or less says you are going to have the economy dictate your aspirations. I understand it dictates what you can and cannot do, but economics was never anything that I understood to say, "We have a depressed world, I think I'll change my ambition as an architect as I have become a depressed architect, and I'll give up desire." That will be a mistake if we don't find the life and vitality emanating from these projects in which a lot of money and creativity was invested. They won't be repeated in that way again. The whole nature of spectacle is constantly morphing. It's always there yet it is constantly morphing. There will be new versions and new forms.

13| Regarding ideas that are more representational in nature such as the projects you just referenced, how do you explore the organizational potential of these ideas? Did you envision the manner in which the Alan—Voo Residence was organized as representational in nature? How are you employing the possibility of organizational strategies that are not just a grid upon which elements are placed? Does this facilitate additional modes of representation?
We wanted the house to be more of an emergent thing rather than a plugged-on project. Because plugging on is, as stated earlier, a reference to one thing accomplishing one thing. We wanted the addition to be launched out of the house even though on the courtyard side it looks just attached to the existing house. This will be modified in the second phase as the continuous surface will turn and move around the entire project. It's going to be its own morphology. Its emergent qualities will be even more clear and logical. It became clear that it was best that we not be collage artists or an "incisionist" employing those as avant-garde techniques. We wanted a certain degree of alignment and seamlessness although the addition has nothing to do with the architectural nature of the existing house.

15| As the design progresses, how do you link the more ephemeral or poetic intentions of your design to the pragmatic, functional and performance concerns? While it took six months to come up with the different site strategies, it took two days to get the program clear as to the clients' needs. As the design progressed, what framed the debate? Would you say because of the nature of the project you were primarily focusing on poetic expressions?
The issue of color will articulate this. On the exterior, unlike the interior, the clients were happy to entertain color. The articulation of the reveal between the windows and the stucco panels emerged and implied that the surface could be, with joints, organized in many ways, that it could possibly be a tri-color surface. It could be anything. There was always an instinct that color would be integrated into the design. The clients were not uninterested in color; they just felt like they wanted to look at it when they wanted to look at it, but not all the time as in the interior. In relation to the conceptual use of color, we went through months discussing intentions regarding levels of artificiality, levels of reference to the printed world, the commercial world, the aquatic world, etc.

The clients wanted something Zen-like. So, we migrated the colors close to each other. The sensibility of reflecting the sky and the garden emerged as the most obvious conditions to naturalize the house in its setting. Every color study came with a discussion that was always prefaced with, "I do or do not instinctively like these colors, but even if we don't like it instinctively, let's sit down and talk about it." I always wanted, as they did, to have conversations that were probing through cultural history and references, rather than simple taste or instance. Nothing is ever relegated to simple taste in the project. We vetted it on a cultural level.

This house represented connectivity to their spirit, to their values or ethos. It returns us to how these were representational considerations to the clients and are examples of a series of decisions exploring a poetic dimension of the house at the most subjective or personal level.

10.1| Moving forward in time design-wise the house is essentially designed. We are now looking at the final refining aspects, and I would like to return to the use of design intentions that are adding depth or range to your initial intentions.
We can cite the engineer here. The ergonomics of the space, which is not big, entered in. The space is very compressed in section, and figuring out how to make the space workable, the distance between the stair and the first V column had to be comfortable enough so that you did not feel you would run into it. We couldn't get away from it. We explored this very thoroughly in the digital model.

We could have asked the engineer to design a vertical and diagonal to make half of a K brace. One would get off the stair, and there would be nothing to encumber you. You walk right into the space. That might have been logical though it would have challenged the other half

A surface is a surface, and it will be painted, and it will be abstract. My interests were all about graphic and atmospheric qualities representing the primary intentions of the projects. I like that there is a new space to explore somewhere between flatness, depth, materiality, something like a 2.5-D world or post material world, like 3.5-D.

of the space. A better logic was to locate the column in the middle of the space but not have it become an obstinate device. That is where the V column entered in. It was envisioned as part of the underlying vector system while permitting additional functional options. You can walk through it, you can place a table in between it. Even if those are only thought of as ergonomic performance considerations representing significant design factors determining how it should work, there was the additional architectural consideration. In that sense, the V column solution represents the apex of many factors worked out on many levels.

16.1| Even though we earlier discussed the more sublime material representations in the project, there is a side of your work where materials are secondary to larger spatial or even global intentions. I would like to return to the question on materiality and its role. Did you envision the materials to be expressive regarding their embedded nature? When did the notion of material intentionality, or diminishing of material representation, become important in the Alan-Voo Residence?

It starts at the very beginning because, even before I built anything, materials, per se, as expressive components were less interesting to me. There was steel, aluminum, drywall and ordinary things; the early obsession was never about surface tactility. It was about tectonics. Those were the materials you make a tectonic project out of. My investigations weren't with any exotic materials or considering them.

If you studied at Cooper Union, you might be drawing a leather wall meeting gravel. In other words direct material considerations. I was never that way, I was always interested in the robustness of tectonics. I thought of

My cultural goal is to not raise the level of form making to a frenzy, but to try to see if there are ways in which the techniques for which lives are being experienced, i.e. in the two dimensional world, could the find their way into architecture.

Formally, the project was about lines, edges, and profiles.

the material world as directly connected to the industrial world. In the Alan Voo residence we wanted it to appear as one material, yet we could not build it out of one substrate. We built it out of three substrates. We wanted, in the end, the graphic encoding to be the primary expression. We didn't want anyone to know the materials. In a sense that is a follow-through from the clients but also from us. A surface is a surface, and it will be painted, and it will be abstract. A little bit different than, let's say, the way Frank Gehry approaches his work. For him, wood is wood, metal is metal, drywall is white, so you paint it white, sheet metal is sheet metal, corrugated is corrugated, galvanized is galvanized and that is what you build buildings out of. That's his level of modernist honesty. In that sense, it is a very materialist approach. I have never really thought of architecture that way.

Because I started my career working in interiors where one is not dealing with waterproofing and building envelope related issues, my interests were all about graphic and atmospheric qualities representing the primary intentions of the projects. The irony in our projects is that everybody wants to touch everything because it is so smooth. You want to touch it because you don't see any imperfections. There is no grain. There is no bumpiness. There is no emboss. It is like a skin. It is an interesting sensibility to achieve because everybody wants to have tactility out of nothingness. There's a body aspect to it. These interests lie at the heart of a tense and very complex spatial, even cognitive relationship between flatness and depth, or our perception of the world through media versus the haptic nature of the material world. Most architects deal with this issue, but with much less instrumentally than I do. I like that there is a new space to explore somewhere between flatness, depth, materiality, something like a 2.5-D world or post material world, like 3.5-D.

I like using the word sublime. It reminds me of Louis Barrigan saying that we need more quiet architecture. Not that yours is quiet, but on some level it is sublime.

I always say that I am a soundtrack composer rather than a rock star, a really good sound track composer, not a boring one. I try to make the work atmospheric. I relate to Brian Eno who makes worlds using music. They don't jump in your face, but they are super memorable and powerful at the same time. I think that our work is analogous to that.

17| How did you conceptualize the organization of the joint between materials in the Alan-Voo Residence and relate it to early intentions?

The aluminum drip edge extrusion is totally functional. We wanted to employ it in a different way than most California architects do, those who take advantage of the fact that there isn't much rain in California. The ¾" depth of the extrusion allows the surface to read as a laminate, a very extruded laminate. The panels relate to the idea of stop action photography, in that you can read it like a series of panels. This promotes the idea that the surface has its own performance characteristics, its own thickness, and its own sense of flatness. This allows the soffit to visually connect to the ceiling inside producing a relationship between flatness and depth, between an apparent mass and an apparent sensibility of thinness of the two-dimensional. They collaborate together and they are not working at cross-purposes. It is then our moment to experiment with the way in which architecture is clarified and is absolutely serious about being a spatial device and not trying to play out illusionistic effects that are cheap or inauthentic. I think there is a deep level of authenticity to the world we live in relative to the nature of the two-dimensional. It would be wrong to moralize against that world. Architecture is like a protection device, the guardian of the real. I'm not the guardian of the real. Let other discourses interact and affect it, yet this represents our early experiments with depth vs. flatness.

I posit that most lives, in their conscious sense, operate in the world of the two-dimensional. Architecture is seldom so obvious to a layperson that it is noticeable. You have to get to the level of spectacle as an attention-getting device to make someone aware of architecture. Otherwise, it is all just infill in a city in which 99% of our buildings derive from a repetitive, standardized system making it is hard to differentiate anything. For the most part the idea of architecture is that it is just there and it operates as a servicing device. What has become more memorable for people are conversations with others and more specifically, and relatively recently, technology based information and interface. It could be a movie, a TV show, a film, a poster, even the words on the page of a book, a magazine, a textbook, or a website.

You can see through that the topics of the two-dimensional, the joint and how they relate to broader themes. Now we work and play in the immaterial world without using architecture to compensate or overcompensate for the fact that it is nothing more than a background feature. What can we do? My cultural goal is to not raise the level of form-making to a frenzy, but to see if there are methods in which the techniques for which lives are being experienced in the two-dimensional world, could the find their way into architecture. When information

My desire is for architecture to be more engaged and noticeable, purposeful. How can architecture perform, generate comfort, but also awaken the senses in a way other than just being a private and poetic language,

is retained, life is experienced; it is the dominance of the digital world. This is post cinematic. This is everyday life and everyday occurrence happening at an earlier and earlier age. Architecture shouldn't be relegated to some heavy necessity to keep the rain out, and then one pays a surplus for design. It relegates architects with certain kinds of ambitions to work only for the richest, the most educated or the most discerning. The reality is that's what we do. My desire is for architecture to be more engaged and noticeable, purposeful. It is hard to add real hard-core information to architecture, like how it really works, because that is all supplemented by technology, infrastructure, furniture, automobiles, hand held devices, all things that are mass produced and disposable, whereas buildings are not supposed to be that.

So, that's been my curiosity over the last ten years. How can architecture perform, generate comfort, but also awaken the senses in a way other than just being a private and poetic language, as in you either like that artist's work or you don't. I'd like for our work to do more than that. In the High Line building although it's a private world, it's right on the High Line. It's going to be a dramatically public building at the object level. Thousands of people are going to see this thing, and they are going to see it from a unique frontal viewpoint, not obliquely. That helps my two-dimensional-based argument. It will be interesting to hear the feedback.

In a residence, mechanical systems are not often overtly expressed. What was your thinking regarding the expression or lack thereof of the systems in the Alan-Voo Residence? What organizational or representational strategies were contemplated?

They appear, in some ways, in the pouche' of the walls. The walls accommodate the ductwork in a way that creates some offsets and things that don't align at certain places.

You wanted, or you were forced to accommodate, the offsets?

We were forced to accommodate. By their own insistence, they are sort of there at one level. This is a house for which systems are not extensive.

18| In refining the design, did you select areas, programmatic or architectural elements, to privilege? If so, how were the privileging concepts expansions or counter points to earlier conceptual intensions? Everything in the house is pretty tightly banded together. The stair, though, is not a single monolithic element. Was there a different design intention or strategy for the stair suggesting different intentions such as ideas concerned with or expressing assembly or thinness? The stair is different.

It's good you point that out. There is a story about that. My first instinct was, "Yeah, it is going to be dry wall with a solid balustrade and a soffit etc." One day the project architect drew the stairs as these floating planes and I mentioned we at least need a stringer, not because of structure, but because I wanted the diagonal line as formally, the project was about lines, edges, and profiles. We were not getting that out of a series of staggered planes. It didn't resonate. That was my instinct. I just left it alone and came back to it. We all sat down, and I said, we should pursue the levitating stair for the main reason that it needed to be dematerialized. I wanted it to go away. No stringer, no guardrail, no infill on the riser, it turns out it was the right decision because the space is too small to place something more massive in it. That became very clear for me. The sky space would have been too encumbered by loading it up with a mass. It works perfectly by being more minimal.

I think back to the *Gyroscopic Horizons* book and there seems to be a secondary narrative. In many projects represented in the book once the continuity of the shell is established, there is an articulated tectonic contained within. In some ways, it does follow through on that, even if it wasn't the initial thought.

That is part of my history—that point is an on-going transition. I think my particular agenda is very far from that at this point. Building itself has offered lessons in what generates the greatest amount of experiential effect. Before I was interested in the decorative effects of tectonics vis-à-vis modernism, deployed in an ironic non-functional way. For example, the reglets are not painted. We leave them anodized aluminum because it is still one of my favorite finishes. Those almost become like a surrogate for all of my interest in tectonics. I go to great lengths to make my fasteners go away. I'm less and less interested in all that tectonic expression. If it comes up, it comes up. I always demand flush fasteners, no Phillips-head, only allen-heads. That retains the energy, the aspect of assembly.

That is one of those organizational and/or representational interactions. It is both organizational in that you are saying everything needs to be organized flush, and yet embedded in that is the representation of the continuity of the surface expressing broader, more representational explorations. It's a useful combination.

Well, as I said, I hope the process leads to awakening senses. ■

TEN

Enrique Norten

National School of Theater

Located in Mexico City, the National School of Theater was a part of a politically influenced effort to construct buildings in a very short period of time, establishing a new civic presence for the school. Design commenced in 1993 and construction was completed in 1994. The building provided a new home for the School of Theater and tested the limits of a design-build process in which multiple design decisions were made during construction. The program includes practice dance rooms, two theaters, one being a black box, a library and classrooms. In honoring a previous custom and necessity to conduct rehearsals outdoors, a large curved canopy defining extensive covered exterior space maintains that tradition while simultaneously creating a larger civic presence.

Buildings often address multiple scalar issues. The National School of Theater provides clear documentation of the use of design intentions addressing this issue, both functionally and symbolically. Building on a necessary and long-established use of exterior space, the theater re-establishes the concept of outdoor performance through a re-interpretation allowing the creation of multiple exterior spaces that include a major plaza along with smaller gathering destinations on the roofs of programmed areas, all remaining protected from wind, rain and sun by the overhead canopy. Simultaneously the canopy provides an armature for establishing a civic presence beyond the scope of the program. The change in scale affords architectural opportunities to explore numerous scalar readings of the building. While an adjacent freeway permits glimpses from passing automobiles, outdoor performance spaces and a diverse set of architectural "events" under the curved canopy provide more intimate experiences. Multiple sensory encounters at different paces and scales, some fleeting some intimate, are achieved.

The meaning of every project is about building up a complexity and complexity is all about gathering and organizing information.

Architecture is about a setting up or inventing certain types of order and it is in those moments of invention where you start defining the multiple types of order required.

1| Tom Diehl: As you start the design of a project, do you have ordering or organizing themes, broad interests you are drawn to for which the project might become a vehicle, or are there project specific issues?

Enrique Norten: It is very project specific. It varies and changes from project to project. As we all know, architecture is quite complex. The meaning of every project is about building up a complexity, and complexity is all about gathering and organizing information. Every one of us processes information in a different way—which leads you to a program that in turn leads you to form and space. I believe initially we begin to put together information—organizing it in a manner that sets up different planes of information. For example, one could be learning about the physical site, about cultural issues, or you may be learning about necessities of the client, the community, or whomever has the responsibility for the project. That is another plane of information. You start to continuously gather all that information That is where the project starts, which is way before you sit with a piece of paper waiting to take pencil in hand.

You would say most of your initial thoughts are about processing multiple or different planes of information that you are receiving, whether from an initial site visit or from a client brief...

Yes, it's true, but not totally passive because it is part of your creative process. So one is being selective about the information, organizing it in different manners. When you start relating the information through different schematic approaches, you create different intentions regarding what the project will become architecturally.

6| So in that regard what are your initial concerns? What I mean by that is...obviously an initial concern could be to fit the project onto the site or to accommodate the

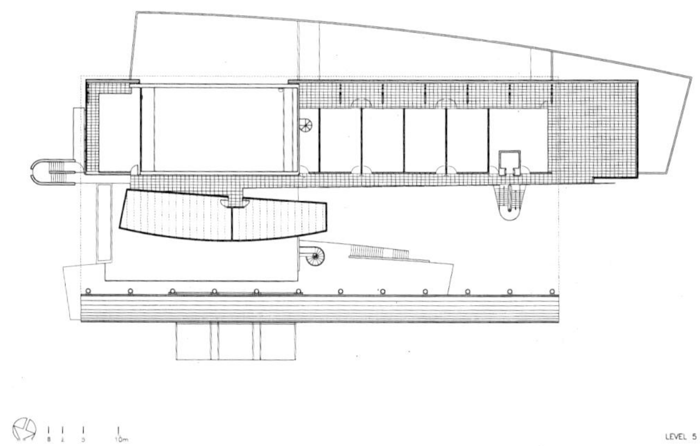

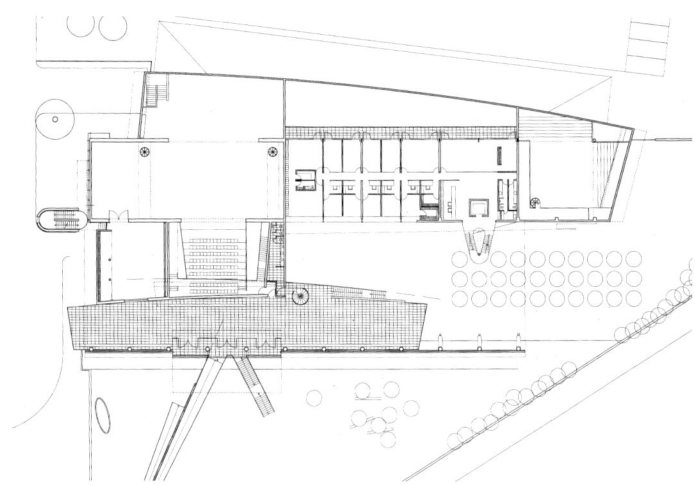

Floor levels 2, 5, plans

parking...but in terms of what you were just describing, in the sense that there are multiple intentions, when does the architectural sense of those concerns appear?

It is always architecture. I don't think architectural considerations start the moment you put the first line on paper. It is before that because you are trying to understand what kind of information you need, and what to do with the information. You are already making architectural decisions. Architecture is about setting up certain types of order and it is in those moments of invention where you start defining the multiple types of order required. I'm sure that If you investigate my use of information and compare it to somebody else's, it will be very different.

4| In relation to the concept of order, what interests guide your thinking beyond those concerned with the program and the site? Does a sense of what order might mean months down the road become one of those concerns?

It is not totally conscious, but it is a concern. One is setting up certain conditions and certain parameters for a project, and they are not always clear. They vary with each project, and issues concerning form, shape, and space may pop up very early in the process and sometimes they don't.

Do you believe that in your conceptualization of a project there is a concern for a particular order or organization that might define a certain representational interest in that you might want the building to "express purity" or be "rhythmic" or something similar? Every architect might bring with him or her that concern, yet in your sense would you say, "Yes, I am processing information, but I'm also considering that I want this 'bar', or this 'module' or this 'arc'. I can see that as an order-giving response to the site." Would that be fair to say?

Sometimes concerns of order or form pop up very early—sort of like a clear impulse to follow.

If not, would you say a desire to establish an order is always there? Do you want to find that?

Yes, I want to find that order but, and this is very typical, at the beginning I do not know what that order is; it comes from the exploration.

Are concerns of order, to the extent that they are part of initial design interests, more often of an organizational or representational nature or of some other nature? Would you say that this order is questioned,

We worked very hard to keep the shell as thin as possible. We wanted it very thin, very light. By no means could it have huge beams or anything similar. Why? Because in the thinness is where the poetry lies.

We had to design and construct a building with a civic presence way beyond its program. ...the building was "enlarged" with voids, un-programmed space, not programmed area, representing more than half of the building's volume.

I want to find that order but, and this is very typical, at the beginning I do not know what that order is; it comes from the exploration.

I don't think that figurative or representative conditions become so clear, not at the beginning. The expression of a design intention and then you have to make it happen, the ordering systems are inventions, not preconceptions. We start with information and the order derives from that.

There was an intention that was quite clear. The big canopy was, as I said, of the urban scale, the scale of the moving automobile. But once you come closer, we wanted a different scale, a smaller scale. We wanted to bring additional articulated interest to the arrival sequence and to the definition of the exterior lobby space.

That was an additional design intention as we wanted to express all of the components of the project, to give them their own personality. We thought there was an opportunity given the diverse nature of the program. Once we had made the unifying gesture with the canopy there was space for the growth, development, and expression of individual pieces and elements.

analyzed, or searched for in the sense of "What am I trying to represent with this order?" As your design progresses and moves forward are your concerns for order more organizational or more representational?

It is both. I don't think that figurative or representative conditions become so clear, not at the beginning. There comes a moment where, yes, we become very committed to the expression of a design intention and then you have to make it happen. The ordering systems are inventions, not preconceptions. We start with information and the order derives from that.

7| In the design of the National School of Theater, were there global architecturally transcendent themes you were interested in at the beginning of the design process, or conversely what interests arose once you started your investigation?

As it's been a few years and as the design process is never linear that is a difficult question. This project was constructed in 1994 and was a very politically driven project. It was a project that had to be built very fast and there was a very limited budget. So...I don't know if that's where we started, but it was definitely a driving force. We had to design and construct a building needing to have a civic presence way beyond its program.

So there were cultural or political aspirations beyond the building's program that were intertwined in the project's "brief" suggesting it be a noteworthy building?

It was part of a collection of projects that were all being constructed simultaneously. The whole complex was built in a year, everything. It was the last year of President Salinas de Gorti's administration. The political pressures were huge, and the pressures on us were huge. Another concern was the site for our building was the most awkward area of the entire complex. In addition to being between two major roads, it was totally inaccessible. Our initial decisions were governed by the reality that this was the one piece of the entire complex located at an intersection. In addition, the only way to see the project was from a car or an elevated portion of the subway, but not as a pedestrian. Nevertheless, when you are moving through the city, the site is "iconic," so we felt a solution was required that was abstract enough to be perceived while moving in a car. If the building was too complex, you would simply overlook it in the complexity of the city. We wanted to create a big, bold statement that one could just "get." But we had no budget.

We had an additional, yet related, problem in that the School of Theater had a smaller program than the other

There are not common materials; there are not rich materials. It's not about that, there are different materials you can use for either purely expressive reasons or because there are materials for a particular application.

We used the studios and the classrooms, the more commonplace programmatic elements to create a backdrop "wall" to further define the space.

buildings, and we did not want the building to seem smaller than the others in the complex. Similarly, the people in the theater community were expecting to have a similar presence in relation to the other buildings in the complex. To accomplish that the building was "enlarged" with voids, un-programmed space, not programmed area, representing more than half of the building's volume. The programmed space comprises a very simple building, very structurally rational, very buildable, very inexpensive and efficient. Those concerns were an issue.

So the mere fact that the construction aspects of the building had to be relatively straightforward was a critical factor. Let me try to reframe that a bit. I noticed when viewing the building plans that the studio spaces on Level 2 are square and then on Levels 3 and 4 above the square is divided in half. Was that a preference for clear geometric expressions, or was the square geometry simply an outcome of the functional needs of the programmed spaces? Is there another aspect not grounded by economics? Does it reflect a desire for the clarity achieved through a clear organizational system?
Part of it is that. The other part is programmatic as the program came out of two considerations. One was the size we needed for the theater space and the studios, which were effectively big lofts, close to being a cube. That geometry was almost programmed in. The second issue was that I started spending some time at the previous School of Theater. The teachers had classrooms, but they spent a lot of time outside because the school was near a park. The students and teachers created their exercises, improvisations and so on in the little square near the school. That's where the concept about creating exterior, un-programmed space originated. We realized we could give them performance platforms on the roofs of the programmed spaces. This was an environmental decision. The exterior spaces created were protected by the canopy from the wind, the rain, and the sun without having to be conditioned. We saw it as an opportunity. We noticed that it was not going to be possible to keep the students inside, in their black box theater. Additionally, we noticed a lack of climactic response in their theater. If the sun became very strong, the rooms became very warm and half of the year it rains, so they were unable to practice in their invented exterior performance spaces.

9| I would like to move a little further into the use of additional conceptual interests.
Were there transcendent issues or representational intentions arising from an analysis of the site, the program, or emanating from outside the domain of

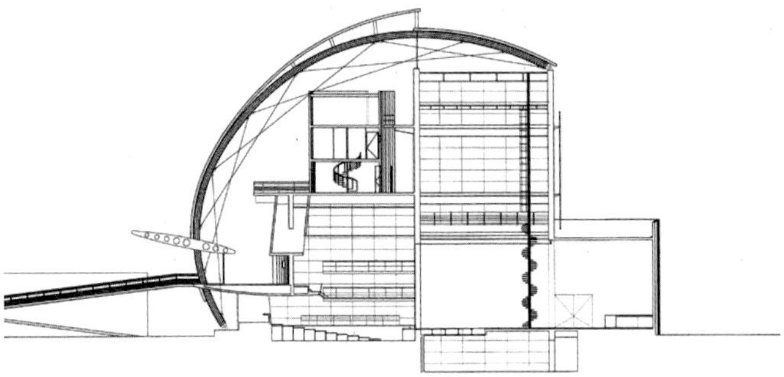

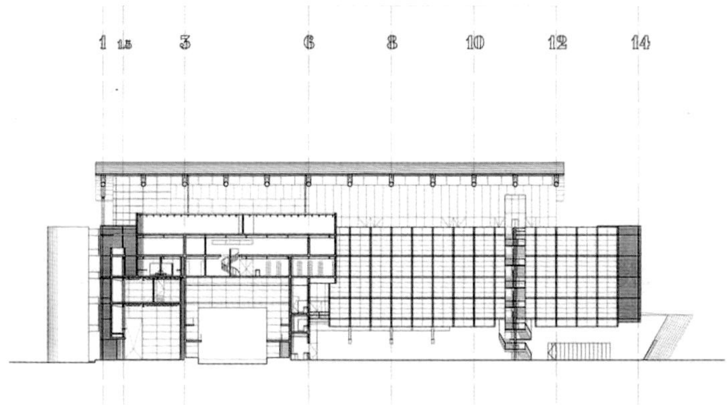

In the end our work, regardless of the result, has very clear geometries and modulations.

architecture? As an example, what was your intention regarding the wall plane that penetrates through the arched canopy?

We need to back up. It was very unfortunate that this project proceeded so fast. It became chaotic; people were making decisions on site. The general contractors and construction administrators were on site 24 hours a day making decisions. Additionally, the director of the school, the bureaucrats, were all involved in an unstructured decision making process. Because of this unorthodox process the place of arrival became completely transformed. I think that's where this project does not work. We wanted to create a stair and a ramp, creating a dramatic entrance to a really prominent lobby space. The idea was that students would come freely into the portico space underneath the canopy. That became completely transformed. Now they have a little wooden ramp functioning as an "entrance" instead approaching the building through a field of gravel providing a transition from the surroundings. The ramp then was to provide a break, another transition, from that exterior field into the exterior space under the canopy. We wanted the ground-floor space under the arched canopy to be a very open student place. We wanted it to function as a fluid portico where people were moving around it from corner to corner. This space was envisioned as a grand outdoor foyer.

The gravel was to "disconnect" the space form the surrounding paving?

Yes, and it was to make the entry into the programmed spaces continuous. People could just flow in and out—it was to be vey public. Now there is just a tiny, little wooden bridge that people walk on to come into the main exterior space. The other reason that we separated the covered exterior space is that I envisioned it as the real lobby. People would gather here, go to the presentations, look down, hang out. What they did when the entry sequence was changed was to transform the approach via the ramp that nobody uses. They killed a major feature of the entry. The intention was that the covered exterior space was a place for students, the community, and the visitors who were all coming to connect to one another. The other intention for the entry sequence was to highlight the fabrication room where the students build and store their theater props by placing it adjacent to the entry sequence. It has a big window to allow visitors to observe the students' preparations from the balcony because this is a student theater, not a professional one. Students are here all day. They end up doing their work here. The space was also to be very flexible with a center stage and some seating in the canopied area.

On one level the building became a very rational construct because of programmatic issues, budget issues and architectural intentions. With the ramp, the strategy changes. It may not have been part of the design or it might have been organized perpendicular to the building. Beyond the entry intention mentioned earlier were there other intentions regarding the use of the ramp and the wall it wraps around?

In addition to the portico space created by the canopy, we really wanted people to occupy the outside plaza in front of the building. The ramp was to establish an open arm and a connecting link. We wanted to celebrate the ramp, yet we didn't want it to become this singular exterior object, so it became part of a spatial intention.

The diagonal placement of the ramp allows the exterior space to be more activated. If we look at that a different way, the ramp with the stair, and the addition of the canopy, something occurs regarding the tectonic elements penetrating through the sleek skin of the canopy. Were there intentions exploring these types of material or assembly concepts?

There was an intention that was quite clear. The big canopy was, as I said, of the urban scale, the scale of the moving automobile. But once you come closer, we wanted a different scale, a smaller scale. We wanted to bring additional articulated interest to the arrival sequence and to the definition of the exterior lobby space. We used this articulation to celebrate the public and the individual. Additionally we wanted the arrival process to celebrate the works of the students. That is why this entry penetration and material detail became so prominent.

10| With that thought in mind, how did you add additional depth to initial, more global, intentions?

The global condition of our work comes from a very conscious intention to integrate our work into the larger discourse on architecture by incorporating the general vocabulary of modern architecture. More and more our generation is the first to fully accept a totally interconnected world. We are part of one community and one civilization; that's a fact. Our predecessors fought that, but we grew up accepting that and being comfortable with that reality. It's important that my work not be in books merely focusing on "Mexican" architecture or "houses on the beach."

6| In that regard, an expression of continuity with the modernist language is an initial concern?

It is part of that, and the work sustains itself there. Then the specificities of the place, of the culture come forward. They will impact the design if one is aware of the culture and the contextual implications.

Not only organizationally, as a method to relate the interaction of the programmatic components and the space defined by the canopy, they are bound together by the order of the structure in that one depends on the other. They are also bound together environmentally. This project would not work without the canopy; each component becomes a part of the other.

Let's tie that together with the more direct intentions for the National School of Theater where on one hand you can say, "Yes, I am engaged in a larger architectural discourse on the nature of design today." Yet more specifically related to the building there are additional interests, the steel canopy, the wood library, the travertine. There is a solid base of concrete and travertine and then there's the wood cladding the library component above the other programmed spaces, all surrounded by a canopy of steel. What were your intentions in relation to the expression of those elements or materials?

That was an additional design intention as we wanted to express all of the components of the project, to give them their own personality. We thought there was an opportunity given the diverse nature of the program. Once we had made the unifying gesture with the canopy there was space for the growth, development, and expression of individual pieces and elements.

16| Tell me about your intentions relating to the materials you selected. Was it about solid "base" materials and lighter "lifted" materials? Or is it...

Basically our thoughts concerned materiality and its expression. I believe, and have always believed, that there are not good materials and bad materials. There are not common materials; there are not rich materials. It's not about that. There are different materials you can use for either purely expressive reasons or because there are materials for a particular application. Many of the decisions regarding the selection of materials for this project were driven by the construction process. For example, we needed concrete because of seismic conditions present at the site.

Let's discuss those issues of materiality in terms of representational intentions. When you see the wood

You set up an order, but it should not require you be a prisoner under its control. It is a framework allowing you to be free and to invent. If you are a prisoner, you are in trouble as ordering systems can set up a condition that does not allow for design freedom or flexibility.

We always keep our work more rational in the way we put our buildings together.

Design intentions are not always necessarily the solution to a functional condition.

of the library it somewhat strikes you as an icon within an icon.

That's what we wanted to express. We were thinking the brain would be located in the library. It is actually not much of a library, but it still represents their ambition, so we thought, we would put the library, representing knowledge, in a unique location, and then reinforce that aspect with a unique material. In addition, there is an outdoor reading area located outside the library, on the roof of the space below. This was to expand the experiential nature of learning. When you arrive on one of these platforms, you also return to the communal space defined by the canopy and are simultaneously in two worlds.

So there is an intent for this library to be honored as a unique destination, yet you can get a book, take it out, and read it in this space that is very much about the public realm

Yes, everybody "lives" in that big space; students live in the big space, the public, the scholars. They all come back to this space.

I noticed that while every other material is aligned or jointed very precisely, on a module, the wood cladding is not. The wood cladding the library is freer in its offset jointing strategy.

Many decisions were a consequence of specific materials available at the time of construction. I cannot recall our precise thinking, yet related to a similar intention we curved the profile of the library to make it more expressive.

11| Under that theme, did you "name" or prioritize specific architectural elements or programmatic areas to differentiate, or give a particular expression to larger global intentions?

The open un-programmed space became the most important hierarchical condition of the building. We used the studios and the classrooms, the more commonplace programmatic elements to create a backdrop "wall" to further define the space.

I was intrigued by the text on the glass screen lining the wall. Tell me about your intentions for the glass wall and the text on it.

We wanted a screen to separate what was occurring in the more private classrooms and studios from the open, outdoor "stage." First we thought we should have a transparent screen echoing the technologically themed assemblies of the canopy and entry elements. We started with clear sheets of glass, but we wanted texture, a graphic. We added text to the glass that honors theatrical themes. All of the quotes originate from and relate to the theater—some are poems, some are paragraphs.

12| As the design developed, did you use different attributes of the organizational and representational conceptual fields to mature or cross-reference each other? The manner in which the curved canopy frames and activates the stage below can be seen as a vibrant counterpoint playing off the orthogonal configuration of the "wall" and representing a dynamic framework defining the space of the stage and the public space in front. In this blending of the organizational and representational do you tend to see a prioritizing of one over the other, or are they intended to be more interactive, more related?

Yes, absolutely, it's both. In the end all concepts have to come together to express one building to make it cohere. There are not two completely distinct conditions defining the project. It is one building. Not only organizationally, as a method to relate the interaction of the programmatic components with the space defined by the canopy; they are also bound together by the order of the structural system in that one depends on the other. They are also bound together environmentally. This project would not work without the canopy. Each component becomes a part of the other.

In your design the canopy is obviously connected via its structural module relating to the structural module of the elements it frames. Similarly, if I look at the western elevation, I see lines of extension that visually unite the upper canopy through other clear relationships to the elements below such as the upper edge of the lifted canopy aligning with the left side of opening in the stair tower. Is the goal to visually validate methods through which you are organizing forms, and what they are trying to represent, through very precise and obvious relationships?

I am very obsessed about that type of precision; it is a personal thing. In the end our work, regardless of the result, has very clear geometries and modulations. There are many explanations for that. It can be as basic as permitting a simplified construction process or providing for easier maintenance of the building. I have been reflecting on these types of issues and their relationship to the formal range of architectural production occurring today. In that regard the very expressive work of some of my colleagues, whom I admire and respect, does not make sense or can be questioned in relation to issues of constructability. We always keep our work more rational in the way we put our buildings together. I come from construction. I know construction very well and understand the process very well. I don't come from an overly conceptual viewpoint, from the new tools of computers that many of our students and younger colleagues easily manipulate into unique configurations...I don't come from that mind-set.

This relates to my own way of looking at the world and the necessity of a certain preciseness or ordering strategy to inform multiple decisions.

It relates to maintaining continuity toward the thinness of edges. That's part of an overall intention and overall system, from the canopy to the details.

14| Did you see the organizational framework employed in the National School of Theater building needing additional architectural intentionality because as an organizational/ordering system the building was under conceptualized?

Well, you set up an order, but it should not require you be a prisoner under its control. It is a framework allowing you to be free and to invent. If you are a prisoner, you are in trouble as ordering systems can set up a condition that does not allow for design freedom or flexibility.

15| Relating to strategies that can be too restrictive, how do you link the ephemeral, poetic intentions of your design to the pragmatic, functional performance concerns as the design progresses? When we look at the structure supporting the canopy, we see in its design development a more "poetic" or tectonic quality with the cables and the articulated connections. In that assembly there are obviously additional design interests. Could you describe your intentions?

It is interesting to use the word "poetic" because that is where one uses non-rational or non-ordered methods to explain something. For example, we worked very hard to keep the shell as thin as possible. We wanted it very thin, very light. By no means could it have huge beams or anything similar. Why? Because we wanted it thin, because in the thinness is where the poetry lies.

Was that a specific intention regarding the canopy or a more general interest in expressing thinness versus volume?

There was a clear idea that we would be moving from the masses defining the program spaces into very thin elements defining the canopy over the un-programmed stage space. Other than the tubes we don't have structural elements in the canopy. We didn't want to fill the bays between the tubes with additional structure. That's what brought us to select a corrugated ribbed material as it could span the distance between the structural tubes. The space was to be defined by very thin reflective materials, metal, and glass. They create the thin envelope and surface characteristics, which was the quality we were looking for.

Here we can say that the organizational framework was not something that could handle the poetic side of your intentions and that thinness becomes a representational device to honor the space.

At this point design intentions are not always necessarily the solution to a functional condition. We could have resolved the definition of the exterior space in many other ways. Your statement is very valid. Why didn't we use standard, heavier structural beams? That's not what we wanted. We wanted lightness. It comes out of the process.

16.1| While we discussed aspects of materiality earlier, was the expressive representational nature of the materials, or how you deployed them, important in the design of the National School of Theater? When did the notion of the expressiveness of your material pallet, or lack thereof, become important? In terms of the travertine, concrete, the delicate metalwork, the wood cladding on the library, or the thinness of the membrane... when do you start thinking of materials used in the building in relation to what they might represent?

I would say that in this case we decided very early on which elements we wanted to distinguish from the others. Initially we focused on the repetitive studios and classroom programmatic elements creating the "bar." Later, certain elements started popping up as opportunities to be programmatically identified through material

At this point design intentions are not always necessarily the solution to a functional condition. Why didn't we use standard, heavier structural beams? That's not what we wanted, we wanted lightness, it comes out of the process.

conditions, such as the library. Yet many of the material issues of the building had to do with construction or structural solutions. How are you going to build the building? Because of seismic conditions and from a pure construction standpoint we needed a concrete base. We made the decision, "Okay, let's leave it". Because we were looking for transparency we knew there was going to be glass and we knew there was to be expressed steel because of the light construction and aesthetic solution it provided.

You realized early on that this concrete base makes sense, primarily in response to the seismic conditions found in Mexico City. If we tie that back to the thinness of the steel canopy, there is a nice dichotomy between the two. You have something very solid, very stereotomic, and then something very thin, very tectonic. Do you remember how these materials, the wood, the travertine, fall somewhere in between? Was that an intention or was that an interest?

Actually that is one of the things that has always been important, that each material has a very different way of expressing itself. Wood has a softness...I am now remembering back to the discussion surrounding the floating box, the library, sitting up on top it was an uncomfortable mass. It wasn't totally fitting in; we needed a material that would represent lightness. It couldn't be a glass because it was going to be a totally solid box. We didn't want a heavy concrete or stone element in that perched situation, which is why we went to wood. It could have been a form of plastic, but we could not use plastic. That's very important to mention. This project is the last generation of projects built in a country that was totally closed to exterior markets. Up to this time Mexico, and many other countries, were not open to globalization. You could import nothing. Obviously we were not closed to the world in regards to information, but it was huge if we wanted to order anything. It was just not a possibility. Because of that the emphasis on local materials remains a constant in our work. Now that we are building in diverse and multiple locations, it remains a constant. It is important to use the available labor with its perspective and the traditions of construction you have in a given place.

Let's return to some of the details and how they relate to the way one conceptualizes organizational or compositional issues relating to the joining of materials. How did they relate to earlier organizational compositional intentions? For example,

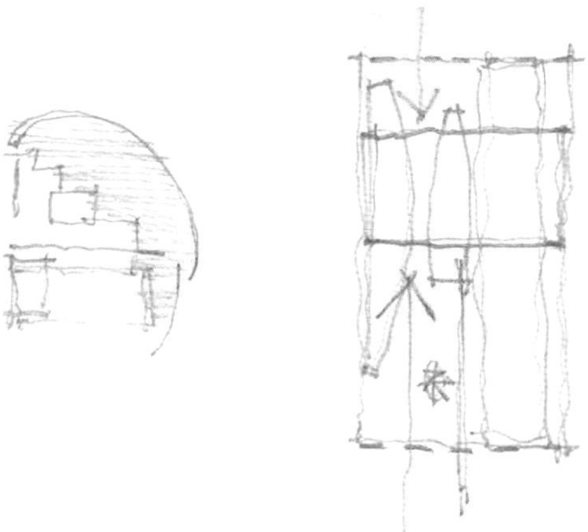

You work very hard at first to set up the regulating lines, to create the alignments, but once you've got them then those detailing decisions fall into place.

There was a clear idea that we would be moving from the masses defining the program spaces into very thin elements defining the canopy.

there's always a thinness associated with jointing and connecting. There is the thin metal banding around the stone, which has a detail continuity with the thin metal door jamb conditions. The stair railing is similarly defined with thin metal elements. My question is, what themes were guiding decisions reflected in these more detailed conditions?
For us that was a simple proposition. It relates to maintaining continuity toward the thinness of edges. That's part of an overall intention and overall system, from the canopy to the details. Once you set up an overall ordering system, you already know, for example, how certain details will be organized or expressed. It would be inconsistent not to use it.

You are describing a logic that implies there is an overall rationale as to why elements are organized in the manner in which they are, including the details... Are you interested in those aspects in the manner in which they allow the building to provide a clarity or readability in relation to the rules governing the relationships among the elements?
Yes, for example when one has to decide where to place light fixtures in an elevation you have been designing and the elevation has lines and relationships between materials created by rules or organization, every intersection has already been "marked" where the lights should go. That's part of an organizational strategy. Similarly, anybody here in the office would know that if you are going to set a light or a toilet paper holder there are only two ways of doing that. It's either at the intersection of two panels or at the center of a panel. It's already set up for you. You work very hard at first to set up the regulating lines, to create the alignments, but once you've got them, then those detailing decisions fall into place.
This relates to my own way of looking at the world and the necessity of a certain preciseness or ordering strategy to inform multiple decisions.

18| What was your thinking regarding expression, or lack thereof, of the systems within the building? What organizational or representational strategies were contemplated in your decision to express the systems?
There are no systems. Most of the building is not air-conditioned. The only air-conditioned space is the black box, and in there the systems are totally expressed. The rest of the building employs passive design strategies with shading and louvers. While there is no air-conditioning or heating system in the building, I do not have a problem expressing those components.

The building employs passive design strategies with shading and louvers.

Would it be correct to state that you would have a general interest in the expression of systems, whether mechanical or structural, as a part of the authenticity of the building? Does the expression of building systems resonate with you in the sense that you prefer to express multiple components constituting the make-up or assembly of a building or they represent a validation of a more complete design process?
I'm not obsessive about it. If there is an opportunity for the expression of systems that will bring added visual interest or value because of their conceptual expression, then yes, I will commit to expressing them. In my buildings in New York one has to fireproof everything, so it is not easy to express the structural systems. It depends upon many factors, yet if there is an opportunity, I will take it.

Regarding details, talk a little bit about your use of the thin line joint between the metal panels at the classrooms and studios.
It's a way of putting together the walls. Those are not pre-existing systems; we were inventing them. We wanted to clean up many walls and let them remain neutral and let a material organization pop out somewhat, yet we needed to invent a system. We could have hidden them. Why didn't we? We had the opportunity, so we decided to express the joints. While there was not a large philosophical position underlying these decisions, many did fall under a larger design interest of expressing many elements underlying the building's design.

19| In refining the design did you select programmatic areas or architectural elements to privilege? If so, how were the privileging concepts expansions on, or counterpoints to, earlier conceptual intentions? If I use the glazing detail, the pin you used to hold the glass in, I don't know if that is "privileging" the detail but it is expressing an idea of assembly.
We were looking for a simple straightforward way of putting together the glass screen to hold it and to easily change the glass if needed.

That's the functional answer, fair enough. There probably are, I would like to argue, additional reasons. This gets very minute, but someone ultimately decided this. For example, here's the line that is separating the two panels, and then here's the line that is the pin holding the glass frame, and here's the line below. They are linear lines, this is a relatively linear building, a linear plane. The roof is a thin-curved linear plane. These might be intuitive decisions, or decisions that just have to be made, but that is what I want to return to. Obviously there could have been a screw used to install the glass fixing but the solution used here is nicer than that. It is a more elegant way even if it is simply pragmatic. I am wondering if the detail expresses an overall interest in thinness or expressing assembly which helps inform the detail in a manner that prevents you from putting in a hex head screw.

I'm not sure that's true. When I am studying those kind of decisions...the opportunity to design those things is when you have paper in front of you. In this project many of those decisions were very spontaneous. I would go to the site almost every day, and I would have employees there, yet the building was constructed at such a rapid pace that many, many, many decisions were made at the site. Because everything was moving so fast, there were many changes. There were modifications not only as we were designing and drawing but also when the building was under construction. There were a significant number of details that were just not on the plans. I'd come to the site and the contractor would say, "How do we do this?" A lot of decisions were made at the site.

That truly represents a design reality relating to the scheduling demands of construction. While not "philosophical" as you mentioned earlier, I imagine there was a certain design ethos, if not overt intention, underlying many of those decisions. In expressing the fasteners as one of "many elements" underlying various design interests and decisions, even if field decisions, was there not an intention, basically representational in nature, providing a "rule" you were employing, even if in the field?
Yes, there is some accuracy to that. While we were required to provide solutions at the site, we were continuing to employ and respond to some of our primary interests in the elemental nature of the design. We wanted to achieve that continuity, whether the decisions were made in the office or at the construction site. It goes back to decisions falling into place and providing overall coherency to the design. ◘

Eric Owen Moss Architects

Eric Owen Moss

Samitaur Tower

Architecturally and functionally Samitaur Tower provides multiple linkages to the surrounding area. On one hand becoming an icon for the visually oriented media companies, graphic designers and office tenants residing in the evolving Culver City area and, on the other, creating a series of observation platforms that allow distant views to the surrounding areas. At grade level the tower also incorporates a projection screen and an excavated amphitheater-like seating area to facilitate performances by local speakers and artists. Completed in 2010 and constructed primarily of exposed steel, the tower rises 72 feet above grade with the excavated seating area creating another 12 feet of height on its southern side. Five offset steel rings create specific angles of orientations for projection screens, permitting inclinations to pedestrians and individuals commuting in highly trafficked circulation routes adjacent to the tower.

The Samitaur Tower resides in the realm of architectural design where "function" may be transcendent versus integrated. The function of buildings and structures attempting to define aspirations through architectural expression, or provide vehicles for the examination of values, resides primarily in the language domain of architectural representation. Subscribing to no particular architectural language, the tower invites debate and confronts the rules often used to establish aesthetic norms and asks "Why"? Not eschewing organizational and representational conceptual domains, the tower permits added scrutiny regarding how and in what manner architectural languages communicate.

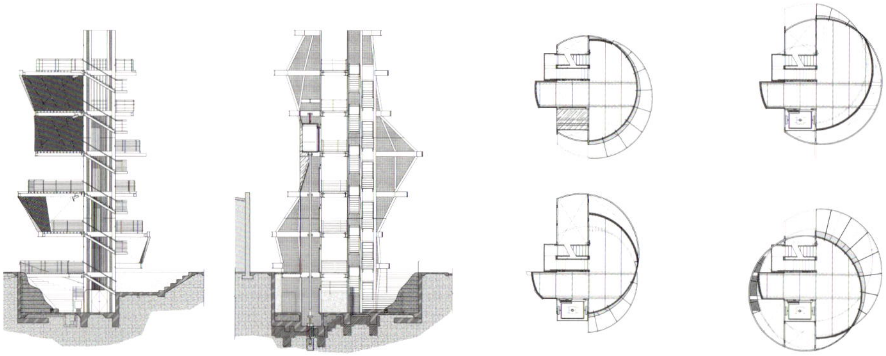

Samitaur Tower Sections, floor plans

Helmet Head #2, Henry Moore

1| Tom Diehl: What value, potential, or use do you see in order? This is a framing question. When we move into the discussion of the Gateway Tower; I'll come back to this issue.

Eric Owen Moss: The problem with this form of a discussion in architecture, but probably almost anything, has to do with whether there are issues you can get at without using either a predictable or an idiosyncratic type of discourse or language. If you use the standard language, which, in belonging to so many people, belongs to nobody, the meaning of the words gets lost over a period of time. If you say it's clean, or you say it's a context, or you say it's porosity, or you say it's digital, etc., there are a lot of words like that which aren't particularly useful in revealing personal intention, although they may respond to something that is more generic, which people may share. I would prefer to define whatever it is I think, or I do, based on some kind of construction that allows me to explain it as an individual, not that my concrete is necessarily different than your concrete. The Gnostic book is a little like that, although it is criticized from time to time for being not sufficiently accessible. I'm not saying it's so, I'm just saying...

When I wrote *Gnostic Architecture* with John Franco, the original request from him was around the time that Koolhaas's *SML* book came out. He asked me to do something that from his vantage point of my vantage point was the inverse, the reverse, or the reciprocal of that book. The *Gnostic* book is interesting just because it is a serious attempt to define a conceptual vocabulary in which I work. So it's not so much a question of whether you say order, disorder, reorder, no order...What that book does, and I don't want to go through some long-winded exegesis, but essentially it's somewhere between the Bible, the building code, and the dictionary—a combination of allegedly authoritative sources. It uses a sculpture called "The Helmet." There's actually a series of helmets that are relatively small by Henry Moore. It's an interesting kind of helmet because it's not like Achilles's helmet or LaDainian Tomlinson's helmet. It is not a matter of something congruent, such as eyes, nose, ears, helmet. There's a separation between the two. There's an external piece, a space, and an internal piece, which is to some extent covered and protected by the external piece. So the sections of the book are related to what we call the outside of the outside, inside of the outside, the glue, the outside of the inside and the inside of the inside. It is not a literal model; it is a conceptual model for the inner relationship of pieces in a building and the tension between those pieces. It is an argument for something, more fragile, less predetermined, and more exploratory than a standard allegiance. If you look around at architecture, what you find over a period of time is that even the most exploratory kind of work seems to become more predictable as what is unknown and part of a discovery process becomes, after a while, a formula, an allegiance, a system, or a method that is a way of dealing with a conception of order, suggesting an inner relationship of parts. That's the best definition I have of what an idea of order means as it relates to an association of pieces. In total it makes something that is never one thing. The thing that it makes is an argument with itself.

My definition of order is "understandably," but not necessarily related to anything having to do with a particular formal system or specific language.

Understandability to you, to me or...

To an observer.

Somebody who is engaged. The reason I'm asking about understandability is that people may not always perceive the term or issue in the same way. If you explain baseball to your kid and you explain baseball to a guy from Vienna who only knows soccer, it's different. So, the question is to whom are you explaining. I remember people would say if the president or the secretary of defense or the vice president were speaking on a subject, we should pay attention as they know much more about the issues they're talking about than anybody else; therefore, we ought to defer to their knowledge. You have to be careful about experts.

Well, in architecture of course we can't explain intentions to anybody except possibly the client and a few choice users. From a teaching standpoint, dealing with students who don't have a real sense of the significance of visual thinking or of the necessity of a conceptual underpinning for aesthetics, it is more of a grounding issue, one providing a potential methodology for providing coherence. As students begin to become curious about these issues, themes of order and organization are necessary to prevent the design process from becoming a formal manipulation exercise. Therefore, one has to get into these kinds of discussions. I chose to start these interviews with the concept of order as a way of asking an underlying question that might almost be existential in nature. In that regard, maybe the audience is unknown, but a subset of that unknown is the uninformed student, at least visually uninformed. What I'm trying to do, by using this discussion on order as a framing question, is to get at the point that when they design something, if they are going to be serious architects, there has to be a sense of intentionality that will come through. I'm starting with concepts of order. There might be site-based concepts, the proper use of material, and so on. That's where the question is coming from.

If you look around at architecture, what you find over a period of time is that even the most exploratory kind of work seems to become more predictable as what is unknown and part of a discovery process becomes, after a while, a formula, an allegiance, a system, or a method that is a way of dealing with a conception of order, suggesting an inner relationship of parts.

The best definition I have of what an idea of order means as it relates to an association of pieces (is that). In total it makes something that is never one thing. The thing that it makes is an argument with itself.

Gnostic Architecture was...actually cognizant of internal differences, which are not so easy to spell out because one is really talking about the tensions between possibilities.

Broadway Boogie Woogie, Piet Mondrian

In your work, there is, I think, a heartfelt attempt at bringing meaning to the constructions—even if the meaning is a challenging one or challenging to some. Yet that is what makes the work interesting and relevant to a discussion one can have with students, or this book can have with students and interested practitioners. They can look at Eric Owen Moss's work, or anyone else's, and say "Oh, now I can understand that."

I'll give you another example. I have a friend who owns a painting called *Broadway Boogie Woogie*. It is a Piet Mondrian painting with right angles and painted with red, blue, yellow, black, white, and gray colors. So, if you look at a reproduction of that painting in somebody's book or in a slide, you see one image. If you physically see the painting, the painting is falling apart. It's made out of tape. It's made out of all kinds of things. It has very different qualities as it deteriorates over time, which is a function of how he made it. And now it has, interestingly enough, other kinds of essentials. If the essential idea is a sort of austerity, and if that is supposed to endure beyond all the frivolity, it doesn't. So, the painting has two arguments. One, is a conceptual argument. Somebody is saying, "This is my idea of order, right angle, right angle, straight line, red, blue, yellow, and so on." That's the formal language of the painting. On the other hand it also has textures which don't belong to that discussion. So, I think the reality of discussions of order or theories of order are very different. I mean if you wanted to put the painting up to discuss Mondrian's "argument," would you discuss the painting falling apart, the painting just after it was completed, a photograph of the painting? So, what I would argue is that the argument doesn't account for the painting and this was the argument we made to Monacelli (the publisher of *Gnostic Architecture*) that *Gnostic Architecture* was a different kind of argument. It was actually cognizant of internal differences which are not so easy to spell out because one is really talking about the tensions between possibilities.

There is something interesting that is that neither side, regardless of the particulars of this argument, necessarily accounts for the entirety of the subject. One can argue that making an argument is itself a matter of insisting on certain things and getting rid of others. In my work, I'm trying to make an argument that doesn't get rid of anything. It's a different kind of argument." And of course, you can't do that any more than you can do the other thing. They run into each other. One person says it's only about this, and the other person says it's about everything. It can never be about everything, and it can never only be about this. And being cognizant of ideas and the history of ideas, and the discussion of ideas makes me aware, in an intellectual way, of the limits of some of these kinds of discussions. The idea of putting up this image and putting up this text and saying "You see this. Now you'll understand it." I'm not sure that works except to the extent that it eliminates what's intricate about certain kinds of ideas. You actually don't want to put in front of a student an argument, which will allow him or her to simply go out and fill in the blanks, i.e., this is a chessboard, this is what you do with a rook, this is what you do with a queen. Want to win? Do this and this and this...checkmate. I think in some ways you want it to be a little bit more open and critical.

I agree. I will take away the word order and substitute it with a broader theme, the meaningfulness of ideas represented in a building. In that case, I'm going to be more specific because I'm interested in your thoughts on this matter. If I refer to the meaningfulness of design intentions realized in a building, there's obviously a strategy employed. Your work has an interest in contrast, counterpoints, and ambiguities. Yet, there is a play between something very clear, at least in the way we understand geometry as representing clarity or a dimension of order, yet it is always confronted with that which is not geometric. I'm using that as a...

A friend of mine came by; a Chinese guy who has an office in Shanghai. He came by yesterday, and he was looking at the Samituar Tower, and he said, referencing an older project of mine called The Wall, What Wall? project, he said the older "wiggly one" is fast geometry and the Samitaur Tower is slow geometry. I think he was trying to find a way, just like you're trying to find a way, to fit the projects into a broader architectural discussion. I don't mind the discussion I'm just not sure I agreed with his position. It is interesting though to see the two structures next to each other because in terms of the evolution of the digital capacity to plasma-cut everything or to 3D print or vacuum-form everything—they are out of sequence. The odd one, or the odder one, the Wall, What Wall? project, is much earlier. So if there is supposed to be a chronology in this discussion, and I don't know if there is, it's not our chronology.

Well, I have one concern that manifests itself. My concern is for students' mental actualization and use of ideas affecting the direction of design in a relatively short period of time, five years. They graduate, and the majority of them haven't internalized the rigorous use of concepts that animate the designs of creative architects.

Maybe the problem is you're trying to talk to 500 people and you should be trying to talk to five.

Right, but there's something. Let's then say this is an altruistic enterprise.

On your part?

I think the best advice for students and architects, and I don't think a lot of architects take it, has to do with listening in a critical way.

Over a period of time, coming to understand how numerous design variables are emphasized and deemphasized or organized by particular conceptual sensibilities and logic that can move a discussion of architecture and make it different, is critical.

In my work, I'm trying to make an argument that doesn't get rid of anything. It's a different kind of argument.

Top: Umbrella

Middle: Samitaur

Bottom: What Wall?

Yes, on my part. To provide a vehicle, or a portion of a vehicle, allowing those who are curious or who do gravitate to design that appears grounded on something beyond a perfunctory level of investigation. They may not know what it's grounded on, but they are drawn to it for reasons, let's hope, that interesting design attracts people. In that regard, it is the intentionality of what you do or the others I'll be talking to do, that underpins the work and gives it a life. So, I will go back and have a discussion...
With me or with your students?

With students, yet in the end our work does represent itself in the public realm, and the idea of intentionality becomes a grounding issue relating to what makes a work cohere, even if cohering is not...
You don't have to put words in my mouth. I'm not arguing against coherence.

I know, and that's what I would like to explore.
There are people who argue that what we're doing is incoherent. I don't think it is.

I don't either. That's one of my biggest fears, and this has nothing to do with your work. It could be the work of any number of the architects that I am speaking with.
Well, I think we have a particular problem in that regard, and I assume the people, and I don't know who you're talking to, but I assume different people have different issues. I was talking to Wolf Prix about that—and this was sort of an odd discussion, maybe it has too much self-pity in it—we were talking about which architects have a proclivity toward large projects. We were saying if you do big projects then "they" say you've gone commercial. If you do little projects, "they" say you can't do big projects. Damned if you do, damned if you don't.
I think the best advice for students and architects, and I don't think a lot of architects take it, has to do with listening in a critical way. Over a period of time, coming to understand how numerous design variables are emphasized and deemphasized or organized by particular conceptual sensibilities and logic that can move a discussion of architecture and make it different, is critical. I've always been interested in that, and I didn't say "better," I would never argue that the world gets better I really don't think the world gets better. I can remember a kind of progressiveness...I was talking to my wife this morning, and we were talking about unions, early unions, and arguments for unions. We were also talking about the voice of women in the 1920s and 1940s. The arguments do not necessarily get stronger. In fact, some of the strengths of certain arguments get lost. You may not be the first in a sequence. You may be the first and last, and there is no sequence.

Well, the dilemma that I face in my design work, that you face in your design work, is ultimately that we have to shift the balls on the table so that people know things are different, and they have to figure it out and, hopefully, they are at least curious about it. Or we have some hope, or false hope, that we are lifting the bar or moving it forward. In either case, we both have to deal with intentions.
Well, it also has to do with that you're talking about issues very abstractly. It has to do with something that you believe. If one believes that the game changes, and you change it, then you might go after that. If you believe the game doesn't change, for example in the Bible, the book of Ecclesiastes effectively says there is nothing new under the sun, and I think there's something true about that then you pursue other objectives. There are some

In the end, you may not know what one is really asking or the question may be, "What am I doing with this project?"

things that get different, but it's not that everything gets different. Many things get different faster, and faster yet some things stay the same. But if one is prepared to say, "It's moving" and your aspiration is to move it, then one of the reasons you move things is because they can't fit into the context of a preexisting discussion. I'm not sure that's really a choice. It may be a theoretical choice; maybe it has to do with the way people are, in a certain essential way.

I can give you an example that's interesting, although I haven't looked at it for while. When you look at a writer like James Joyce, an early 20th-century writer, what's novel about his work is that nobody's following it! So, he's a pioneer, he's Daniel Boone, and nobody's coming after him, hardly anybody. And he says, "Oh this is a sentence like your kid is learning in school." Capital letter, noun, verb, period, sentence. Like what you pick up in the *New York Times*, or whatever is left of the *LA Times*. They write in those kinds of sentences. You pick up books and they're written in sentences. Joyce comes along and says, "Wait a minute." That's not adequate for me to say what I need to say. Many people will discuss, particularly in this culture, his motives.

In Le Corbusier's book, *Creation is a Patient Search*, there is a poem at the beginning called "The Acrobat." It has a lot of self-pity in it. It's probably not the greatest poem, but it essentially says that the architect is an acrobat. He's always accused of showing off, and if he falls, nobody gives a damn. That's a paraphrase, but it basically says that. So with Le Corbusier one has a combination of a self-portrait and a portrait of himself as he thinks other people have represented him. I don't think motives are useful in these discussions. What is done is done, and you have to try to make some sense out of it. All I'm

If you look at the wiggle of the building or the movement of the structure, you can make a very good pragmatic argument.

saying is, in a personal way, your motivation, if you think the world will move, as in shifting the balls on the table—is not so much as if somebody will move or somebody won't, which is the way I understood what you said, it is that some will move it, some won't. I'll move it, not because somebody will move it, but because I have to move it. Why? Because I can't do what they want me to do. Joyce said, in effect, "I couldn't write a sentence that way, I just can't write it."

Similarly, we were doing a book, and nobody would touch it. They would touch it, but only on their terms. It's 40 projects spanning 20 years. It's an interesting project; it was actually inspired by somebody at Thames and Hudson. They said, "No, this is too much. You have to cut it." So, now who's doing it? The Chinese. Everybody you send it to, including my buddies over there at Monacelli, say this is very interesting...it's too expensive, too much going on. Make it shorter, and then we'll talk to you. So, we go to the Chinese guys who got it at 10:30 AM and at 10:45 AM said, "We'll do whatever you like." So, again, what I'm saying is somebody can say we're showing off, somebody can say we're acting like idiots, or somebody can say we're doing something profound. I do know we wanted to do something we thought would be useful internally and would also explain to you, to students, and to others, even if it's only three people, what we're doing, and why we're doing it.

4| My interest is actually what you've just said, yet focusing on one project you are designing and what is underlying your specific pursuits would be a very fair way of restating goals. In that regard, let's talk about the Samitaur Tower. Did interests regarding preliminary design intentions focus on themes generated by the site and program or were design interests originating form sources lying outside those considerations?

What I finally figured out with the effort to publish the *Gnostic Architecture* book, and an earlier essay entitled, "Which Lie Do You Want To Tell?" is that there are a lot of ways and many vantage points to direct what you are doing. In the end, you may not know what one is really asking or the question may be, "What am I doing with this project?"

An existential issue.

Maybe. But, the question is how intrigued are you about those kinds of questions. The local newspaper published a small article about the Samitaur Tower, in a friendly way, not in a negative way, but, I think, with a certain amount of skepticism. The Samituar Tower is being built next to a new light rail line. That was finished in 2010 and runs from downtown south to USC, then west to a train stop at La Cienega and Jefferson. Then it goes into Culver City and stops. So one, "What am I doing with this project?" topic of conversation could be strictly in terms of the tower's relationship to a series of viewing points along the light rail line.

So in that regard there's a series of screens, it's a tower and it wiggles, and it wiggles nominally in order to face particular vantage points. There's rear projection behind all of the screens to produce information. Although the caveat, in terms of its approval by the city, is that it's not commercial information, yet the "commercial" side of the project is interesting vis-à-vis, all these "billboards" showing up on buildings all over the world, in the Ginza district in Tokyo, in Times Square, etc.

If you look at the wiggle of the building or the movement of the structure, you can make a very good

So maybe that's why some of this is not a matter of art; it's a matter of psychology or a matter of the intersection of art and psychology and how do you think, how do you know, how do you understand, and how do you imagine? I think those are all open questions forever.

pragmatic argument. The top of the Tower faces the the train station stop at La Cienega and Jefferson, two major north-south, east-west streets in Los Angeles. When you get out of the train or you get onto the train, there is a screen. There is another screen at a different level, and there are five levels altogether, facing the Santa Monica freeway which is a major east-west artery connecting the west side of Los Angeles to downtown. There's another screen with a different orientation facing the new train station on the other side of the Tower. The fourth screen faces National Boulevard, which, depending on your point of view, is either the most obnoxious street in LA because of traffic, or it's a great venue because there are red lights and you get a captive audience. Using these vantage points one can account for the configuration of the screens on the Tower and shape of the Tower.

On the opposite side of the Tower there will be a small outdoor seating area that seats about 150 people on a rake as the Tower goes down into a hole, into an open space. Extending back into the parking lot you can seat maybe about 800 people. On that side, there's another screen oriented to the tenants. They are an interesting mix: AOL, Nike, Ogilvy, Cineon, Kodak, Anonymous, etc. You know, some of these new experimental characters so the developer's game looks like it worked as it gets fancy people in a very kinetic city like LA to dump Santa Monica, to dump Century City and come to this cool place, whatever that means. As a commercial strategy, he used the architecture in a very strategic way. You could use it as a kind of vertical park and set events up there. So whether he loves architecture or not, he used it in a strategic way. Those tenants can come out and use that 5th screen in order to gather in one place.

An outdoor gathering or performance area?

Something like that. There are a lot of ways, in terms of art exhibition programs, to use the Tower. It's very much architecture, although it's form, and it's purpose is not conventional. That doesn't mean it's not a building. It's interesting people assume that everything has to fall into conventional categories, just like the earlier discussion about writing a conventional sentence and the rules that one follows. If you don't write a sentence that way, it's not a sentence. If you don't write a book that fits into, its "type" is it history? Is it poetry? People have difficulty with that. The question is, whose problem is it? Is it the publisher's problem, or it is the writer's problem? The publisher probably says it's the writer's problem. A critic of the building may say it's my problem. I don't think it's my problem.

However, that is the program for the Samitaur Tower in the conventional sense. It's a complicated one for the project. It has to do with the delivery of information through a series of venues that are large public venues. There are traffic-based venues that surround the site and then one on the site. There is more of a local pedestrian venue. That's it. That's what the project is.

Now I would like to re-phrase that question. You just gave me the definition of what the Semitaur Tower is in terms of prose. Now I would like you to give me what the Samitaur Tower is as an exploration. Not what it is as based upon site and program but in its "Joycian" or the "Mossian" understanding of "wiggle" or similar interests.

The reason that I said there was an essay entitled "Which Lie Do You Want to Tell?" actually I got it wrong. That was the original name of the essay. David Morton, a friend of mine, is an editor at Rizzoli. He said, "Moss, you had better not do that. You're going to lose some clients. Why don't you change it to, 'Which Truth Do You Want to Tell?'" The essay now says, "Which Truth Do You Want to Tell?" So it is fair to say that there is an argument for the project, which is just the argument I gave, which is a fair argument, a valid argument and part of the explanation.

But it's not the only argument.

No, but the argument I just gave is what clever architects are doing to validate conceptual ideas that seem to be, I don't know at this point, outlandish. Assuming there are ideas that depart from some type of norm, the way you validate that is to redefine the norm. The way you redefine the norm in a contemporary discussion is to use issues of technical fabrication, design engineering, other complicated ones and justify them. Today, in particular, we do that in terms of green sustainable issues. So the wind is doing this, the turbines are doing that, and the surface of the building allows you to do so and so. So when somebody says, "Gee, this is somewhat weird. How come it's like that?" The answer is given a technical spin.

I was on a jury a few months ago in Beijing, and Foster's office was one of the competitors. It was a huge project, six high rises, and he didn't come to the presentation. I thought that very strange, but all his guys came and they all made the argument about that double-glazing, and triple-glazing, and the gardens, and the sky, and so on. Technically the project had a very sophisticated look as if those arguments were self-justifying, meaning that if you solve those problems, you, ipso facto, have a great project, which is crap. That's the truth.

The point is that something is seen as genuine in a technical way, but disingenuous in a sort of "What are you really trying to do here?" position. What I'm interested in is moving conventional ways of thinking about

The way I begin to work on something is, by intention, to misrepresent what is conventionally the representation of a particular typology.

What I'm interested in is moving conventional ways of thinking about building types to a different position. ...If you want to do what I just said, regarding moving conventional ways of thinking, you have to be, in principle, dissatisfied with conditions as you find them.

building-types to a different position. Because, again, nobody who has ever read a history book should argue that the way it is today is the way it was yesterday or the way it should be tomorrow. If you want to do what I just said, regarding moving conventional ways of thinking, you have to be, in principle, dissatisfied with conditions as you find them.

There's an old Bernard Shaw line, "You see things; and you say, 'Why?' But I dream things that never were; and I say, 'Why not?' This is a little bit romantic, maybe a little bit adolescent, but I do think there's a kind of inertia in me responding to so many things that I would prefer to see differently. Then you could say that if they were different, you'd want them again different. So maybe that's why some of this is not a matter of art:; it's a matter of psychology or a matter of the intersection of art and psychology and how you think, how you know, how you understand, and how you imagine. I think those are all open questions forever.

I agree, yet, that's not the point actually. Your position also expresses an attitude implying that if one says, "I'm dissatisfied," or saying, "I have a concern." I may not solve my dissatisfaction or the general dissatisfaction, but I am motivated to address it. That is where a willingness to explore enters in. That's where one can begin to explore the relevance of "wiggle" or similar concerns.

Though in the language that I speak. In other words, if one designs a housing project in response to a shortage of housing, its realization in response to a perceived or recognized utilitarian social need. It adds to the discussion that everybody knew they were having. With my projects or language, I'm contributing to a discussion, except nobody's in the discussion. Not nobody... Tom Mayne may be in the discussion; Wolf Prix may be in the discussion, but there are just a few people in the discussion.

Adolf Loos is in the discussion with his statement regarding the "function" of funeral monuments in that they represent pure architecture. You have some function, but it's a different kind of function. So, that begs the question about why it "wiggles."

It doesn't wiggle very much.

Tempered wiggling then. Obviously the sense that there is, under what I'm now labeling as a concern, a desire to say, "Look, there are other paths that we should be exploring and those paths have validity." I'm now using the term "wiggle" in the sense of, "I'm interested in additional meanings in my work." I tell my students they must have at least two defenses of their conceptual statements. There's the practical defense, which you gave me regarding the views, and then there's the philosophical defense, or design intent defense, or whatever.

There may be audiences, lecture audiences, art audiences, etc., that are interested in those discussions. Certainly there is a lot of interest in those discussions. However, that argument does not always work. If you're talking to the Government Services Administration, you have to tell them it's going to cost this, it is going to solve this, it accommodates this, this is how you go up, this is how you go down, this is how you come out. There's a kind of utilitarian context that exists, and I think that is, in fact, a part of the discussion.

The more personal, or conceptual, or spiritual side is different...there are many ways to be serious about those issues. Somebody asked me the other day, "How do you start a project?" This is a little bit like your discussion,

There's an essential need to move the architectural discussion into an area of operation that separates it from a conventional way of thinking and understanding. ...In other words, you enlarge the discussion beyond what would conventionally be understood, in relation to what's possible, in any form, whether in making the project, the book, etc.

not exactly, but close. I said, what I do, as an example, if somebody comes to me and asks me to do a hospital, the first thing I do, and they don't know it, the first thing I do is make a jail. I just make a jail. It has nothing to do with a hospital. When I get done with the jail, I make the jail into the hospital. So, this belongs to me. I can't blame anybody for that. I never heard anybody argue that, but there's an essential need to move the architectural discussion into an area of operation that separates it from a conventional way of thinking and understanding. Now whether this is acrobatics, vanity, profundity, I don't know, but that was the answer to the question of how I begin a project. And I think it's largely true. In other words, you enlarge the discussion beyond what would conventionally be understood, in relation to what's possible, in any form, whether in making the project, the book, etc.

So is the answer, a "modern" answer, by that I mean from an "I'm ok you're ok" perspective, that all answers are OK?

I was just saying that the way I begin to work on something is, by intention, to misrepresent what is conventionally the representation of a particular typology. There are many examples of towers, which are investigations of technical capacity, or were created as vantage points from which to see the city. Similarly, there are vantage points in the city from which to see the tower, and they have an iconic role that belongs inevitably to a particular time in terms of representing meaning in a very abstract way. Some do it better...like the Samitaur Tower. It is more an iconic archetype as it is not very big, but relative to its surroundings, it is large in comparison to the built infrastructure around it because the other structures were limited in height, for whatever reason, and they let us get away with making the tower substantially higher. So, it has a meaning as an object in a landscape

So, it has a meaning as an object in a landscape of very different objects. It sets up the possibility that one could understand shape, space, and the interrelationship of pieces, elements, or components in a very different way than the way that you might normally understand...it makes for other ways of understanding, going forward, more doable because every time something like that doesn't get done it pushes us backwards. Every time it does get done, in the aggregate, it adds to the ammunition for moving forward.

of very different objects. It sets up the possibility that one could understand shape, space, and the interrelationship of pieces, elements, or components in a very different way than the way that you might normally understand so if the sentence is always capital, noun, verb, period now there's a different kind of sentence and it makes the original idea of the sentence, if not antiquated, it at least stretches the definition of what's possible. If it stretches it intelligently, it makes for other ways of understanding, going forward, more doable because every time something like that doesn't get done it pushes us backwards. Every time it does get done, in the aggregate, it adds to the ammunition for moving forward.

Or just moving.

Forward probably wouldn't be the word, moving differently and enlarging a vocabulary. It's funny to think about vocabulary like a dictionary. The language itself changes. If you look in a dictionary, you probably wouldn't find "Google" 20 minutes ago or "iPhone" 20 minutes ago or even the way language is used in terms of various courtesies or relationships. It changes. This is also true in architecture. The language changes. I was talking to a local developer, Eric Cobb, who's building a project in Century City that he has been working on for many years. They are bitching at him for knocking down a building, an old building. The argument is it's an iconic building. My argument is they are knocking down a hotel in Century City that was a piece of junk, as far as I'm concerned. It could just as easily be in Sao Paulo or Tel Aviv or so on. It doesn't matter. It's been there for a while, and so they're criticizing him for removing this piece of LA history. For that building it is not a very intelligent argument, but I think the point is, if a position is successful, you can change things. The Samitaur Tower potentially changes the discussion of what's conceivable. If you show that project to a student, it might make a big difference. Maybe not to 500 students, but maybe to five students. They know not only that it's possible to think differently, but some crazy guy will build it. Ultimately there are a lot of pedagogical, poetic, didactic, philosophical, as well as practical issues. Look, you're putting up steel. Every piece of steel, every pipe, all that stuff is certainly not a new idea as exposed. How are you going to keep it from rusting? There're all sorts of technical issues. Because we only had one stair, we had to sprinkle the whole thing. There are a lot of those kinds of problems which are also part of the discussion. All of that, so you can come at it in a lot of different ways and you can talk about it in a lot of different ways. It's not that a single way of talking about it is the real way. When we did the *Gnostic* book,

But I think the point is, if a position is successful, you can change things. The Samitaur Tower potentially changes the discussion of what's conceivable.

the inside of the inside is supposed to represent the most introspective way of understanding architecture. The outside of the outside was supposed to represent the most public or extroverted way, but the composite is still the composite. Now you might say what it is really about is the inside of the inside, but the model doesn't necessarily ratify that. You could use the model in a lot of different ways. It's not necessarily from 1 to 5, 1 being the most internal, 5 being the most external, but it could be.

For some it will be. So, a summation, not the summation, is, the Samitaur Tower wiggles for pragmatic reasons, and it wiggles for other, less pragmatic, reasons. You start a hypothetical hospital by envisioning it as a jail with the summation point being the goal of moving the process or the project differently? The prospect.

The prospect, better word. To permit the possibility of moving.

That's right.

So, let's pose the issue as exploring the known and unknown as a dialectic you would like to see through those types of oppositions. Like Henry Moore's "The Helmet" project, make the project read at more levels. Might be level five, might be level one, might be two and a half. In that manner there appears to be a strategy that relies on the certainty, the clarity of geometry, or other types of ordering conventions and opposes those sensibilities with shaping, ornamental, or jointing counterpoints that are obviously in opposition to that. In 3535 Hayden it's the old arches coming out of an existing building. They are set within a clear framework. In the "Wall, What Wall" project a "normal" wall is counterpointed with individually constructed CMU blocks to create a different dialogue in relation to the norm. It is the wiggle within an otherwise very structured stair tower. Are there interests relating to this desire to inform, this desire to move the discussion along that work into your architectural strategies?

Maybe the desire to inform has a corollary, as in who are you informing. I think the reality is you are probably informing the people who are making the project before you are informing the people who will see it or use it. So there's a self-informing, and that has to do with learning.

But here I'm saying you are now an architect, you've established a paradigm, and there's the hospital as a jail or whatever. You've sold it to the client. They don't have a clue about the jail, but you've sold it as a hospital. So now, you're back at the office, and you're further exploring the matter. At some point, you're going to have to say the jail is precise, and the hospital is imprecise, or vice versa or whatever. And you do that, and that's what I want to hear about.

We don't actually work that way. And that may be because many of the clients I work with now, I've worked with for a while. We work on things in a certain way. Nobody has to say anything. In fact, I remember a few years ago I gave a talk at UCLA. One of the guys in the office came to the talk and afterwards he came up to me and said, "Is that what we've been doing?"

Well, the issue here is not to create some false argument. The issue is to allow a reader to sense that even though the outcome is not trying to be predetermined or suggest moving forward or backward, it is to say

Maybe I'm trying to make people comfortable being uncomfortable.

But if an analysis is required, it would be, in the end, an analysis that would say this is about the incapacity of the architect to ever develop an allegiance to anything except a perpetual non-allegiance.

that what I employ as an architect is no different than what Joyce employs when he rewrites or redefines the sentence. In that regard, people need to know something about that. I'm trying to center the discussion on something one can observe, understand, or maybe even grow from.

Maybe I'm trying to make people comfortable being uncomfortable. That doesn't mean comfortable being comfortable. That doesn't mean uncomfortable being uncomfortable. It means comfortable being uncomfortable, meaning one can be comfortable with a contradictory condition, which it seems to me, is just endemic to culture and good architecture.

Is it fair to say, at least in an approach to the idea of establishing something of comfort, that there is something knowable? In that regard, I will use "knowable" to refer to the use of geometry in your projects. As soon as that is established, a shift or a destruction of the knowable is employed to assert a tension that is uncomfortable. The goal being to educate, by saying, "Look, we know what comfort is, but we don't know what discomfort is, and my goal is to make you comfortable with discomfort."

I think my objective is not exactly that way. It would be like running a race because you can't know exactly where you are finishing, like running a race and they keep moving the finish line. You are running a race in which you never get to the end, and if you do get to the end, then the game has become different. I think this sort of exploration of how we develop something, which first is, in itself, a value to the people who experience and use it, and as an analysis, maybe second or last. But if an analysis is required, it would be, in the end, an analysis that would say, "This is about the incapacity of the architect to ever develop an allegiance to anything except a perpetual non-allegiance." From time to time in some of the clearer presentations of this work, I think I have called that a provisional paradigm. Provisional because you have to insist on it in a certain time frame, but you have to understand the limits of insisting on it in a longer time frame. So, it has to do with a kind of perpetual, self-critical discussion. You are trying to set up a kind of regular space which intersects an irregular space. This is similar to the norm and the exception, the rule and the exception. I don't necessarily look at it that way because I'm not sure the rule even exists. Never mind the exception to the rule.

There's an interesting critic, Jeff Kipnis. We did an installation, and we were supposed to discuss the installation and a friend of mine was telling me that Kipnis was talking about it and said, "Well, I don't really have to say anything because Moss will argue both sides." I don't know whether that was meant as a criticism or a compliment, or neither, or either, or both, but I think there is something in that which is a kind of intrinsic dissatisfaction with everything. What I also would say every once in a while one hits a note, and the note is such an anomaly that all of the things you say in words about how it does not work go away. I can think of a couple of spaces that we made or things we've drawn that haven't been made, that fall into that category. They sort of escape this kind of didactic, thesis argument, because I think one makes the argument in order to escape an argument. But mostly you don't escape it. If the architecture is exceptional, unusual, what you think of as a life experience, those are the moments where you get out of it. But usually the way you get out of it is the act of the architecture allowing you to escape the contradiction that you're arguing for. So you're arguing for something on one hand, and you're trying to find a way out of it on the other.

What you're saying in relation to a strategy is, well, my strategy is to have a non-strategy or to show that I am...

No, it's simpler than that. I would say I would be a democrat if I could sit somewhere and say, "OK, I'm a democrat. I'll sign up for that, and I'll vote for that." But since I can't, I can't be a democrat. I can't be a post modernist, a neo-modernist, a digital guy, a deconstructivist, or an environmentalist because none of those things fit. It is not that those things don't fit anybody. They fit a lot of people. But if they don't fit, then don't put them on.

In essence, even if it is in some sort of diametrically opposed context, you are concerned about the human condition.

I think it is about the human condition.

And I think that's where the issue resides. Other concerns there might be, but in this regard we are forced to employ strategies allowing us to come to terms with what we feel we can do to address the issue. I'm not a critic; I'm a teacher and a practicing architect. When I look at the Arnoff Guest House or Samitaur, or the Samitaur Tower there is a strategy employed to make people think, and therefore become uncomfortable, but learn.

Comfortable being uncomfortable.

Yes, but there are enough continuities in your projects that make it possible to argue a position reflecting this concern, a concern regarding this interest that is evaluated through a construct providing enough knowledge, enough order, enough geometry—if that is what we have to use as a construct because that's the history of architecture—that you give to the user and then take it away. That is the point of reference from which I would like to continue the discussion.

But the awkwardness is like a little kid learning to walk who doesn't quite know how to walk yet. This is where I want to be.

If you looked at the smaller building, the Wall, What Wall project next to the Samitaur Tower, that project has 1,000 blocks, and every one of those blocks is an 8 x 8 x 8 concrete block, yet every single block is cut differently. This project was realized before CNC processes. People now associate it with a digital process, but it was constructed before that opportunity existed. In the sense there is a recognizable alphabet identified through, the use of CMU blocks to create a recognizable sentence or a recognizable module created for construction, through repetition a certain type of building logic is understood. Now there is an argument for a somewhat different kind of application, if not a bastardization of the entire motivation for making concrete block in the first place. We didn't actually pour that concrete, which we could have done. We made it out of the pieces that everybody said, "You can't make this out of that." In your terms of a knowable construct, there is the unit. There's a concrete block wall, and that's the unit, like the alphabet, which is recognizable in architectural ways, technical ways, engineering ways, spatial ways, etc. We all know what you can do with that unit, right? Wrong, we don't actually.

If you talk to the mason who built the Wall, What Wall project, one understands that he learned the rules of masonry, and for many years he didn't build the way we were asking him to construct the wall. But his capacity to use reinforcing steel, to cut blocks, to make things fit, to follow a new process—because he built the wall using a model and a series of cardboard profiles, which we made in the office, allowed to him to "start over." I think, in that sense, what we are seeing is that what was once impossible is now possible. What's inconceivable is now conceivable and the spatial experience of that is, especially on the inside, a very powerful experience. Some of

You can't do nothing and you can't do everything... there are limits, they are the poles. I think what I'm trying to do in some ways is push the poles.

it is clumsy. I don't want to say it's completely awkward, and by the time we get into the project in Kazakhstan, it may not be awkward at all. But the awkwardness is like a little kid learning to walk who doesn't quite know how to walk yet. This is where I want to be.

I don't want to learn to walk unless I can learn to run, jump, or skip. I want to be able to sustain that, and I believe nobody thinks one can do that, that it is possible.

You want to make people more aware, and more understanding of the fact that there's more to the world than making a concrete block wall out of an 8 x 8 x 8 module and stacking it one way. That is an important realization, and while you can argue that it is for a few interested, curious, talented people, "the five," our public realm responsibilities suggest that it goes beyond that.

I agree with that. I think it depends at what level one understands that issue. Somebody may go to Red Square, Tiananmen Square, etc., and say the scale of those things...like Nuremburg, has a spatial purpose and a political purpose, similar to walking up the steps at a temple in the Yucatan. These conditions tend to dwarf or trivialize the individual. There are many ways to talk about these things. I wouldn't say that building means everything to everybody or nothing to most people. All I'm saying is it may mean more to some people, in different ways, than it means to other people. If nothing else, it's a curiosity. I don't think it's a matter of either it's everything or it's nothing. I think for most people it's probably somewhere in between. I think you could break art theory into, if you wanted to simplify everything... somebody could be Rothko, could be Mondrian, almost nothing or almost everything, and although you can't do nothing and you can't do

I think a lot of the things we've done, for a number of reasons, are complex. You have to be very patient to realize them in a spatial way. I'm not the guy that says it has to be made out of this or that.

I'm interested in the kind of hybridization of a materiality and purpose in a spatial way, not in a technical way.

After you work on ideas for a while there are a number of possibilities, and in this office they keep moving. I think in other offices once a language or frame of reference is established limits accrue. For us it is a little more complicated than that.

I think rigor shouldn't be so easy to discover. It should not be something that is so translatable.

everything there are limits. They are the poles. I think what I'm trying to do in some ways is push the poles.

16| Let me use that as a reference for a slightly different part of the conversation. Materiality, or lack there of, or the discounting thereof, define your thoughts on your perception of materials and their use.

I'm not interested in material as a priority in the way that a spatial idea would be a priority. I would concede, if I had to pay for something, that I would probably be prepared to pay for what it took to make the space. To pay for what the space should be, what it would be if it were made out of adobe, bamboo, carbon fiber, or poured concrete or whatever. There is a kind of materiality that drives a certain kind of architecture. In other words, it is concrete before it's anything. I think a lot of the things we've done, for a number of reasons, are complex. You have to be very patient to realize them in a spatial way. I'm not the guy that says it has to be made out of this or that.

One of the reasons for my skepticism for computer drawings and renderings is that they're very ethereal. More and more younger people, people that really do Catia, are without a kind of material sensibility. You know that one has to learn from experience that if you bite something hard, you break your jaw. You punch the wall made out of gypsum, you put your arm through it. You punch the wall made out of granite you break you arm. In some ways, it's like the difference between walking down Grand Avenue or Michigan Avenue. There are different sensibilities.

We've been very interested in the use of glass and the qualities of glass. We did a project for the Smithsonian. It didn't work. We made it for Nike, and it didn't work. Now we're making it for a Culver City project using the glass cylinders. I'm interested in the kind of hybridization of a materiality and purpose in a spatial way, not in a technical way. I think the argument for a technologically inspired architecture is complete nonsense in that it is an end in itself. I gave a talk the other day in Seoul, Korea and I showed guys in Alamogordo, New Mexico gathering around talking about the atomic bomb, which as far as I know, is scientific progress, because it adds knowledge. If you can split the atom, you know something you didn't know before, but the application of science is technology and the application of that is discovery. For instance, in the Smithsonian, we made trusses using glass vertical tubes...we did not win that competition. We tied it with Sir Norman Foster. Aaron Betsky ran the jury. Then he left, and ultimately, they gave the project to Foster's office. They thought what we were talking about couldn't be done, as it is a big roof over the Smithsonian in Washington, DC.

A roof similar to Foster's renovation and enclosing roof at the British Museum?

That's one of the reasons he got it. And one of the reasons we didn't. So, we're trying to build it now. But, yes, that's exactly the project. We had a series of trusses, very beautiful. I think it worked. But the trusses were glass. The chords were glass. We can do it, we know how to do it, we are going to do it. They thought we couldn't do it, couldn't build it, couldn't pay for it. It would fall down and somebody would get sued or somebody would get killed. But what is interesting about that is that there is an interest in the kind of expansive interrogatory about technology. Our truss substitutes what is a conventional chord of a truss with glass and gives it a completely different quality, a completely different meaning.

Obviously there is a parallel with the idea of glass used as a truss and in the exploration of making people comfortable with uncomfortable-ness.

Well, that's another one, although I'm not so sure about that. You know it's funny when you say that. Regarding the glass truss we are doing now, we have a hearing with the City Council coming up and people ask me if the trusses are going to fall on their heads. So, this isn't some sort of bullshit theoretical discussion. This is not somebody speculating for students. It is a retail project, including restaurants, with human occupants. Some will be saying, "Gee, what the hell is going on?" I like that in a way, in the abstract.

You mean you like the question or the concern?

I like the question in a sense that I think it implies something that, in a philosophical form, I would support. What's difficult about it, and this is back to what lie you are going to tell, is that if they think it's going to fall down, and they're certain, then they will not go for it. If they don't support it, you don't build it. So, in a way, this is a different kind of contradiction. It has to do with a public perception of something, and I think this is why we lost the competition in DC. They thought we were going to kill everybody.

There's an interesting sort of authentic/inauthentic issue in the sense of, well, it is authentic, in that the glass truss has been engineered. It works, but it creates an inauthentic reading of what we think glass can do. It makes us anxious.

Good point actually, because the conventional structural idea of what glass requires has nothing to do with the chords of the truss. In a different way it takes us back to the conventional idea of what a concrete block is, what it represents, and how you construct with it. So

However, the double plates, the stiffeners, all these elements were developed as the building evolved, they were very much a part of our frame of reference for making the tower. We don't want expressions or design resolutions grounded on practicality as the only determinant of the outcome.

what's unsettling about a glass truss is, in a philosophical way, good. In an approval way, because you're actually asking people to understand the use of a glass truss, it is different. The top horizontal member is a steel tube. The bottom member is a cable and the vertical cords are glass. I don't think about it as unsettling in a literal way yet it obviously turned out to be a very literal issue. It is going to the planning department so we will see what happens.

Returning to the Samitaur Tower, at the level of a diagram this tower can be understood as two interacting towers with two beams slicing through to hold a series of circular diaphragms. What was the value of the circular elements? What was the impact of site constraints? Was the program a factor in determining a certain size? What I am interested in is what interests governed the decision to make one move or another?
From your vantage point, I do not think you will ever find an answer to all of them. Obviously you cannot make a circle that is bigger than the site; you cannot build over someone else's property. After you work on ideas for a while there are a number of possibilities, and in this office they keep moving. I think in other offices once a language or frame of reference is established, limits accrue. For us it is a little more complicated than that. It finds a way of repeating itself. And this goes back to that article on radicalism in architecture published in *Architecture Review* about renewing a point of view rather than repeating a point of view and looking for ways to undo what you have done before. So why exactly was this thing done in the way it was done could be explained as a response to our previous projects.

Depending to whom you are speaking, it is perfectly plausible to explain the tower in pragmatic terms. You

I am very interested in the power of objects and the power of space in an overwhelming way. I am also interested in the capacity to implement something in architecture that you couldn't say you knew before you came to it.

can look at it from different directions, and it works. What else do you need? I am very interested in the power of objects and the power of space in an overwhelming way. I am also interested in the capacity to implement something in architecture that you couldn't say you knew before you came to it. It could be a way of looking at life. You have to be willing to do that. That is a completely different kind of discussion. What you are talking about tries to organize an idea based on a whole series of pragmatic needs; how much, how high, what is the setback, what are the programmatic requirements and somehow if you could add all those up, you would arrive at a conclusion.

4.1| Actually, I am trying to get past that. Other than the issues surrounding the program and site, what intentions underlie the design of the Samitaur Tower? That is what I want to expand upon. As a link here is a quote from *Gnostic Architecture*, "The process of making a building is a process of making cerebral subject matter the experience of the building. If you can sense that contradictory quality distinctly without necessarily dealing with it in an intellectual way, then it is there. It's not so much that there is a particular rationale to validate the project, but the project is validated by rendering the dialectic so sharply, so insightful that a transcendent lyrical experience becomes available in the architecture." I think that's fantastic, but obviously it has little to do with program.

What it really says is that the experience has to transcend the argument. You can make a lot of interesting arguments, with a lot of intelligence, and yet in the end, it has to be something. I think the word "lyrical" is a word for that. And maybe another phrase, dialectical lyrical

It doesn't look like a typical tower, which means that its motivating factor must, to some extent, be different than what is programmed into or organizing a typical project. But all of that is of no value if pursuing those qualities does not have an experiential value. If is does not have an experiential attribute, it is of no consequence.

argument, which I have thought about. There exists an intellectual world of thinking about ideas in architecture and a dialectic, meaning a contradiction, so in an intellectual way, there is a very fundamental contradiction in the experience of these buildings. It's not a believer's building; it is a Gnostic's building. A gnostic, at least historically, has a private way of thinking or feeling or believing, which is not necessarily so far from an agnostic, who might acknowledge that there is one way of believing, but they don't know what it is.

Then there's the dialectical side, in which there could be arguments—it could be this, but it could be that, it could stand up, it might fall down. It moves outside of traditional recognition factors for a building of this type, in this case, a tower. It doesn't look like a typical tower, which means that its motivating factor must, to some extent, be different than what is programmed into or organizes a typical project. But all of that is of no value if pursuing those qualities does not have an experiential value. If it does not have an experiential attribute, it is of no consequence, and there are a lot of experiences like that. Love could be an experience like that. Hate could be an experience like that. There are a lot of things that are emotive before they are cerebral. And I think the business that you are in, and that almost everyone is in, is somehow analytical and theoretical and those kinds of arguments, as we all know, at a certain point have their limit, however interesting they are. There are a lot of religious books that reference that topic, and there are a lot of philosophical books, as philosophical as they are, that realize that those things have to be somehow transcendent.

In other words, if you have yourself a system, and you can teach it, and you can learn it, it is too late and that is not what I am interested in. What I am more interested in is where it is before it is what it will ultimately become.

In our office we want to teach you, let you experience what we don't yet know what we are talking about. We want to develop a capacity to see the world differently, one that we haven't yet developed.

I think authenticity comes from the ability for one not to accept it as a rule, but to invent it in a personal way and then define it in a manner that makes it belong to the architect, the architecture, or the process as opposed to a generic formulation of construction techniques.

Describe procedures or processes, whether conceptual or practical, where construction rigor was used to achieve a particular design intention.

Well the problem with words is that you have to use words! Rigor, I think, implies a system, a method, a discipline, and probably in architecture a legible discipline. I think rigor shouldn't be so easy to discover. It should not be something that is so translatable. I don't want anybody to be able to learn how to do this.

This, meaning what?

What we do. Things are often interesting before they come to be what they finally come to be. In other words, if you have a system, and you can teach it, and you can learn it, it is too late, and that is not what I am interested in. What I am more interested in is where it is before it is what it will ultimately become. By that I mean what it might suggest in a more fragile, speculative, exploratory, experimental stage of development when you don't really know exactly what it'll be, or whether it will be, or whether it will completely fail and disappear. You don't know that.

How does that relate to the idea of education?

Ha, it means that education is too late! It means education is no good. Because, I think what you have to do when you educate someone, and this is only part of that discussion, is that you have to teach someone to unlearn what he or she is being taught. And a lot of people aren't receptive to that. In fact, if you set that down as a dictum, you probably won't get very many students. In our office we want to teach you, let you experience what we don't yet know what we are talking about. We want to develop a capacity to see the world differently, one that we haven't yet developed.

For example, if you were Columbus, and you said, "OK, I'm going to get on a boat and find India." You had an idea, you set off with a destination in mind, and you figured it out because you have to figure something out, at least hypothetically. In the end you land somewhere new. It was very interesting, it is useful, and it turns out, if you were Columbus, you didn't even know where you landed, but it wasn't what he thought it was. That's a good model.

That is a good model. Now that we are at the tower site let's see if we can carry that forward. I would like to start with an issue that caught my interest by starting at the ground and moving up. On one, maybe all of the circular rings, there are steel plates attached apparently to add additional structural rigidity.

Are you talking about the vertical stiffeners between the flanges?

Yes. And while I cannot speak to the engineering requirements, there is...

We do our own engineering, and we don't. In other words, this thing was pretty definite before the Arup engineering guys got a hold of it. That doesn't mean we don't know how to work with engineers. We know how to work with engineers very well, but I think we consider them through a more comprehensive idea of defining the content so as to control it as comprehensively as possible. Therefore, the process is not like I made a sketch on an airplane, gave it to a group of engineers and they returned an engineered solution without any conversation. However, the double plates, the stiffeners, all these elements were developed as the building evolved. They were very much a part of our frame of reference for making the tower. We don't want expressions or design resolutions grounded on practicality as the only determinant of the outcome.

You want it to be expressive in a realm that supports a transcendent side.

That's right. Everything is pursuant to that objective. We probably would have created the stair without a handrail if we could have gotten away with it. But obviously there are conditions here one cannot avoid. You have to have a tread; you have to have a riser. There are limits within multiple arenas, but the idea is that everything you put into the building is pursuant to the conceptual content of the building.

The focus is to make sure that decisions do not appear to be unintended or unanticipated. In the expressiveness of the concrete, how does that relate to larger intentions?

I think there's an old discussion that shouldn't be accepted at face value but has to do with an interest in, for maybe more than a century, the way in which buildings are constructed. Understanding construction techniques and technology as a part of what a building is to become then allows it to be a part of the outcome. That's different than having a kind of a priori image. In putting a building together it is obvious that it will become large, yet in turn it is constructed from small pieces. Now we are having a discussion about a channel, a metal deck, the concrete. It is a discussion about the angles. It is a discussion about the rods. All of those elements come together, so in the aggregate, you are looking at many different visual interrelationships, technical issues, all of that.

How does that relate to your conceptualizing in terms of authenticity? Is that part of it or is it envisioned as an aspect of assembly?

I think authenticity comes from the ability for one not to accept it as a rule, but to invent it in a personal way

The objective is to deliver an experience that is not so predictable that can be read as, "Oh, we've come to a corner, we must then go 12" to the left and 12" to the right."

and then define it in a manner that makes it belong to the architect, the architecture, or the process as opposed to a generic formulation of construction techniques. To some extent authenticity belongs to something; it is part of a history, or it belongs to our era. To another extent it belongs to a personal rendition of something that has a more general meaning.

That is no different than the "dead man" here where you see their tops expressed. They imply that there was a big hole here. Many people walk up and down this sidewalk. They are probably just out for a walk, and they walk right over them. They do not notice the deadmen or pay any attention. Yet if you were to walk on the next million side-walks from here to Barcelona you probably won't find this detail expressed. It is not automatically intelligible, yet it is something and suggests that an action occurred here. It repeats itself around the perimeter. It could be something that someone informed like you might read into the situation, or it could be something that is a little more enigmatic.

It provides an opportunity for engagement.

It suggests that it is a possibility. To some extent, and this is true for many things in life, it's up to the person to engage with the event or element or to simply keep walking. You walk in somewhere, you are having a cigarette, or you argue with your girlfriend, and you are not paying attention to anything but your current state of affairs. Yet on the other hand, if you are musing on the inconsistencies of human affairs, it may strike you perfectly. It may have an impact.

Historically speaking, or even walking around a mall in Houston and seeing the concrete one probably does not perceive it in a manner similar to what we have been

But obviously there are conditions here one cannot avoid. You have to have a tread; you have to have a riser. There are limits within multiple arenas, but the idea is that everything you put into the building is pursuant to the conceptual content of the building.

discussing. This is, in part, a way of looking at what you see and what you are used to seeing. We see a hunk of concrete. It is a curb. It runs for 50 feet, and so on. Yet the interrelationship between the tools, or what represents a vision for its form or its materiality, or ultimately what might be a slightly different way of looking at concrete is part of the equation.

Let's talk about the corner conditions at the railings. A lot of architects would say, "I either have a corner post, or I don't have a corner post but each support point is 36" from here and then the next support point is 36" from here, and so on." What I am curious about is you set up a module for the railing baluster spacing, and then you just allow it to run, regardless of the specific lengths of each side of the platform. When you come to a corner there's not a fixation with being concerned about how the module corresponds to a larger dimension.

If you wanted to look at the corner you could say, "There's a corner." If you look a little closer, the dimensions are all different, so a uniform module wouldn't measure out right on each side. The objective is to deliver an experience that is not so predictable that can be read as, "Oh, we've come to a corner. We must then go 12" to the left and 12" to the right." The railing supports do not run on a module. Even the module is malleable, based on the idea that turning the corner, which is a historic discussion in architecture, is always a slightly different experience.

At the entry walkway one sees two parallel steel I-beams, which are offset inwardly from the steel panels on the adjacent side-walls on either side, one containing the elevator and the other the stair core. My question is, "Are the steel beams holding the various floor levels pulled in from the elevator and stair core to suggest a non-standard use of structure or are they representing something else?" What were your thoughts in relation to the beams, their location, and expression?

You are referencing that they are not sitting on the walls of the elevator core and the stair core and ,yet the answer is not automatic. You can support something by aligning it over a column or over a beam, or you can hold something adjacent, but you have to grab it. This gets subjective to the point where I'm not sure I can make a verbal case for it. There are different arguments for supporting the beams in one way and there is a different argument for supporting them in another. For me if you split the core and then let the beams run in between, they then run from end to end. They don't visually stop at the core, they run all the way through. And the core grabs that piece and supports it. That's the way it works. When you walk in you get the experience of the beams expressed running all the way through. The stair core and the elevator core then remain discreet and the structural system supporting the cantilevered floors also remains discrete or expressive.

In that regard you want to privilege the entry, maybe circulation or supporting the floor plates?

I think it means the directional condition and the force of that condition have to maintain visual priority, visual expression. I think it's less so if it melts into the cores.

If you shove those beams into the face of the elevator core and the stair core, it would change those conditions substantially yet you could do it. There are numerous solutions. I could push the beam in so the web essentially sits over the wall. You could push it part way in so that it obviates the cores but still hangs out. You could push it all the way in, which would mean essentially that

In a literal sense experiencing the components of the systems moving through the tower is actually very important. ...In the end, part of the thinking underlying the tower is to not allow the kinds of decisions typically made where one is going to hide this and bury that regarding the expression of utilities.

the outside edge of the flange is aligned with the wall of the core. There remain multiple ways of integrating the beams that could be accomplished. Similarly, it is interesting observing the conduits and all the utilities. As you get higher that changes. It's different on every floor as there are fewer and fewer components as you get higher. If you shove the beam in there, just for the sake of argument, and you have to punch 500 holes in the beam for the conduit lines then it is not a beam anymore. So some of it has to do with reconciling various kinds of experiences and how you put together 10 different things.

18| How do you allow for something so conventional sounding as building systems to have their own zone, their own qualities letting them have an expression?
The hole in the stair core, and the pipes running up and through is an analogy to an organ loft. I remember seeing one that was very beautiful that Utzon did in a church outside of Copenhagen. Frank Gehry did a nice one at the Disney Hall. And even though this is not a pipe organ, in a literal sense experiencing the components of the systems moving through the tower is actually very important. In addition, they also function as a railing as they are alongside a spatial void in the tower. Therefore, there is a need for a railing, yet there is no longer a railing in the conventional sense because a "pipe organ" is a surrogate for a rail. So, when you start thinking about it, it gets a little more complicated.

The idea is of different pipes all at different spacing running through the building. In the end, part of the thinking underlying the tower is to not allow the kinds of decisions typically made where one is going to hide this and bury that regarding the expression of utilities. We had to move all of that and spread it all around the building. In addition we had to incorporate the sound system and the projection system. In all cases the spacing between the various elements is intentionally different.

It is very elegant. The spacing issue addresses the same kind of issues discussed concerning the deadmen.
It is also relates to themes underlying the detail condition of turning corners with the railings. There are different kinds of spacing, and you don't quite know what they are as they change from level to level. Then there is different spacing between the pipes, the balusters, all of that. That generates a kind of enigmatic quality as part of the building.

10| I'm glad you made that reference as it is important. Would it be fair to say that the enigmatic quality carries right through to how elements are organized, or more properly stated, intentionally unorganized? That aspect has something to do with the idea of adding depth, whether depth of engagement or an intentional enigma.
If you added all of these things up, whether it is the railing or the deadmen, the pipes or many other things, you start to come to a conclusion about how this tower is conceived.

15| Then the art or the poetic or the lyrical starts entering in, let's relate that to a material question. The material qualities are in a long "Mossian" tradition representing an ambiguous use of material. Yet at the same time there are material conditions representing a very crisp and clear expression which I think is also part of a tradition. In that regard I am interested in how you were envisioning the conceptual role of glass.
Why glass on the elevator? Well there are a lot of

The steel has a has a certain visual role, I did not want to obviate that role by putting it contiguous with another opaque material with another visual "weight" as opposed to putting it against something transparent, a material not having those qualities of weight, color, or materiality. You have something that governs the building and supports the building playing against something that is more ethereal. That's what glass does.

Materials are important and materials are unimportant. But you have to work with both conditions, then the question is when is it one and when is it the other?

answers. Which lie do you want to tell; which truth do you want to tell? The steel has a certain visual role, I did not want to obviate that role by putting it contiguous with another opaque material with another visual "weight" as opposed to putting it against something transparent, a material not having those qualities of weight, color, or materiality. You have something that governs the building and supports the building playing against something that is more ethereal. That's what glass does. Of course with the elevator being transparent you can look out.

In thinking of your larger body of work, I would argue that to you, materials are both important and in another way not important, yet you have used multiple materials over the span of your projects. They often have a kind of dematerialized quality in the sense that there's an apparent interest in having a texture of some sort, yet there remains underlying expressions of intention. Is that argument similar to what you're describing about the glass and its lightness vs. the solidity of the panels at the elevator? In the tower there is the glass with its dematerialized qualities and the steel, which is more or less allowed to maintain a material essence. I am probing for an area where you would say you have interests that move from project to project.

You said it accurately. Materials are important and materials are unimportant. But you have to work with both conditions. Then the question is when is it one and when is it the other?

Regarding the assembly of various components, I can imagine many architects stating, "This structure is obviously a steel tectonic assembly. Let's install the steel plate and expose all the fasteners." But the stair and elevator cores, and the steel cladding are smooth, with no fasteners exposed. Was the issue about expressing a constructed language, including the fasteners, or was the design intention more focused on achieving a certain material texture, a less tectonic essence?

It is welded, and it is ground down. The tower is not a solid; it is a frame, a frame that is clad. What holds the building together structurally is less a solid and more of a frame. Witness the fact that there are big holes within the tower. But to give it the sense of an object as opposed to a frame with holes in it, both become, to a certain extent, solid. That is the way it was envisioned so the point, in this case, was not to make every seam or fastener an issue.

Because of the interest of wanting the tower to read more as a solid and less as a frame, tell me about the stair and its top side and bottom side. It could have been two layers of checker plate but you have a smooth side on the bottom of the stair and a textured side, with the checked plate, on the top. Is there a similar conceptual interest in that smooth/rough duality as described regarding the duality between the solidity of the object and the more open frame?

What is interesting is that the only place you get that is on the edge of the star. It is a little bit like reading the metal deck and the concrete expressed on the edge of the bridge, which is a clue to how the concrete was poured with the metal deck supporting it. If you only see the support for the checker plate, you will never know of the other expression. You don't necessarily perceive the bottom by looking at the top, or the top by looking at the bottom. But you get the relationship or duality of the materials when you see it from the side.

Under the larger themes that you have been elaborating it is interesting to see those issues continue to become incorporated at the detail level. Standing on the second level, one also reads the solidity of one of the cores as well as the frame of the core.

To me it becomes a little more ambivalent. It is a solid, and then it isn't, or it is open. There are big panels and at those locations it is pretty clear how the frame works. In a way it is a single solid reading at the stairwell, and in another sense it is two pieces. The stair core itself is not so solid, compared to the elevator core which is more so. It really has to do with identity of shapes and ideas and whether you can see it, and read it, and understand it—in a sense similar to an experience where one can look down the Champs-Elysées and see the Arc de Triomphe and say, "Wow." There you know what this is from top to bottom. What this tower requires is that you walk around and examine it, assuming you want to do that. However, what you learn is that what you thought you saw isn't what's there.

Similarly, depending on how you look at the tower if we are at the outside, then the frame is the inside. From one side you don't see it as a frame and from another side you do. On the other hand, when you look at the core from "this" outside, it presents as a solid, yet at the same time you see the core from within. You see the inside of the other outside. So there you are looking at the outside of the outside; now you're looking at inside of the outside.

One other area that appears to have design intentions expressing an interest in providing a narrative is the base of the tower, including the grass. Discuss your thoughts about the grass or the conceptual side of placing the tower lower into the ground.

As opposed to setting the "building" on the land...When you cut into the land, there is a record of it. The deadmen give this a qualitative aspect, an expression and reading of land and what the land does, that the land does something different than what manmade things do....The grass becomes another condition similar to that experienced with the screens, something more transitory or visceral.

That is a big issue for us in terms of the interrelationship between the building and the land. As opposed to setting the "building" on the land, I am interested in building into the land. It makes it so integral to the process. It goes down into the ground and the ground obligates it. One manifestation of that relationship to the earth is the deadmen, which indicate the whole thing has been excavated in a substantial way. It is a very complicated foundation, with very big piles because of the cantilevers and so on.

When you cut into the land, there is a record of it. The deadmen give this a qualitative aspect, an expression and reading of land and what the land does, that the land does something different than what manmade things do. So, the tower is in the land, and the land presents a different qualitative experience relating to the world and what it produces vis a vis the tower. That becomes another contradiction. It has an excavated hole, it has a technical aspect with the deadmen, but it also has another kind of experiential quality. Relating to the grass, it obviously grows seasonally. It comes and goes. It is softer in a way. It's not as tough and harsh and abrasive and aggressive as the building. The grass becomes another condition similar to that experienced with the screens, something more transitory or visceral .

What I'm saying is there's a landscape experience, object experience, and then a use experience through the exhibits and projections. They all give the tower another purpose. In the Samitaur Tower experiencing the film/media events, even the grass, gives it a different kind of life. It is not so abstract. It personalizes it and gives it other meanings. ■

TWBT

Tod Williams/Billie Tsien

American Folk Art Museum

A project whose program is both singular and unique, the American Folk Art Museum epitomizes the apogee of building types to which architects aspire. However, given the idiosyncratic nature of the art form for which it was built, the museum presented multiple design challenges. The 40,000 square foot museum, located on a narrow 40 x 100 foot site adjacent to the Museum of Modern Art was completed in 2001. Because of a narrow site, two levels, housing larger and more opaque program components including an auditorium, classrooms and administrative offices, were placed below grade. This allowed the galleries and public areas to benefit from a building section activated by light filtering in from a large north-facing skylight. Plan and section organization also enabled light to penetrate into the lower levels of the building.*

TWBT Architects, looking for balance and wholeness to organize a diverse collection without an artistic center, distributed the artwork throughout the building, including locating it among structural elements and circulation pathways. Multiple circulation routes and sectional spaces become organizing elements allowing the diverse collection to be viewed as a singular whole. Circulation, space and light then permit design intentions to imbue the building with intentions not singularly focused on the program. Starting with fundamental criteria relating to program distribution, and site considerations, ultimate interests underlying the design of the American Folk Art Museum support an intimacy deriving from the small scale nature of the artwork. A connection is established that reaches to the hand-wrought, as well as the intellect, to provide a basis for design intentions guiding the realized outcome..

* The Folk Art Museum was purchased by the Museum of Modern Art and demolished in 2014.

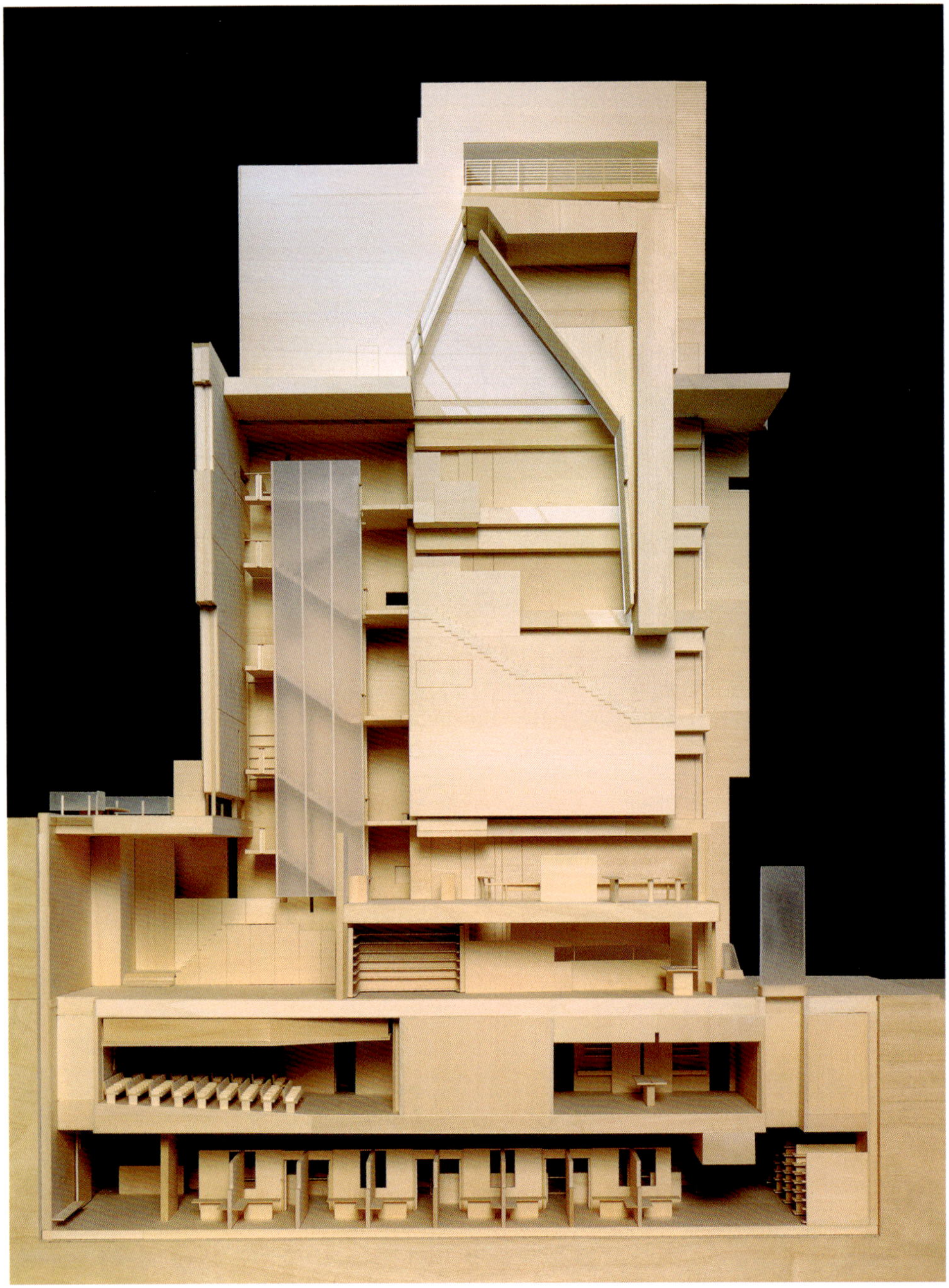

We perceive experiences in a sequential, almost narrative way and and not as independent, drawn pieces.

1| Tom Diehl: What value, potential, or use do you see in order?

Billie Tsien: Envisioning the program as separate components or small buildings and then exploring the relationship between them I think is, in a way, an ordering or disordering mechanism that we've used throughout the time we've been working. If you look at various projects, although maybe less true with the Folk Art Museum because it is a singular building, you can pull apart programmatic components and understand them as separate buildings. They are very interesting as separate entities with spatial relationships between them. In the Neurosciences Institute it could have been one building, but instead it is three buildings, and there is space in between. At the scale of elements, there are similar aspects in the Folk Art Museum

Tod Williams: I think space is a true ordering device. It is the dynamic relationship between components and the continuously changing relationship between them we are interested in. It certainly continues to be about understanding elements and allowing them to exist in an ordered relationship to one another.

I think an example of order could be a gridding. I started out as a young man looking at grids and regulating lines and fairly soon realized that architecture, spatial architecture, is much more complex than that. And so, we do, in fact, use ordering systems that are sometimes ghosts of organizing systems. They appear to order a space. Certain angles you just pointed to are probably not the same degree, but we knew that a chamfer might relate to a chamfer and the precise dimension may be unimportant to us or the precise angle may be unimportant to us but experiencing the design intention and its realized quality as you move through the space is our primary goal.

Plan, section Sketches

I think space is a true ordering device. It is the dynamic relationship between components and the continuously changing relationship between them we are interested in.

The negative space is also a part of the ordering. The space between buildings and various elements is as important as the space occupied by the building.

It is the ordering of materials, it's the ordering of systems, of mechanical systems or the ordering of structure. ...The order is there and it finds itself expressed in the building but is never a singular ordering device. ...I would say that we often wait for the order to emerge. Instead of imposing order, say placing a grid on a plan, we will wait to see how it emerges

I am sensing there is an interest in order not created through not some overarching system but the identification of objects or elements that then become "ordered" in the way in which they are spatially linked.
BT: Yes. The negative space is also a part of the ordering. The space between buildings and various elements is as important as the space occupied by the building.

TW: But I don't think it is just about space, although space is certainly a strong preoccupation. It is the ordering of materials, it's the ordering of systems, of mechanical systems or the ordering of structure. Structure never really becomes the primary element in our work, but it's the underlying principle of virtually all of the work. For example, the basic root of a building is usually a concrete foundation that sits somewhere on Mother Earth and from that ordering device, the grounding of the building into the earth, one begins to see the building emerge. The order is there and it finds itself expressed in the building but is never a singular ordering device such as a grid might be. It's not the primary organizing device but one of the many. We choose to recognize that reality. That seems logical to us. We will think of structure in that way.

So, while there is some use of classic modernist tools of regulating lines, lines of extension, that provide a certain system used to relate diverse parts, the larger issue is the experiential nature of the building. You want to achieve an "order," or experiential quality, that is based more upon something that has to do with a narrative quality rather than focusing on whether components are ordered by some...
BT: Yes, because we perceive experiences in a sequential, almost narrative way and not perceiving them as independent drawn pieces.

TW: For example, you find a person who has a certain character. You can describe an image of the person, the feeling of the person, and the actions of the person. In the end buildings operate in the same way, that is, how they operate spatially, how they operate emotionally, how they operate in time. All of these things give weight to a larger sense of the building's place in time and space and history. So we look for a building to last longer than our own lives, and we expect that it will change its performance characteristics as it grows, as society grows around it. We are really interested in how it interacts.

2| How do concepts of order manifest themselves in your design thinking or processes? What does order mean to you architecturally? Are you interested in concepts of order that exist outside the specific disciplines of architecture?
BT: I think it is manifested within the experiential confines of the individual and rooted in construction and assembly.

TW: I think order is ultimately rooted in the world of architecture. The world of architecture is broad enough to absorb all things. It is an extremely rich world, and as you look deeper, it becomes deeper itself. I would say that we often wait for the order to emerge. Instead of imposing order, say placing a grid on a plan, we will wait to see how it emerges, and that is sometimes frustrating. People think of us as being interested in materials. The fact is, it comes out of research, and often it comes slowly, and we may not know many of the materials until we get to know the project better. We are waiting for the order to emerge as we search through the project, trying to find its deeper meaning.

If order comes from experience, marking the ground, research, etc., that has led to a particular direction or position, at what point do you find yourself using ordering systems to make spatial, or formal connections, "rational" or not, making evident boundaries or space defining conditions? Is there a sense of that tying into your definition of order, or would you say those aspects are less important to you, that it is not a critical part of your process?
TW: I think we know a duality, whether literally or experientially, is present. We are often thinking in terms of a balance or wholeness in the final product, a sense of wholeness which is not always known in the ongoing process when one is moving elements around and separating the program into a series of pieces and making opposites. But in the end there is a desire to make it whole, to make it ordered.

So then wholeness might derive from, as an example, lining elements up, and yet sometimes it may come from intentionally not lining them up, which ever might support the larger goal of balance or wholeness.
TW: Totally correct. You start out with a process where one is hoping for and believing in wholeness. It doesn't come by the stroke of the pen or a singular inspiration, but it is still the goal. What one does is look at the various parts and try to find the way they actually relate to one another. Sometimes the coincidence is so strong as to make them seem to be whole when they shouldn't be, so we might try and slide them apart or push them apart to ensure that there is a kind of a blur and that you are constantly aware that wholeness is not a given. It's not something that we can mandate. It is by the grace of our struggle that it comes.

4| Then do design interests, extending beyond those concerned with fitting the building to the site or

There are sources that have nothing to do with architecture. They aren't history, they aren't really theory, but they are sources that move us. Dance, theater, nature come back into our work in direct ways. ...Can we incorporate aspects that are more idiosyncratic, ones not simply found through looking at materials and arranging spaces? That is a very important part of what we do, of our approach to design.

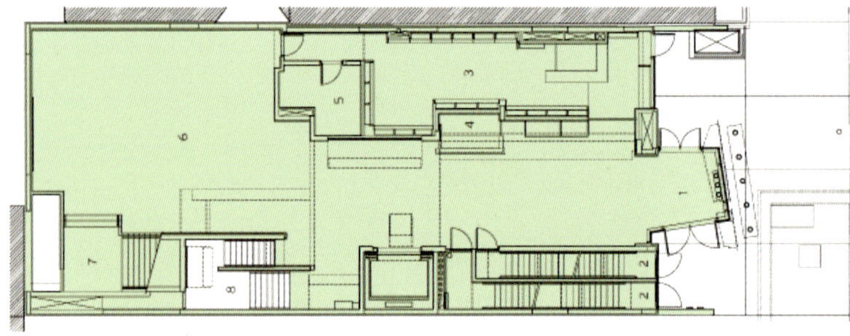

First floor plan

facilitating the distribution of the program, originate, for you, within the discipline of architecture or from sources lying outside of it?

BT: It is discipline based, but there are sources that have nothing to do with architecture. They aren't history, they aren't really theory, but they are sources that move us. Dance, theater, nature come back into our work in direct ways.

So the more architectural criteria you referred to earlier do not constitute a singular focus directing your design interests or intentions?

BT: Not always. They may come from a piece of poetry about whiteness or quietness, a gingko tree whose yellow color in the fall is really iridescent. Can we find a way to incorporate that spirit or quality inside? Can we incorporate aspects that are more idiosyncratic, ones not simply found through looking at materials and arranging spaces? That is a very important part of what we do, of our approach to design.

TW: I would also argue that program is, in fact, not what we do. Certainly we respect the program, but it is actually the place that is not program where the life of architecture occurs. For example, if someone gives me a program for a room of 120 square feet, it is 10 feet x 12 feet with an eight-foot-high ceiling. To me the question of what goes on in that space functionally is critical, but the more important question is what goes on outside that space. Somebody has already programmed what goes on inside that space; my responsibility is to determine what goes on outside that space. For example, I could call you a program element and identify you by your green shirt, your mustache, etc. Similarly for Billie, but the more important aspect is the space between us. As "program" elements, that is the powerful and important thing we are talking about. So I would say that it is always the experience, what is not programmed that is the most critical part. Certainly you have to order the program—you have to be on that side of the table, and we have to be on this side, and so on. But that which is between us, or even inside you, that is what we care about.

What you both just described represents a fairly high interest in transcendent issues, those existing outside the base considerations of architectural design. Would you call that a global interest or intention, or is it more project specific and varies from project to project?

BT: I think it is not project specific; it is life oriented. I think that different influences are occurring all the time. It is not like we would look at a site and draw a line connecting it to another site that somehow...it's not about formal ordered relationship. It's emotional or even sensuous influences that come from outside and are constantly filtering their way into the work. It is never a "this relates to this," so we draw a line here in order to line it up with something there. Neither is it particularly based on a theory; we are not trying to prove something with the building.

TW: I would also say that in teaching it is not a bad thing at all to use program and program relationships as a basis for learning. As we have become older, we have recognized that we have to transcend those issues. We have to go beyond them. So what is merely obvious when we were younger ultimately becomes more richly developed as we get older. It could put us in a transcendent place which isn't really what we are after, but I suppose as one moves closer to death you actually move into a kind of transcendent state. When you are young, to ask for that is a lot, because it is certain that we could have learned in more interesting and rich ways than we were taught. But you need to use these building blocks to start from in order to move to the more complex relationships we ultimately seek.

5| So how do these interests, whether transcendent or foundational, impact your thinking in relation to the methods employed to architecturally organize and/or represent your intentions? Whether from a book you have read or from an issue discovered in conversation with a client but not necessarily derived from the program or a site, how are the elements utilized to document design interests organized? How do they impact your thinking? At some point we have to organize things, at some point we have to decide what regulates the components, the space.

TW: I would say a couple of things. First, the formal method by which we attack the problem is that if someone tells us the programmatic elements are ABCDEF...and they represent the net square footage of a building, we say we are interested in the gross. At the onset we are interested in the space between, in issues beyond ABCDEF. And we do that so much that we often physically pull things apart allowing the outside in.

When you say the gross, are you saying that you are interested in the gestalt?

TW: Yes, the circulation system, the environmental systems, everything is considered. I'm more interested in the sound of the car outside than I am interested in the program itself. But I still have to organize it somehow. We do start with the simple building blocks. The building has to be made and constructed somehow. We think about where it's being made, and what materials are available at a given location, at the very simplest and dumbest level. We will wonder whether the foundation will be made out of poured in place concrete or block, what it

It is actually the place that is not program where the life of architecture occurs. ...So I would say that it is always the experience, what is not programmed that is the most critical part.

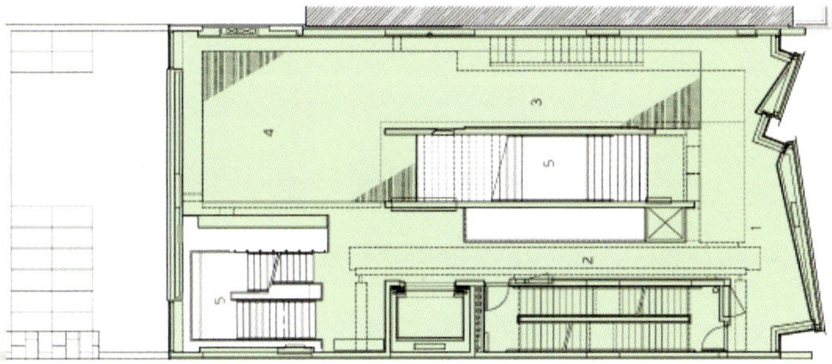

Second floor plan

will bear on, what the aggregate of the concrete or block might be and so on. So it is very much asking what is available in the place where you are going to make the work. We are simultaneously thinking about the ineffable condition of the space in between, but we are actually starting with some very pragmatic things. People come and say, "Wow, you must really enjoy just speculating about materials!" but we don't at all. We work from what we know can work in a place, what seems to a given. We of course question it; we ask what can it bring to the table. Like a contractor or a client, we are always asking what can be brought to the table, even from very specific situations or conditions.

6| Given your comments, what are your initial concerns when you begin your design work on a project? Moving beyond the conceptual aspects, and including issues that arise from the site and the program, are you more interested in those considerations or are in these larger issues we've been discussing? Is there typically a specific interest that initiates the design process?

BT: I would say site first.

TW: Site is very, very important. We try to digest it many times, not only to understand it, but to also ask, "What has been done with this site before?" For example, we went to India. In Mumbai, we both tried to discover how they build, what kind of materials might be appropriate, etc. But we might also say, "We're foreigners that came to India and have been asked to do work here. Why don't we think about how other people have thought about their entrance into this other world?" Many people have worked in a given locale. Some have made a mess, and some have done inspired work. So you also look at how other people have reacted to it. You're both investigating the place first-hand, and, at the same time, you're looking historically into the site to try to more deeply understand how one reacts to the specific condition and where one is in relation to it.

At the Neurological Sciences Institute, working with Dr. Edelman who is its head and also worked at the Salk Institute, it would be rather foolish for us not to have considered Louis Khan. That is a fairly logical thing, although the site for the NSI is completely different from that of the Salk. It is not looking at the ocean. It is an inward turning site in a different way. There's no particular view, etc.

We generally believe that the architecture should be in dialogue with the site, and if anything subservient to it. In other words, the building should not dominate the site. We are also asking how the site can have a presence or a power that balances the building.

BT: We really try not to have a preconception.

TW: We try not to, but, of course, we come with preconceptions. We come with research, with our own baggage.

7| Now let's bring the discussion to the Museum of American Folk Art itself and to your design interests. Given the limitations of the site, when you started the design were there global architecturally transcendent themes you were investigating? What was on your mind that might have transcended the program or the site?

BT: Certainly the nature of the art, because it is quite different. It can be something that is seen as traditional as a decoy, or it can be work that is done under the name "outsider" art, those that are challenged whether physically, or in jail, or are mentally challenged. So

We are simultaneously thinking about the ineffable condition of the space in between, but we are actually starting with some very pragmatic things.

We thought about intimacy as a theme.

We wanted to drive the art through every piece and fabric of the entire building so it was intimately attached to all surfaces and could not be "removed" from a wall in relation to the quality of the space.

it is a very big gamut, but what they have always felt unites the work is that it is created by people that are not necessarily trained to be artists but are, in some way, expressing themselves. I think this idea of having a very strong connection—not through the intellect—but from the desire of your hand, without channeling that through theory, over intellectualization, or historical referencing is at the heart of the art at the Folk Art Museum. It was very interesting to us to explore how that process was then expressed in a building, a building that feels in some way hand made.

TW: In the end, it is not only all that Billie just described, but also that the art is not made with a lot of mechanical assistance. In fact, it is made by individuals. So there is something inherently personal and small in scale and intimate about it. We thought about intimacy as a theme. The design of the building responds to an art that is created through a process less concerned with rational precepts, more oriented to personal or emotional themes.

TW: That's right. It has a kind of gut reaction. At the same time, I'm sorry we are architects. We have been trained. And we must recognize that we cannot become—yet we thought about it—how irrational can we be? Or how much can we forget our training? It was a dilemma. We determined that we couldn't be the fools. We couldn't imagine that we had not had an excellent education. We also, while accepting and embracing that quality of the art itself, said, "Ok, we need to look out and see what's been done, what actually is appropriate and relevant to the Folk Art Museum and its place in the city." It was very clear. We've talked about this before. We looked at the Guggenheim and thought about what defines the most important and very personal museum in the city. We looked at the Whitney, which is another relatively small building. We looked at John Soanes' work in London and Dullich Picture Gallery. We looked at Henry Mercer museum in Doylestown, Pennsylvania—all of which we felt were pertinent to the issue at hand. So it took two forms, and they were nearly simultaneous. One was recognizing that the art was different. It came from different sources. And at the same time we recognized that we weren't those people. We knew who we were. Our training was different from the people who were making art. As much as we respect them and their art, we are architects who could step back from our gut and actually look at history. We could hardly not do that. That was our obligation and our pleasure.

The desire to make a façade that would be a symbol and sign for the museum and express the contents in a certain way was very important.

8| Moving further into the process, what other conceptual criteria did you employ to anchor initial intentions? At some point you have to start organizing the program. You have to represent some kind or architectural position or intention. You know a bit about the project. You know the nature of the...

TW: To be clear, it was the program. This was a small site, and they knew very well what could fit on the site. They had already thought about it. They came to us and said, "We need three floors of galleries." One floor is for traditional folk art, the blankets, decoys, and paintings from 1700s and 1800s. The other is contemporary folk art or outsider art. There were two different kinds of people who collect these distinct art forms, two groups who often had very different ideas about the Folk Art Museum. They each wanted a floor for their work. Then they wanted one for changing exhibits. They said, "We also want to have classrooms, we need to have offices and we need a shop, and the shop must be on the first floor." They were very clear about where the programmatic components were to be located.

We said, "Ok, let's think about that." We came back to them and we diagrammed that exact organization of space. We said, "Let's think about it a different way." We said we believe that they should have an additional floor and mix their art more completely so that they weren't clearly delineated. So we did another diagram. We wanted to drive the art through every piece and fabric of the entire building, so it was intimately attached to all surfaces and could not be "removed" from a wall in relation to the quality of the space.

We wanted it to feel embedded in the building, that it should be much harder to separate the art from the building than say in the Museum of Modern Art. We went right through that.

So instead of putting the offices on the top floor, you put them in the lowest level, below grade. That means you've given over that upper space to the "public," yet of course we have to provide a quality environment for those working in the building. That means that those who are living in the building have to be able to receive natural light. They need wonderful spaces to work in, and it should be easy to engage with the building rather than isolating yourself.

We very, very clearly came at this by thinking about programming, yet while analysis of the program directed

Circulation, and making it experiential, was a major organizational issue for us.

The solution, while all about the program, was not about solving the "program."

As a representational element I think there is also a desire to connect people to a more humble building.

an investigation, the solution, while all about the program, was not about solving the "program."

BT: Additionally, from another standpoint we were very aware that it was a very small building next to the MoMA, which was going to become a very, very large building. The desire to make a façade that would be a symbol and sign for the museum and express the contents in a certain way was very important. Also, we were thinking about how it could separate itself from MoMA in terms of material and its unique identity.

9| So then what specific organizational or representational intentions arising from this analysis of the site and program were employed to organize and ultimately express your conceptual interests?
TW: Circulation was important. Everyone assumed that we would have two elevators. Why would you not in a seven-story building? One would break or would be serviced. We said, "Don't install two elevators; challenge yourselves. Make one. Make sure it's a good one, a big one. It could be used for art as well as people. And then use your senses to move between the floors via the stairs instead of the elevator." So circulation, and making it experiential, was a major organizational issue for us. Circulation was a conceptual idea that we believed was critical for them to rethink and for us to rethink as we had a narrow seven-story building.

That is similar to the point you were making about art distributed uniformly to ensure that the experience, to the extent that we can control or facilitate it, becomes of equal distribution. You're not segmenting the experience by continually going into the elevator.
TW: That's right. The circulation and experiencing the art was envisioned as a continuum.

9| 10|

We like to build with concrete because it feels very solid. ...In the Folk Art Museum it seemed appropriate as it allowed us to work with its texture. We knew that we would have more finished elements in the building returning us to that conceptual duality of being rough and smooth, warm and cool.

Considering the practicalities and realities of egress in relation to codes, there appears to be only one fire stair.
BT: There are two fire stairs. It's a scissor stair. There are two means of egress on every floor. We convinced ourselves, and ultimately the code officials. If you were in, let's say the northeast corner of the building and a fire occurred, and you ran to the stair, but there was a blockage in front of you, you could go the opposite way around the atrium and go to the other entrance. The building has a very, very small atrium. Today, this atrium would not be permitted in this manner. We also have a smoke evacuation system. At any rate there are two means of egress from every single floor.

So in relation the organizational strategies how did they impact your creation of a formal/spatial configuration?
TW: As mentioned, the large stair in the middle of the space was clearly an idea to not only facilitate the experience of the building, but also to be understood as part of the architectural language. You can see it from above and below. It is clogging the space. In a certain way it both binds and separates the three-dimensional spatial quality of the building.

That would, then, be an example of something that functions organizationally and representationally, organizationally in the sense that you want this core element as a circulating system to keep people embedded in the space yet it is representing a type of hearth, another type of core.
TW: Absolutely, it double functions in that regard.

BT: As a representational element I think there is also a desire to connect people to a more humble building. Although it is not an all concrete building, a lot of concrete is exposed, and the stair provides a material counterpoint.

In that case is the connection one of...are you saying that concrete has sort of representational quality, a humbleness? Was the material selection, with the concrete having the humble expression, at that time did you also know that there would be another material palette that you would be playing off of? Or was it a case of the concrete being an anchor?
BT: We like to build with concrete because it feels very solid. Second of all, in the Folk Art Museum it seemed appropriate as it allowed us to work with its texture. And third, I think that we knew that we would have more finished elements in the building returning us to that conceptual duality of being rough and smooth, warm and cool.

Do you think that the duality issue was "something that we do," or did it arise from your understanding of the nature of the Folk Art Museum as you got further into this particular design process?
TW: I would say it was both. Because there's an inherent duality between our different interests we were keenly aware of this potential. So, we look for it, and we find it there, and there, and there. In this case it was relatively easy because we were presented with a building that had gone before several different architects who had not been able to proceed because there had been a fight between those on the board who collect traditional folk art and those who were interested in contemporary folk art. Two very different kinds of constituent members. But at the same time we were looking for those opportunities. Because of the nature of the museum clientele and our general interests, the moment we sensed this opportunity we began to see it, and see it, and see it. We were looking for those qualities, and they emerged.

So there was, in effect, a duality in the very programmatic nature of the client. Similarly, there is a certain duality that your office has grown into and has accepted as a part of your make-up, i.e., you accept that the two of you are not going to march lock step and so, in the end, that has become an understanding that there is going to be a certain tussle over this issue of duality regardless of the commission.
TW: Absolutely.

10| At this point I'd like to move to a time further in the design process. The client has accepted the basic programmatic organization of the building, the section is resolved, and you are now into more purely architectural issues. How do you add additional depth to your initial intentions?
TW: I think we are always hoping for that depth. One of the ways that it happens is that you actually have to take your time and allow the project to breathe that depth in. You just have to allow it to speak to you as you've spoken to it. So I'd say it is similar to what Kahn said about asking the brick what it wants to be. Speak. So we look forward to that happening. As an example, we weren't thinking about the mechanical systems as much as we should have been at the beginning of the design process. We said, "These mechanical components are going to be at the bottom, or they're going to be at the top. They can't be in the middle." The stair is in the middle. We knew the top is the place you would be able to search for air. We knew the bottom was where the services came in. Purely logical. So we also look for the form that begins to unite those two things as we moved from bottom to top.

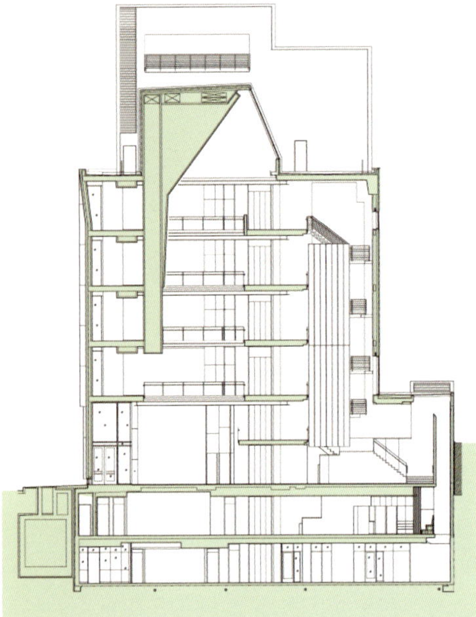

The large Y-shaped section is not just a way to shape the light, it is actually accommodating larger ducts above and distributing them down the building, acknowledging that they get smaller and smaller as they are not required to provide as much air as various ducts peel off.

As we developed the design we were trying to get each element to speak in quiet and subtle ways, in ways that may seem mysterious, but if you track them through there's an intention for everything and it is fairly common.

Those two things being the different service and mechanical components?

TW: Yes, service components, structure too. But in the longitudinal section the pouch filling in the large Y-shaped section is not just a way to shape the light; it is actually accommodating larger ducts above and distributing them down the building, acknowledging that they get smaller and smaller as they are not required to provide as much air as various ducts peel off. Another example is the issue of the Sheetrock vs. concrete. At one point we began to conceptually understand the building as a concrete frame instead of a concrete box. In that regard we did not want to express the necessary concrete block infill. We only wanted to express the concrete frame. Therefore, we used Sheetrock to mask the concrete block and reveal the concrete frame. The concrete system began to reveal itself in different cases; the surface as ground, i.e., the surface of the slab, the surface thinned out as frame, the surface thickened, etc.

In the mechanical example I was referring to, that being the Sheetrock volume, we were trying to turn it into a form that was understood conceptually as we did with the concrete frame. We wanted it to be part of the experience rather than just slathering Sheetrock over the ductwork.

BT: Yet again, it was also two issues coming together. The form also has a function to it, that being the ductwork. Our decisions are made with a layering of reason and logic. We're not just making shapes. (At this point, Billie Tsien was no longer available to participate in the interview.)

TW: And here we see the shaft where we have actually stacked branching mechanical elements into a collector, actually a Sheetrock collector, because we couldn't make this element into a light fixture. Local law wouldn't permit us to make it, and the cost wouldn't allow it. So, very, very slowly we began to massage each of these elements to see where we could make them speak at the right time and at the right moment, privileging experience, asking the mechanical system to come forward at the right time, asking it to back off at a certain time. This was the same with the structure system. So I would say we are now orchestrating the various elements to the service of the space.

The first image you showed us was an interesting one. It showed the bottom of the concrete stair, with the slope and the cantilevered treads. The stair is fairly simple. It is basically a bent beam, sloping down without a column at the end, wrapping around and bending back to the floor above. From that we wanted to express the saw-toothed element of the stair, which, had we extended it all the way across it, would not have revealed itself in as evocative a manner. As we developed the design, we were trying to get each element to speak in quiet and subtle ways, in ways that may seem mysterious, but if you track them through, there's an intention for everything, and it is a fairly common.

Then the depth of the intentions is understood, in part, by how one sees issues of fabrication affecting the design, whether in the expressed assembly of the components involved in the fabrication of the stair and handrail, or in relation to incorporating the AC duct work into the building. The intentions became realized in both architectural and performance-oriented responses. Billie was adding, "Well it is that, but it is also this quality of light that we are trying to articulate given the opportunity". So intentions that relate to the practical, in the form of fabrication, and to the experiential in the form of mystery are intertwined.

TW: Light appearing in little slivers of space, which may not appear to be there but are there. Just dropping one plane down ever so slightly from another plane means that I am slightly more aware of this space than I am of that space. So we now have three layers of space. Sometimes we have tried to terminate things. Other times we are trying to make them slide through for variety of different understandings.

Let me build on that for a moment. In relation to the Folk Art Museum is your intention to deliberately offset

I see the architect as a kind of a conductor of all these different symphonic elements that sometimes are not even to be used. Many architects won't even recognize that we have these instruments out there, or they will see them and think that they are just dumb instruments or ones that belong to someone else. They belong to the architect.

Sometimes we have tried to terminate things. Other times we are trying to make them slide through for a variety of different understandings.

elements to allow for the greater expression of each individual material component. Is that interpretation correct?

TW: That, and space, little slivers of transparent space are so terribly important. The gaps allow linkages that multiply spatial experiences. For instance, when we extend a beam beyond a slab, this allows it to say, "I'm a beam. See me."

11| Did you name or prioritize architectural elements or programmatic areas to differentiate or give hierarchy to the larger global intentions. For example, you talked about the "core" of the stair, or in this case you want the beam to have a more pronounced expression. How do you see those issues, such as naming something to help define its importance to the designer or to the design? Is it an interest that the design has a richer story to tell, one that must express the multiple components that are its essence?

TW: The latter is true. As I mentioned, we want to express more components. We can be criticized sometimes for over expressing that, and we can be criticized at other times for under-expressing that. And I would criticize myself the same way. At least we want to take a shot at understanding what these pieces are and how they can best be expressed. We go back over and over again in plan and section, elevation, detail, and they're constantly chattering to one another ,and we are trying to figure out where each one stands in relationship to each other. They are speaking so many different languages. Each one has its own language, and each one wants to talk about itself. We are trying to say, "Come on, Ok. Be quiet. We don't need you now." That is basically the orchestration; I see the architect as a kind of a conductor of all these different symphonic elements that sometimes are not even to be used. Many architects won't even recognize that we have these instruments out there, or they will see them and think that they are just dumb instruments or ones that belong to someone else. They belong to the architect. The architect is there to talk to them and to try to hear them and to try to orchestrate the overall symphony that should be architecture.

Under this notion of prioritizing, you seem to be saying, "Does this room or building want to be quiet or does this want to shout?"

TW: It is a continuous discourse that we have from the moment a building design begins in the studio to the time we send it out. We just yesterday sent out the drawings for the Barnes Foundation. Now that the working drawings are done, I am realizing that some elements

are telling me, "Hey, you didn't listen to me. You didn't look." That's something to be aware of, and I can sense probably a dozen right now. We do get to some of it later. Maybe we will buck it up and do justice to it. Design never stops talking, it's just like a child. You send them off to college, yet they continue to speak to you all the time.

12| As the design developed did you use the different attributes of the organizational and representational conceptual fields to mature or cross-reference each other? They are never seen as something that needs to be a fixed idea. You would not see yourselves as a firm stating there are underlying organizational systems that become fixed once we have established them. They are always in play.

TW: Of course we have to fix them. We have to fix them to make certain...they are fixed, just like the working drawings that we sent out are fixed...but if they are not in play to some extent we will have a building that is stiffened when we finished our working drawings. Actually, it stiffened some weeks ago, but design never ends.

13| Regarding ideas that are more representational in nature, how do you explore the organizational potential of these ideas? There are concerns that you have to deal with. For example, as Billie was stating, the front façade of the building speaks at some representational level to distinguish the Folk Art Museum as a museum with folk art and craft as its underpinning. That doesn't necessarily explain the three facets of the façade. So one has a need for a strong representational component. How do you go about organizing something of that nature?

TW: That was a tough one. We were obviously aware of Louis Khan's work at the Salk when we were working on the Folk Art Museum. We were also aware that we didn't know what Tanaguchi would do at MoMA. We thought that they would do something fairly slick. We thought we should separate the Folk Art Museum from that so the outer edges of the façade, which are made of Tombasill, actually separate themselves from the building envelope. A little further in the design process we made sure that we had a shadow reveal between ourselves and the surrounding buildings. The panels orient inward from the adjacent buildings in a U shape, and they tip in to allow the sun to strike the left, or west, panel in the morning, the full façade at midday, and the eastern side in the evening, often in shadow. We were also trying to, by tipping the façade, enable one to see it a little bit better walking down the street. After all, 40 feet is potentially 14 strides, and you're gone. You've just stepped by it. That happens all the time. As people walk to MoMA, they

We want to express more components. ...We want to take a shot at understanding what these pieces are and how they can best be expressed.

don't really notice it's there. We were trying to give it a little punch or presence on the street.

So there were at least two organizational criteria affecting the design of the façade beyond the idea that it was to represent the unique quality of the museum. One was to facet the panels allowing for a play of light, and the other was to give the façade some depth, allowing it to differentiate itself from the flatness of the MoMA, allowing the building to shout a little bit.
TW: The reveals, or gaps, at the edge have windows behind them. We called them reentrant windows. They allow a person on the inside to walk up and "re-enter" the street at an oblique angle to look down to the populace below. While that began with an intention concerning the façade, these gaps separating the panels from the building's frame became a way by which people could look out, becoming a great additional experience.

I will segue into jointing strategies, yet not as a technical issue but as an architectural one. The façade is created via a series of dimensionally irregular rectangles. What was driving your thought on that organization?
TW: When we began to cast the panels we thought that the largest panel we could cast, which would remain flat and be sensible to transport, would be a 10-foot long panel. Later we learned that when we made a 10-foot panel, it sort of warped like a potato chip. We didn't know that when we started. A 6 x 10-foot panel made sense. At the foundry, we were casting panels that they could cut into smaller pieces. The ten-foot dimension was more or less a cannon. The additional dimension meant that there would be no panel wider than six feet. That meant we could get a syncopated pattern crossing the façade from one side to the other. That turned out to be so much more difficult than I ever expected because we didn't really track through the system of hanging, the system of fabrication, etc. That informed the logic for the organizing pattern. We also insisted on slipped relationships. We believed that there were certain panels that couldn't be too narrow. I should also say we tried very hard not to let all of the panels come down to the floor or the street.

Why?
TW: In order to allow the plane of the façade to literally become a mask. Now it would not be incorrect to reference the work of John Hedjuk, whom I taught with for years, to say that the mask is not to some extent a device that we knew from his work and from teaching at Cooper. And I'm not too pleased about that. But it is simply a façade, and in this case, more than any other building, this mask is something that we put on the building. And the mask says to the street, "Look at me. I'm an entity."

It would be difficult for one to argue against that, given what you have already said about the scale of the building and the scale of its neighbors. It would be irresponsible not to ask "How do I address my clients' needs?" On the syncopation issue, I think you used the term slipping. Why not just put it in a grid or....
TW: We always wanted them to be sliding panels in relationship to one another, to heal together, to be an overall form or three forms becoming one. It also had to do with the hanging of the panels. It's a rain screen, and there is a horizontal channel. As we worked that out, we were actually channeling the water behind every single panel down one joint to the joint below. The horizontal channels allowed us to set those panels in a consistent way on the façade.

To allow the plane of the façade to literally become a mask.

The horizontal lines became established in large part as a water collection system?
TW: That's correct. And hanging points.

The vertical joints are then in part water collection system and in part a desire to have an offset play of the jointing system?
TW: Correct. The detail, when you come up to it, you can actually grab a panel with both hands. You can feel the thickness. That was utterly critical. You come in contact with the panel as you touch it. You can put it in your hand and walk around it.

14| Did you see the organizational framework employed in the Folk Art Museum as needing additional architectural expression because it was under conceptualized? Was its essence envisioned as a, or the, significant aspect of the building.
TW: It was. The essence of the organizational aspect of the building is the essence of the building. That's correct.

What I have learned is that the organizational strategy, through what I will call "universal distribution," was important, whether it is bringing light far in to the building, shifting panels off of a surface to allow a connectivity from one space to another or whether it is taking the artwork itself and truly not putting in a room designated as "art A" or "art B." Everything truly flows through as light flows through a building. There was not an organizational overlay system. The organization came about through the spatial criteria, and it appears that an additional primary organizational criteria was the distribution of the artwork. Am I overplaying that?
TW: No, there are many organizational systems in the building and sub systems within the building. We tried to engage them all. We tried to move the project forward

We tried to move the project forward while having them say what they needed to say as independent elements and then speak to one another. In that regard it is loaded with organizational systems.

The value of material palates is like the value of any of the expressive elements that one begins with. It's the possibility to communicate.

Material expression is one of the tools architects can employ, and we should take advantage of that gives a building its sense of place, a sense of personality, the possibility of further communication—particularly with all people—not just those who are elite, but to those who are simply walking by.

while having them say what they needed to say as independent elements and then speak to one another. In that regard it is loaded with organizational systems. Some are obvious, and some are not.

15| How did you link ephemeral, poetic intentions of your design to the pragmatic, functional performance concerns as the design progressed? You have already mentioned this in terms of refining the top of the building. Would that be described as a poetic issue?
TW: It was a difficult concern. There is no question about that. First, the slope of the gypsum board form relates to what was behind it, which are the air conditioning supply ducts. They are larger at the top of the building and smaller as they extend to the floors below. At the same time we wanted to establish design continuity with planes denoting areas of light, referencing that the exterior of the building is made of planes set at an angle to capture light. They are not the same angle, but they share a common purpose in their intent to capture and reflect light. Similarly, the jointing helps to identify them, not as a mass but as a series of planes. That was a hard one. The concrete wall runs through the building. There is no question about that. It is the "foundation" of the building extending all the way to the top. It is on the top of the concrete wall that the gypsum board walls were set. The east side actually runs past that wall and runs down to the floor, becoming a surface on which art hangs. The walls on the west side, which are faceted, sit in front of the concrete wall, and they then become light catchers. The reveal establishes the difference between the light catcher or the picture plane on which paintings occur and the wall itself.

You are saying the angled nature of these upper walls, of these gyp-board walls, reflects the angled nature of the planes at the front of the building, and the fact that they are offset from the concrete walls is to identify their role as light or...
TW: Light, and it happens to be a literal mask of the ductwork. The other wall on the opposite side along the stairwell. Is, in fact, a wall for paintings and these walls are themselves objects. I remember struggling with this, whether we ought to detach the angled face from the flat face. It sits on the railing as if it's another plane. We intentionally chose to detach it to create a slot between the two planes making space for a wonderful window. All of that is extremely formal in some ways, yet it also touches on some of the additional organizational themes mentioned earlier. We are trying to privilege different surfaces.

Your goal, in part, is to give these elements, in terms of the language of the light volume, a clear expression of the three surfaces. It wasn't intended to be a singular monolith.
TW: That's correct. I see them as one, because they are all one. I see them as two because there is the north south bent one. And then there are three...Actually the happiest moment for me is the little space between where we actually pull the reveal that we are using between the planes, and we made a place for a person to stand and look through.

16| These things don't happen by accident. One realizes there was a very clear sense of allowing that slip, to honor or create the gap. Moving on to material considerations, was the expressive or representational nature of the materials, or how you employed them, important in the design of the Folk Art Museum? When did the notion of material intentionality, or diminishing thereof, become important in the project?
TW: From the moment we started it. We were constantly orchestrating the conceptual use of materials from the moment we first spoke with the client down to the removal of wood cladding toward the very end when we realized it was not needed. People today think of us as architects who will bring a certain material sensitivity to the project. Therefore, from the onset we talked about it, and we didn't know what that material was, but we tried to loosen them up by throwing out some very goofy ideas just so they wouldn't get stuck. Sometimes we suggest inappropriate materials to loosen everyone up and give us some distance, some room to maneuver.

So there was some level of intentionality attached to the use of materials because, right or wrong, there was an interest in material expression instead of an abstract palate.
TW: They came to us, in part, because of that. In the initial interviews we discussed the issue of materiality as being critical to the project, because of the nature of this type of museum and because of our known use of diverse materials.

Then speak to that issue if you would, as we did not touch on that in relation to a global intention. What were the thoughts regarding the value of a diverse material palate versus a more minimal one.
TW: I would say the value of material palates is like the value of any of the expressive elements that one begins with. It's the possibility to communicate. Its also a possibility to miscommunicate. I think that looking at materiality through the lens of history, one of the questions in contemporary architecture has been that in the 20th century we slowly began to abandon materiality as a design element. We can look back at the Bauhaus and say, "Look at that concrete work, it is so thin or so white

We wanted to establish design continuity with planes denoting areas of light, referencing that the exterior of the building is made of planes set at an angle to capture light.

To me, if there is an organizing principle to virtually all of our work, it is the stair. This building is about the stairs, there is no question about it. I want them to be rich and varied and interesting and engaging

or so irregular." There was some material information there, early metal windows and so on, but in general, as one has come to a more rational architecture, one has abandoned the idea of the maker, and one is increasingly seeing the tectonics of the machine. Therefore, in fact, the person has disappeared.

Today, with the incredible potential of materials and computer fabrication, the material culture will not disappear. It is how we use them that's important to us. Looking back at the Folk Art Museum, people that I care deeply about think that we over-expressed the exterior. That may be so. However, I'm not sure. To them we didn't need it to be so sensually powerful. I still feel great about it, but I hear that. Where I feel more deeply is why didn't we allow the material to penetrate deeper into the interior of the building? Why is it sitting as a mask on the face? At any rate material expression is one of the tools architects can employ, and we should take advantage of that. It gives a building its sense of place, a sense of personality, the possibility of further communication—particularly with all people—not just those who are elite, but to those who are simply walking by. It's great. I have become friends with one of the individuals who sells African arts on the street in front of the Folk Art Museum. He got it. This guy really appreciates the material presence at the street. It has a kind of emotional resonance. These are our tools. It is our responsibility to say they are in our control.

Furthering the material discussion, all of the stairs are concrete with the exception of the stair on the side at the upper levels. Is it because it was a secondary stair, or is it because that part of the project seemed not to require the kind of material presence that other areas might have?

TW: I must say that for a long time the building committee didn't understand the stair. In fact, the studio, our employees, didn't understand that stair, yet it was a favorite of my own. I couldn't justify it for almost the entire life of the project. It came in rather late when I finally began to understand it. One of the reasons the stair is not concrete is that concrete is an expensive, slow moving component of the project ,so we knew that we might not get to use it everywhere we wanted. We might lose the stair. So I needed that stair not to be a deal breaker but an accent, a grace note. In that respect it was easier to conceptualize it out of steel. I say it is steel because it is steel clad in wood. The wood is not a spanning element; it is a cladding on the top and underneath side of the steel plate bridging between two stringers. I

If architecture is about space, the stair is the way by which we move physically from one space to another. The elevator is certainly one way we can also imagine ourselves moving between space, but the stair is the one that makes your heart move up and down.

wanted it to be a kind of grace note, a kind of secret. It is almost like a piece of cabinet-work. I described it to them as a kind of stair leading up to a grandmother's attic.

It has that kind of feeling. It has a sense of surprise to it.
TW: It's a small enough building that you can overlook it ,yet it is also an interesting enough piece that you can catch it. It adds a kind of an exclamation mark to your experience. Or it says walk down me, but if you walk down me, you will not walk down the other stair and that means you're going to have to come up another way. The building becomes more experiential.

You mentioned early on how the stairs and circulation were of concern from the beginning.
TW: It always is. I've talked about this. If architecture is about space, the stair is the way by which we move physically from one space to another. The elevator is certainly one way we can also imagine ourselves moving between space, but the stair is the one that makes your heart move up and down. And it slows you down or speeds you up sufficiently so that you actually are very aware of your presence in the building. I believe stairs are ultimately scalar humanizing elements within a building.

They are of the very highest level of expression that we can give a building. To me, if there is an organizing principle to virtually all of our work, it is the stair. Interestingly, we have just recently interviewed for a project, and I said I wanted there to be no stairs and no elevator. But it's just because it is in a way to challenge my utter obsession with stairs. This building is about the stairs; there is no question about it. I want them to be rich and varied and interesting and engaging.

This goes back to how one adds depth to ideas. If you conceptually understand the stair as a core idea, you feel its value in terms of movement through the building and space. In the particular stair we have been discussing you accomplished that primary goal. Yet there are two other stairs...
TW: The center stair is really the symbol. It is more than a symbol. It is a fact—an element that grounds you and establishes a tactile relationship with the space that surrounds you.

17| How do you conceptualize and organize the assembly or composition between joints? We started that conversation in relation to the front façade.
TW: I would almost always call them reveals. A reveal in almost all cases should separate materials. In various soffit conditions in the building I would identify them

Between any two materials one should have a reveal defining which one is dominant. One is established as the primary and another material is set in contrast or even against it.

Concrete... is the ground to the plates that sit on the ceiling... yet it also grounds the building.

as separating a plate material from a base material, which are often more important in the Folk Art Museum. Concrete is not a plate. Concrete is a liquid, so it becomes primarily a base form, but within that we sometimes have put it in planes and sometimes in plates, but generally a single piece of material, like metal, comes in a plated form. We're trying to establish the form of the plate. Between any two materials one should have a reveal defining which one is dominant. One is established as the primary and another material is set in contrast or even against it. You need to find your tolerance relative to their relationship, and it helps aesthetically set one off from the other.

So you are identifying a material that is a poured vs. a material that is a plate. In various applications one is dominant, and one is secondary. To identify the plate material as part of an organizational strategy, it becomes understood that to be expressed as an element it has to be offset or extended.
TW: Correct.

18| What was your thinking about your expression of systems in the building? What strategies were contemplated in your decision to express the systems? I would like to talk about the ceilings. There's a very clear layering quality to them. You have the concrete as a base structure.
TW: And that should always be. It is the ground to the plates that sit on the ceiling or the Sheetrock that sits on the ceiling. Yet, it also grounds the building. It is also deformed because we made an indentation for plates, so it is a little over-articulated, but that is certainly the ground for the light rail shoe, and it becomes the ground for the metal plate that is the light shield.

So you are envisioning materials in a certain representational mode. Some are anchoring materials, which in the Folk Art Museum is typically concrete. But then subsequent materials, which are not concrete, are always understood as cladding or plates
TW: In this case, I think it is interesting to note that the concept allows us to conceptually integrate something as basic as a fire exit door. The doors are set behind the plane of the concrete. It is clearly to honor the conceptual grounding role we give to concrete as the more important surface. Your eye should go to that rather than the recessive one of the fire door, yet the fire door can be conceptually understood as a plate.

So then it is important to honor the concrete by presenting it, giving it hierarchy, so other material or surface relationships can be conceptually grounded through their relation to concrete. That presents a clear conceptual integration with the front of the building represented as a mask or architectural layer, I see it in the family of layers you were describing as the planes at the front becoming a plate to the larger context of...
TW: The building, which is grounded behind it.

Exactly. So there is a core faced by a layer or plate at the front elevation with similar concrete cores or grounding elements within the building for additional elements, layers, or details to counterpoint. Those linkages are nice to see.
TW: It ultimately affects secondary or tertiary materials such as laminates. Laminate is not a material to me. You just assume it is a void. It is no more than a reveal itself. Although we have to use them in certain circumstances, Sheetrock and such from time to time, I regard them as lesser materials, yet, they can, or have to be,

integrated in some way. They may be refined in some ways, but the mother material would be concrete or its equivalent.

In that regard are you saying that when you use laminate, you will try to separate or diminish it somehow?
TW: I'll try to separate it. We often use this color called Raven, because the laminate joint falls into a shadow and your eye isn't drawn to it. Mostly we are saying, "Don't look at me."

19| In refining the design did you select programmatic areas or architectural elements to privilege? If so, how were the privileging concepts expansions on or counterpoints to earlier conceptual intentions?
TW: Although used earlier, privilege is not my favorite word. Emphasize would be better.

In relation to that, utilizing specific materials, components, and details to frame the north window in the lobby, conceptually links it to the language employed to frame displayed objects. There is a common organizational tool in the form of details or a representational language-based intention. It is no longer a "window" but one of many architectural display cases.
TW: Correct. And knowing that north is the best light for a space, everything is bathed in light. And we knew that a building would be behind it, or Tanaguchi would be behind it. But we knew that you could see through that, and we didn't care what you looked at. It happens to be a miserable looking place at the moment. We saw that it was a picture of life and therefore it was framed. It was a picture of whatever life, happened to be in that image. It was the ordinary image framed in a manner that related it to other "ordinary" components displayed in the museum.

As some of the craft displayed could be deemed "ordinary" in relation to high art.
TW: Yes, as life itself is ordinary—living, breathing, a piece of garbage sitting out there. Whatever comes into that frame is important. Nobody ever talks about that window. I like that window a lot. ■

Internal And External

In analyzing the thesis of internal *versus* external as outlined in the first chapter of the book, and then more thoroughly developed in the subsequent interviews, it must be restated that there is an intended focus on expanding design methodologies useful for creating developed and inclusive architectural languages. This in not for the purpose of creating languages readable and understandable only by a subset of individuals with a heightened interest in conceptual themes underlying the design of buildings, but rather to elevate the overall outcome of building design. The purpose is intended to advance the growth of architectural languages through the development of strategies that inform the design process with multiple levels of intentionality, beginning with the initial sketch. While the attention has been on language-based concepts regarding the organization and representation of form, whether in object, spatial, or material considerations, it is now desirable to incorporate design mindfulness concerning the "external" aspects of the design process, topics most frequently originating from matters relating to and affected by the site and program.

What are referenced as external aspects of the design process in the internal/external duality is not to suggest these considerations contain secondary content or relevance; quite the contrary as a missed opportunity relating to site design or a misunderstanding related to the program or client values will significantly diminish or misdirect design opportunities. Additionally, leaving the external aspects of the design process in a realm defined only by information relevant to practical and functional solutions undermines the design process, undercutting the validity of any resultant ideas emanating from considerations evolving from external factors. It is a necessary procedure that various aspects of the design process be confirmed via information-based content and understandings which are then brought into an analytical process linking information to broader, more inclusive design interests.

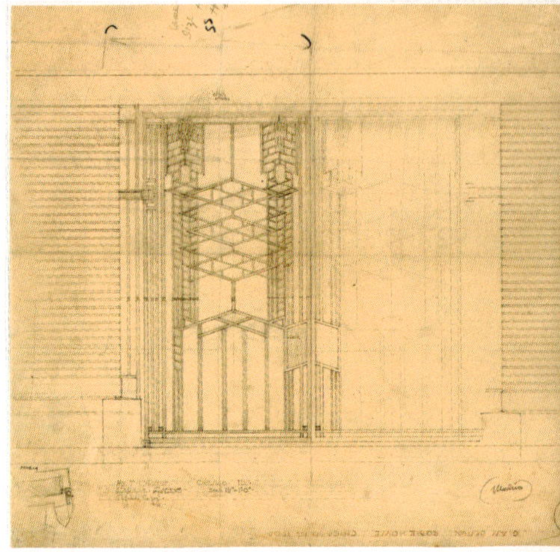

Frank Lloyd Wright
Robie House

However, when external-based information masquerades as ideas impacting aesthetic directions and become a consequential source for language development, conflicts can arise. In an attempt to represent themselves visually, information based decisions such as program related considerations, issues affected by the necessity to comply with a building code or a site characteristic suggesting a particular massing, become marginalized. External-based intentions, as discussed earlier, contain a diminished ability to provide for language development and coherence relating to intentions exploring broader considerations. Those intentions are usually expressed or realized through language-based concepts. As stated in the first chapter, external-based information possesses limited ability to communicate intentions more global or holistic in nature as its role integrating the development of architectural languages is limited.

Similarly, unintended consequences relating to a singular focus on language-based themes must also be acknowledged. When a design process focuses too much conceptual energy on the development of aesthetic architectural themes and resultant "languages" become drivers of design decisions overriding the content of external site and program related considerations the approach can lead to scenographic outcomes. These results may give the design an experiential high but do not typically imbue it with long-term meaningfulness or a deeper richness. Integrating external factors, with the varied performance-related content they possess, generates material informing the design process, permitting a dialectical approach to occur. This process thus becomes synthetic in nature, enabling an informing and refining of language-based concepts.

A common failure of an over reliance on language-based themes in a design process is exemplified when a representational design interest slips into a metaphorical realm. Outcomes become image based versus giving evidence of a process incorporating numerous integrated design decisions that are cognizant of strategies linking the internal

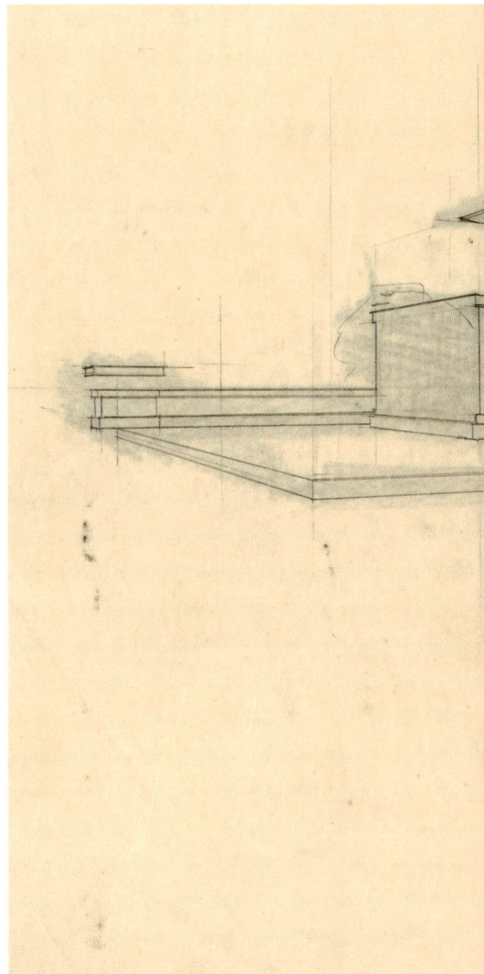

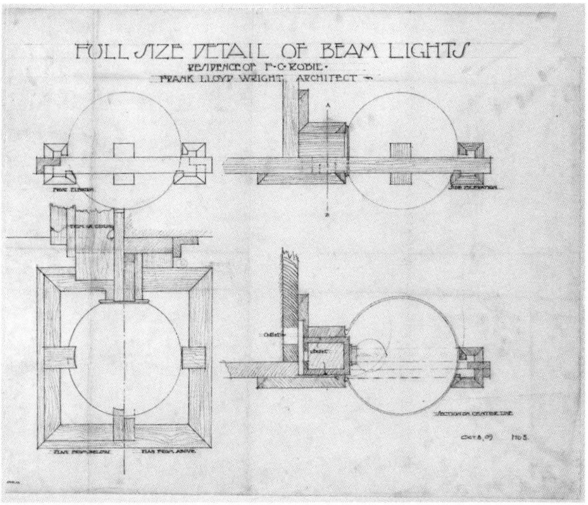
FULL SIZE DETAIL OF BEAM LIGHTS
RESIDENCE OF F. C. ROBIE.
FRANK LLOYD WRIGHT, ARCHITECT

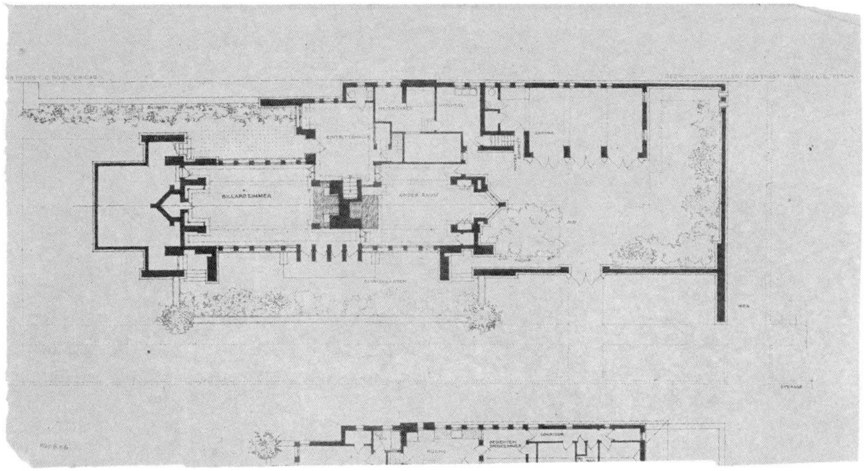

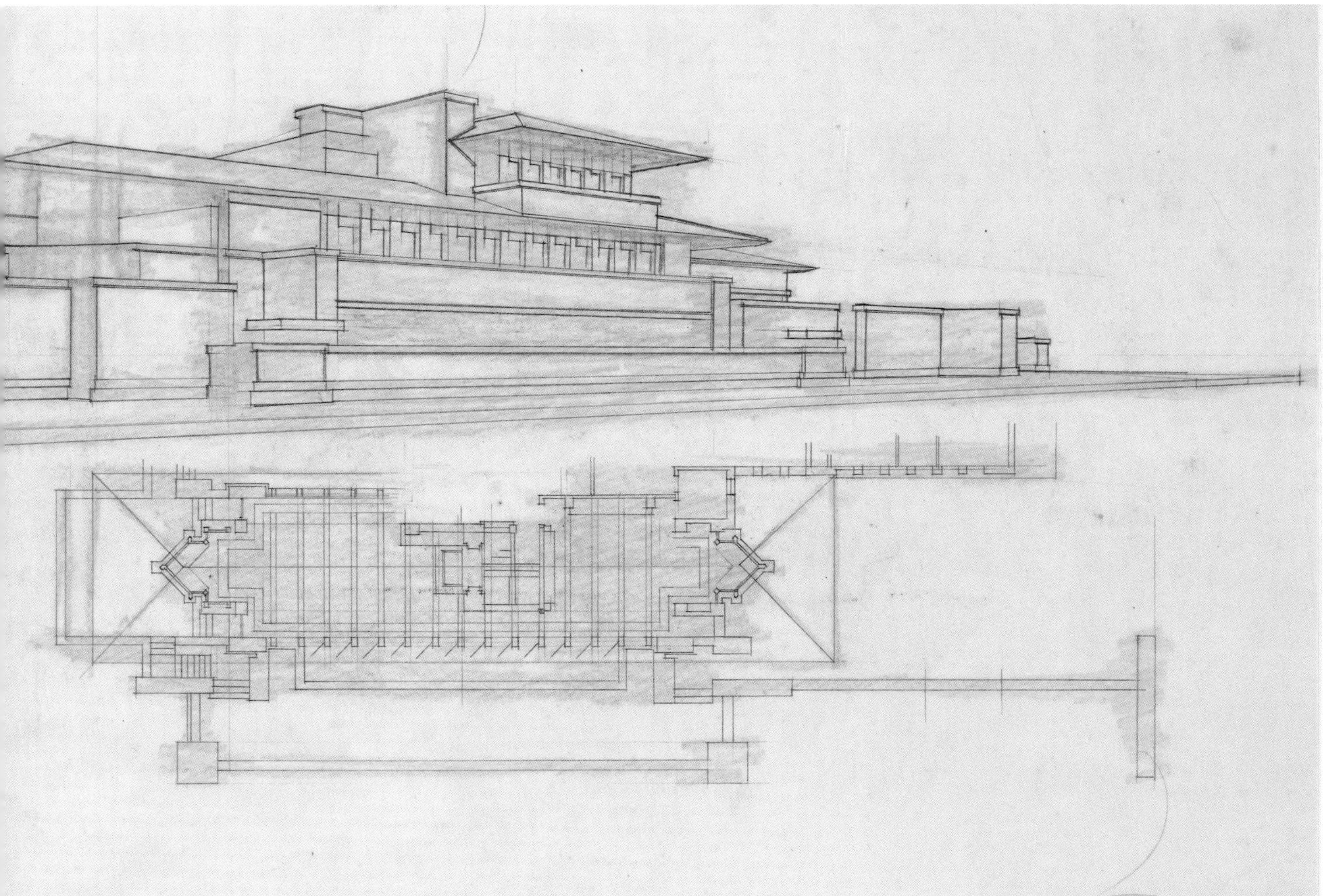

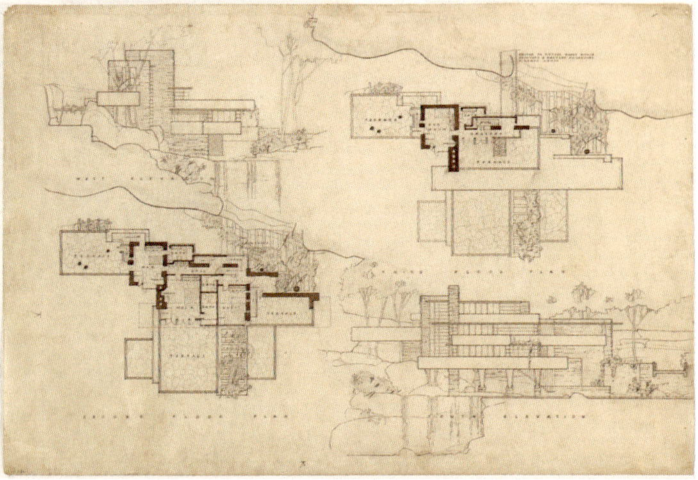

All fine architectural values are human values, otherwise they are not valuable.

The thing always happens that you really believe in; and the belief in a thing makes it happen.

Form follows function—that has been misunderstood.
Form and function should be one, joined in a spiritual union.

The space within becomes the reality of the building.

The architect should strive continually to simplify; the ensemble of the rooms should then be carefully considered that comfort and utility may go hand in hand with beauty.

— Frank LLoyd Wright

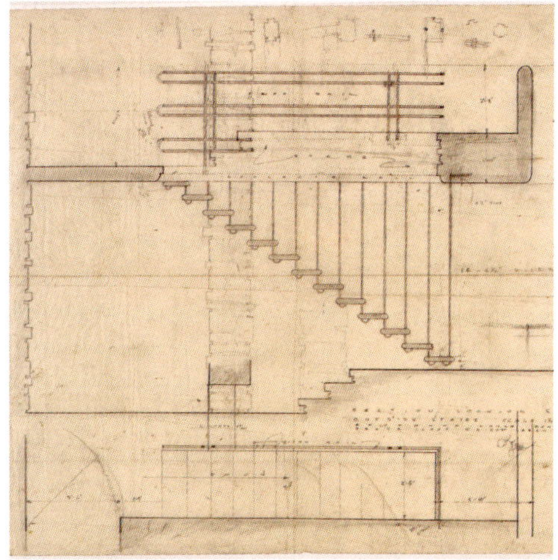

Frank Lloyd Wright
Fallingwater

and external domains. An imbalance occurs in that extracting ideas only from an internal conceptual domain will primarily define each outcome aesthetically and a collaborative internal/external dialectical design process does not ensue. Intentions intended to elicit meaning and experiential enrichment are not matured by being informed with the content provided by external design influences.

Contrasting a diagrammatic or sceneographic high, a similar yet opposite question concerning the relationship between internal and external design factors can be asked. Today, in the search for novel directions meant to add a "Bilbao effect" to the design of buildings aspiring to greater relevance, one can ask, "Does a reliance on factors external to language-based considerations represent an approach to design which appears undervalued, even prosaic or boring?" Have external factors, with their limited ability to provide a comprehensive basis for establishing a language, become of less interest? Or is the question more correctly stated, "Is the design of 'buildings' an undervalued endeavor in relation to the design of 'architectural statements'?"

Of course, as in so many issues underlying the design process, and certainly in relation to the language-based themes, the answer is often "it depends." Even the subtitle of this book raises the question through the use of the somewhat ambiguous word "informed." The word itself implies that for the outcome of a design process to have enhanced results and aspire to more meaningful outcomes it must become more inclusive than one focusing strictly on considerations resulting from the specificities of the site and program. Add to those realities the variabilities which client preferences or institutional values bring to the decision-making process boundaries can accrue and design outcomes easily become under-informed. Addressing the realities of multiple client needs and functional requirements, as well as additional architectural interests the "it depends" argument can be answered in both the affirmative and negative. From a

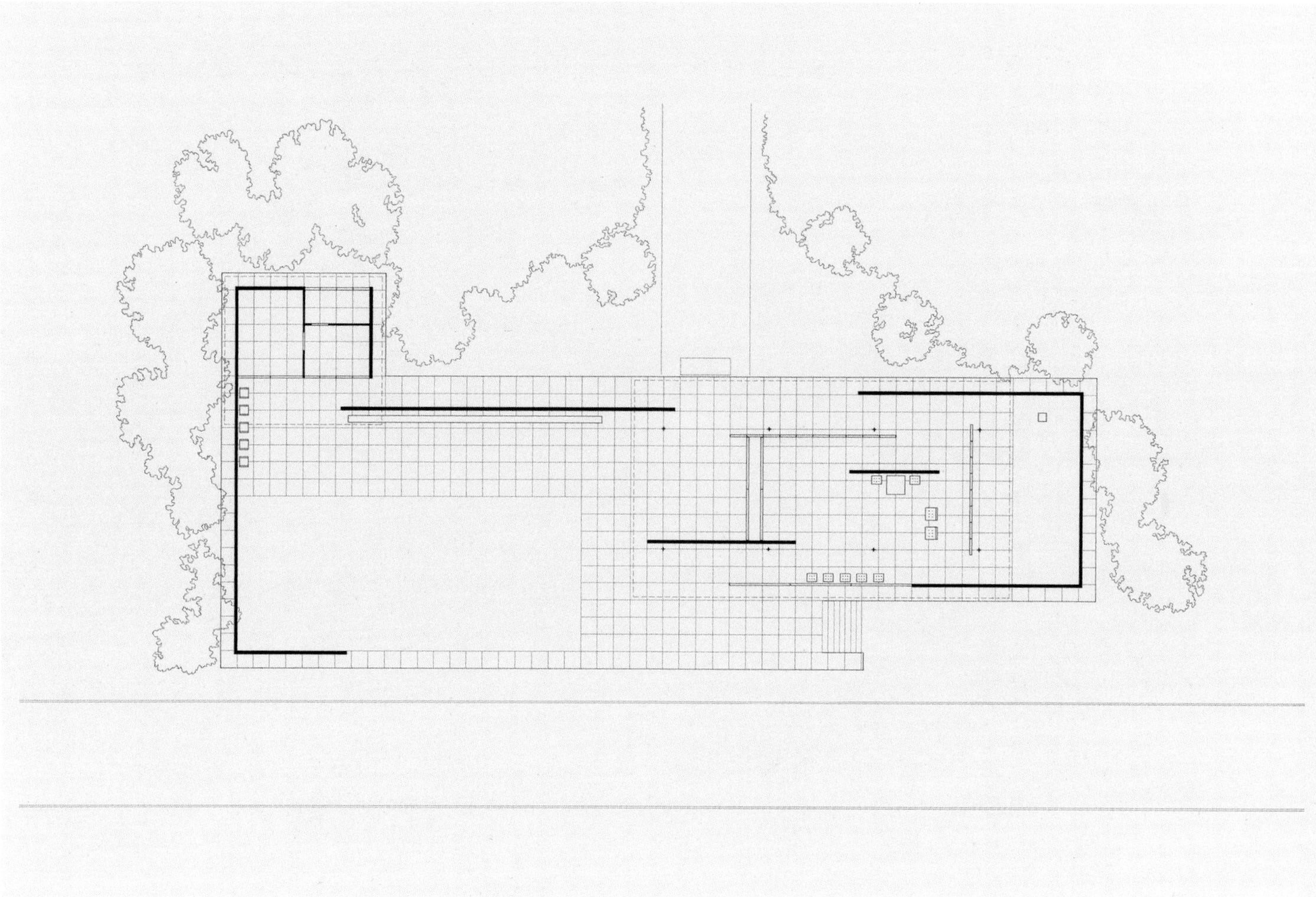

Ludwig Mies van der Rohe
Barcelona Pavilion

user's perspective the building typically meets the required needs, provides appropriate life safety, and is overall satisfactory, yet the "architecture" is realized through a default solution represented by an under-conceptualization of language-based attributes.

However, a well designed "background" building, informed by multiple external and internal factors will authenticate elevated design outcomes created through the use and synthesis of these conceptual domains. Outcomes governed by internal language-based concepts and rules will impart added design depth and coherence to the building and experiential delight for its users. Developing a more complete and informed design process provides an arena with the greatest potential to activate the design and allow architecture to claim its inclusion as an artform.

The goal underlying the questions and, hopefully, answers provided in the interviews is to spotlight more complete and integrated design processes used to develop

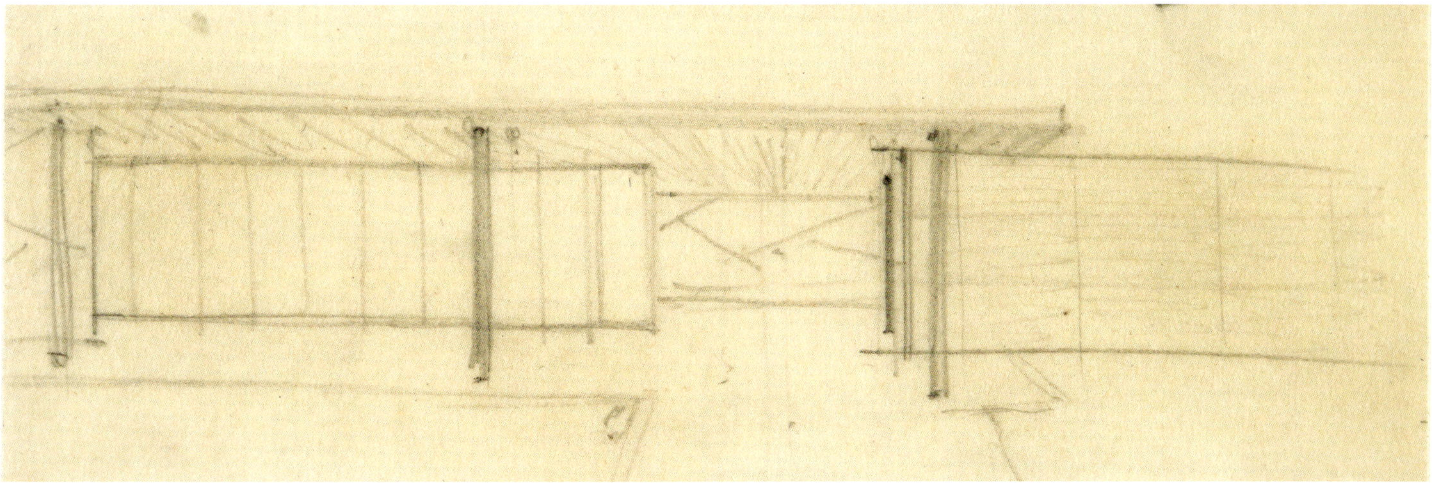

We refuse to recognize problems of form, but only problems of building. Form is not the aim of our work, but only the result. Form, by itself, does not exist. Form as an aim is formalism; and that we reject.

Architecture depends on facts, but its real field of activity lies in the realm of the significance.

Means must be subsidiary to ends and to our desire for dignity and value.

It is much better to have just one idea, and if the idea is clear, then you can fight for it. That is how you can get things done.

Architecture is always the will of the age conceived as space—nothing else. Until this simple truth is clearly recognized, the struggle over the foundation of a new architecture confident in its aims and powerful in its impact cannot be realized; until then, it is destined to remain a chaos of uncoordinated forces.

— Ludwig Mies van der Rohe

more informed and therefore enriched architectural languages. The title, *Internal*, was selected to identify an interpretation of architectural design less singularly reliant on attributes residing in the external realm of design, ones possessing fewer language-based features propelling the design of a building. The subtitle of the book, *Developing Informed Architectural Languages*, amplifies language aspects of the design process that aid in the enhancement of those attributes regardless of a given aesthetic direction. The diversity of the programmatic types and sizes of the projects included in the book along with the diverse architectural directions represented, suggest that developing an informed language is not a result of a particular approach to design. As suggested in the diagram created by Charles Jencks located in the introduction, the diversity of directions constituting the range of contemporary architecture will likely continue unabated. What is hoped for is that internal language-based design intentions are advanced and merged with external conditions to inform the design process in a manner that is knowable and understandable, one applicable to projects of all scales and architectural directions. The goal is to create coherence, depth of meaning, and experiential qualities in the realization of more inclusive design outcomes.

It might be worth ending with the question: What is an "informed" language?

The issue of what constitutes an informed language will continue to be debatable as many descriptions underlining the meaning of the term will remain unclear, providing no overriding definition. Is its meaning suggestive of outcomes more fully reliant on solutions stemming from external-based considerations of design or is it more specifically linked to the language-based aspects of building design that has been the primary thesis of this book? As has been continually referenced, *Internal*, in focusing on the use of language-based concepts, defines an approach to design that is intended to be inclusive. The intent is to support the formation of more richly designed buildings, places, and spaces through

Ludwig Mies van der Rohe
Farnsworth

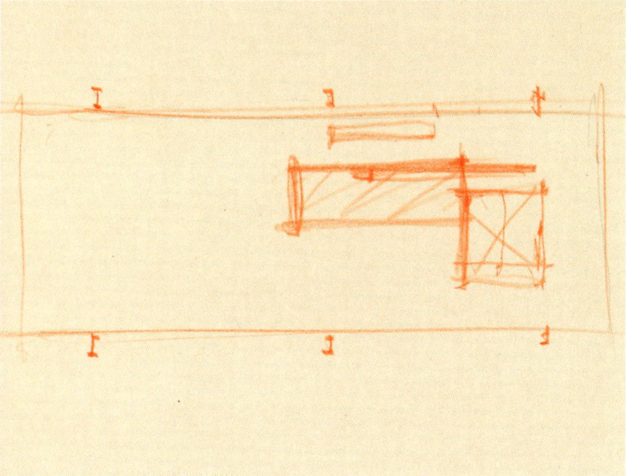

To create architecture is to put in order. Put what in order? Function and objects.

Space and light and order. Those are the things that men need just as much as they need bread or a place to sleep.

The truthfulness of materials of constructions, concrete, bricks, and stone, shall be maintained in all buildings constructed or to be constructed.

The purpose of construction is to make things hold together; of architecture—to move us.

The history of architecture is the history of the struggle for light.

— Le Corbusier

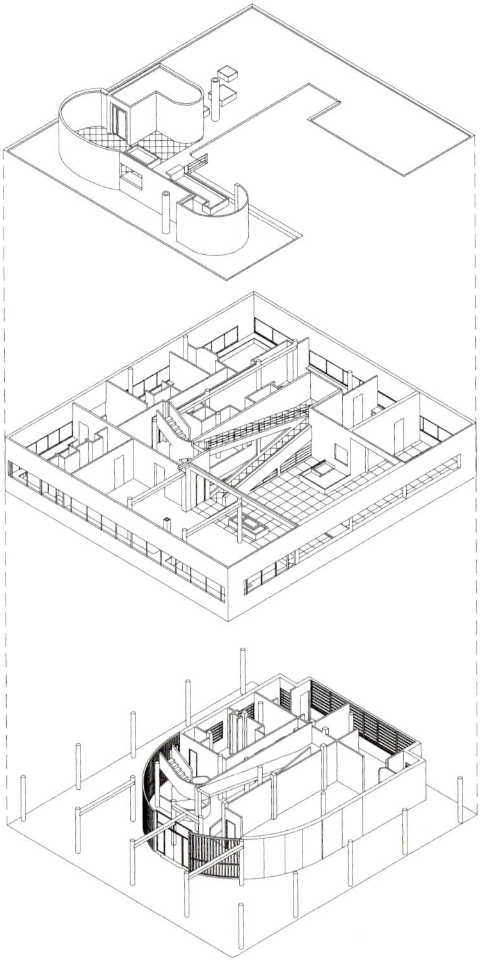

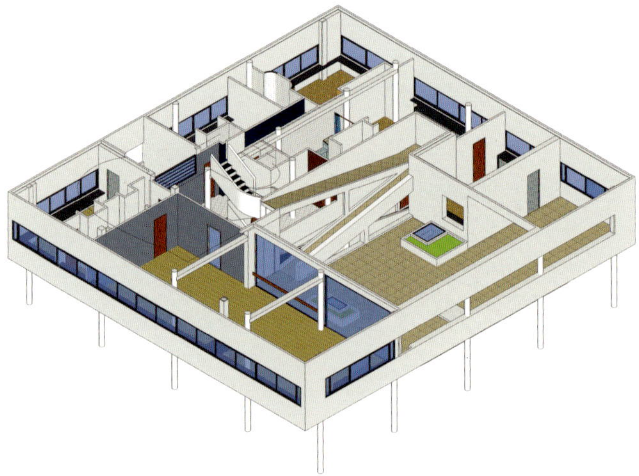

Le Corbusier
Villa Savoye

advancing a design process more consciously incorporating language-based criteria versus a process that remains unintentionally allied to design criteria that are "external" to the creation of languages. These internal language-based intentions, as have been discussed in the interviews, must carry both organizational and representational conceptual accountability to expand the design methodology in a manner that advances experiential and meaningful design outcomes–thus becoming more informed.

Expanding on a methodology for informing the design process and developing architectural languages requires that an additional issue be raised. Even if seemingly tangential the issue touches on the distinction between the terms creativity and originality. Relating to the organizational and representational domains underlying language-based attributes of design this understanding, or misunderstanding, of the differences between the terms becomes consequential.

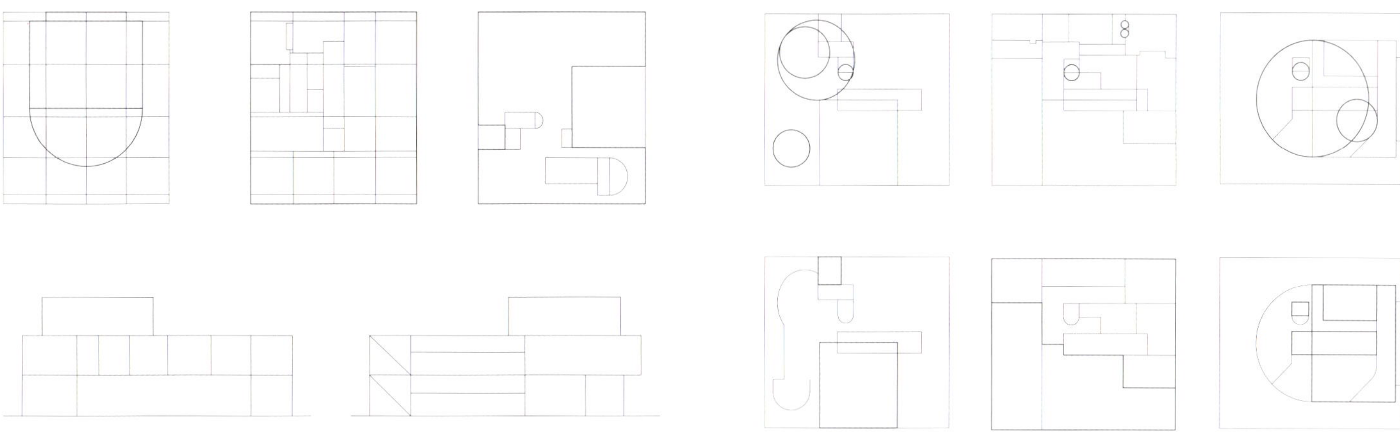

Le Corbusier
Notre Dame du Haut, Ronchamps

Too often acceptance of equality between these terms and their role influencing a building's realization suggests a willingness to misinterpret the difference between creativity and originality in the design process. Often the distinct differences between the two words are conflated. Creativity, by its very definition is linked to the idea of a process whereas originality typically relates to independent and often unrelated ideas, even if they represent potential value to an underlying essence of a building. In the design of a building, singular events of great originality do not necessarily generate outcomes of overall quality in that originality does not lend itself to the idea of synthesis. Solutions defining isolated yet "original" ideas often require that they be further *informed* by additional creative input through a practice that embeds added layers of intentionality into the design process. In the creation of architectural languages design intentions need to be understood within, and benefit from, an understanding that refined outcomes derive from an integration of external and internal factors. If informed architectural languages are to develop the entirety of the creative *process* must remain synthetic and inclusive, incorporating external and internal considerations and an understanding of organizational and representational domains as a part of a design methodology merging meaningful and integrated design decisions infused with intentionality. ◘

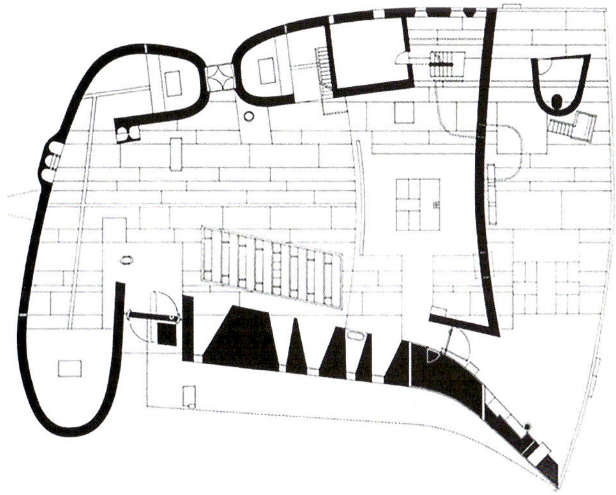

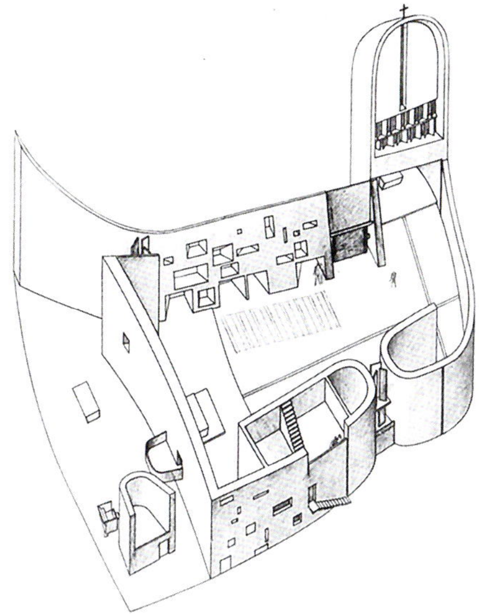

Selected bibliography

General

Agrest, Diana, *Design Versus Non Design*, Oppositions 6, New York, NY, Fall 1976

Banham, Reyner, *Theory and Design in the First Machine Age* (2nd ed), Praeger, Westport CT, 1967

Eisenman, Peter, *Post Functionalism*, Oppositions 6, New York, NY, Fall 1976

Frampton, Kenneth, *Studies in Tectonic Culture*, MIT Press, Cambridge MA, 1995

Hayes, Michael, *Architecture Theory Since 1968*, MIT Press, Cambridge MA, 2000

Jencks, Charles, *Modern Movements in Architecture*, Anchor Press, New York, NY, 1973

Jencks, Charles, *The Language of Post-Modern Architecture*, Rizzoli, New York, NY, 1977

Perez-Gomez, Alberto, *Architecture and the Crisis of Modern Science*, MIT Press, Cambridge MA, 1983

Reisner, Yael, *Architecture and Beauty*, John Wiley & Sons, Hoboken, NJ, 2010

Rowe, Colin, *Five Architects: Eisenman, Graves, Gwathmey, Hejduk, Meier*, Introduction by Colin Rowe, Wittenborn, 1972

Stern, Robert A. M., *Architecture on the Edge of Post-Modernism*, Yale University Press, New Haven, CT, 2009

Tschumi, Bernard, *Architectural Disjunction*, MIT Press, Cambridge, MA, 1996

Venturi, Robert, *Complexity and Contradiction in Architecture*, The Museum of Modern Architecture Press, New York, NY, 1966

Ventrui, Robert, Denise Scott Brown, Steven Izenour *Learning from Las Vegas*, MIT Press, Cambridge, MA, 1977

Brian MacKay-Lyons

Robert McCarter; Brian MacKay-Lyons, Talbot Sweetapple, *The Work of Maykay-Lyons Sweetapple Architects: Economy As Ethic*, Thames & London, 2017

Brian MacKay-Lyons; Robert McCarter, *Local Architecture Building Place, Craft and Community*, Princeton Architectural Press, New York, NY, 2015

Brian MacKay-Lyons; Peter Buchanan, *Ghost: Building an Architectural Vision*, Princeton Architectural Press, New York, NY, 2008

Malcolm Quantrill, *Plain Modern: The Architecture of Brian MacKay-Lyons*, Princeton Architectural Press, New York, NY, 2005

Brian Carter, *Brian MacKay-Lyons: Selected Projects 1986-1997*, TUNS Press, Halifax N.S., 2000

Brian MacKay-Lyons; Brian Carter, *Brian MacKay-Lyons*, TUNS Press, Halifax N.S., 1998

Patkau Architects

Patkau Architects, *Patkau Architects: Material Operations*, Princeton Architectural Press, New York, NY, 2017

Kenneth Frampton, *Five North American Architects*, Lars Muller Publishers, Zurich, Newy York, NY, 2012

Patkau Architects, *Patkau Architects*, Monacelli Press, New York, NY, 2006

Brian Carter, *Patkau Architects*, TUNS Press, Halifax, N.S., 2005

Patkau Architects, *Patkau Architects: Selected Projects 1983-1993*, Technical University of Nova Scotia, 1994

Tom Kundig

Tom Kundig, Mark Rozzo, Michael Chaiken, *Tom Kundig*, Princeton Architectural Press, Hudson, NY, 2020

Tom Kundig, *Tom Kundig: Works*, Princeton Architectural Press, New York, NY, 2015

Tom Kundig, *Tom Kundig: Houses 2*, Princeton Architectural Press, New York, NY, 2012

Dung Ngo, *Tom Kundig: Houses*, Princeton Architectural Press, New York, NY, 2006

Thom Mayne

Thom Mayne, *Morphosis: 2004-2018*, Rizzoli, New York, NY, 2019

Thom Mayne, *Combinatory Urbanism, The Complex Behavior of Collective Form*, Stray Dog Café/Morphosis Architects, Culver City, CA, 2011

Thom Mayne, Peter Cook, *Morphosis: 1998-2004*, Rizzoli, New York, NY, 2006

Thom Mayne, Val K Warke, *Morphosis Architects*, Phaidon, London, New York, NY 2003

Jeffery Kipnis, Todd Gannon, *Morphosis – Diamond Ranch High School*, Source Books in Architecture, The Monacelli Press, New York, NY 2001

Morphosis, *Planet Architecture Morphosis: Recent Works*, In-D Press, Los Angeles CA, 2000

Neil Denari

Neil Denari, Kara Moore, Bure Q. Lan, Linda Hart, MASSX: *Neil M. Denari Architects 2000-2017*, AADCU, Beijing, 2018

Neil Denari, *Gyroscopic Horizons*, Thames and Hudson, London, 1999

Neil Denari, *The Baumer Lectures*, Applied Research + Design, Novato, California, 2018

Neil Denari, Stephen Deters, *Megavoids: UCLA Suprastudio*, UCLA Architecture and Urban Design, Los Angeles, CA, 2015

Enrique Norten

Enrique Norten, Carolina Orloff, *TEN Architectos/Enrique Norten*, Princton Architectural Press, Hudson, NY 2018

Enrique Norten, *TEN Arguitectos*, Princeton Architectural Press, New York, NY, 2017

Enrique Norten, Deyan Sudjic, *Enrique Norten/TEN Architectos, Working: 20 Projects in Process*, The Monacelli Press, New York, NY, 2017

Brooke Hodge, Andrew Bush, *Enrique Norten: A House in the City*, Harvard Design School, Cambridge, MA, 2003

Witold Rybczynski, *The Look of Architecture*, Oxford University Press, New York, NY, 2001

Eric Owen Moss

Eric Owen Moss, *The New City: I'll See It When I Believe It, Rizzoli*, New York, NY, 2016

Todd Gannon (editor) *Eric Owen Moss Architects/3585 Source Books In Architecture*, Applied Research + Design Publishing, San Francisco, CA, 2016

Eric Owen Moss, *Construction Manual 1998 - 2008*, AADCU, China, 2009

Eric Owen Moss, *Gnostic Architect*, Monacelli Press, New York, NY, 1999

Richard Meier,, *Eric Owen Moss: Buildings and Projects 3*, Rizzoli, New York, NY, 2002

Anthony Vidler, *Eric Owen Moss: Buildings and Projects 2*, Rizzoli, New York, NY, 1996

Wolf Prix, *Eric Owen Moss: Buildings and Projects 1*, Rizzoli, New York, NY, 1991

Tod Williams/Billie Tsien

Tod Williams, Billie Tsien, Octavia Giovannini-Torelli, Michael Moran, *The Architecture of the Barnes Foundation*, Skira Rizzoli, New York, NY, 2012

Raymund Ryan, *Cool Construction*, Thames & Hudson, London, 2001

Tod Williams, Billie Tsien, Hadley Soutter Arnold, *Work Life: Tod Williams, Billie Tsien*, Monacelli Press, New York, NY, 2000

Tod Williams, Billie Tsien, Peter Zumthor, Will Bruder, *Williams Tsien (2G International Architecture Review, 9)*, Editorial Gustavo Gili, Barcelona,1999

Photo credits

Introduction

p.3	Sydney Opera House	Shutterstock
p.3	Evolutionary Tree Diagram	Charles Jencks, Architectural Review, July 2000, p.77 (scan)
p.5	Façade 1	Noritaka Minami, 1972 – Nakagin Capsule Tower

Internal versus External

p.19	Crawford Residence, plan	Morphosis Architects
p.19	Diamond Ranch section	Morphosis Architects
p.21	41 Cooper Square, plan, section	Morphosis Architects
p.25	Rachofsky House/Gallery drawings	Richard Meier & Partners Architects
p.25	Rachofsky House photograph	Duke Fleshman
p.27	Diamond Ranch plan, elevation	Morphosis Architects
p.29	BMW Central drawings	Zaha Hadid Architects
p.29	BMW Central photographs	Werner Huthmacher
p.30	Nasher Sculpture Center section	Renzo Piano Building Workshop
p.31	Nasher Sculpture Center drawings	Renzo Piano Building Workshop
p.31	Nasher Sculpture Center photo	Michel Denance

MLSA - Hill House

p.47	Hill House, sketch	MLS Architects
p.48	Hill House, plans, elevations	MLS Architects
p.49	Hill House collage, model	MLS Architects
p.51	Photograph	Steven Evans
p.52	Photograph	Raoul Manuel Snell
p.55	Photographs top, bottom left	Steven Evans
p.56	Photograph	Raoul Manuel Snell
p.57	Photograph	Steven Evans
p.58	Diagram	BMLS Architects
p.58	Photographs, top, bottom left	Steven Evans
p.58	Photograph, bottom right	Undine Pröhl
p.60	Photograph	Steven Evans
p.60	Hill House, elevations	BMLS Architects
p.63	Photograph	Steven Evans
p.64	Photograph	Steven Evans
p.65	Photograph	Steven Evans

Patkau Architects - Strawberry Vale Elementary School

p.67	SVES, roof plan	Patkau Architects
p.68	Photograph	James Dow
p.69	SVES, model photos	Patkau Architects
p.69	Photograph	James Dow
p.70	Photograph	James Dow
p.71	Photograph	James Dow
p.72	Photograph	James Dow
p.74	Photograph	James Dow
p.75	SVES, floor plan, sections	Patkau Architects
p.77	Photograph	James Dow
p.78	Photographs	James Dow
p.79	Photograph	James Dow
p.80	Photographs	James Dow
p.81	Photographs	James Dow
p.82	Photograph	James Dow
p.83	Photograph	James Dow
p.85	Photograph	James Dow

Olson Kundig Architects - Chicken Point Cabin

p.87	Chicken Point Cabin, sketches	Tom Kundig
p.88	Chicken Point Cabin, sketch	Tom Kundig
p.89	Chicken Point Cabin, sketch, drawing	Tom Kundig
p.89	Photographs	Benjamin Benschneider
p.90	Axonometric drawing	Olson Kundig Architects
p.90	Photograph	Benjamin Benschneider
p.91	Chicken Point Cabin, sketch	Tom Kundig
p.92	Chicken Point Cabin, plan	Olson Kundig Architects
p.96	Photograph	Benjamin Benschneider
p.97	Photograph	Benjamin Benschneider
p.98	Photograph	Benjamin Benschneider
p.100	Photograph	Benjamin Benschneider
p.101	Photograph	Benjamin Benschneider
p.102	Photograph	Benjamin Benschneider
p.104	Photograph	Benjamin Benschneider

Morphosis Architects - Caltrans District 7 Headquarters

p.109	Caltrans, sketch	Morphosis Architects
p.110	Crawford Residence, model	Tom Bonner
p.112	Caltrans, plan, section	Morphosis Architects
p.113	Photo, top	Roland Halbe
p.114	Photograph	Roland Halbe
p.115	Photograph	Roland Halbe
p.116	Photograph, top	Tim Griffith
p.116	Photograph, bottom	Roland Halbe
p.117	Photograph, right	Roland Halbe
p.122	Photograph, right	Roland Halbe

p.123	Photograph, bottom	Roland Halbe
p.125	Photographs, middle, lower	Roland Halbe
p.127	Hypo Bank, plan, section	Morphosis Architects
p.128	Photograph	Roland Halbe
p.131	Caltrans, drawings	Morphosis
p.131	Caltrans, model	Morphosis Architects

NMDA - Alan-Voo Residence

p.135	Alan-Voo, axonometric	NMDA Architects
p.137	Alan-Voo, section	NMDA Architects
p.138	Vertical Smoothouse, top	NMDA Architects
p.138	Gallery MA, bottom	NMDA Architects
p.139	Photograph	Benny Chan
p.140	Diagram, unfolded façade	NMDA Architects
p.141	Photograph	Benny Chan
p.143	Photograph	Benny Chan
p.145	Photograph	Benny Chan
p.146	Photograph	Neil Denari
p.151	Photograph	Benny Chan
p.153	Photograph (detail crop)	Benny Chan
p.154	Photograph	Benny Chan

TEN – National School of Theater

p.161	NST, electronic sketch	TEN Architects
p.162	NST, Floor plans	TEN Architects
p.163	Photograph	TEN Architects
p.164	Photograph, left, sketch	TEN Architects
p.165	Photograph	TEN Architects
p.166	Photographs	TEN Architects
p.167	Photograph	TEN Architects
p.168	NST, sections	TEN Architects
p.169	Photograph	TEN Architects
p.172	Photograph	TEN Architects
p.173	NST, sketches, photograph	TEN Architects
p.174	Photograph	TEN Architects

EOM Architects - Samitaur Tower

p.177	Samitaur Tower	EOM Architects
p.178	Samitaur Tower, plans, sections	EOM Architects
p.178	Helmet Head, Henry Moore	© 2021 Artists Rights Society (ARS), New York/VG Build-Kunst, Bohn
p.179	Broadway Boogie Woogie, Piet Mondrian	Digital Image © The Museum of Modern Art/ Licensed by SCALA/Art Resource, NY
p.180	Photographs	Tom Bonner
p.181	Photograph	Tom Bonner
p.182	Photograph	Tom Bonner
p.184	Samitaur Tower model photograph	Tom Bonner
p.185	Photograph	Tom Bonner
p.186	Photograph, left	Tom Bonner
p.187	Photographs	Tom Bonner
p.188	Photograph	Tom Bonner

p.190	Photograph	Tom Bonner
p.191	Photograph	Tom Bonner
p.192	Photograph	Tom Bonner
p.193	Photograph, lower right	Tom Bonner
p.194	Photograph	Tom Bonner
p.195	Photographs	Tom Bonner

TWBT Architects – American Folk Art Museum

p.203	American Folk Art Museum, sketch	TWBT Architects
p.204	American Folk Art Museum, model photograph	Michael Moran
p.205	American Folk Art Museum, plan, section sketches	TWBT Architects
p.206	American Folk Art Museum, first floor plan	TWBT Architects
p.207	American Folk Art Museum, second floor plan	TWBT Architects
p.207	Photographs	Michael Moran
p.210	Photographs	Michael Moran
p.211	Photograph	Giles Ashford
p.212	American Folk Art Museum, section	TWBT Architects
p.213	Photograph	Giles Ashford
p.215	Photograph	Michael Moran
p.216	Photograph, bottom	Giles Ashford
p.217	Photograph	Michael Moran
p.219	Photograph, right	Giles Ashford
p.220	Photograph, center	Giles Ashford
p.220	Photograph, right	Michael Moran
p.221	Photographs	Giles Ashford
p.223	Photograph	Michael Moran

Internal and External

p.179	Broadway Boogie Woogie, Piet Mondrian	Digital Image © The Museum of Modern Art/Licensed by SCALA/Art Resource, NY
p. 226	Gate	© 2021 Frank Lloyd Wright Foundation, Scottsdale, AZ. All rights reserved
p. 227	Detail, plan, perspective	© 2021 Frank Lloyd Wright Foundation, Scottsdale, AZ. All rights reserved
p. 228	Perspectives (2), plans, elevations	© 2021 Frank Lloyd Wright Foundation, Scottsdale, AZ. All rights reserved
p. 229	Detail	© 2021 Frank Lloyd Wright Foundation, Scottsdale, AZ. All rights reserved
p.230	Plan	© 2021 Artists Rights Society (ARS), New York/VG Build-Kunst, Bohn
p.231	Photograph, sketch	© 2021 Artists Rights Society (ARS), New York/VG Build-Kunst, Bohn
p.233	Photograph, sketches	© 2021 Artists Rights Society (ARS), New York/VG Build-Kunst, Bohn
p.234	Axonometric drawings	Ben Kalgovas
p.235	Diagrams	Ben Kalgovas
p.236	Axonometric drawing	Web source: www.digits2widgets.com
p.237	Plan architectural	moleskineblogspot.com

All other photographs credited to Tom Diehl.